# THE SCOPE OF RECOGNITION

## Thought and Vision

JILL BOHLANDER
Pierce College

HOLT, RINEHART AND WINSTON, INC.
*New York, Chicago, San Francisco*
*Atlanta, Dallas, Montreal, Toronto*

to my son, Eric Bohlander:
to the flight of his imagination,
to the endurance of his magic,
which is alive.

# The Wayfarer,

The wayfarer,
Perceiving the pathway to truth,
Was struck with astonishment.
It was thickly grown with weeds.
"Ha," he said,
"I see that none has passed here
"In a long time."
Later he saw that each weed
Was a singular knife.
"Well," he mumbled at last,
"Doubtless there are other roads."

STEPHEN CRANE

# Preface

I believe in the sacred and the profane within man and his universe; the sacred as the infinite potential within each man to reach toward knowing and creating, the profane as allowing or forcing any man to impose limits upon his imagining.

Young minds want to extend themselves. Frequently all they lack is a profound sense that the material to which they are exposed is something that really matters. The materials that compose this collection do matter.

Students gravitate toward material with which they themselves can be energetically involved. This book is a result of having heard the appetites of my students. These materials are theirs, mine, and now yours. Neither this book nor its organization should be used as a straitjacket. The organization is merely a reflection of my own convenience. The materials have been chosen to involve the minds of the students and the instructors that they may engage in fertile dialogue, an on-going uncovering of the art within this book and within themselves. I hope that each of these selections helps provide what Dylan Thomas calls, "the rhythmic, inevitably narrative, movement from overclothed blindness to naked vision."

The instructor's manual contains the identifying notes on the montages and the film. The discussion and writing suggestions that I have found successful in my own classes are there. Their exclusion from the text is intentional, and based on the belief that each selection is a work of art which must not be confined to one point of view.

Let the recognition in each color these pages.

Jill Bohlander

Santa Monica, California
January, 1972

# Acknowledgments

I express my gratitude to the following people without whose advice, encouragement, and cooperation this project, the book, the montages, and the film could never have been completed. To Everett Jones for his guidance and faith in an experimental teacher; to Richard Dodge, Alan Casty, and Tony DiNiro for their advice and encouragement; to Raymond Keller — a patient and versatile artist; to Jill Dunner for help in difficult times; to Hope Blacker, my faithful friend and secretary whose intelligent advice and endurance made my work easier; to Professor Irwin Blacker for his patient answers to endless questions; to Steve Wallis and associates for cooperating with my head and its trips; to Malory Pearce for patience and enthusiasm and many pats upon a weary head; to Ben Adelson, my department chairman at Pierce College for his strong backing of me and my rather unconventional methods — he provided me with the sense of academic freedom which was necessary for this book to grow. To all of these friends I say thank you. To all of my students who helped me to sustain my enthusiasm and who taught me how to learn from them I express my unending gratitude. To Holt and my editor, Jane Ross, I say thank you for your confidence in me and your support.

# Contents

## I.  Seeing Another

> "And all night long we have
> not stirred,
> And yet God has not said
> a word."
> ROBERT BROWNING

## II.   Seeing the Self

"To days of childhood that
are still unexplained."
RAINER MARIA RILKE

## III.   Love and Hate

"nobody, not even the rain,
has such small hands."
E. E. CUMMINGS

# IV.   The Artist and His Art

> "Indeed, whatever exists
> in the universe. . . . the
> painter has first in his
> mind and then in his hands."
>                    LEONARDO DA VINCI

# V.   Art As Social Commentary

> "pity this busy monster manunkind,
> not"
>                    E. E. CUMMINGS

# VI.  The Necessity of Myth

"There he hath lain for
ages, and will lie
Battening upon huge sea
worms in his sleep."
ALFRED, LORD TENNYSON

# VII.   The Sense of Evil

"Let others complain that times are
bad; I complain that they are petty
because they lack passion. . . . Men's
thoughts are too petty to be sinful.
A worm might consider such thoughts
to be sinful, but not a man created
in the image of God. Their pleasures
are circumspect and boring; their passions
sleep."

SOREN KIERKEGAARD

# VIII.   Humor

"Even God likes a good joke."

# IX.   Alienation

"Till human voices wake us
and we drown."
T. S. ELIOT

# I
## SEEING ANOTHER

*"And all night long we have
not stirred,
And yet God has not said
a word."*

*Robert Browning*

# DRY SEPTEMBER

## William Faulkner

## PART 2

She was thirty-eight or thirty-nine. She lived in a small frame house with her invalid mother and a thin, sallow, unflagging aunt, where each morning between ten and eleven she would appear on the porch in a lace-trimmed boudoir cap, to sit swinging in the porch swing until noon. After dinner she lay down for a while, until the afternoon began to cool. Then, in one of the three or four new voile dresses which she had each summer, she would go downtown to spend the afternoon in the stores with the other ladies, where they would handle the goods and haggle over the prices in cold, immediate voices, without any intention of buying.

She was of comfortable people—not the best in Jefferson, but good people enough—and she was still on the slender side of ordinary looking, with a bright, faintly haggard manner and dress. When she was young she had had a slender, nervous body and a sort of hard vivacity which had enabled her for a time to ride upon the crest of the town's social life as exemplified by the high school party and church social period of her contemporaries while still children enough to be unclassconscious.

She was the last to realize that she was losing ground; that those among whom she had been a little brighter and louder flame than any other were beginning to learn the pleasure of snobbery—male—and retaliation—female. That was when her face began to wear that bright, haggard look. She still carried it to parties on shadowy porticoes and summer lawns, like a mask or a flag, with that bafflement of furious repudiation of truth in her eyes. One evening at a party she heard a boy and two girls, all school-mates, talking. She never accepted another invitation.

She watched the girls with whom she had grown up as they married and got homes and children, but no man ever called on her steadily until the children of the other girls had been calling her "aunty" for several years, the while their mothers told them in bright voices about how popular Aunt Minnie had been as a girl. Then the town began to see her driving on Sunday afternoons with the cashier in the bank. He was a widower of about forty—a high-colored man, smelling always faintly of the barber shop or of whisky. He owned the first automobile in town, a red runabout; Minnie had the first motoring bonnet and veil the town ever saw. Then the town began to say: "Poor Minnie." "But she is old enough to take care of herself," others said. That was when she began to ask her old school-mates that their children call her "cousin" instead of "aunty."

It was twelve years now since she had been relegated into adultery by public opinion, and eight years since the cashier had gone to a Memphis bank, returning for one day each Christmas, which he spent at an annual bachelors' party at a hunting club on the river. From behind their curtains the neighbors would see the party pass, and during the over-the-way Christmas day visiting they would tell her about him, about how well he looked, and how they heard that he was prospering in the city, watching with bright, secret eyes her haggard, bright face. Usually by that hour there would be the scent of whisky on her breath. It was supplied her by a youth, a clerk at the soda fountain: "Sure, I buy it for the old gal. I reckon she's entitled to a little fun."

Her mother kept to her room altogether now; the gaunt aunt ran the house. Against that background Minnie's bright dresses, her idle and empty days, had a quality of furious unreality. She went out in the evenings only with women now, neighbors, to the moving pictures. Each afternoon she dressed in one of the new dresses and went downtown alone, where her young "cousins" were already strolling in the late afternoons with their delicate, silken heads and thin, awkward arms and conscious hips, clinging to one another or shrieking and giggling with paired boys in the soda fountain when she passed and went on along the serried store fronts, in the doors of which the sitting and lounging men did not even follow her with their eyes any more.

# BLOOD-BURNING MOON

## Jean Toomer

Up from the skeleton stone walls, up from the rotting floor boards and the solid hand-hewn beams of oak of the pre-war cotton factory, dusk came. Up from the dusk the full moon came. Glowing like a fired pine-knot it illumined the great door and soft showered the Negro shanties aligned along the single street of factory town. The full moon in the great door was an omen. Negro women improvised songs against its spell.

Louisa sang as she came over the crest of the hill from the white folk's kitchen. Her skin was the color of oak leaves on young trees in fall. Her breasts, firm and uppointed like ripe acorns. And her singing had the low murmur of winds in fig trees. Bob Stone, younger son of the people she worked for, loved her. By the way the world reckons things he had won her. By measure of that warm glow which came into her mind at thought of him, he had won her. Tom Burwell, whom the whole town called Big Boy, also loved her. But working in the fields all day, and far away from her, gave him no chance to show it. Though often enough of evenings he had tried to. Somehow, he never got along. Strong as he was with hands upon the axe or plow, he found it difficult to hold her. Or so he thought. But the fact was that he held her to factory town more firmly than he thought, for his black balanced, and pulled against the white of Stone, when she thought of them. And her mind was vaguely upon them as she came over the crest of the hill, coming from the white folk's kitchen. As she sang softly at the veil face of the full moon.

A strange stir was in her. Indolently she tried to fix upon Bob or Tom as the cause of it. To meet Bob in the canebrake as she was going to do an

From *Cane* by Jean Toomer by permission of Liveright Publishers. Copyright © 1951 by Jean Toomer.

hour or so later, was nothing new. And Tom's proposal which she felt on its way to her could be indefinitely put off. Separately, there was no unusual significance to either one. But for some reason they jumbled when her eyes gazed vacantly at the rising moon. And from the jumble came the stir that was strangely within her. Her lips trembled. The slow rhythm of her song grew agitant and restless. Rusty black and tan spotted hounds, lying in the dark corners of porches or prowling around back yards, put their noses in the air and caught its tremor. They began to plaintively yelp and howl. Chickens woke up, and cackled. Intermittently, all over the country-side dogs barked and roosters crowed as if heralding a weird dawn of some ungodly awakening. The women sang lustily. Their songs were cottonwads to stop their ears. Louisa came down into factory town and sank wearily upon the step before her home. The moon was rising towards a thick cloud-bank which soon would hide it.

> Red nigger moon. Sinner!
> Blood-burning moon. Sinner!
> Come out that fact'ry door.

## 2

Up from the deep dusk of a cleared spot on the edge of the forest a mellow glow arose and spread fan-wise into the low-hanging heavens. And all around the air was heavy with the scent of boiling cane. A large pile of cane-stalks lay like ribboned shadows upon the ground. A mule, harnessed to a pole, trudged lazily round and round the pivot of the grinder. Beneath a swaying oil lamp, a Negro alternately whipped out at the mule, and fed cane-stalks to the grinder. A fat boy waddled pails of fresh ground juice between the grinder and the boiling stove. Steam came from the copper boiling pan. The scent of cane came from the copper pan and drenched the forest and the hill that sloped to factory town, beneath its fragrance. It drenched the men in circle seated round the stove. Some of them chewed at the white pulp of stalks, but there was no need for them to, if all they wanted was to taste the cane. One tasted it in factory town. And from factory town one could see the soft haze thrown by the glowing stove upon the low-hanging heavens.

Old David Georgia stirred the thickening syrup with a long ladle, and ever so often drew it off. Old David Georgia tended his stove and told tales about the white folks, about moonshining and cotton picking and about sweet nigger gals, to the men who sat there about his stove to listen to him. Tom Burwell chewed cane-stalk and laughed with the others till someone mentioned Louisa. Till someone said something about Louisa and Bob Stone, about the silk stockings she must have gotten from him. Blood ran up Tom's neck hotter than the glow that flooded from the stove. He sprang up, glared at the men and said, "She's my gal." Will Manning laughed. Tom strode over to him, yanked him up, and knocked him to the ground. Several of Manning's friends got up to fight for him. Tom whipped out a long knife and would have cut them to shreds if they hadn't ducked into the woods. Tom had had enough. He nodded to old David Georgia and swung down the path to factory town. Just then, the dogs started barking and the roosters began to crow. Tom felt funny. Away from the fight, away from the stove, chill got to him. He shivered. He shuddered when he saw the full moon rising towards the cloud-bank. He who didn't give a godam for the fears of old women. He forced his mind to fasten on Louisa. Bob Stone. Better not be. He turned into the street and saw Louisa sitting before her home. He went towards her, ambling, touched the brim of a marvelously shaped, spotted, felt hat, said he wanted to say something to her, and then found that he didn't know what he had to say, or if he did, that he couldn't say it. He shoved his big fists in his overalls, grinned, and started to move off.

"Youall want me, Tom?"

"That's what us wants sho, Louisa."

"Well, here I am—"

"An' here I is, but that ain't ahelpin' none, all th' same."

"You wanted to say something. . . . ?"

"I did that, sho. But words is like th' spots on dice; no matter how y' fumbles 'em there's times when they jes won't come. I dunno why. Seems like th' love I feels fo' yo' done stole m' tongue. I got it now. Whee! Louisa, honey, I oughtn't tell y', I feel I oughtn't cause yo' is young an' goes t' church an' I has had other gals, but Louisa I sho do love y'. Lil' gal I'se watched y' from them first days wen youall sat right here befo' yo' door befo' th' well an sang sometimes in a way that like t' broke m' heart. I'se carried y' with me into th' fields, day after day, an' after that, an' I sho can plow when yo' is ther, an' I can pick cotton. Yassur! Come near beatin' Barlo yesterday. I sho did. Yassur! An' next year if ol'e Stone'll trust me, I'll have a farm. My own. My bales will buy yo' what y' gets from white folks now. Silk stockings, an' purple dresses—course I don't believe what some folks been whisperin' as t'how y' gets them things now. White folks always did do for niggers what they likes. An' they jes can't help alikin' yo, Louisa. Bob Stone like y'. Course he does. But not th' way folks is awhisperin'. Does he, hon?"

"I don't know what you mean, Tom."

"Course y' don't. I'se already cut two niggers. Had t' hon, t' tell 'em so. Niggers always tryin' t' make somethin' out a'nothin'. An' then besides, white folks ain't up t' them tricks so much nowadays. Godam better not be. Leastwise not with yo'. Cause I wouldn't stand f' it. Nassur."

"What would you do, Tom?"

"Cut him jes like I cut a nigger."

"No, Tom—"

"I said I would an' there ain't no mo' to it. But that ain't th' talk f' now. Sing, honey Louisa, an' while I'm listenin' t' y' I'll be makin' love."

Tom took her hand in his. Against the tough thickness of his own, hers felt soft and small. His huge body slipped down to the step beside her. The full moon sank upward into the deep purple of the cloud-bank. An old woman brought a lighted lamp and hung it on the common well whose bulky shadow squatted in the middle of the road, opposite Tom and Louisa. The old woman lifted the well-lid, took hold of the chain, and began drawing up the heavy bucket. As she did so, she sang. Figures shifted, restlesslike, between lamp and window in the front rooms of the shanties. Shadows of the figures fought each other on the grey dust of the road. Figures raised the windows and joined the old woman in song. Louisa and Tom, the whole street, singing:

> Red nigger moon. Sinner!
> Blood-burning moon. Sinner!
> Come out that fact'ry door.

Bob Stone sauntered from his veranda out into the gloom of fir trees and magnolias. The clear white of his skin paled, and the flush of his cheeks turned purple. As if to balance this outer change, his mind became consciously a white man's. He passed the house with its huge open hearth which in the days of slavery was the plantation cookery. He saw Louisa bent over the hearth. He went in as a master should, and took her. Direct, honest, bold. None of this sneaking that he had to go through now. The contrast was repulsive to him. His family had lost ground. Hell no, his family still owned the niggers, practically. Damned if they did, or he wouldn't have to duck around so. What would they think if they knew? His mother? His sister? He shouldn't mention them, shouldn't think of them in this connection. There in the dusk he blushed at doing so. Fellows about town were all right, but how about his friends up north? He could see them incredible, repulsed. They didn't know. The thought first made him laugh. Then, with their eyes still upon him, he began to feel embarrassed. He felt the need of explaining things to them. Explain hell. They wouldn't understand, and moreover who ever heard of a Southerner getting on his knees to any Yankee, or anyone. No sir. He was going to see Louisa tonight, and love her. She was lovely—in her way. Nigger way. What way was that? Damned if he knew. Must know. He'd known her long enough to know. Was there something about niggers that you couldn't know? Listening to them at church didn't tell you anything. Looking at them didn't tell you anything. Talking to them didn't tell you anything,— unless it was gossip, unless they wanted to talk. Of course about farming, and licker, and craps,—but those weren't niggers. Nigger was something more. How much more? Something to be afraid of, more? Hell no. Who ever heard of being afraid of a nigger? Tom Burwell, Cartwell had told him that Tom went with Louisa after she reached home. No sir. No nigger had ever been with his girl. He'd like to see one try. Some position for him to be in. Him, Bob Stone, of the old Stone family, in a scrap with a nigger over a nigger girl. In the good old days. . . . Ha! Those were the days. His family had lost ground. Not so much, though. Enough for him to have to cut through old Lemon's canefield by way of the woods, that he might meet her. She was worth it. Beautiful nigger gal. Why nigger? Why not, just gal? No, it was because she was nigger that he went to her. Sweet . . . The scent of boiling cane came to him. Then he saw the rich glow of the stove. He heard the voices of the men circled round it. He was about to skirt the clearing when he heard his own name mentioned. He stopped. Quivering. Leaning against a tree, he listened.

"Bad nigger. Yassur he sho' is one bad nigger when he gets started."
"Tom Burwell's been on th' gang three times fo' cuttin' men."
"What y' think he's agwine t' do t' Bob Stone?"
"Dunno yet. He ain't found out. When he does—Baby!"
"Ain't no tellin'."
"Young Stone ain't no quitter an' I ken tell y' that. Blood of th' old uns in his veins."
"That's right. He'll scrap sho."
"Be gettin' too hot f' niggers 'round this away."
"Shut up nigger. Y' don't know what y' talking 'bout."
Bob Stone's ears burnt like he had been holding them over the stove. Sizzling heat welled up within him. His feet felt as if they rested on red hot coals. They stung him to quick movement. He circled the fringe of the glowing. Not a twig cracked beneath his feet. He reached the path that led to factory town. Plunged furiously down it. Half way along, a blindness within him veered him aside. He crashed into the bordering canebrake. Cane leaves cut his face and lips. He tasted blood. He threw himself down and dug his fingers in the ground. The earth was cool. Cane-roots took the fever from his hands. After a long while, or so it seemed to him, the thought came to him that it must be time to see Louisa. He got to his feet, and walked calmly to their meeting place. No Louisa. Tom Burwell had her. Veins in his forehead bulged and distended. Saliva moistened the dried blood on his lips. He bit down on his lips. He tasted blood. Not his own blood; Tom Burwell's blood. Bob drove through the cane, and out again upon the road. A hound swung down the path before him towards factory town. Bob couldn't see it. The dog loped aside to let him pass. Bob's blind rushing made him stumble over it. He fell with a thud that dazed him. The hound yelped. Answering yelps came from all over the country-side. Chickens cackled. Roosters crowed, heralding the blood-shot eyes of south-

ern awakening. Singers in the town were silenced. They shut their windows down. Palpitant between the rooster crows, a chill hush settled upon the huddled forms of Tom and Louisa. A figure rushed from the shadow and stood before them. Tom popped to his feet.

"What's y' want?"

"I'm Bob Stone."

"Yassur—an' I'm Tom Burwell. What's y' want?"

Bob lunged at him. Tom side stepped, caught him by the shoulder, and flung him to the ground. Straddled him.

"Let me up."

"Yassur—but watch yo' doin's Bob Stone."

A few dark figures, drawn by the sound of scuffle, stood about them. Bob sprang to his feet.

"Fight like a man Tom Burwell an' I'll lick y'."

Again he lunged. Tom side stepped and flung him to the ground. Straddled him.

"Get off me you godam nigger you."

"Yo' sho has started somethin' now. Get up."

Tom yanked him up and began hammering at him. Each blow sounded as if it smashed into a precious, irreplacable soft something. Beneath them, Bob staggered back. He reached in his pocked and whipped out a knife.

"That's my game, sho."

Blue flashed, a steel blade slashed across Bob Stone's throat. He had a sweetish sick feeling. Blood began to flow. Then he felt a sharp twitch of pain. He let his knife drop. He slapped one hand against his neck. He pressed the other on top of his head as if to hold it down. He groaned. He turned, and staggered toward the crest of the hill in the direction of white town. Negroes who had seen the fight slunk into their homes and blew the lamps out. Louisa, dazed, hysterical, refused to go indoors. She slipped, crumbled, her body loosely propped against the wood-work of the well. Tom Burwell leaned against it. He seemed rooted there.

Bob reached Broad Street. White men rushed up to him. He collapsed in their arms.

"Tom Burwell . . ."

White men like ants upon a forage rushed about. Except for the taut hum of their moving, all was silent. Shotguns, revolvers, rope, kerosene, torches. Two high powered cars with glaring search lights. They came together. The taut hum rose to a low roar. Then nothing could be heard but the flop of their feet in the thick dust of the road. The moving body of their silence preceded them over the crest of the hill into factory town. It flattened the Negroes beneath it. It rolled to the wall of the factory, where it stopped. Tom knew that they were coming. He couldn't move. And then he saw the search lights of the two cars glaring down on him. A quick shock went through him. He stiffened. He started to run. A yell went up from the mob. Tom wheeled about and faced them. They poured on him. They swarmed. A large man with dead white face and flabby cheeks came to him and almost jabbed a gun-barrel through his guts.

"Hands behind y' nigger."

Tom's wrists were bound. The big man shoved him to the well. Burn him over it, and when the wood-work caved in, his body would drop to the bottom. Two deaths for a godam nigger. Louisa was driven back. The mob pushed in. Its pressure, its momentum was too great. Drag him to the factory. Tom moved in the direction indicated. But they had to drag him. They reached the great door. Too many to get in there. The mob divided, and flowed around the walls to either side. The big man shoved him through the door. The mob pressed in from the sides.Taut humming. No words. A stake was sunk into the ground. Rotting floor boards piled around it. Kerosene poured on the rotting floord boards. Tom bound to the stake. His breast bare. Nail scratches let little lines of blood trickle down, and mat into the hair. His face, his eyes were set and stony. Except for irregular breathing, onc would havc thought him already dead. Torches were flung onto thc pilc. A great flare muffled in black smoke shot upward. The mob yelled. The mob was silent. Now Tom could be seen within the flames. Only his head, erect, like a blackened stone. Stench of burning flesh soaked the air. Tom's eyes poped. His head settled downward. The mob yelled. Its yell echoed against the skeleton stone walls and sounded like a hundred yells. Like a hundred mobs yelling. Its yell thudded against the thick front wall, and fell back. Ghost of a yell slipped through the flames, and out the great door of the factory. It fluttered like a dying thing down the single street of the factory town. Louisa, upon the step before her home, did not hear it, but her eyes opened slowly. They saw the full moon glowing in the great door. The full moon, an evil thing, an omen, soft showering the homes of folks she knew. Where were they these people? She'd sing, and perhaps they'd come out and join her. Perhaps Tom Burwell would come. At any rate, the full moon in the great door was an omen which she must sing to:

Red nigger moon. Sinner!
Blood-burning moon. Sinner!
Come out that fact'ry door.

# LAZARUS, COME FORTH

## Eldridge Cleaver

### THE BLOOD LUST

The boxing ring is the ultimate focus of masculinity in America, the two-fisted testing ground of manhood, and the heavyweight champion, as a symbol, is the real Mr. America. In a culture that secretly subscribes to the piratical ethic of "every man for himself"—the social Darwinism of "survival of the fittest" being far from dead, manifesting itself in our ratrace political system of competing parties, in our dog-eat-dog economic system of profit and loss, and in our adversary system of justice wherein truth is secondary to the skill and connections of the advocate—the logical culmination of this ethic, on a person-to-person level, is that the weak are seen as the natural and just prey of the strong. But since this dark principle violates our democratic ideals and professions, we force it underground, out of a perverse national modesty that reveals us as a nation of peep freaks who prefer the bikini to the naked body, the white lie to the black truth, Hollywood smiles and canned laughter to a soulful Bronx cheer. The heretical mailed fist of American reality rises to the surface in the velvet glove of our every institutionalized endeavor, so that each year we, as a nation, grind through various cycles of attrition, symbolically quenching the insatiable appetite of the *de facto* jungle law underlying our culture, loudly and unabashedly proclaiming to the world that "competition" is the law of life, getting confused, embarrassed, and angry if someone retorts: "Competition is the Law of the Jungle and Cooperation is the Law of Civilization."

Our mass spectator sports are geared to disguise, while affording expression to, the acting out in elaborate pageantry of the myth of the fittest in the process of surviving. From the Little League to the major leagues, through the orgiastic climax of the World Series; from high school football teams, through the college teams, to the grand finale of the annual bowl washouts; interspersed with the subcycles of basketball, track, and field meets—all of our mass spectator sports give play to the basic cultural ethic, harnessed and sublimated into national-communal pagan rituals.

But there is an aspect of the crystal of our nature that eschews the harness, scorns sublimation, and demands to be seen in its raw nakedness, crying out to us for the sight and smell of blood. The vehemence with which we deny this obvious fact of our nature is matched only by our Victorian hysteria on the subject of sex. Yet, we deny it in vain. Whether we quench our thirst from the sight of a bleeding Jesus on the Cross, from the ritualized sacrifice in the elevation of the Host and the consecration of the Blood of the Son, or from bullfighting, cockfighting, dogfighting, wrestling, or boxing, spiced with our Occidental memory and heritage of the gladiators of Rome and the mass spectator sport of the time of feeding Christians and other enemies of society to the lions in the Coliseum— whatever the mask assumed by the impulse, the persistent beat of the drum over the years intones the chant: Though Dracula and Vampira must flee the scene with the rising of the sun and the coming of the light, night has its fixed hour and darkness must fall. And all the lightbulbs ever fashioned, and all the power plants generating electricity, have absolutely no effect on the primeval spinning of the earth in its orbit.

In America, we give maximum expression to our blood lust in the mass spectator sport of boxing. Some of us are Roman enough to admit our love and need of the sport. Others pretend to look the other way. But when a heavyweight championship fight rolls around, the nation takes a moral holiday and we are all tuned in—some of us peeping out of the corner of our eye at the square jungle and the animal test of brute power unfolding there.

Every institution in America is tainted by the mystique of race, and the question of masculinity is confused by the presence of both a "white" man and a "black" man here. One was the master and the other was the slave until a moment ago when they both were declared to be equal "men"; which leaves American men literally without a unitary, nationally viable self-image. Whatever dim vision of masculinity they have is a rough-and-ready, savage mishmash of violence and sexuality, a dichotomized exercise and worship of physical force/submission to and fear of physical force —which is only one aspect of the broken-down relationship between men and women in America. This is an era when the models of manhood and womanhood have been blasted to dust by social upheaval, as the most alienated males and females at the bottom of society move out of "their places" and bid for their right to be "man" and "woman" on an equal basis with the former masters and mistresses. These, in turn, are no longer seen by themselves and others as supermen and superwomen, but only as men and women like all other. And in this period of social change and sexual confusion, boxing, and the heavyweight championship in particular, serves as the ultimate test of masculinity, based on the perfection of the body and its use.

## THE NEGRO CELEBRITY

The murder of Malcom X, the exile of Robert F. Williams, who was forced to flee to Cuba with the combined terrors of the FBI and the minions of Southern justice snapping at his heels, and the exile of the late W. E. B. DuBois, who, in the sunset of a valiant life, made three symbolic gestures as a final legacy to his people (renouncing his American citizenship, "returning" to Africa to become a citizen of Ghana, and cursing capitalism while extolling communism as the hope of the future)—these events on the one hand, and on the other hand the award of a Nobel Prize to Martin Luther King and the inflation of his image to that of an international hero, bear witness to the historical fact that the only Negro Americans allowed to attain national or international fame have been the puppets and lackeys of the white power structure—and entertainers and athletes.

One tactic by which the rulers of America have kept the bemused millions of Negroes in optimum subjugation has been a conscious, systematic emasculation of Negro leadership. Through an elaborate system of sanctions, rewards, penalties, and persecutions—with, more often than not, members of the black bourgeoisie acting as hatchet men—any Negro who sought leadership over the black masses and refused to become a tool of the white power structure was either cast into prison, killed, hounded out of the country, or blasted into obscurity and isolation in his own land and among his own people. His isolation was assured by publicity boycotts alternated with character assassination in the mass media, and by the fratricidal power plays of Uncle Toms who control the Negro community on behalf of the white power structure. The classic illustrations of this quash-the-black-militant policy are the careers of Marcus Garvey, W. E. B. DuBois, and Paul Robeson.

Garvey, who in the first quarter of this century sparked a black mass movement based in America but international in scope and potential, was cast into federal prison and then exiled to England. W. E. B. DuBois, one of the intellectual giants of the modern world, was silenced and isolated in America as viciously and effectively as the racist regime in South Africa has silenced and isolated such leaders of the black masses as Chief Albert Luthuli, or as the British, in Kenya, once silenced and isolated Jomo

Kenyatta. After attempts to cast him into prison on trumped-up charges had failed, DuBois went into exile in Ghana and later renounced the bitter citizenship of the land of his birth.

Paul Robeson was at the apex of an illustrious career as a singer and actor, earning over $200,000 a year, when he began speaking out passionately in behalf of his people, unable to balance the luxury of his own life with the squalor of the black masses from which he sprang and of which he was proud. The response of the black masses to his charisma alarmed both the Uncle Toms and the white power structure, and Paul Robeson was marked for destruction. Through a coordinated, sustained effort, Robeson became the object of economic boycott and character assassination. Broken financially, and heartbroken to see black Uncle Toms working assiduously to defeat him and keep their own people down, Robeson's spirit was crushed, his health subverted, and his career destroyed.

By crushing black leaders, while inflating the images of Uncle Toms and celebrities from the apolitical world of sport and play, the mass media were able to channel and control the aspirations and goals of the black masses. The effect was to take the "problem" out of a political and economic and philosophical context and place it on the misty level of "goodwill," "charitable and harmonious race relations," and "good sportsmanlike conduct." This technique of "Negro control" has been so effective that the best-known Negroes in America have always been—and still are—the entertainers and athletes (this is true also of white America). The tradition is that whenever a crisis with racial overtones arises, an entertainer or athlete is trotted out and allowed to expound a predictable, conciliatory interpretation of what's happening. The mass media rush forward with grinding cameras and extended microphones as though some great oracle were about to lay down a new covenant from God; when in reality, all that has happened is that the blacks have been sold out and cooled out again— *"One more time, boom! One more time, boom!"*

When the question of segregation in the armed services arose during the '40s, the then heavyweight champion of the world, Joe Louis, and Louis Satchmo Armstrong, who was also noted for blowing a trumpet, were more likely to be quoted on the subject than A. Philip Randolph or W.E.B. Du-Bois. And more recently, at the peak of a nationwide epidemic of sit-ins and demonstrations, Attorney General Robert Kennedy called together a group of "influential" Negro entertainers and athletes to meet with him in secret, to get the message from The Man and carry the gospel back to the restless natives. It actually seemed possible to this intelligent Enforcer of the Establishment Will that Queen of the Mellow Mood, Lena Horne, and Harry Belafonte, quarterbacked by James Baldwin, were qualified—not to say "willing," which they weren't—to say or do something to make the black and white hordes of insurgents "freeze" for a cooling-off period.

Obviously, the move made sense to Kennedy. It was worth trying, because Kennedy knew that it was based on a solid tradition which had worked for years. But times had changed, fundamentally, and Kennedy's attempted cool-out was greeted with hoots of scorn and contempt from Negroes— entertainers and athletes included. Just as funnyman Dick Gregory got himself shot trying to "cool off" revolting Negroes in Watts, the celebrities knew that their standing in the black community, which suddenly had become important to them, could easily be destroyed if the impression got out that they were cooperating in an Uncle Tom cool-out this late in the game. The stakes were growing higher, and Negroes everywhere were becoming eager and anxious to bet their lives against the *status quo*. The stupidity of the Uncle Tom cool-out reached perhaps its most grotesque incarnation when, after Negroes had rioted and burned in Harlem, the black friends of the white power structure issued a pamphlet with the headline COOL IT, BABY!

But proof that the power structure never learns can be found in the ludicrous action of the wheels within wheels who rule Los Angeles. After the biggest, most violent Negro uprising since the Civil War—the burning of Watts—the blind, tradition-bound reactionaries of L.A. sought to placate the aroused Negro community by appointing John Roseboro, a baseball player, "ace catcher for the Los Angeles Dodgers," to the position of consultant on community relations. One of his tasks being to spread "goodwill" between Negroes and Chief Parker's Police Department!

It is against this background—of the traditional role of the Negro entertainer and athlete in racial crisis and the rebellion against that tradition— that the Muhammad Ali–Floyd Patterson fight for the world heavyweight championship must be viewed.

## THE MUHAMMAD ALI–PATTERSON FIGHT

It is tempting to say that the Muhammad Ali-Floyd Patterson fight was an "internal affair" of the Negro people. But how could that be, if it is true that both fighters and the boxing game itself, like everything else in America, are more or less owned and controlled by whites? The fight was, ideologically, a pivotal event, reflecting the consolidation of certain psychic gains of the Negro revolution. However, the diplomatic fiction of the "internal affair," no longer operative in international politics, is also inoperative here. Both black and white America, looking on, were sucked into the vortex of the event, feeling somehow a profound relationship to what was being enacted in that ring. They knew that a triumph and a defeat were taking place with consequences for America, transcending the fortunes of the two men squaring off in the ring to test their strength.

The simplistic version of the fight bandied about in the press was that there was a "white hope" and a "black hope" riding on this fight. The white hope for a Patterson victory was, in essence, a counterrevolutionary desire to force the Negro, now in rebellion and personified in the boxing world by Ali, back into his "place." The black hope, on the contrary, was to see Lazarus crushed, to see Uncle Tom defeated, to be given symbolic proof of the victory of the autonomous Negro over the subordinate Negro.

The broad support for Muhammad Ali among Negroes had nothing to do with the black Muslims' racist ideology. Even the followers of the late beloved Malcolm X, many of whom despise Muhammad Ali for the scurvy remarks he made about the fallen Malcolm, nevertheless favored him over Patterson as the lesser of two evils—because Ali was more in harmony with the furious psychic stance of the Negro today, while Patterson was an anachronism light years behind. In time of war, in the very center of the battle, the man of peace cannot command the ear of his people and he loses ground to the man of war. The revolutionary rage in the black man's soul today, which boiled over and burned Watts to the ground, means nothing if it doesn't mean business, and it was focused in cold, deadly hatred and contempt upon Floyd Patterson and the bootlicking art of the puppet in the style of his image.

There is no doubt that white America will accept a black champion, applaud and reward him, as long as there is no "white hope" in sight. But what white America demands in her black champions is a brilliant, powerful body and a dull, bestial mind—a tiger in the ring and a pussycat outside the ring. It is a hollow, cruel mockery to crown a man king in the boxing ring and then shove him about outside, going so far as to burn a cross on his front doorstep, as whites did when Floyd Patterson tried to integrate a neighborhood. "A man's home is his castle" is a saying not meant for Negroes; a Negro's castle exists only in his mind. And for a black king of boxing the boundaries of his kingdom are sharply circumscribed by the ropes around the ring. A slave in private life, a king in public—this is the life that every black champion has had to lead—until the coming of Muhammad Ali.

Muhammad Ali is the first "free" black champion ever to confront white America. In the context of boxing, he is a genuine revolutionary, the black Fidel Castro of boxing. To the mind of "white" white America, and "white" black America, the heavyweight crown has fallen into enemy hands, usurped by a pretender to the throne. Muhammad Ali is conceived as "occupying" the heavyweight kingdom in the name of a dark, alien power, in much the same way as Castro was conceived as a temporary interloper "occupying" Cuba. It made no difference that, when Patterson announced that he would beat Ali and return the crown to America, Ali protested vigorously, asking, "What does he mean? I'm an American too!" Floyd Patterson was the symbolic spearhead of a counterrevolutionary host, leader of the mythical legions of faithful darkies who inhabit the white imagination, whose assigned task it was to liberate the crown and restore it to its proper "place" in the Free World. Muhammad Ali, in crushing the Rabbit in twelve—after punishing him at will so there could be no doubt, so that the sports writers could not rob him of his victory on paper—inflicted a psychological chastisement on "white" white America similar in shock value to Fidel Castro's at the Bay of Pigs. If the Bay of Pigs can be seen as a straight right hand to the psychological jaw of white America, then Las Vegas was a perfect left hook to the gut.

Essentially, every black champion until Muhammad Ali has been a puppet, manipulated by whites in his private life to control his public image. His role was to conceal the strings from which he was suspended, so as to appear autonomous and self-motivated before the public. But with the coming of Muhammad Ali, the puppet-master was left with a handful of strings to which his dancing doll was no longer attached. For every white man, feeling himself superior to every black man, it was a serious blow to his self-image; because Muhammad Ali, by the very fact that he leads an autonomous private life, cannot fulfill the psychological needs of whites.

The heavyweight champion is a symbol of masculinity to the American male. And a black champion, as long as he is firmly fettered in his private life, is a fallen lion at every white man's feet. Through a curious psychic mechanism, the puniest white man experiences himself as a giant-killer, as a superman, a great white hunter leading a gigantic ape, the black champion tamed by the white man, around on a leash. But when the ape breaks away from the leash, beats with deadly fists upon his massive chest and starts talking to boot, proclaiming himself to be the greatest, spouting poetry, and annihilating every gunbearer the white hunter sics on him (the white hunter not being disposed to crawl into the ring himself), a very serious slippage takes place in the white man's self-image—*because that by which he defined himself no longer has a recognizable identity.* "If that black ape is a man," the white hunter asks himself, "then what am I?"

It was really Sonny Liston who marked the coming of the autonomous Negro to boxing. But he was nonideological and so the scandal he caused could be handled, albeit with difficulty and pain. The mystique he exuded was that of a lone wolf who did not belong to his people or speak for them. He was for Liston and spoke only for Liston, and this was not out of harmony with the competitive ethic undergirding American culture. If every man is for himself, it was rational for Liston to be for *him*self. Although even this degree of autonomy in a Negro was bitterly resented, white America could tolerate it with less hysteria, with less of a sense of being threatened. But when the ideological Negro seized the heavyweight crown, no front of cool could conceal the ferocious emotional eruption in white America and among the embarrassed Uncle Toms, who were also experiencing an identity crisis. Yes, even old faithful Uncle Tom has a self-image.

*Blood Lust* by Raymond Keller

*Black Bondage* by Raymond Keller

*Whose Horn of Plenty?* by Raymond Keller

*Vision or Nightmare?* by Raymond Keller

All men must have one or they start seeing themselves as women, women start seeing them as women, then women lose their own self-image, and soon nobody knows what they are themselves or what anyone else is—that is to say, the world starts looking precisely as it looks today. For there to be so deep an uproar over Muhammad Ali should indicate that there is something much more serious than a boxing title at stake, something cutting right to the center of the madness of our time.

The New Testament parable of Jesus raising Lazarus from the dead is interpreted by the Black Muslims as a symbolic parallel to the history of the Negro in America. By capturing black men in Africa and bringing them to slavery in America, the white devils *killed* the black man—killed him mentally, culturally, spiritually, economically, politically, and morally— transforming him into a "Negro," the symbolic Lazarus left in the "grave-yard" of segregation and second-class citizenship. And just as Jesus was summoned to the cave to raise Lazarus from the dead, Elijah Muhammad had been summoned by God to lift up the modern Lazarus, the Negro, from his grave.

"Come out of her, my people!" cries Elijah Muhammad.

Cassius Clay, shedding his graveyard identiy like an old dead skin, is one who heeded Elijah's call, repudiating the identity America gave him and taking on a new identity—Muhammad Ali. Floyd Patterson did not heed Elijah.

The America out of which Elijah Muhammad calls his people is indeed doomed, crumbling, burning, if not by the hand of God then by the hand of man, and this doomed America was partly buried in the boxing ring at Las Vegas when Muhammad Ali pounded a die-hard Lazarus into submission. With the America that is disappearing, the Lazarus-man created in the crucible of its hatred and pain is also vanishing. The victory of Muhammad Ali over Floyd Patterson marks the victory of a New World over an Old World, of life and light over Lazarus and the darkness of the grave. This is America recreating itself out of its own ruins. The pain is mighty for every American, black or white, because the task is gigantic and by no means certain of fulfillment. But there are strong men in this land and they will not be denied. Their task will not be ended until both Paul Bunyan and John Henry can look upon themselves and each other as men, the strength in the image of the one not being at the expense of the other.

Harsh, brutal, and vicious though it may be, no one can deny Muhammad Ali his triumph, and though you comb the ghettos of your desperate cities and beat the bushes of your black belts for another puppet who will succeed where the Rabbit failed, your search will be in vain. Because even as you search you, yourself, are being changed, and you will understand that you must continue to change or die. Yes, the Louisville Lip is a loudmouthed braggart. Yes, he is a Black Muslim racist, staunch enough in the need of his beliefs to divorce his wife for not adopting his religion; and firing his trainer, who taught him to "float like a butterfly and sting like a bee," for the same reason. But he is also a "free" man, determined not to be a white man's puppet even through he fights to entertain them; determined to be autonomous in his private life and a true king of his realm in public, and he is exactly that. A racist Black Muslim heavyweight champion is a bitter pill for racist white America to swallow. Swallow it—or throw the whole bit up, and hope that in the convulsions of your guts, America, you can vomit out the poisons of hate which have led you to a dead end in this valley of the shadow of death.

# A CLEAN, WELL-LIGHTED PLACE

## Ernest Hemingway

It was late and every one had left the café except an old man who sat in the shadow the leaves of the tree made against the electric light. In the day time the street was dusty, but at night the dew settled the dust and the old man liked to sit late because he was deaf and now at night it was quiet and he felt the difference. The two waiters inside the cafe knew that the old man was a little drunk, and while he was a good client they knew that if he became too drunk he would leave without paying, so they kept watch on him.

"Last week he tried to commit suicide," one waiter said.

"Why?"

"He was in despair."

"What about?"

"Nothing."

"How do you know it was nothing?"

"He has plenty of money."

They sat together at a table that was close against the wall near the door of the café and looked at the terrace where the tables were all empty except where the old man sat in the shadow of the leaves of the tree that moved slightly in the wind. A girl and a soldier went by in the street. The street light shone on the brass number on his collar. The girl wore no head covering and hurried beside him.

"The guard will pick him up," one waiter said.

"What does it matter if he gets what he's after?"

"He had better get off the street now. The guard will get him. They went by five minutes ago."

The old man sitting in the shadow rapped on his saucer with his glass. The younger waiter went over to him.

"What do you want?"

The old man looked at him. "Another brandy," he said.

"You'll be drunk," the waiter said. The old man looked at him. The waiter went away.

"He'll stay all night," he said to his colleague. "I'm sleepy now. I never get into bed before three o'clock. He should have killed himself last week."

The waiter took the brandy bottle and another saucer from the counter inside the café and marched out to the old man's table. He put down the saucer and poured the glass full of brandy.

"You should have killed yourself last week," he said to the deaf man. The old man motioned with his finger. "A little more," he said. The waiter poured on into the glass so that the brandy slopped over and ran down the stem into the top saucer of the pile. "Thank you," the old man said. The waiter took the bottle back inside the café. He sat down at the table with his colleague again.

"He's drunk now," he said.

"He's drunk every night."

"What did he want to kill himself for?"

"How should I know."

"How did he do it?"

"He hung himself with a rope."

"Who cut him down?"

"His niece."

"Why did they do it?"

"Fear for his soul."

"How much money has he got?"

"He's got plenty."

"He must be eighty years old."

"Anyway I should say he was eighty."

"I wish he would go home. I never get to bed before three o'clock. What kind of hour is that to go to bed?"

"He stays up because he likes it."

"He's lonely. I'm not lonely. I have a wife waiting in bed for me."

"He had a wife once too."

"A wife would be no good to him now."

"You can't tell. He might be better with a wife."

"His niece looks after him. You said she cut him down."

"I know."

"I wouldn't want to be that old. An old man is a nasty thing."

"Not always. This old man is clean. He drinks without spilling. Even now, drunk. Look at him."

"I don't want to look at him. I wish he would go home. He has no regard for those who must work."

The old man looked from his glass across the square, then over at the waiters.

"Another brandy," he said, pointing to his glass. The waiter who was in a hurry came over.

"Finished," he said, speaking with that omission of syntax stupid people employ when talking to drunken people or foreigners. "No more tonight. Close now."

"Another," said the old man.

"No. Finished." The waiter wiped the edge of the table with a towel and shook his head.

The old man stood up, slowly counted the saucers, took a leather coin purse from his pocket and paid for the drinks, leaving half a peseta tip.

The waiter watched him go down the street, a very old man walking unsteadily but with dignity.

"Why didn't you let him stay and drink?" the unhurried waiter asked. They were putting up the shutters. "It is not half-past two."

"I want to go home to bed."

"What is an hour?"

"More to me than to him."

"An hour is the same."

"You talk like an old man yourself. He can buy a bottle and drink at home."

"It's not the same."

"No, it is not," agreed the waiter with a wife. He did not wish to be unjust. He was only in a hurry.

"And you? You have no fear of going home before your usual hour?"

"Are you trying to insult me?"

"No, hombre, only to make a joke."

"No," the waiter who was in a hurry said, rising from pulling down the metal shutters. "I have confidence. I am all confidence."

"You have youth, confidence, and a job," the older waiter said. "You have everything."

"And what do you lack?"

"Everything but work."

"You have everything I have."

"No. I have never had confidence and I am not young."

"Come on. Stop talking nonsense and lock up."

"I am of those who like to stay late at the café," the older waiter said. "With all those who do not want to go to bed. With all those who need a light for the night."

"I want to go home and into bed."

"We are of two different kinds," the older waiter said. He was now dressed to go home. "It is not only a question of youth and confidence although those things are very beautiful. Each night I am reluctant to close up because there may be some one who needs the café."

"Hombre, there are bodegas open all night long."

"You do not understand. This is a clean and pleasant café. It is well lighted. The light is very good and also, now, there are shadows of the leaves."

"Good night," said the younger waiter.

"Good night," the other said. Turning off the electric light he continued the conversation with himself. It is the light of course but it is necessary that the place be clean and pleasant. You do not want music. Certainly you do not want music. Nor can you stand before a bar with dignity although that is all that is provided for these hours. What did he fear? It was not fear or dread. It was a nothing that he knew too well. It was all a nothing and a man was nothing too. It was only that and light was all it needed and a certain cleanness and order. Some lived in it and never felt it but he knew it all was nada y pues nada y nada y pues nada. Our nada who art in nada, nada be thy name thy kingdom nada thy will be nada in nada as it is in nada. Give us this nada our daily nada and nada us our nada as we nada our nadas and nada us not into nada but deliver us from nada; pues nada. Hail nothing full of nothing, nothing is with thee. He smiled and stood before a bar with a shining steam pressure coffee machine.

"What's yours?" asked the barman.

"Nada."

"Otro loco mas," said the barman and turned away.

"A little cup," said the waiter.

The barman poured it for him.

"The light is very bright and pleasant but the bar is unpolished," the waiter said.

The barman looked at him but did not answer. It was too late at night for conversation.

"You want another copita?" the barman asked.

"No thank you," said the waiter and went out. He disliked bars and bodegas. A clean, well-lighted café was a very different thing. Now, without thinking further, he would go home to his room. He would lie in the bed and finally, with daylight, he would go to sleep. After all, he said to himself, it is probably only insomnia. Many must have it.

# PORPHYRIA'S LOVER

## Robert Browning

The rain set early in to-night,
    The sullen wind was soon awake,
It tore the elm-tops down for spite,
    And did its worst to vex the lake:
I listened with heart fit to break.
When glided in Porphyria; straight
    She shut the cold out and the storm,
And kneeled and made the cheerless grate
    Blaze up, and all the cottage warm;
Which done, she rose, and from her form
Withdrew the dripping cloak and shawl,
    And laid her soiled gloves by, untied
Her hat and let the damp hair fall,
    And, last she sat down by my side
And called me. When no voice replied,
She put my arm about her waist,
    And made her smooth white shoulder bare
And all her yellow hair displaced,
    And, stooping, made my cheek lie there,
And spread, o'er all, her yellow hair,
Murmuring how she loved me—she
    Too weak, for all her heart's endeavor,
To set its struggling passion free
    From pride, and vainer ties dissever,
And give herself to me forever.
But passion sometimes would prevail.

Nor could to-night's gay feast restrain
A sudden thought of one so pale
   For love of her, and all in vain:
So, she was come through wind and rain.
Be sure I looked up at her eyes
   Happy and proud; at last I knew
Porphyria worshipped me; surprise
   Made my heart swell, and still it grew
While I debated what to do.
That moment she was mine, mine, fair,
   Perfectly pure and good: I found
A thing to do, and all her hair
   In one long yellow string I wound
Three times her little throat around,
And strangled her. No pain felt she;
   I am quite sure she felt no pain.
As a shut bud that holds a bee,
   I warily oped her lids: again
Laughed the blue eyes without a stain.
And I untightened next the tress
   About her neck; her cheek once more
Blushed bright beneath my burning kiss:
   I propped her head up as before,
Only, this time my shoulder bore
Her head, which droops upon it still:
   The smiling rosy little head,
So glad it has its utmost will,
   That all it scorned at once is fled,
And I, its love, am gained instead!
Porphyria's love: she guessed not how
   Her darling one wish would be heard.
And thus we sit together now,
   And all night long we have not stirred.
   And yet God has not said a word!

# THE SÉANCE

## Isaac Bashevis Singer

*Translated by*
*H. Klein and Cecil Hemley*

It was during the summer of 1946, in the living room of Mrs. Kopitzky on Central Park West. A single red bulb burned behind a shade adorned with one of Mrs. Kopitzky's automatic drawings—circles with eyes, flowers with mouths, goblets with fingers. The walls were all hung with Lotte Kopitzky's paintings, which she did in a state of trance and at the direction of her control—Bhaghavar Krishna, a Hinda sage supposed to have lived in the fourth century. It was he, Bhaghavar Krishna, who had painted the peacock with the golden tail, in the middle of which appeared the image of Buddha; the otherworldly trees hung with elflocks and fantastic fruits; the young women of the planet Venus with their branch-like arms and their ears from which stretched silver nets—organs of telepathy. Over the pictures, the old furniture, the shelves with books, there hovered reddish shadows. The windows were covered with heavy drapes.

At the round table on which lay a Ouija board, a trumpet, and a withered rose, sat Dr. Zorach Kalisher, small, broad-shouldered, bald in front and with sparse tufts of hair in the back, half yellow, half gray. From behind his yellow bushy brows peered a pair of small, piercing eyes. Dr. Kalisher had almost no neck—his head sat directly on his broad shoulders, making him look like a primitive African statue. His nose was crooked, flat at the top, the tip split in two. On his chin sprouted a tiny growth. It was hard to tell whether this was a remnant of a beard or just a hairy wart. The face was wrinkled, badly shaven, and grimy. He wore a black corduory jacket, a white shirt covered with ash and coffee stains, and a crooked bow tie.

When conversing with Mrs. Kopitzky, he spoke an odd mixture of Yid-

Reprinted with the permission of Farrar, Straus and Giroux, Inc. from *The Séance and Other Stories* by Isaac Bashevis Singer, copyright © 1965, 1966, 1968 by Isaac Bashevis Singer.

dish and German. "What's keeping our friend Bhaghavar Krishna? Did he lose his way in the spheres of heaven?"

"Dr. Kalisher, don't rush me," Mrs. Kopitzky answered. "We cannot give them orders . . . they have their motives and their moods. Have a little patience."

"Well, if one must, one must."

Dr. Kalisher drummed his fingers on the table. From each finger sprouted a little red beard. Mrs. Kopitzky leaned her head on the back of the upholstered chair and prepared to fall into a trance. Against the dark glow of the red bulb, one could discern her freshly dyed hair, black without luster, waved into tiny ringlets; her rouged face, the broad nose, high cheekbones, and eyes spread far apart and heavily lined with mascara. Dr. Kalisher often joked that she looked like a painted bulldog. Her husband, Leon Kopitzky, a dentist, had died eighteen years before, leaving no children. The widow supported herself on an annuity from an insurance company. In 1929 she had lost her fortune in the Wall Street crash, but had recently begun to buy securities again on the advice of her Ouija board, planchette, and crystal ball. Mrs. Kopitzky even asked Bhaghavar Krishna for tips on the races. In a few cases, he had divulged in dreams the names of winning horses.

Dr. Kalisher bowed his head and covered his eyes with his hands, muttering to himself as solitary people often do. "Well, I've played the fool enough. This is the last night. Even from kreplach one has enough."

"Did you say something, Doctor?"

"What? Nothing."

"When you rush me, I can't fall into the trance."

"Trance-shmance," Dr. Kalisher grumbled to himself. "The ghost is late, that's all. Who does she think she's fooling? Just crazy—meshugga."

Aloud, he said: "I'm not rushing you, I've plenty of time. If what the Americans say about time is right, I'm a second Rockefeller."

As Mrs. Kopitzky opened her mouth to answer, her double chin, with all its warts, trembled, revealing a set of huge false teeth. Suddenly she threw back her head and sighed. She closed her eyes, and snorted once. Dr. Kalisher gaped at her questioningly, sadly. He had not yet heard the sound of the outside door opening, but Mrs. Kopitzky, who probably had the acute hearing of an animal, might have. Dr. Kalisher began to rub his temples and his nose, and then clutched at his tiny beard.

There was a time when he had tried to understand all things through his reason, but that period of rationalism had long passed. Since then, he had constructed an antirationalistic philosophy, a kind of extreme hedonism which saw in eroticism the *Ding an sich,* and in reason the very lowest stage of being, the entropy which led to absolute death. His position had been a curious compound of Hartmann's idea of the Unconscious with the Cabbala of Rabbi Isaac Luria, according to which all things, from the smallest grain

of sand to the very Godhead itself, are Copulation and Union. It was because of this system that Dr. Kalisher had come from Paris to New York in
1939, leaving behind in Poland his father, a rabbi, a wife who refused to
divorce him, and a lover, Nella, with whom he had lived for years in Berlin
and later in Paris. It so happened that when Dr. Kalisher left for America,
Nella went to visit her parents in Warsaw. He had planned to bring her over
to the United States as soon as he found a translator, a publisher, and a
chair at one of the American universities.

In those days Dr. Kalisher had still been hopeful. He had been offered a
cathedra in the Hebrew University in Jerusalem; a publisher in Palestine was
about to issue one of his books; his essays had been printed in Zurich and
Paris. But with the outbreak of the Second World War, his life began to
deteriorate. His literary agent suddenly died, his translator was inept and,
to make matters worse, absconded with a good part of the manuscript, of
which there was no copy. In the Yiddish press, for some strange reason, the
reviewers turned hostile and hinted that he was a charlatan. The Jewish
organizations which arranged lectures for him cancelled his tour. According
to his own philosophy, he had believed that all suffering was nothing more
than negative expressions of universal eroticism: Hitler, Stalin, the Nazis
who sang the Horst Wessel song and made the Jews wear yellow armbands,
were actually searching for new forms and variations of sexual salvation.
But Dr. Kalisher began to doubt his own system and fell into despair. He
had to leave his hotel and move into a cheap furnished room. He wandered
about in shabby clothes, sat all day in cafeterias, drank endless cups of
coffee, smoked bad cigars, and barely managed to survive on the few dollars
that a relief organization gave him each month. The refugees whom he met
spread all sorts of rumors about visas for those left behind in Europe, packages of food and medicines that could be sent them through various
agencies, ways of bringing over relatives from Poland through Honduras,
Cuba, Brazil. But he, Zorach Kalisher, could save no one from the Nazis.
He had received only a single letter from Nella.

Only in New York had Dr. Kalisher realized how attached he was to his
mistress. Without her, he became impotent.


2

Everything was exactly as it had been yesterday and the day before.
Bhaghavar Krishna began to speak in English with his foreign voice that
was half male and half female, duplicating Mrs. Kopitzky's errors in pro-
nunciation and grammar. Lotte Kopitzky came from a village in the Car-
pathian Mountains. Dr. Kalisher could never discover her nationality—
Hungarian, Rumanian, Galician? She knew no Polish or German, and little
English; even her Yiddish had been corrupted through her long years in

America. Actually she had been left languageless and Bhaghavar Krishna spoke her various jargons. At first Dr. Kalisher had asked Bhaghavar Krishna the details of his earthly existence but had been told by Bhaghavar Krishna that he had forgotten everything in the heavenly mansions in which he dwelt. All he could recall was that he had lived in the suburbs of Madras. Bhaghavar Krishna did not even know that in that part of India Tamil was spoken. When Dr. Kalisher tried to converse with him about Sanskrit, the Mahabharata, the Ramayana, the Sakuntala, Bhaghavar Krishna replied that he was no longer interested in terrestrial literature. Bhaghavar Krishna knew nothing but a few theosophic and spiritualistic brochures and magazines which Mrs. Kopitzky subscribed to.

For Dr. Kalisher it was all one big joke; but if one lived in a bug-ridden room and had a stomach spoiled by cafeteria food, if one was in one's sixties and completely without family, one became tolerant of all kinds of crack-pots. He had been introduced to Mrs. Kopitzky in 1942, took part in scores of her séances, read her automatic writings, admired her automatic paintings, listened to her automatic symphonies. A few times he had borrowed money from her which he had been unable to return. He ate at her house— vegetarain suppers, since Mrs. Kopitzky touched neither meat, fish, milk, nor eggs, but only fruit and vegetables which mother earth produces. She specialized in preparing salads with nuts, almonds, pomegranates, avocados.

In the beginning, Lotte Kopitzky had wanted to draw him into a ro-mance. The spirits were all of the opinion that Lotte Kopitzky and Zorach Kalisher derived from the same spiritual origin: *The Great White Lodge.* Even Bhaghavar Krishna had a taste for matchmaking. Lotte Kopitzky constantly conveyed to Dr. Kalisher regards from the Masters, who had connections with Tibet, Atlantis, the Heavenly Hierarchy, the Shambala, the Fourth Kingdom of Nature and the Council of Sanat Kumara. In heaven as on the earth, in the early forties, all kinds of crises were brewing. The Powers having realigned themselves, the members of the Ashrams were preparing a war on Cosmic Evil. The Hierarchy sent out projectors to light up the planet Earth, and to find esoteric men and women to serve special purposes. Mrs. Kopitzky assured Dr. Kalisher that he was ordained to play a huge part in the Universal Rebirth. But he had neglected his mission, dis-appointed the Masters. He had promised to telephone, but didn't. He spent months in Philadelphia without dropping her a postcard. He returned with-out informing her. Mrs. Kopitzky ran into him in an automat on Sixth Avenue and found him in a torn coat, a dirty shirt, and shoes worn so thin they no longer had heels. He had not even applied for United States citizen-ship, though refugees were entitled to citizenship without going abroad to get a visa.

Now, in 1946, everything that Lotte Kopitzky had prophesied had come true. All had passed over to the other side—his father, his brother, his sisters, Nella. Bhaghavar Krishna brought messages from them. The Masters still remembered Dr. Kalisher, and still had plans for him in connection with the Centennial Conference of the Hierarchy. Even the fact that his family had perished in Treblinka, Maidanek, Stutthof was closely connected with the Powers of Light, the Development of Karma, the New Cycle after Lemuria, and with the aim of leading humanity to a new ascent in Love and a new Aquatic Epoch.

During the last few weeks, Mrs. Kopitzky had become dissatisfied with summoning Nella's spirit in the usual way. Dr. Kalisher was given the rare opportunity of coming into contact with Nella's materialized form. It happened in this way: Bhaghavar Krishna would give a sign to Dr. Kalisher that he should walk down the dark corridor to Mrs. Kopitzky's bedroom. There in the darkness, near Mrs. Kopitzky's bureau, an apparition hovered which was supposed to be Nella. She murmured to Dr. Kalisher in Polish, spoke caressing words into his ear, brought him messages from friends and relatives. Bhaghavar Krishna had admonished Dr. Kalisher time and again not to try to touch the phantom, because contact could cause severe injury to both, to him and Mrs. Kopitzky. The few times that he sought to approach her, she deftly eluded him. But confused though Dr. Kalisher was by these episodes, he was aware that they were contrived. This was not Nella, neither her voice nor her manner. The messages he received proved nothing. He had mentioned all these names to Mrs. Kopitzky and had been questioned by her. But Dr. Kalisher remained curious: Who was the apparition? Why did she act the part? Probably for money. But the fact that Lotte Kopitzky was capable of hiring a ghost proved that she was not only a self-deceiver but a swindler of others as well. Every time Dr. Kalisher walked down the dark corridor, he murmured, "Crazy, meshugga, a ridiculous woman."

Tonight Dr. Kalisher could hardly wait for Bhaghavar Krishna's signal. He was tired of these absurdities. For years he had suffered from a prostate condition and now had to urinate every half hour. A Warsaw doctor who was not allowed to practice in America, but did so clandestinely nonetheless, had warned Dr. Kalisher not to postpone an operation, because complications might arise. But Kalisher had neither the money for the hospital nor the will to go there. He sought to cure himself with baths, hot-water bottles, and with pills he had brought with him from France. He even tried to massage his prostate gland himself. As a rule, he went to the bathroom the moment he arrived at Mrs. Kopitzky's, but this evening he had neglected to do so. He felt a pressure on his bladder. The raw vegetables which Mrs. Kopitzky had given him to eat made his intestines twist. "Well, I'm too old for such pleasures," he murmured. As Bhaghavar Krishna spoke, Dr. Kalisher could scarcely listen. "What is she babbling, the idiot? She's not even a decent ventriloquist."

The instant Bhaghavar Krishna gave his usual sign, Dr. Kalisher got up. His legs had been troubling him greatly but had never been as shaky as tonight. "Well, I'll go to the bathroom first," he decided. To reach the bathroom in the dark was not easy. Dr. Kalisher walked hesitantly, his hands outstretched, trying to feel his way. When he had reached the bathroom and opened the door, someone inside pulled the knob back. It is she, the girl, Dr. Kalisher realized. So shaken was he that he forgot why he was there. "She most probably came here to undress." He was embarrassed both for himself and for Mrs. Kopitzky. "What does she need it for, for whom is she playing this comedy?" His eyes had become accustomed to the dark. He had seen the girl's silhouette. The bathroom had a window giving on to the street, and the shimmer of the street lamp had fallen on to it. She was small, broadish, with a high bosom. She appeared to have been in her underwear. Dr. Kalisher stood there hypnotized. He wanted to cry out, "Enough, it's all so obvious," but his tongue was numb. His heart pounded and he could hear his own breathing.

After a while he began to retrace his steps, but he was dazed with blindness. He bumped into a clothes tree and hit a wall, striking his head. He stepped backwards. Something fell and broke. Perhaps one of Mrs. Kopitzky's otherworldly sculptures! At that moment the telephone began to ring, the sound unusually loud and menacing. Dr. Kalisher shivered. He suddenly felt a warmth in his underwear. He had wet himself like a child.

"Well, I've reached the bottom," Dr. Kalisher muttered to himself. "I'm ready for the junkyard." He walked toward the bedroom. Not only his underwear, his pants also had become wet. He expected Mrs. Kopitzky to answer the telephone; it happened more than once that she awakened from her trance to discuss stocks, bonds, and dividends. But the telephone kept on ringing. Only now he realized what he had done—he had closed the living-room door, shutting out the red glow which helped him find his way. "I'm going home," he resolved. He turned toward the street door but found he had lost all sense of direction in that labyrinth of an apartment. He touched a knob and turned it. He heard a muffled scream. He had wandered into the bathroom again. There seemed to be no hook or chain inside. Again he saw the woman in a corset, but this time with her face half in the light. In that split second he knew she was middle-aged.

"Forgive, please." And he moved back.

The telephone stopped ringing, then began anew. Suddenly Dr. Kalisher glimpsed a shaft of red light and heard Mrs. Kopitzky walking toward the telephone. He stopped and said, half statement, half question: "Mrs. Kopitzky!"

Mrs. Kopitzky started. "Already finished?"

"I'm not well, I must go home."

"Not Well? Where do you want to go? What's the matter? Your heart?"

"Everything."

"Wait a second."

Mrs. Kopitzky, having approached him, took his arm and led him back to the living room. The telephone continued to ring and then finally fell silent. "Did you get a pressure in your heart, huh?" Mrs. Kopitzky asked. "Lie down on the sofa, I'll get a doctor."

"No, no, not necessary."

"I'll massage you."

"My bladder is not in order, my prostate gland."

"What? I'll put on the light."

He wanted to ask her not to do so, but she had already turned on a number of lamps. The light glared in his eyes. She stood looking at him and at his wet pants. Her head shook from side to side. Then she said, "This is what comes from living alone."

"Really, I'm ashamed of myself."

"What's the shame? We all get older. Nobody gets younger. Were you in the bathroom?"

Dr. Kalisher didn't answer.

"Wait a moment, I still have *his* clothes. I had a premonition I would need them someday."

Mrs. Kopitzky left the room. Dr. Kalisher sat down on the edge of a chair, placing his handkerchief beneath him. He sat there stiff, wet, childishly guilty and helpless, and yet with that inner quiet that comes from illness. For years he had been afraid of doctors, hospitals, and especially nurses, who deny their feminine shyness and treat grownup men like babies. Now he was prepared for the last degradations of the body. "Hell, I'm finished, *kaput.*" . . . He made a swift summation of his existence. "Philosophy? what philosophy? Eroticism? whose eroticism?" He had played with phrases for years, had come to no conclusions. What had happened to him, in him, all that had taken place in Poland, in Russia, on the planets, on the far-away galaxies, could not be reduced either to Schopenhauer's blind will or to his, Kalisher's, eroticism. It was explained neither by Spinoza's substance, Leibnitz's monads, Hegel's dialectic, or Heckel's monism. "They all just juggle words like Mrs. Kopitzky. It's better that I didn't publish all that scribbling of mine. What's the good of all these preposterous hypotheses? They don't help at all. . . ." He looked up at Mrs. Kopitzky's pictures on the wall, and in the blazing light they resembled the smearings of school children. From the street came the honking of cars, the screams of boys, the thundering echo of the subway as a train passed. The door opened and Mrs. Kopitzky entered with a bundle of clothes: a jacket, pants, and shirt, and underwear. The clothes smelled of mothballs and dust. She said to him, "Have you been in the bedroom?"

"What? No."

"Nella didn't materialize?"

"No, she didn't materialize."

"Well, change your clothes. Don't let me embarrass you."

She put the bundle on the sofa and bent over Dr. Kalisher with the devotion of a relative. She said, "You'll stay here. Tomorrow I'll send for your things."

"No, that's senseless."

"I knew that this would happen the moment we were introduced on Second Avenue."

"How so? Well, it's all the same."

"*They* tell me things in advance. I look at someone, and I know what will happen to him."

"So? When am I going to go?"

"You still have to live many years. You're needed here. You have to finish your work."

"My work has the same value as your ghosts."

"There *are* ghosts, there are! Don't be so cynical. They watch over us from above, they lead us by the hand, they measure our steps. We are much more important to the Cyclic Revival of the Universe than you imagine."

He wanted to ask her: "Why then, did you have to hire a woman to deceive me?" but he remained silent. Mrs. Kopitzky went out again. Dr. Kalisher took off his pants and his underwear and dried himself with his handkerchief. For a while he stood with his upper part fully dressed and his pants off like some mad jester. Then he stepped into a pair of loose drawers that were as cool as shrouds. He pulled on a pair of striped pants that were too wide and too long for him. He had to draw the pants up until the hem reached his knees. He gasped and snorted, had to stop every few seconds to rest. Suddenly he remembered! This was exactly how as a boy he had dressed himself in his father's clothes when his father napped after the Sabbath pudding: the old man's white trousers, his satin robe, his fringed garment, his fur hat. Now his father had become a pile of ashes somewhere in Poland, and he, Zorach, put on the musty clothes of a dentist. He walked to the mirror and looked at himself, even stuck out his tongue like a child. Then he lay down on the sofa. The telephone rang again, and Mrs. Kopitzky apparently answered it, because this time the ringing stopped immediately. Dr. Kalisher closed his eyes and lay quietly. He had nothing to hope for. There was not even anything to think about.

He dozed off and found himself in the cafeteria on Forty-second Street, near the Public Library. He was breaking off pieces of an egg cookie. A refugee was telling him how to save relatives in Poland by dressing them up in Nazi uniforms. Later they would be led by ship to the North Pole, the South Pole, and across the Pacific. Agents were prepared to take charge of them in Tierra del Fuego, in Honolulu and Yokohama. . . . How strange, but that smuggling had something to do with his, Zorach Kalisher's, philosophic system, not with his former version but with a new one, which blended eroticism with memory. While he was combining all these images, he asked himself in astonishment: "What kind of relationship can there be between sex, memory, and the redemption of the ego? And how will it work in infinite time? It's nothing but casuistry, casuistry. It's a way of explaining my own impotence. And how can I bring over Nella when she has already perished? Unless death itself is nothing but a sexual amnesia." He awoke and saw Mrs. Kopitzky bending over him with a pillow which she was about to put behind his head.

"How do you feel?"

"Has Nella left?" he asked, amazed at his own words. He must still be half asleep.

Mrs. Kopitzky winced. Her double chin shook and trembled. Her dark eyes were filled with motherly reproach.

"You're laughing, huh? There is no death, there isn't any. We live forever, and we love forever. This is the pure truth."

# MEMPHIS BLUES
# AGAIN

## Bob Dylan

Ah, the ragman draws circles
Up and down the block.
I'd ask him what the matter was
But I know that he don't talk,

And the ladies treat me kindly,
And they furnish me with tape.
Deep inside my heart
I know I can't escape.

Oh, mama, can this really be the end,
To be stuck inside of Mobile
With the Memphis Blues again?

Well, Shakespeare, he's in the alley
With his pointed shoes and his bells
Speaking to some French girl
Who says she knows me well,

And I would send a message
To find out if she's talked,
But the Post Office has been stolen,
And the mail box is locked.

Oh, mama, can this really be the end,
To be stuck inside of Mobile
With the Memphis Blues again?

Mona tried to tell me
To stay away from the train-line.
She said that all the railroad men
Just drink up your blood like wine,

And I said, "Oh, I didn't know that,
But then again there's only one I've met,
And he just smoked my eyelids
And punched my cigarette.

Oh, mama, can this really be the end,
To be stuck inside of Mobile
With the Memphis Blues again?

Granpa died last week,
And now he's buried in the rocks,
But everybody still talks about
How badly they were shocked,

But me, I expected it to happen,
I knew he'd lost control
When I saw he'd built a fire on Main Street
And shot it full of holes.

Oh, mama, can this really be the end
To be stuck inside of Mobile
With the Memphis Blues again?

Now the Senator came down here
Showing everyone his gun
Handing out free tickets
To the wedding of his son,

And me, I nearly got busted,
And wouldn't it be my luck
To get caught without a ticket
And be discovered beneath the truck.

Oh, mama, can this really be the end
To be caught inside of Mobile
With the Memphis Blues again?

Now, the T-preacher looked so baffled
When I asked him why he dressed
With twenty pounds of headlines
Stappled to his chest,

But he cursed me when I proved to him,
Then I whispered, said, "not even you can hide,
You see you're just like me,
I hope you're satisfied."

Oh, mama, can this really be the end
To be stuck inside of Mobile
With the Memphis Blues again?

Now, the rain-man gave me two cheers;
Then he said, "Jump right in."
The one was Texas medicine;
The other was just railroad gin,

And like a fool I mixed them,
And it strangled up my mind,
And now people just get uglier,
And I have no sense of time.

Oh, mama, can this really be the end
To be stuck inside of Mobile
With the Memphis Blues again?

When Ruthie says come see her
In her honky-tonk lagoon
Where I can watch her waltz for free
'Neath the pandamonium moon,

And I say, "Aw, come on, now,
You know you know about my debutant,"
And she says, "Your debutant just knows what you need,
But I know what you want."

Oh, mama, can this really be the end
To be stuck inside of Mobile
With the Memphis Blues again?

Now the bricks lay on Grand Street
Where the neon madmen climb.
They all fall there so perfectly
It all seems so well-timed,

And here I sit so patiently
Waiting to find out what price
You have to pay to get out of
Going through all these things twice.

# THE LIAR

## Imamu Amiri Baraka (LeRoi Jones)

What I thought was love
in me, I find a thousand instances
as fear. (Of the tree's shadow
winding around the chair, a distant music
of frozen birds rattling
in the cold.
        Where ever I go to claim
my flesh, there are entrances
of spirit. And even its comforts
are hideous uses I strain
to understand.
        Though I am a man
who is loud
on the birth
of his ways. Publicly redefining
each change in my soul, as if I had predicted
them,
    and profited, biblically, even tho
    their chanting weight,
        erased familiarity
        from my face.
           A question I think,
an answer; whatever sits
counting the minutes
till you die.

When they say, "It is Roi
who is dead?" I wonder
who will they mean?

# A POEM
# FOR
# SPECULATIVE
# HIPSTERS

## Imamu Amiri Baraka
## (LeRoi Jones)

He had got, finally,
to the forest
of motives. There were no
owls, or hunters. No Connie Chatterleys
resting beautifully
on their backs, having casually
brought socialism
to England.
      Only ideas,
and their opposites.
        Like,
   he was *really*
   nowhere.

# BLACK CHURCH
# ON SUNDAY

## Joseph M. Mosley, Jr.

Exiled
     from places of honor about the Throne of Grace
in Saint Mary's Cathedral
These overdressed Black men, women and children
hold fast the Faith—not of *their* Fathers—
returning now from Religion's Baptist sing-song
in the rickety storefront Church all peeling paint
and creaking plaster, down the street from the
Liquor Store across from the Homosexual Bar.
Exiles
     from polished Pine pews and Redwood kneelers
they attend the God of Abraham—not Christ Jesus—
though they bathe in His Name.
More kin than kind to Hebrew Pawnbrokers and
    Candy Store merchants on the streets of the world.
Now wrapped from weekday wrongs and run-over shoes
    they go, encased in fine linens which startle their
Black bodies to a strange new stiffness, their Black
faces still reflecting Light from communion with
the Unknown God.

# MY COUSIN AGUEDA

## Ramón López Velarde

My godmother invited my cousin
Agueda to spend the day
with us, and my cousin
came with a conflicting
prestige of starch and fearful
ceremonious weeds.

Agueda appeared, sonorous
with starch, and her green eyes
and ruddy cheeks protected
me against the fearsome
weeds.

      I was a small boy,
knew O was the round one,
and Agueda knitting,
mild and persevering,
in the echoing gallery,
gave me unknown shivers.
(I think I even owe her the heroically
morbid habit of soliloquy.)

At dinner-time in the quiet
shadowy dining-room,
I was spellbound by the brittle
intermittent noise of dishes
and the caressing timbre
of my cousin's voice.

      Agueda was
(weeds, green pupils, ruddy cheeks)
a polychromatic basket of
apples and grapes
in the ebony of an ancient cupboard.

Reprinted by permission of Indiana University Press from *An Anthology of Mexican Poetry,* edited by Octavio Paz, translated by Samuel Beckett. Copyright © 1958 by Indiana University Press.

### On a Withered Branch
On a withered branch
a crow has settled—
autumn nightfall.


BASHO


### In the Winter River
In the winter river,
thrown away, a dog's
dead body.


SHIKI

# SUZANNE TAKES YOU DOWN

## Leonard Cohen

Suzanne takes you down
to her place near the river,
you can hear the boats go by
you can stay the night beside her.
And you know that she's half crazy
but that's why you want to be there
and she feeds you tea and oranges
that come all the way from China.
Just when you mean to tell her
that you have no gifts to give her,
she gets you on her wave-length
and she lets the river answer
that you've always been her lover.
   And you want to travel with her,
   you want to travel blind
   and you know that she can trust you
   because you've touched her perfect body
   with your mind.

Jesus was a sailor
when he walked upon the water
and he spent a long time watching
from a lonely wooden tower
and when he knew for certain
only drowning men could see him
he said All men will be sailors then

until the sea shall free them,
but he himself was broken
long before the sky would open,
forsaken, almost human,
he sank beneath your wisdom like a stone.
And you want to travel with him,
you want to travel blind
and you think maybe you'll trust him
because he touched your perfect body
with his mind.

Suzanne takes your hand
and she leads you to the river,
she is wearing rags and feathers
from Salvation Army counters.
The sun pours down like honey
on our lady of the harbour
as she shows you where to look
among the garbage and the flowers,
there are heroes in the seaweed
there are children in the morning,
they are leaning out for love
they will lean that way forever
while Suzanne she holds the mirror.
And you want to travel with her
and you want to travel blind
and you're sure that she can find you
because she's touched her perfect body
with her mind.

### People through Finding

People through finding something beautiful
Think something else unbeautiful,
Through finding one man fit
Judge another unfit.
Life and death, though stemming from each other,
    seem to conflict as stages of change,
Difficult and easy as phases of achievement,
Long and short as measures of contrast,
High and low as degrees of relation;
But, since the varying of tones gives music to a voice
And what is is the was of what shall be,
The sanest man
Sets up no deed,
Lays down no law,
Takes everything that happen as it comes,
As something to animate, not to appropriate,
To earn, not to own,
To accept naturally without self-importance:
If you never assume importance
You never lose it.


LAO TZU


Reprinted by permission of G. P. Putnam's Sons from *The Way of Life According to Lao Tzu,* translated by Witter Bynner. Copyright 1944 by Witter Bynner.

". . . to days of childhood that
are still unexplained,"

Rainer Maria Rilke

# II
# SEEING
# THE SELF

*Ascent into the Heavenly Paradise* (detail) by Hieronymous Bosch (Palazzo Ducale, Venice)

# THE RAW MATERIAL
# OF POETRY

## Rainer Maria Rilke

*Translated by M. D. Herter Norton*

I think I ought to begin to do some work, now that I am learning to see. I am twenty-eight years old, and almost nothing has been done. To recapitulate: I have written a study on Carpaccio which is bad, a drama entitled "Marriage," which sets out to demonstrate something false by equivocal means, and some verses. Ah! but verses amount to so little when one writes them young. One ought to wait and gather sense and sweetness a whole life long, and a long life if possible, and then, quite at the end, one might perhaps be able to write ten lines that were good. For verses are not, as people imagine, simple feelings (those one has early enough),— they are experiences. For the sake of a single verse, one must see many cities, men and things, one must know the animals, one must feel how the birds fly and know the gesture with which the little flowers open in the morning. One must be able to think back to roads in unknown regions, to unexpected meetings and to partings one had long seen coming; to days of childhood that are still unexplained, to parents whom one had to hurt when they brought one some joy and one did not grasp it (it was a joy for someone else); to childhood illnesses that so strangely begin with such a number of profound and grave transformations; to days in rooms withdrawn and quiet and to mornings by the sea, to the sea itself, to seas, to nights of travel that rushed along on high and flew with all the stars— and it is not yet enough if one may think of all this. One must have memories of many nights of love, none of which was like the others, of the screams of women in labor, and of light, white, sleeping women in child-

Reprinted from *The Notebooks of Malte Laurids Brigge* by Rainer Maria Rilke. Translated by M. D. Herter Norton. By permission of W. W. Norton & Company, Inc. Copyright 1949 by W. W. Norton & Company, Inc. Alternative translation by John Linton available, published by the Hogarth Press.

bed, closing again. But one must also have been beside the dying, must have sat beside the dead in the room with the open window and the fitful noises. And still it is not yet enough to have memories. One must be able to forget them when they are many and one must have the great patience to wait until they come again. For it is not yet the memories themselves. Not till they have turned to blood within us, to glance and gesture, nameless and no longer to be distinguished from ourselves—not till then can it happen that in a most rare hour the first word of a verse arises in their midst and goes forth from them.

# REQUIEM:
# TO PAULA
# MODERSOHN-BECKER

## Rainer Maria Rilke

Then when I have learned much
Look simply at the animals until
An essence from them glides into me—
Stand in their eyes awhile and witness
How they put me out again
Gently, incuriously, unjudged.

From *An Anthology of German Poetry from Hölderlin to Rilke,* edited by Angel Flores, Doubleday & Co., Inc.

# FROM SONG OF MYSELF

## Walt Whitman

32

I think I could turn and live with animals, they are so placid and
    self-contain'd,
I stand and look at them long and long.

They do not sweat and whine about their condition,
They do not alike awake in the dark and weep for their sins,
They do not make me sick discussing their duty to God,
Not one is dissatisfied, not one is demented with the mania of owning
    things,
Not one kneels to another, nor to his kind that lived thousands of years ago,
Not one is respectable or unhappy over the whole earth.

So they show their relations to me and I accept them,
They bring me tokens of myself, they evince them plainly in their possession.

I wonder where they get those tokens,
Did I pass that way huge times ago and negligently drop them?

Myself moving forward then and now and forever,
Gathering and showing more always and with velocity,
Infinite and omnigenous, and the like of these among them,
Not too exclusive toward the reachers of my remembrancers,
Picking out here one that I love, and now go with him on brotherly terms.

# A BIRD
# CAME DOWN
# THE WALK

## Emily Dickinson

A Bird came down the Walk—
He did not know I saw—
He bit an Angleworm in halves
And ate the fellow, raw,

And then he drank a Dew
From a convenient Grass—
And then hopped sidewise to the Wall
To let a Beetle pass—

He glanced with rapid eyes
That hurried all around—
They looked like frightened Beads, I thought—
He stirred his Velvet Head

Like one in danger, Cautious,
I offered him a Crumb
And he unrolled his feathers
and rowed him softer home—

Than Oars divide the Ocean,
Too silver for a seam—
Or Butterflies, off Banks of Noon
Leap, plashless as they swim.

# THE END OF MAN
# IS HIS BEAUTY

## Imamu Amiri Baraka
## (LeRoi Jones)

*The end of man is his beauty*
And silence
which proves / but
a referent
to my disorder.
        Your world shakes

cities die
beneath your shape.

      The single shadow

at noon
like a live tree
whose leaves
are like clouds

Weightless soul
at whose love faith moves
as a dark and
withered day.

They speak of singing who
have never heard song; of living
whose deaths are legends
for their kind.

A scream
gathered in wet fingers,
at the top of its stalk.

—They have passed
and gone
whom you thot your lovers

In this perfect quiet, my friend,
their shapes
are not unlike
night's

# from MEMOIRS OF A SHY PORNOGRAPHER

## Kenneth Patchen

### 7

I had found the prettiest wild flowers I could and as Priscilla sat there in the sun with them pinned in her hair I thought it would be a sad thing to be dead.

Children's voices floated across to us like bright toys which the wind was amusing the angels with. Mr. Dickens was telling about how some poor people didn't have any fuel in their house and the snow drifting in on their beds at night. . . .

The little deer walked up and stood very quietly watching us. Its coat was yellow and it held a basket of white roses in its mouth.

"Priscilla . . ." I said softly.

"Yes, Albert, what is it?"

"Don't look up until I tell you to," I said.

"All right, but—"

"Do you believe I love you?"

"Why, yes, of course, Albert—"

"Do you believe I would lie to you?"

"No, Albert, I know you wouldn't."

"Do you believe in—" I was afraid to say what I wanted to say.

"Do I believe in what?"

"In us," I said.

"I do, Albert," she answered.

"Then believe as hard as you can now. Because . . . because there's something standing in front of us which no one else in the world has ever seen before."

"Something standing—"

"Lift your eyes, Priscilla."

As her head raised I tried to think of every beautiful thing I had ever heard of.

"Oh, Albert!" she said. "It's . . . it's . . . why, it's a lovely little faun bringing us flowers!"

"He wants you to go over and pick out the ones you like best," I said, wondering how long I could pray that hard.

She let the book fall to the grass and getting out of her wheel chair she started to walk over to him. . . .

He stood very still. And Priscilla took a rose out of the basket and held it up for me to see.

Then suddenly her eyes filled with terror.

"Priscilla," I called, "you've taken only for yourself. . . . Aren't you going to find one for me?"

Slowly she turned back and extended her hand again. This time he raised his head, shaking the basket gently back and forth.

"Why, he wants me to scratch his neck," she said, and she allowed him to nuzzle her fingers.

"Oh, Albert! Albert! He's real! He's real! His nose is all wet!"

I crossed over and put my arm around her, swinging her about so she faced me. . . . Then I pressed my mouth on her forehead.

"Promise me you'll never doubt again, Priscilla," I said.

"I can walk," she said softly. "Oh, Albert, I can walk! I can walk! I'll take all the roses now. . . ."

As she turned and found him gone her eyes filled again with terror.

"Look in your hand, Priscilla," I said, gripping her shoulders.

"The roses," she said. "I still have the roses. . . ."

"Of course," I said. "Would you like another one to come? Perhaps a green one this time."

And she flung out of my arms and ran down among the trees to meet him.

"Oh, this one has purple daffodils," she called, laughing and half-dancing in her excitement. "But where did the first one go, Albert?" she asked, as I came up to her.

"I just wished him away," I said.

She looked at me a long moment before she said slowly:

"Then it is through you they come—that I am able to walk?"

"No, Priscilla," I said, "not through me, but through our love."

"But it was you who believed enough—"

"And now you believe too."

"Yes, Albert, now I believe too," she said, taking another flower from the basket and smelling it.

Then we heard the voice of her mother calling from the house. . . .

And Priscilla sank to the ground, her legs twisting horribly under her.

"Oh, God! O my God!" she sobbed.

The little green deer was gone.

The roses and the daffodils were gone from her hand.

And something was dying away deep inside me.

. . .

# 9

Everything had changed in the house. I would look up to find Mrs. Cumberland watching me like she was a little afraid to have me there anymore. Even Charcoal never jumped onto my lap in the evenings and when the neighbors dropped in there wasn't much laughing or singing—then after a few times they stopped coming altogether.

I'd see faces pulling back from the windows when I went anywhere along the roads.

Only Priscilla tried to make it seem as if it was the same as it had been before.

But her face was sad when she didn't know I was looking at her.

And I knew that the time had come for me to go away for a while.

She told me not to bring the little deer into the orchard again. The time had come for me to go. . . .

"I'll come back soon, Priscilla," I said.

"I'll be here waiting for you, darling," she said.

# FEVER DREAM

## Ray Bradbury

They put him between fresh, clean, laundered sheets and there was always a newly squeezed glass of thick orange juice on the table under the dim pink lamp. All Charles had to do was call and Mom or Dad would stick their heads into his room to see how sick he was. The acoustics of the room were fine; you could hear the toilet gargling its porcelain throat of mornings, you could hear rain tap the roof or sly mice run in the secret walls or the canary singing in its cage downstairs. If you were very alert, sickness wasn't too bad.

He was thirteen, Charles was. It was mid-September, with the land beginning to burn with autumn. He lay in the bed for three days before the terror overcame him.

His hand began to change. His right hand. He looked at it and it was hot and sweating there on the counterpane alone. It fluttered, it moved a bit. Then it lay there, changing color.

That afternoon the doctor came again and tapped his thin chest like a little drum. "How are you?" asked the doctor, smiling. "I know, don't tell me: 'My *cold* is fine, Doctor, but *I* feel awful' Ha!" He laughed at his own oft-repeated joke.

Charles lay there and for him that terrible and ancient jest was becoming a reality. The joke fixed itself in his mind. His mind touched and drew away from it in a pale terror. The doctor did not know how cruel he was with his jokes! "Doctor," whispered Charles, lying flat and colorless. "My *hand,* it doesn't *belong* to me any more. This morning it *changed* into something else. I want you to change it back, Doctor, Doctor!"

The doctor showed his teeth and patted his hand. "It looks fine to me, son. You just had a little fever dream."

"But it changed, Doctor, oh, Doctor," cried Charles, pitifully holding up his pale wild hand. "It *did!*"

The doctor winked. "I'll give you a pink pill for that." He popped a tablet onto Charles' tongue. "Swallow!"

"Will it make my hand change back and become *me* again?"

"Yes, yes."

The house was silent when the doctor drove off down the road in his car under the quiet, blue September sky. A clock ticked far below in the kitchen world. Charles lay looking at his hand.

It did not change back. It was still something else.

The wind blew outside. Leaves fell against the cool window.

At four o'clock his other hand changed. It seemed almost to become a fever. It pulsed and shifted, cell by cell. It beat like a warm heart. The fingernails turned blue and then red. It took about an hour for it to change and when it was finished, it looked just like any ordinary hand. But it was not ordinary. It no longer was him any more. He lay in a fascinated horror and then fell into an exhausted sleep.

Mother brought the soup up at six. He wouldn't touch it. "I haven't any hands," he said, eyes shut.

"Your hands are perfectly good," said Mother.

"No," he wailed. "My hands are gone. I feel like I have stumps. Oh, Mama, Mama, hold me, hold me, I'm scared!"

She had to feed him herself.

"Mama," he said, "get the doctor, please, again. I'm so sick."

"The doctor'll be here tonight at eight," she said, and went out.

At seven, with night dark and close around the house, Charles was sitting up in bed when he felt the thing happening to first one leg and then the other. "Mama! Come quick!" he screamed.

But when Mama came the thing was no longer happening.

When she went downstairs, he simply lay without fighting as his legs beat and beat, grew warm, red-hot, and the room filled with the warmth of his feverish change. The glow crept up from his toes to his ankles and then to his knees.

"May I come in?" The doctor smiled in the doorway.

"Doctor!" cried Charles. "Hurry, take off my blankets!"

The doctor lifted the blankets tolerantly. "There you are. Whole and healthy. Sweating, though. A little fever. I told you not to move around, bad boy."

He pinched the moist pink cheek. "Did the pills help? Did your hand change back?"

"No, no, now it's my other hand and my legs!"

"Well, well, I'll have to give you three more pills, one for each limb, eh, my little peach?" laughed the doctor.

"Will they help me? Please, please, What've I *got?*"

"A mild case of scarlet fever, complicated by a slight cold."

"Is it a germ that lives and has more little germs in me?"

"Yes."

"Are you *sure* it's scarlet fever? You haven't taken any tests!"

"I guess I know a certain fever when I see one," said the doctor, checking the boy's pulse with cool authority.

Charles lay there, not speaking until the doctor was crisply packing his black kit. Then in the silent room, the boy's voice made a small, weak pattern, his eyes alight with remembrance. "I read a book once. About petrified trees, wood turning to stone. About how trees fell and rotted and minerals got in and built up and they look just like trees, but they're not, they're stone." He stopped. In the quiet warm room his breathing sounded.

"Well?" asked the doctor.

"I've been thinking," said Charles after a time. "Do germs ever get big? I mean, in biology class they told us about one-celled animals, amoebas and things, and how millions of years ago they got together until there was a bunch and they made the first body. And more and more cells got together and got bigger and then finally maybe there was a fish and finally here *we* are, and all we are is a bunch of cells that decided to get together, to help each other out. Isn't that right?" Charles wet his feverish lips.

"What's all this about?" The doctor bent over him.

"I've got to tell you this. Doctor, oh, I've got to!" he cried. "What would happen, oh just pretend, please pretend, that just like in the old days, a lot of microbes got together and wanted to make a bunch, and reproduced and made *more——*"

His white hands were on his chest now, crawling toward his throat.

"And they decided to *take over* a person!" cried Charles.

"Take over a person?"

"Yes, *become* a person. *Me,* my hands, my feet! What if a disease somehow knew how to kill a person and yet live after him?"

He screamed.

The hands were on his neck.

The doctor moved forward, shouting.

At nine o'clock the doctor was escorted out to his car by the mother and father, who handed him his bag. They conversed in the cool night wind for a few minutes. "Just be sure his hands are kept strapped to his legs," said the doctor. "I don't want him hurting himself."

"Will he be all right, Doctor?" The mother held to his arm a moment.

He patted her shoulder. "Haven't I been your family physician for thirty years? It's the fever. He imagines things."

"But those bruises on his throat, he almost choked himself."

"Just you keep him strapped; he'll be all right in the morning."

The car moved off down the dark September road.

At three in the morning, Charles was still awake in his small black room. The bed was damp under his head and his back. He was very warm. Now he no longer had any arms or legs, and his body was beginning to change. He did not move on the bed, but looked at the vast blank ceiling space with insane concentration. For a while he had screamed and thrashed, but now he was weak and hoarse from it, and his mother had gotten up a number of times to soothe his brow with a wet towel. Now he was silent, his hands strapped to his legs.

He felt the walls of his body change, the organs shift, the lungs catch fire like burning bellows of pink alcohol. The room was lighted up as with the flickering of a hearth.

Now he had no body. It was all gone. It was under him, but it was filled with a vast pulse of some burning, lethargic drug. It was as if a guillotine had neatly lopped off his head, and his head lay shining on a midnight pillow while the body, below, still alive, belonged to somebody else. The disease had eaten his body and from the eating had reproduced itself in feverish duplicate.

There were the little hand hairs and the fingernails and the scars and the toenails and the tiny mole on his right hip, all done again in perfect fashion.

I am dead, he thought. I've been killed, and yet I live. My body is dead, it is all disease and nobody will know. I will walk around and it will not be me, it will be something else. It will be something all bad, all evil, so big and so evil it's hard to understand or think about. Something that will buy shoes and drink water and get married some day maybe and do more evil in the world than has ever been done.

Now the warmth was stealing up his neck, into his cheeks, like a hot wine. His lips burned, his eyelids, like leaves, caught fire. His nostrils breathed out blue flame, faintly, faintly.

This will be all, he thought. It'll take my head and my brain and fix each eye and every tooth and all the marks in my brain, and every hair and every wrinkle in my ears, and there'll be nothing left of me.

He felt his brain fill with a boiling mercury. He felt his left eye clench in upon itself and, like a snail, withdraw, shift. He was blind in his left eye. It no longer belonged to him. It was enemy territory. His tongue was gone, cut out. His left cheek was numbed, lost. His left ear stopped hearing. It belonged to someone else now. This thing that was being born, this mineral thing replacing the wooden log, this disease replacing healthy animal cell.

He tried to scream and he was able to scream loud and high and sharply in the room, just as his brain flooded down, his right eye and right ear were cut out, he was blind and deaf, all fire, all terror, all panic, all death.

His scream stopped before his mother ran through the door to his side.

It was a good, clear morning, with a brisk wind that helped carry the doctor up the path before the house. In the window above, the boy stood, fully dressed. He did not wave when the doctor waved and called, "What's this? Up? My God!"

The doctor almost ran upstairs. He came gasping into the bedroom.

"What are you doing out of bed?" he demanded of the boy. He tapped his thin chest, took his pulse and temperature. "Absolutely amazing! Normal. Normal, by God!"

"I shall never be sick again in my life," declared the boy, quietly, standing there, looking out the wide window. "Never."

"I hope not. Why, you're looking fine, Charles."

"Doctor?"

"Yes, Charles?"

"Can I go to school *now?*" asked Charles.

"Tomorrow will be time enough. You sound positively eager."

"I am. I like school. All the kids. I want to play with them and wrestle with them, and spit on them and play with the girls' pigtails and shake the teacher's hand, and rub my hands on all the cloaks in the cloakroom, and I want to grow up and travel and shake hands with people all over the world, and be married and have lots of children, and go to libraries and handle books and—*all* of that I want to!" said the boy, looking off into the September morning. "What's the name you called me?"

"What?" The doctor puzzled. "I called you nothing but Charles."

"It's better than no name at all, I guess." The boy shrugged.

"I'm glad you want to go back to school," said the doctor.

"I really anticipate it," smiled the boy. "Thank you for your help, Doctor. Shake hands."

"Glad to."

They shook hands gravely, and the clear wind blew through the open window. They shook hands for almost a minute, the boy smiling up at the old man and thanking him.

Then, laughing, the boy raced the doctor downstairs and out to his car. His mother and father followed for the happy farewell.

"Fit as a fiddle!" said the doctor. "Incredible!"

"And strong," said the father. "He got out of his straps himself during the night. Didn't you, Charles?"

"Did I?" said the boy.

"You did! How?"

"Oh," the boy said, "that was a long time ago."

"A long time ago!"

They all laughed, and while they were laughing, the quiet boy moved his bare foot on the sidewalk and merely touched, brushed against a number of red ants that were scurrying about on the sidewalk. Secretly, his eyes shining, while his parents chatted with the old man, he saw the ants hesitate, quiver, and lie still on the cement. He sensed they were cold now.

"Good-by!"

The doctor drove away, waving.

The boy walked ahead of his parents. As he walked he looked away toward the town and began to hum "School Days" under his breath.

"It's good to have him well again," said the father.

"Listen to him. He's so looking forward to school!"

The boy turned quietly. He gave each of his parents a crushing hug. He kissed them both several times.

Then without a word he bounded up the steps into the house.

In the parlor, before the others entered, he quickly opened the bird cage, thrust his hand in, and petted the yellow canary, once.

Then he shut the cage door, stood back, and waited.

# THE ALLEGORY
# OF THE CAVE

## Plato

Next, said I, here is a parable to illustrate the degrees in which our nature may be enlightened or unenlightened. Imagine the condition of men living in a sort of cavernous chamber underground, with an entrance open to the light and a long passage all down the cave. Here they have been from childhood, chained by the leg and also by the neck, so that they cannot move and can see only what is in front of them, because the chains will not let them turn their heads. At some distance higher up is the light of a fire burning behind them; and between the prisoners and the fire is a track with a parapet built along it, like the screen at a puppet-show, which hides the performers while they show their puppets over the top.

I see, said he.

Now behind this parapet imagine persons carrying along various artificial objects, including figures of men and animals in wood or stone or other materials, which project above the parapet. Naturally, some of these persons will be talking, others silent.

It is a strange picture, he said, and a strange sort of prisoners.

Like ourselves, I replied; for in the first place prisoners so confined would have seen nothing of themselves or of one another, except the shadows thrown by the fire-light on the wall of the Cave facing them, would they?

Not if all their lives they had been prevented from moving their heads.

And they would have seen as little of the objects carried past.

Of course.

Now, if they could talk to one another, would they not suppose that their words referred only to those passing shadows which they saw?

From *The Republic of Plato*, trans. by F. M. Cornford, 1941, pp. 222–226.

Necessarily.

And suppose their prison had an echo from the wall facing them? When one of the people crossing behind them spoke, they could only suppose that the sound came from the shadow passing before their eyes.

No doubt.

In every way, then, such prisoners would recognize as reality nothing but the shadows of those artificial objects.

Inevitably.

Now consider what would happen if their release from the chains and the healing of their unwisdom should come about in this way. Suppose one of them were set free and forced suddenly to stand up, turn his head, and walk with eyes lifted to the light; all these movements would be painful, and he would be too dazzled to make out the objects whose shadows he had been used to see. What do you think he would say, if someone told him that what he had formerly seen was meaningless illusion, but now, being somewhat nearer to reality and turned towards more real objects, he was getting a truer view? Suppose further that he were shown the various objects being carried by and were made to say, in reply to questions, what each of them was. Would he not be perplexed and believe the objects now shown him to be not so real as what he formerly saw?

Yes, not nearly so real.

And if he were forced to look at the fire-light itself, would not his eyes ache, so that he would try to escape and turn back to the things which he could see distinctly, convinced that they really were clearer than these other objects now being shown to him?

Yes.

And suppose someone were to drag him away forcibly up the steep and rugged ascent and not let him go until he had hauled him out into the sunlight, would he not suffer pain and vexation at such treatment, and, when he had come out into the light, find his eyes so full of its radiance that he could not see a single one of the things that he was now told were real?

Certainly he would not see them all at once.

He would need, then, to grow accustomed before he could see things in that upper world. At first it would be easiest to make out shadows, and then the images of men and things reflected in water, and later on the things themselves. After that, it would be easier to watch the heavenly bodies and the sky itself by night, looking at the light of the moon and stars rather than the Sun and the Sun's light in the day-time.

Yes, surely.

Last of all, he would be able to look at the Sun and contemplate its nature, not as it appears when reflected in water or any alien medium, but as it is in itself in its own domain.

No doubt.

And now he would begin to draw the conclusion that it is the Sun that produces the seasons and the course of the year and controls everything in the visible world, and moreover is in a way the cause of all that he and his companions used to see.

Clearly he would come at last to that conclusion.

Then if he called to mind his fellow prisoners and what passed for wisdom in his former dwelling-place, he would surely think himself happy in the change and be sorry for them. They may have had a practice of honouring and commending one another, with prizes for the man who had the keenest eye for the passing shadows and the best memory for the order in which they followed or accompanied one another, so that he could make a good guess as to which was going to come next. Would our released prisoner be likely to covet those prizes or to envy the men exalted to honour and power in the Cave? Would he not feel like Homer's Achilles, that he would far sooner "be on earth as a hired servant in the house of a landless man" or endure anything rather than go back to his old beliefs and live in the old way?

Yes, he would prefer any fate to such a life.

Now imagine what would happen if he went down again to take his former seat in the Cave. Coming suddenly out of the sunlight, his eyes would be filled with darkness. He might be required once more to deliver his opinion on those shadows, in competition with the prisoners who had never been released, while his eyesight was still dim and unsteady; and it might take some time to become used to the darkness. They would laugh at him and say that he had gone up only to come back with his sight ruined; it was worth no one's while even to attempt the ascent. If they could lay hands on the man who was trying to set them free and lead them up, they would kill him.

Yes, they would.

# INTO MY OWN

## Robert Frost

One of my wishes is that those dark trees,
So old and firm they scarcely show the breeze,
Were not, as 'twere, the merest mask of gloom,
But stretched away unto the edge of doom.

I should not be withheld but that some day
Into their vastness I should steal away,
Fearless of ever finding open land,
Or highway where the slow wheel pours the sand.

I do not see why I should e'er turn back,
Or those should not set forth upon my track
To overtake me, who should miss me here
And long to know if still I held them dear.

They would not find me changed from him they knew—
Only more sure of all I thought was true.

# THE FOOL
# ON THE HILL

## John Lennon
## and Paul McCartney

Day after day, alone on a hill, the man with a foolish grin is
     perfectly still
But nobody wants to know him, they can see that he's
     just a fool as he never gives an answer
But the fool on the hill sees the sun going down
And the eyes in his head see the world spinning round.
Well on the way, head in a cloud, the man of a thousand
     voices talking perfectly loud
But nobody ever hears him or the sound he appears to make
     and he never seems to notice
But the fool on the hill sees the sun going down
And the eyes in his head see the world spinning round.
And nobody seems to like him they can tell what he wants to do
And he never shows his feelings but the Fool on the Hill
Sees the sun going down and the eyes in his head see the world
     spinning round.
He never listens to them He knows that they're the fools
They don't like him
The Fool on the Hill sees the sun going down
And the eyes in his head see the world spinning round.

# IN JUST-

## E. E. Cummings

In Just-
spring        when the world is mud-
luscious the little
lame ballonman

whistles        far        and wee

and eddieandbill come
running from marbles and
piracies and it's
spring

when the world is puddle-wonderful

the queer
old balloonman whistles
far        and        wee
and bettyandisbel come dancing

from hop-scotch and jump-rope and

it's
spring
and
       the

              goat-footed

balloonMan      whistles
far
and
wee

# A MAN SAID
# TO THE UNIVERSE

## Stephen Crane

A man said to the universe:
"Sir, I exist!"
"However," replied the universe,
"The fact has not created in me
A sense of obligation."

# TO THE WIND

## Vicente Riva Palacio

When I was a child I lay in dread,
listening to you moaning at my door,
and fancying I heard the sorrowful
and grievous dirge of some unearthly being.

When I was a youth your tumult spoke
phrases with meaning that my mind divined;
and, blowing through the camp, in after years
your harsh voice kept on crying "Fatherland."

Now, in the dark nights, I hear you beating
against my incoercible prison-bars;
but my misfortunes have already told me

that you are wind, no more, when you complain,
wind when raging, wind when murmuring,
wind when you come and wind when you depart.

### The Breath of Life
The breath of life moves through a deathless valley
Of mysterious motherhood
Which conceives and bears the universal seed,
The seeming of a world never to end,
Breath for men to draw from as they will:
And the more they take of it, the more remains.


### The Universe Is Deathless
The universe is deathless,
Is deathless because, having no finite self,
It stays infinite.
A sound man by not advancing himself
Stays the further ahead of himself,
By not confining himself to himself
Sustains himself outside himself:
By never being an end in himself
He endlessly becomes himself.


LAO TZU


Reprinted by permission of G. P. Putnam's Sons from *The Way of Life According to Lao Tzu* translated by Witter Bynner. Copyright 1944 by Witter Bynner.

# THE TRIAL BY EXISTENCE

## Robert Frost

Even the bravest that are slain
    Shall not dissemble their surprise
On waking to find valor reign,
    Even as on earth, in paradise;
And where they sought without the sword
    Wide fields of asphodel fore'er,
To find that the utmost reward
    Of daring should be still to dare.

The light of heaven falls whole and white
    And is not shattered into dyes,
The light forever is morning light;
    The hills are verdured pasturewise;
The angel hosts with freshness go,
    And seek with laughter what to brave—
And binding all is the hushed snow
    Or the far-distant breaking wave.

And from a cliff top is proclaimed
    The gathering of the souls for birth,
The trial by existence named,
    The obscuration upon earth.
And the slant spirits trooping by
    In streams and cross- and counter-streams

Can but give ear to that sweet cry
    For its suggestion of what dreams!

And the more loitering are turned
    To view once more the sacrifice
Of those who for some good discerned
    Will gladly give up paradise.
And a white shimmering concourse rolls
    Toward the throne to witness there
The speeding of devoted souls
    Which God makes His especial care.

And none are taken but who will,
    Having first heard the life read out
That opens earthward, good and ill,
    Beyond the shadow of a doubt;
And very beautifully God limns,
    And tenderly, life's little dream,
But naught extenuates or dims,
    Setting the thing that is supreme.

Nor is there wanting in the press
    Some spirit to stand simply forth,
Heroic in its nakedness,
    Against the uttermost of earth.
The tale of earth's unhonored things
    Sounds nobler there than 'neath the sun;
And the mind whirls and the heart sings,
    And a shout greets the daring one.

But always God speaks at the end:
    "One thought in agony of strife
The bravest would have by for friend,
    The memory that he chose the life;
But the pure fate to which you go
    Admits no memory of choice,
Or the woe were not earthly woe
    To which you give the assenting voice."

And so the choice must be again,
    But the last choice is still the same;
And the awe passes wonder then,
    And a hush falls for all acclaim.
And God has taken a flower of gold
    And broken it, and used therefrom

The mystic link to bind and hold
    Spirit to matter till death come.

'Tis of the essence of life here,
    Though we choose greatly, still to lack
The lasting memory at all clear,
    That life has for us on the wrack
Nothing but what we somehow chose;
    Thus are we wholly stripped of pride
In the pain that has but one close,
    Bearing it crushed and mystified.

# THE BRAIN—
# IS WIDER THAN
# THE SKY

## Emily Dickinson

The Brain—is wider than the Sky—
For—put them side by side—
The one the other will contain
With ease—and—You—beside—

The Brain is deeper than the sea—
For—hold them—Blue to Blue—
The one the other will absorb—
As Sponges—Buckets—do—

The Brain is just the weight of God—
for—Heft them—Pound for Pound—
And they will differ—if they do—
As Syllable from Sound—

# THERE WAS
# A CHILD
# WENT FORTH

## Walt Whitman

There was a child went forth every day,
And the first object he look'd upon, that object he became,
And that object became part of him for the day or a certain part of the day,
Or for many years or stretching cycles of years.

The early lilacs became part of this child,
And grass and white and red morning-glories, and white and red clover,
    and the song of the phoebe-bird,
And the Third-month lambs and the sow's pink-faint litter, and the mare's
    foal and the cow's calf,
And the noisy brood of the barnyard or by the mire of the pond-side,
And the fish suspending themselves so curiously below there, and the
    beautiful curious liquid,
And the water-plants with their graceful flat heads, all became part of him.

The field-sprouts of Fourth-month and Fifth-month became part of him,
Winter-grain sprouts and those of the light-yellow corn, and the esculent
    roots of the garden,
And the apple-trees cover'd with blossoms and the fruit afterward, and
    wood-berries, and the commonest weeds by the road,
And the old drunkard staggering home from the outhouse of the tavern
    whence he had lately risen,
And the schoolmistress that pass'd on her way to the school,
And the friendly boys that pass'd, and the quarrelsome boys,
And the tidy and fresh-cheek'd girls, and the barefoot negro boy and girl,
And all the changes of city and country wherever he went.

His own parents, he that had father'd him and she that had conceiv'd
him in her womb and birth'd him,
They gave this child more of themselves than that,
They gave him afterward every day, they became part of him.

The mother at home quietly placing the dishes on the supper-table,
The mother with mild words, clean her cap and gown, a wholesome odor
falling off her person and clothes as she walks by,
The father, strong, self-sufficient, manly, mean, anger'd, unjust,
The blow, the quick loud word, the tight bargain, the crafty lure,
The family usages, the language, the company, the furniture, the yearning
and swelling heart,
Affection that will not be gainsay'd, the sense of what is real, the thought
if after all it should prove unreal,
The doubts of day-time and the doubts of night-time, the curious whether
and how,
Whether that which appears so is so, or is it all flashes and specks?
Men and women crowding fast in the streets, if they are not flashes and
specks what are they?
The streets themselves and the façades of houses, and goods in the windows,
Vehicles, teams, the heavy-plank'd wharves, the huge crossing at the ferries,
The village on the highland seen from afar at sunset, the river between,
Shadows, aureola and mist, the light falling on roofs and gables of white
or brown two miles off,
The schooner near by sleepily dropping down the tide, the little boat
slack-tow'd astern,
The hurrying tumbling waves, quick-broken crests, slapping,
The strata of color'd clouds, the long bar of maroon-tint away solitary
by itself, the spread of purity it lies motionless in,
The horizon's edge, the flying sea-crow, the fragrance of salt marsh and
shore mud,
These became part of that child who went forth every day, and who now
goes, and will always go forth every day.

*Child's Vision* by Raymond Keller

*Rebirth* by Raymond Keller

*The Link* by Raymond Keller

*Rock Poetry* by Raymond Keller

# THE FORCE THAT THROUGH THE GREEN FUSE DRIVES THE FLOWER

## Dylan Thomas

The force that through the green fuse drives the flower
Drives my green age; that blasts the roots of trees
Is my destroyer.
And I am dumb to tell the crooked rose
My youth is bent by the same wintry fever.

The force that drives the water through the rocks
Drives my red blood; that drives the mountain streams
Turns mine to wax.
And I am dumb to mouth unto my veins
How at the mountain spring the same mouth sucks.

The hand that whirls the water in the pool
Stirs the quicksand; that ropes the blowing wind
Hauls my shroud sail.
And I am dumb to tell the hanging man
How of my clay is made the hangman's lime.

The lips of time leech to the fountain head;
Love drips and gathers, but the fallen blood
Shall calm her sores.
And I am dumb to tell a weather's wind
How time has ticked a heaven round the stars.

And I am dumb to tell the lover's tomb
How at my sheet goes the same crooked worm.

# ILLUMINATIONS

## Arthur Rimbaud

**IV**

I am the saint at prayer on the terrace like the peaceful beasts that graze down to the sea of Palestine.

I am the scholar of the dark armchair. Branches and rain hurl themselves at the windows of my library.

I am the pedestrian of the highroad by way of the dwarf woods; the roar of the sluices drowns my steps. I can see for a long time the melancholy wash of the setting sun.

I might well be the child abandoned on the jetty on its way to the high seas, the little farm boy following the lane, its forehead touching the sky.

The paths are rough. The hillocks are covered with broom. The air is motionless. How far away are the birds and the springs! It can only be the end of the world ahead.

**V**

Let them rent me this whitewashed tomb, at last, with cement lines in relief,—far down under ground.

I lean my elbows on the table, the lamp shines brightly on these newspapers I am fool enough to read again, these stupid books.

At an enormous distance above my subterranean parlor, houses take root, fogs gather. The mud is red or black. Monstrous city, night without end!

Less high are the sewers. At the sides, nothing but the thickness of the globe. Chasms of azure, wells of fire perhaps. Perhaps it is on these levels that moons and comets meet, fables and seas.

In hours of bitterness, I imagine balls of sapphire, of metal. I am master of silence. Why should the semblance of an opening pale under one corner of the vault?

### Existence Is Beyond the Power of Words

Existence is beyond the power of words
To define:
Terms may be used
But are none of them absolute.
In the beginning of heaven and earth there were no
        words,
Words came out of the womb of matter;
And whether a man dispassionately
Sees to the core of life
Or passionately
Sees the surface,
The core and the surface
Are essentially the same,
Words making them seem different
Only to express appearance.
If name be needed, wonder names them both:
From wonder into wonder
Existence opens.

LAO TZU

Reprinted by permission of G. P. Putnam's Sons from *The Way of Life According to Lao Tzu,* translated by Witter Bynner. Copyright 1944 by Witter Bynner.

*"nobody,not even the rain,
has such small hands,"*

E. E. Cummings

# III

## LOVE
## AND HATE

*The Last Judgment* (detail) by Hieronymous Bosch (Gemaldegalerie der Akademie der Bildenden Kunste, Vienna, Austria)

# HEAR ME,
# MY WARRIORS

## Chief Joseph
## of the Nez Perce

Hear me, my warriors; my heart is sick and sad.
Our chiefs are killed,
The old men are all dead
It is cold, and we have no blankets;
The little children are freezing to death.
Hear me, my warriors; my heart is sick and sad.
From where the sun now stands I will fight no more forever!

# SOLILOQUY OF THE SPANISH CLOISTER

## Robert Browing

Gᴿ-ᴿ-ᴿ—there go, my heart's abhorrence!
　　Water your damned flower-pots, do!
If hate killed men, Brother Lawrence,
　　God's blood, would not mine kill you!
What? your myrtle-bush wants trimming?
　　Oh, that rose has prior claims—
Needs its leaden vase filled brimming?
　　Hell dry you up with its flames!

At the meal we sit together:
　　*Salve tibi!* I must hear
Wise talk of the kind of weather,
　　Sort of season, time of year:
*Not a plenteous cork-crop: scarcely*
　　*Dare we hope oak-galls, I doubt:*
*What's the Latin name for "parsley"?*
　　What's the Greek name for Swine's Snout?

Whew! We'll have our platter burnished,
　　Laid with care on our own shelf!
With a fire-new spoon we're furnished,
　　And a goblet for ourself.
Rinsed like something sacrificial
　　Ere 't is fit to touch our chaps—
Marked with L for our initial!
　　(He-he! There his lily snaps!)

*Saint,* forsooth! White brown Dolores
　　Squats outside the Convent bank

With Sanchicha, telling stories,
    Steeping tresses in the tank.
Blue-black, lustrous, thick like horsehairs,
    —Can't I see his dead eye glow,
Bright as 't were a Barbary corsair's?
    (That is, if he'd let it show!)

When he finishes refection,
    Knife and fork he never lays
Cross-wise, to my recollection,
    As do I, in Jesu's praise.
I the Trinity illustrate,
    Drinking watered orange-pulp—
In three sips the Arian frustrate;
    While he drains his at one gulp.

Oh, those melons! If he's able
    We're to have a feast! so nice!
One goes to the Abbot's table,
    All of us get each a slice.
How go on your flowers? None double?
    Not one fruit-sort can you spy?
Strange!—And I, too, at such trouble
    Keep them close-nipped on the sly!

There's a great text in Galatians,
    Once you trip on it, entails
Twenty-nine distinct damnations,
    One sure, if another fails:
If I trip him just a-dying,
    Sure of heaven as sure can be,
Spin him round and send him flying
    Off to hell, a Manichee?

Or, my scrofulous French novel
    On gray paper with blunt type!
Simply glance at it, you grovel
    Hand and foot in Belial's gripe:
If I double down its pages
    At the woeful sixteenth print,
When he gathers his greengages,
    Ope a sieve and slip it in't?

Or, there's Satan!—one might venture
    Pledge one's soul to him, yet leave

Such a flaw in the indenture
   As he'd miss till, past retrieve,
Blasted lay that rose-acacia
   We're so proud of! *Hy, Zy, Hine* . . .
'St, there's Vespers! *Plena gratiâ,*
   *Ave, Virgo!* Gr-r-r—you swine!

# CANDY MAN

## Mississippi John Hurt

All you ladies gather round
The good sweet Candy Man's in town
Candy Man     Candy Man.

He's got some candy that's nine inch long
He sells it fast to all the chewers come
Candy Man     Candy Man.

All heard what Sister Jonah's said
She always takes a candy stick to bed
Candy Man     Candy Man.

All yer stick candy don't melt away
Guess it gets better so the ladies say
Candy Man     Candy Man.

Yes, don't stand close to the Candy Man
He'll ease a stick a candy in your hand
Candy Man     Sweet Candy Man.

Yes, you and Candy Man, you gettin mighty thick
Mmmmm hmmmmm

Uh huh
O yeh
O yeh
Yeh yeh

I said you and the Candy Man, you gettin mighty thick
You must be stuck on the Candy Man's stick.
O yeh
O yeh

# SONNET 73

## William Shakespeare

That time of year thou mayst in me behold,
When yellow leaves, or none, or few do hang
Upon those boughs which shake against the cold,
Bare ruin'd choirs, where late the sweet birds sang.
In me thou seest the twilight of such day,
As after sunset fadeth in the West,
Which by and by black night doth take away,
Death's second self that seals up all in rest.
In me thou seest the glowing of such fire,
That on the ashes of his youth doth lie,
As the death-bed, whereon it must expire,
Consum'd with that which it was nourish'd by.
   This thou perceiv'st, which makes thy love more strong,
   To love that well, which thou must leave ere long.

# SONNET 116

## William Shakespeare

Let me not to the marriage of true minds
Admit impediments, love is not love
Which alters when it alteration finds,
Or bends with the remover to remove.
O no, it is an ever-fixed mark
That looks on tempest and is never shaken;
It is the star to every wand'ring bark,
Whose worth's unknown, although his height be taken,
Love's not Time's fool, though rosy lips and cheeks
Within his bending sickle's compass come,
Love alters not with his brief hours and weeks,
But bears it out even to the edge of doom:
    If this be error and upon me proved,
    I never writ, nor no man ever loved.

# SOMEWHERE I HAVE NEVER TRAVELLED

## E. E. Cummings

somewhere i have never travelled,gladly beyond
any experience,your eyes have their silence:
in your most frail gesture are things which enclose me,
or which i cannot touch because they are too near

your slightest look easily will unclose me
though i have closed myself as fingers,
you open always petal by petal myself as Spring opens
(touching skilfully,mysteriously)her first rose

or if you wish be to close me,i and
my life will shut very beautifully,suddenly,
as when the heart of this flower imagines
the snow carefully everywhere descending;

nothing which we are to perceive in this world equals
the power of your intense fragility:whose texture
compels me with the colour of its countries,
rendering death and forever with each breathing

(i do not know what it is about you that closes
and opens;only something in me understands
the voice of your eyes is deeper than all roses)
nobody,not even the rain,has such small hands

# SPRING IS LIKE
# A PERHAPS HAND

## E. E. Cummings

Spring is like a perhaps hand
(which comes carefully
out of Nowhere)arranging
a window,into which people look(while
people stare
arranging and changing placing
carefully there a strange
thing and a known thing here)and

changing everything carefully

spring is like a perhaps
Hand in a window
(carefully to
and fro moving New and
Old things,while
people stare carefully
moving a perhaps
fraction of flower here placing
an inch of air there)and

without breaking anything.

# SINCE FEELING
# IS FIRST

## E. E. Cummings

since feeling is first
who pays any attention
to the syntax of things
will never wholly kiss you;

wholly to be a fool
while Spring is in the world

my blood approves,
and kisses are a better fate
than wisdom
lady i swear by all flowers.  Don't cry
—the best gesture of my brain is less than
your eyelids' flutter which says

we are for each other: then
laugh, leaning back in my arms
for life's not a paragraph

And death i think is no parenthesis

# IT MAY NOT ALWAYS BE SO

## E. E. Cummings

it may not always be so; and i say
that if your lips, which i have loved, should touch
another's, and your dear strong fingers clutch
his heart, as mine in time not far away;
if on another's face your sweet hair lay
in such a silence as i know, or such
great writhing words as, uttering overmuch,
stand helplessly before the spirit at bay;

if this should be, i say if this should be—
you of my heart, send me a little word;
that i may go unto him, and take his hands,
saying, Accept all happiness from me.
Then shall i turn my face, and hear one bird
sing terribly afar in the lost lands.

# FRANKIE
# AND
# JOHNNY

## Folk Ballad

Frankie and Johnny were lovers.
O my Gawd how they did love!
They swore to be true to each other,
As true as the stars above.
He was her man but he did her wrong.

Frankie and Johnny went walking,
Johnny in a brand new suit.
Frankie went walking with Johnny,
Said: "O Gawd don't my Johnny look cute."
He was her man but he did her wrong.

Frankie went down to Memphis,
Went on the morning train,
Paid a hundred dollars,
Bought Johnny a watch and chain.
He was her man but he did her wrong.

Frankie lived in a crib-house,
Crib-house with only two doors,
Gave her money to Johnny,
He spent it on those parlour whores.
He was her man but he did her wrong.

Frankie went down to the hock-shop,
Went for a bucket of beer,
Said: "O Mr. Bartender
Has my loving Johnny been here?
He is my man but he's doing me wrong."

"I don't want to make you no trouble,
I don't want to tell you no lie,
But I saw Johnny an hour ago
With a girl name Nelly Bly.
He is your man but he's doing you wrong."

Frankie went down to the hotel.
She didn't go there for fun,
'Cause underneath her kimona
She toted a 44 gun.
He was her man but he did her wrong.

Frankie went down to the hotel.
She rang the front-door bell,
Said: "Stand back all you chippies
Or I'll blow you all to hell.
I want my man for he's doing me wrong."

Frankie looked in through the key-hole
And there before her eye
She saw her Johnny on the sofa
A-loving up Nelly Bly.
He was her man; he was doing her wrong.

Frankie threw back her kimona,
Took out a big 44,
Root-a-toot-toot, three times she shoot
Right through that hard-ware door.
He was her man but was doing her wrong.

Johnny grabbed up his Stetson,
Said; "O my Gawd Frankie don't shoot."
But Frankie pulled hard on the trigger
And the gun went root-a-toot-toot.
She shot her man who was doing her wrong.

"Roll me over easy,
Roll me over slow,
Roll me over on my right side
'Cause my left side hurts me so.
I was her man but I did her wrong."

Johnny he was a gambler,
He gambled for the gain;
The very last words he ever said
Were—"High-low Jack and the game."
He was her man but he did her wrong.

"Bring out your rubber-tired buggy,
Bring out your rubber-tired hack;
I'll take my Johnny to the graveyard
But I won't bring him back.
He was my man but he did me wrong.

Lock me in that dungeon,
Lock me in that cell,
Lock me where the north-east wind
Blows from the corner of Hell.
I shot my man 'cause he did me wrong."

Frankie went down to the Madame,
She went down on her knees.
"Forgive me Mrs. Halcombe,
Forgive me if you please
For shooting my man 'cause he did me wrong."

"Forgive you Frankie darling,
Forgive you I never can,
Forgive you Frankie darling
For shooting your only man,
For he was your man though he did you wrong."

It was not murder in the first degree,
It was not murder in the third.
A woman simply shot her man
As a hunter drops a bird.
She shot her man 'cause he did her wrong.

Frankie said to the Sheriff
"What do you think they'll do?"
The Sheriff said to Frankie
"It's the electric chair for you.
You shot your man 'cause he did you wrong."

Frankie sat in the jail-house,
Had no electric fan,
Told her little sister:
"Don't you marry no sporting man.
I had a man but he did me wrong."

Frankie heard a rumbling,
Away down in the ground;
Maybe it was little Johnny
Where she had shot him down.
He was her man, but he did her wrong.

Once more I saw Frankie,
She was sitting in the chair
Waiting for to go and meet her God
With the sweat dripping out of her hair.
He was her man but he did her wrong.

This story has no moral,
This story has no end,
This story only goes to show
That there ain't no good in men.
He was her man, but he did her wrong.

# THE BALLAD OF FRANKIE LEE AND JUDAS PRIEST

## Bob Dyland

Well, Frankie Lee and Judas Priest,
They were the best of friends,
So when Frankie Lee needed money one day,
Judas quickly pulled out a roll of tens
And placed them on a foot stool
Just above the cloudy plain,
Saying take your pick, Frankie Boy,
My loss will be your gain.

Well, Frankie Lee, he sat right down
And put his fingers to his chin,
But with the cold eyes of Judas on him
His head began to spin.
"Could you please not stare at me like that?"
He said, "It's just my foolish pride.
But sometimes a man must be alone,
And this is no place to hide."

Well, Judas, he just winked and said,
"All right, I'll leave you here,
But you'd better hurry up and choose
Which o' these bills you want
Before they all disappear."
"I'm gonna start my pickin' right now.
Just tell me where you'll be."
Judas pointed down the road
And said, "Eternity."

"Eternity?" said Frankie Lee
With a voice as cold as ice.
"That's right," said Judas, "Eternity,
Though you might call it Paradise."

"I don't call it anything,"
Said Frankie Lee with a smile.
"All right," said Judas Priest,
"I'll see you after a while."

Well, Frankie Lee, he sat back down
Feeling low and mean,
When just then a passing stranger
Burst in upon the scene,
Saying, "Are you Frankie Lee, the gambler,
Whose father is deceased?
Well, if you are there's a fella calling
Down the road, and they say his name is Priest."

"Oh, yes, he is my friend,"
Said Frankie Lee in fright.
"I do recall him very well.
In fact he just left my sight."

"Yes, that's the one," said the stranger
As quiet as a mouse.
"Well, my message is he's down the road,
Stranded in a house."

Well, Frankie Lee, he panicked.
He dropped everything and ran
Until he came onto the spot
Where Judas Priest did stand.

"What kind of house is this?" he said,
"Where I have come to roam?"
"It's not a house," said Judas Priest,
"It's not a house, it's a home."

Well, Frankie Lee, he trembled;
He soon lost all control
Over everything which he had made
While the mission bells did toll.
He just stood there staring at that big house
As bright as any sun,
With four and twenty windows,
And a woman's face in everyone.

Well, up the stairs ran Frankie Lee
With a soulful bounding leap,
And foaming at the mouth,
He began to make his midnight creep.
For sixteen nights and days he raved,
But on the seventeenth he burst
Into the arms of Judas Priest,
Which is where he died of thirst.

Noone tried to say a thing
When they carried him out in jest
Except, of course, the little neighbor boy
Who carried him to rest,
And he just walked along alone
With his guilt so well-concealed
And muttered underneath his breath,
"Nothing is revealed."

Well, the moral of this story,
The moral of this song
Is simply that one should never be
Where one does not belong.
So when you see your neighbor carrying something,
Help him with his load
And don't go mistaking paradise
For that home across the road.

### The Cat
Sleeping, then waking
and giving a great yawn, the cat
goes out love-making.


### In the House
At the butterflies
the caged bird gazes, envying—
just watch its eyes!


### A Summer Day
High noon:
save for reed-sparrows, the river
makes no sound.


ISSA

# MISS LONELYHEARTS,
# HELP ME, HELP ME

## Nathanael West

The Miss Lonelyhearts of The New York *Post-Dispatch* (Are-you-in-trouble?—Do-you-need-advice?—Write-to-Miss-Lonelyhearts-and-she-will-help-you) sat at his desk and stared at a piece of white cardboard. On it a prayer had been printed by Shrike, the feature editor.

Soul of Miss L, glorify me.
Body of Miss L, nourish me
Blood of Miss L, intoxicate me.
Tears of Miss L, wash me.
Oh good Miss L, excuse my plea,
And hide me in your heart,
And defend me from mine enemies.
Help me, Miss L, help me, help me.
In sæcula sæculorum. Amen.

Although the deadline was less than a quarter of an hour away, he was still working on his leader. He had gone as far as: "Life *is* worth while, for it is full of dreams and peace, gentleness and ecstasy, and faith that burns like a clear white flame on a grim dark altar." But he found it impossible to continue. The letters were no longer funny. He could not go on finding the same joke funny thirty times a day for months on end. And on most days he received more than thirty letters, all of them alike, stamped from the dough of suffering with a heart-shaped cookie knife.

On his desk were piled those he had received this morning. He started through them again, searching for some clue to a sincere answer.

*Dear Miss Lonelyhearts—*

*I am in such pain I dont know what to do sometimes I think I will kill myself my kidneys hurt so much. My husband thinks no woman can be a good catholic and not have children irregardless of the pain. I was married honorable from our church but I never knew what married life meant as I never was told about man and wife. My grandmother never told me and she was the only mother I had but made a big mistake by not telling me as it dont pay to be inocent and is only a big disapointment. I have 7 children in 12 yrs and ever since the last 2 I have been so sick. I was operatored on twice and my husband promised no more children on the doctors advice as he said I might die but when I got back from the hospital he broke his promise and now I am going to have a baby and I dont think I can stand it my kidneys hurt so much. I am so sick and scared because I cant have an abortion on account of being a catholic and my husband so religious. I cry all the time it hurts so much and I dont know what to do.*

> *Yours respectfully,*
> *Sick-of-it-all*

Miss Lonelyhearts threw the letter into an open drawer and lit a cigarette.

*Dear Miss Lonelyhearts—*

*I am sixteen years old now and I dont know what to do and would appreciate it if you could tell me what to do. When I was a little girl it was not so bad because I got used to the kids on the block makeing fun of me, but now I would like to have boy friends like the other girls and go out on Saturday nites, but no boy will take me because I was born without a nose —although I am a good dancer and have a nice shape and my father buys me pretty clothes.*

*I sit and look at myself all day and cry. I have a big hole in the middle of my face that scares people even myself so I cant blame the boys for not wanting to take me out. My mother loves me, but she crys terrible when she looks at me.*

*What did I do to deserve such a terrible bad fate? Even if I did do some bad things I didnt do any before I was a year old and I was born this way. I asked Papa and he says he doesn't know, but that maybe I did something in the other world before I was born or that maybe I was being punished for his sins. I dont believe that because he is a very nice man. Ought I commit suicide?*

> *Sincerely yours,*
> *Desperate*

The cigarette was imperfect and refused to draw. Miss Lonelyhearts took it out of his mouth and stared at it furiously. He fought himself quiet, then lit another one.

*Dear Miss Lonelyhearts—*

*I am writing to you for my little sister Gracie because something awfull hapened to her and I am afraid to tell mother about it. I am 15 years old and Gracie is 13 and we live in Brooklyn. Gracie is deaf and dumb and biger than me but not very smart on account of being deaf and dumb. She plays on the roof of our house and dont go to school except to deaf and dumb school twice a week on tuesdays and thursdays. Mother makes her play on the roof because we dont want her to get run over as she aint very smart. Last week a man came on the roof and did something dirty to her. She told me about it and I dont know what to do as I am afraid to tell mother on account of her being liable to beat Gracie up. I am afraid that Gracie is going to have a baby and I listened to her stomack last night for a long time to see if I could hear the baby but I couldn't. If I tell mother she will beat Gracie up awfull because I am the only one who loves her and last time when she tore her dress they loked her in the closet for 2 days and if the boys on the blok hear about if they will say dirty things like they did on Peewee Conors sister the time she got caught in the lots. So please what would you do if the same hapened in your family.*

*Yours truly,*
*Harold S.*

He stopped reading. Christ was the answer, but, if he did not want to get sick, he had to stay away from the Christ business. Besides, Christ was Shrike's particular joke. "Soul of Miss L, glorify me. Body of Miss L, save me. Blood of . . ." He turned to his typewriter.

Although his cheap clothes had too much style, he still looked like the son of a Baptist minister. A beard would become him, would accent his Old-Testament look. But even without a beard no one could fail to recognize the New England puritan. His forehead was high and narrow. His nose was long and fleshless. His bony chin was shaped and cleft like a hoof. On seeing him for the first time, Shrike had smiled and said, "The Susan Chesters, the Beatrice Fairfaxes and the Miss Lonelyhearts are the priests of twentieth-century America."

A copy boy came up to tell him that Shrike wanted to know if the stuff was ready. He bent over the typewriter and began pounding its keys.

But before he had written a dozen words, Shrike leaned over his shoulder. "The same old stuff," Shrike said. "Why don't you give them something new and hopeful? Tell them about art. Here, I'll dictate:

*"Art Is a Way Out.*

"Do not let life overwhelm you. When the old paths are choked with the débris of failure, look for newer and fresher paths. Art is just such a path. Art is distilled from suffering. As Mr. Polnikoff exclaimed through his fine

Russian beard, when, at the age of eighty-six, he gave up his business to learn Chinese, 'We are, as yet, only at the beginning. . . .'

"*Art Is One of Life's Richest Offerings.*

"For those who have not the talent to create, there is appreciation. For those . . .

"Go on from there."

# THE BIRTHMARK

## Nathaniel Hawthorne

In the latter part of the last century there lived a man of science, an eminent proficient in every branch of natural philosophy, who not long before our story opens had made experience of a spiritual affinity more attractive than any chemical one. He had left his laboratory to the care of an assistant, cleared his fine countenance from the furnace smoke, washed the stain of acids from his fingers, and persuaded a beautiful woman to become his wife. In those days when the comparatively recent discovery of electricity and other kindred mysteries of Nature seemed to open paths into the region of miracle, it was not unusual for the love of science to rival the love of woman in its depth and absorbing energy. The higher intellect, the imagination, the spirit, and even the heart might all find their congenial aliment in pursuits which, as some of their ardent votaries believed, would ascend from one step of powerful intelligence to another, until the philosopher should lay his hand on the secret of creative force and perhaps make new worlds for himself. We know not whether Aylmer possessed this degree of faith in man's ultimate control over Nature. He had devoted himself, however, too unreservedly to scientific studies ever to be weaned from them by any second passion. His love for his young wife might prove the stronger of the two; but it could only be by intertwining itself with his love of science, and uniting the strength of the latter to his own.

Such a union accordingly took place, and was attended with truly remarkable consequences and a deeply impressive moral. One day, very soon after their marriage, Aylmer sat gazing at his wife with a trouble in his countenance that grew stronger until he spoke.

"Georgiana," said he, "has it never occurred to you that the mark upon your cheek might be removed?"

"No, indeed," said she, smiling; but perceiving the seriousness of his

*Mom* by Raymond Keller

*Love* by Raymond Keller

*Is This Your Peace?* by Raymond Keller

*Rage* by Raymond Keller

manner, she blushed deeply. "To tell you the truth it has been so often called a charm that I was simple enough to imagine it might be so."

"Ah, upon another face perhaps it might," replied her husband; "but never on yours. No, dearest Georgiana, you came so nearly perfect from the hand of Nature that this slightest possible defect, which we hesitate whether to term a defect or a beauty, shocks me, as being the visible mark of earthly imperfection."

"Shocks you, my husband!" cried Georgiana, deeply hurt; at first reddening with momentary anger, but then bursting into tears. "Then why did you take me from my mother's side? You cannot love what shocks you!"

To explain this conversation it must be mentioned that in the centre of Georgiana's left cheek there was a singular mark, deeply interwoven, as it were, with the texture and substance of her face. In the usual state of her complexion—a healthy though delicate bloom—the mark wore a tint of deeper crimson, which imperfectly defined its shape amid the surrounding rosiness. When she blushed it gradually became more indistinct, and finally vanished amid the triumphant rush of blood that bathed the whole cheek with its brilliant glow. But if any shifting motion caused her to turn pale there was the mark again, a crimson stain upon the snow, in what Aylmer sometimes deemed an almost fearful distinctness. Its shape bore not a little similarity to the human hand, though of the smallest pygmy size. Georgiana's lovers were wont to say that some fairy at her birth hour had laid her tiny hand upon the infant's cheek, and left this impress there in token of the magic endowments that were to give her such sway over all hearts. Many a desperate swain would have risked life for the privilege of pressing his lips to the mysterious hand. It must not be concealed, however, that the impression wrought by this fairy sign manual varied exceedingly, according to the difference of temperament in the beholders. Some fastidious persons—but they were exclusively of her own sex—affirmed that the bloody hand, as they chose to call it, quite destroyed the effect of Georgiana's beauty, and rendered her countenance even hideous. But it would be as reasonable to say that one of those small blue stains which sometimes occur in the purest statuary marble would convert the Eve of Powers to a monster. Masculine observers, if the birthmark did not heighten their admiration, contented themselves with wishing it away, that the world might possess one living specimen of ideal loveliness without the semblance of a flaw. After his marriage—for he thought little or nothing of the matter before—Aylmer discovered that this was the case with himself.

Had she been less beautiful—if Envy's self could have found aught else to sneer at—he might have felt his affection heightened by the prettiness of this mimic hand, now vaguely portrayed, now lost, now stealing forth again and glimmering to and fro with every pulse of emotion that throbbed within her heart; but seeing her otherwise so perfect, he found this one defect grow more and more intolerable with every moment of their united lives. It was the fatal flaw of humanity which Nature, in one shape or another, stamps ineffaceably on all her productions, either to imply that they are temporary and finite, or that their perfection must be wrought by toil and pain. The crimson hand expressed the ineludible gripe in which mortality clutches the highest and purest of earthly mould, degrading them into kindred with the lowest, and even with the very brutes, like whom their visible frames return to dust. In this manner, selecting it as the symbol of his wife's liability to sin, sorrow, decay, and death, Aylmer's sombre imagination was not long in rendering the birthmark a frightful object, causing him more trouble and horror than ever Georgiana's beauty, whether of soul or sense, had given him delight.

At all the seasons which should have been their happiest, he invariably and without intending it, may, in spite of a purpose to the contrary, reverted to this one disastrous topic. Trifling as it at first appeared, it so connected itself with innumerable trains of thought and modes of feeling that it became the central point of all. With the morning twilight Aylmer opened his eyes upon his wife's face and recognized the symbol of imperfection; and when they sat together at the evening hearth his eyes wandered stealthily to her cheek, and beheld, flickering with the blaze of the wood fire, the spectral hand that wrote mortality where he would fain have worshipped. Georgiana soon learned to shudder at his gaze. It needed but a glance with the peculiar expression that his face often wore to change the roses of her cheek into a deathlike paleness, amid which the crimson hand was brought strongly out, like a bas-relief of ruby on the whitest marble.

Late one night when the lights were growing dim, so as hardly to betray the strain on the poor wife's cheek, she herself, for the first time, voluntarily took up the subject.

"Do you remember, my dear Aylmer," said she, with a feeble attempt at a smile, "have you any recollection of a dream last night about this odious hand?"

"None! none whatever!" replied Aylmer, starting; but then he added, in a dry, cold tone, affected for the sake of concealing the real depth of his emotion, "I might well dream of it; for before I fell asleep it had taken a pretty firm hold of my fancy."

"And you did dream of it?" continued Georgiana, hastily; for she dreaded lest a gush of tears should interrupt what she had to say. "A terrible dream! I wonder that you can forget it. Is it possible to forget this one expression?—'It is in her heart now; we must have it out!' Reflect, my husband; for by all means I would have you recall that dream."

The mind is in a sad state when Sleep, the all-involving, cannot confine her spectres within the dim region of her sway, but suffers them to break forth, affrighting this actual life with secrets that perchance belong to a deeper one. Aylmer now remembered his dream. He had fancied himself with his servant Aminadab, attempting an operation for the removal of the birthmark; but the deeper went the knife, the deeper sank the hand, until at length its tiny grasp appeared to have caught hold of Georgiana's heart; whence, however, her husband was inexorably resolved to cut or wrench it away.

When the dream had shaped itself perfectly in his memory, Aylmer sat in his wife's presence with a guilty feeling. Truth often finds its way to the mind close muffled in robes of sleep, and then speaks with uncompromising directness of matters in regard to which we practise an unconscious self-deception during our waking moments. Until now he had not been aware of the tyrannizing influence acquired by one idea over his mind, and of the lengths which he might find in his heart to go for the sake of giving himself peace.

"Aylmer," resumed Georgiana, solemnly, "I know not what may be the cost to both of us to rid me of this fatal birthmark. Perhaps its removal may cause cureless deformity; or it may be the stain goes as deep as life itself. Again: do we know that there is a possibility, on any terms, of unclasping the firm gripe of this little hand which was laid upon me before I came into the world?"

"Dearest Georgiana, I have spent much thought upon the subject," hastily interrupted Aylmer. "I am convinced of the perfect practicability of its removal."

"If there be the remotest possibility of it," continued Georgiana, "let the attempt be made at whatever risk. Danger is nothing to me; for life, while this hateful mark makes me the object of your horror and disgust—life is a burden which I would fling down with joy. Either remove this dreadful hand, or take my wretched life! You have deep science. All the world bears witness of it. You have achieved great wonders. Cannot you remove this little, little mark, which I cover with the tips of two small fingers? Is this beyond your power, for the sake of your own peace, and to save your poor wife from madness?"

"Noblest, dearest, tenderest wife," cried Aylmer, rapturously, "doubt not my power. I have already given this matter the deepest thought— thought which might almost have enlightened me to create a being less perfect than yourself. Georgiana, you have led me deeper than ever into the heart of science. I feel myself fully competent to render this dear cheek as faultless as its fellow; and then, most beloved, what will be my triumph when I shall have corrected what Nature left imperfect in her fairest work! Even Pygmalion, when his sculptured woman assumed life, felt not greater ecstasy than mine will be."

"It is resolved, then," said Georgiana, faintly smiling. "And, Aylmer, spare me not, though you should find the birthmark take refuge in my heart at last."

Her husband tenderly kissed her cheek—her right cheek—not that which bore the impress of the crimson hand.

The next day Aylmer apprised his wife of a plan that he had formed whereby he might have opportunity for the intense thought and constant watchfulness which the proposed operation would require; while Georgiana, likewise, would enjoy the perfect repose essential to its success. They were to seclude themselves in the extensive apartments occupied by Aylmer as a laboratory, and where, during his toilsome youth, he had made discoveries in the elemental powers of Nature that had roused the admiration of all the learned societies in Europe. Seated calmly in this laboratory, the pale philosopher had investigated the secrets of the highest cloud region and of the profoundest mines; he had satisfied himself of the causes that kindled and kept alive the fires of the volcano; and had explained the mystery of fountains, and how it is that they gush forth, some so bright and pure, and others with such rich medicinal virtues, from the dark bosom of the earth. Here, too, at an earlier period, he had studied the wonders of the human frame, and attempted to fathom the very process by which Nature assimilates all her precious influences from earth and air, and from the spiritual world, to create and foster man, her masterpiece. The latter pursuit, however, Aylmer had long laid aside in unwilling recognition of the truth—against which all seekers sooner or later stumble—that our great creative Mother, while she amuses us with apparently working in the broadest sunshine, is yet severely careful to keep her own secrets, and, in spite of her pretended openness, shows us nothing but results. She permits us, indeed, to mar, but seldom to mend, and, like a jealous patentee, on no account to make. Now, however, Aylmer resumed these half-forgotten investigations; not, of course, with such hopes or wishes as first suggested them; but because they involved much physiological truth and lay in the path of his proposed scheme for the treatment of Georgiana.

As he led her over the threshold of the laboratory, Georgiana was cold and tremulous. Aylmer looked cheerfully into her face, with intent to reassure her, but was so startled with the intense glow of the birthmark upon the whiteness of her cheek that he could not restrain a strong convulsive shudder. His wife fainted.

"Aminadab! Aminadab!" shouted Aylmer, stamping violently on the floor.

Forthwith there issued from an inner apartment a man of low stature, but bulky frame, with shaggy hair hanging about his visage, which was grimed with the vapors of the furnace. This personage had been Aylmer's underworker during his whole scientific career, and was admirably fitted for that office by his great mechanical readiness, and the skill with which, while incapable of comprehending a simple principle, he executed all the details of his master's experiments. With his vast strength, his shaggy hair, his smoky aspect, and the indescribable earthiness that incrusted him, he seemed to represent man's physical nature; while Aylmer's slender figure, and pale, intellectual face, were no less apt a type of the spiritual element.

"Throw open the door of the boudoir, Aminadab," said Aylmer, "and burn a pastil."

"Yes, master," answered Aminadab, looking intently at the lifeless form of Georgiana; and then he muttered to himself, "If she were my wife, I'd never part with that birthmark."

When Georgiana recovered consciousness she found herself breathing an atmosphere of penetrating fragrance, the gentle potency of which had recalled her from her deathlike faintness. The scene around her looked like enchantment. Aylmer had converted those smoky, dingy, sombre rooms, where he had spent his brightest years in recondite pursuits, into a series of beautiful apartments not unfit to be the secluded abode of a lovely woman. The walls were hung with gorgeous curtains, which imparted the combination of grandeur and grace that no other species of adornment can achieve; and as they fell from the ceiling to the floor, their rich and ponderous folds, concealing all angles and straight lines, appeared to shut in the scene from infinite space. For aught Georgiana knew, it might be a pavilion among the clouds. And Aylmer, excluding the sunshine, which would have interfered with his chemical process, had supplied its place with perfumed lamps, emitting flames of various hue, but all uniting in a soft, impurpled radiance. He now knelt by his wife's side, watching her earnestly, but without alarm; for he was confident in his science, and felt that he could draw a magic circle round her within which no evil might intrude.

"Where am I? Ah, I remember," said Georgiana, faintly; and she placed her hand over her cheek to hide the terrible mark from her husband's eyes.

"Fear not, dearest!" exclaimed he. "Do not shrink from me! Believe me, Georgiana, I even rejoice in this single imperfection, since it will be such a rapture to remove it."

"Oh, spare me!" sadly replied his wife. "Pray do not look at it again. I never can forget that convulsive shudder."

In order to soothe Georgiana, and, as it were, to release her mind from the burden of actual things, Aylmer now put in practice some of the light and playful secrets which science had taught him among its profounder lore. Airy figures, absolutely bodiless ideas, and forms of unsubstantial beauty came and danced before her, imprinting their momentary footsteps on beams of light. Though she had some indistinct idea of the method of these optical phenomena, still the illusion was almost perfect enough to warrant the belief that her husband possessed sway over the spiritual world. Then again, when she felt a wish to look forth from her seclusion, immediately, as if her thoughts were answered, the procession of external existence flitted across a screen. The scenery and the figures of actual life were perfectly represented, but with that bewitching, yet indescribable difference which always makes a picture, an image, or a shadow so much more attractive than the original. When wearied of this, Aylmer bade her cast her eyes upon a vessel containing a quantity of earth. She did so, with little interest at first; but was soon startled to perceive the germ of a plant shooting upward from the soil. Then came the slender stalk; the leaves gradually unfolded themselves; and amid them was a perfect and lovely flower.

"It is magical!" cried Georgiana. "I dare not touch it."

"Nay, pluck it," answered Aylmer—"pluck it, and inhale its brief perfume while you may. The flower will wither in a few moments and leave nothing save its brown seed vessels; but thence may be perpetuated a race as ephemeral as itself."

But Georgiana had no sooner touched the flower than the whole plant suffered a blight, its leaves turning coalblack as if by the agency of fire.

"There was too powerful a stimulus," said Aylmer, thoughtfully.

To make up for this abortive experiment, he proposed to take her portrait by a scientific process of his own invention. It was to be effected by rays of light striking upon a polished plate of metal. Georgiana assented; but, on looking at the result, was affrighted to find the features of the portrait blurred and indefinable; while the minute figure of a hand appeared where the cheek should have been. Aylmer snatched the metallic plate and threw it into a jar of corrosive acid.

Soon, however, he forgot these mortifying failures. In the intervals of study and chemical experiment he came to her flushed and exhausted, but seemed invigorated by her presence, and spoke in glowing language of the resources of his art. He gave a history of the long dynasty of the alchemists, who spent so many ages in quest of the universal solvent by which the golden principle might be elicited from all things vile and base. Aylmer appeared to believe that, by the plainest scientific logic, it was altogether within the limits of possibility to discover this long-sought medium; "but," he added, "a philosopher who should go deep enough to acquire the power would attain too lofty a wisdom to stoop to the exercise of it." Not less singular were his opinions in regard to the elixir vitæ. He more than intimated that it was at his option to concoct a liquid that should prolong life for years, perhaps interminably; but that it would produce a discord in Nature which all the world, and chiefly the quaffer of the immortal nostrum, would find cause to curse.

"Aylmer, are you in earnest?" asked Georgiana, looking at him with amazement and fear. "It is terrible to possess such power, or even to dream of possessing it."

"Oh, do not tremble, my love," said her husband. "I would not wrong either you or myself by working such inharmonious effects upon our lives; but I would have you consider how trifling, in comparison, is the skill requisite to remove this little hand."

At the mention of the birthmark, Georgiana, as usual, shrank as if a redhot iron had touched her cheek.

Again Aylmer applied himself to his labors. She could hear his voice in the distant furnace room giving directions to Aminadab, whose harsh, uncouth, misshapen tones were audible in response, more like the grunt or growl of a brute than human speech. After hours of absence, Aylmer reappeared and proposed that she should now examine his cabinet of chemical products and natural treasures of the earth. Among the former he showed her a small vial, in which, he remarked, was contained a gentle yet most powerful fragrance, capable of impregnating all the breezes that blow across a kingdom. They were of inestimable value, the contents of that little vial; and, as he said so, he threw some of the perfume into the air and filled the room with piercing and invigorating delight.

"And what is this?" asked Georgiana, pointing to a small crystal globe containing a gold-colored liquid. "It is so beautiful to the eye that I could imagine it the elixir of life."

"In one sense it is," replied Aylmer; "or, rather, the elixir of immortality. It is the most precious poison that ever was concocted in this world. By its aid I could apportion the lifetime of any mortal at whom you might point your finger. The strength of the dose would determine whether he were to linger out years, or drop dead in the midst of a breath. No king on his guarded throne could keep his life if I, in my private station, should deem that the welfare of millions justified me in depriving him of it."

"Why do you keep such a terrific drug?" inquired Georgiana in horror.

"Do not mistrust me, dearest," said her husband, smiling; "its virtuous potency is yet greater than its harmful one. But see! here is a powerful cosmetic. With a few drops of this in a vase of water, freckles may be washed away as easily as the hands are cleansed. A stronger infusion would take the blood out of the cheek, and leave the rosiest beauty a pale ghost."

"Is it with this lotion that you intend to bathe my cheek?" asked Georgiana, anxiously.

"Oh, no," hastily replied her husband; "this is merely superficial. Your case demands a remedy that shall go deeper."

In his interviews with Georgiana, Aylmer generally made minute inquiries as to her sensations and whether the confinement of the rooms and the temperature of the atmosphere agreed with her. These questions had such a particular drift that Georgiana began to conjecture that she was already subjected to certain physical influences, either breathed in with the fragrant air or taken with her food. She fancied likewise, but it might be altogether fancy, that there was a stirring up of her system—a strange, indefinite sensation creeping through her veins, and tingling, half painfully, half pleasurably, at her heart. Still, whenever she dared to look into the mirror, there she beheld herself pale as a white rose and with the crimson birthmark stamped upon her cheek. Not even Aylmer now hated it so much as she.

To dispel the tedium of the hours which her husband found it necessary to devote to the processes of combination and analysis, Georgiana turned over the volumes of his scientific library. In many dark old tomes she met with chapters full of romance and poetry. They were the works of philosophers of the middle ages, such as Albertus Magnus, Cornelius Agrippa, Paracelsus, and the famous friar who created the prophetic Brazen Head. All these antique naturalists stood in advance of their centuries, yet were imbued with some of their credulity, and therefore were believed, and perhaps imagined themselves to have acquired from the investigation of Nature a power above Nature, and from physics a sway over the spiritual world. Hardly less curious and imaginative were the early volumes of the Transactions of the Royal Society, in which the members, knowing little of the limits of natural possibility, were continually recording wonders or proposing methods whereby wonders might be wrought.

But to Georgiana the most engrossing volume was a large folio from her husband's own hand, in which he had recorded every experiment of his scientific career, its original aim, the methods adopted for its development, and its final success or failure, with the circumstances to which either event was attributable. The book, in truth, was both the history and emblem of his ardent, ambitious, imaginative, yet practical and laborious life. He handled physical details as if there were nothing beyond them; yet spiritualized them all, and redeemed himself from materialism by his strong and eager aspiration towards the infinite. In his grasp the veriest clod of earth assumed a soul. Georgiana, as she read, reverenced Aylmer and loved him more profoundly than ever, but with a less entire dependence on his judgment than heretofore. Much as he had accomplished, she could not but observe that his most splendid successes were almost invariably failures, if compared with the ideal at which he aimed. His brightest diamonds were the merest pebbles, and felt to be so by himself, in comparison with the inestimable gems which lay hidden beyond his reach. The volume, rich with achievements that had won renown for its author, was yet as melancholy a record as ever mortal hand had penned. It was the sad confession and continual exemplification of the shortcomings of the composite man, the spirit burdened with clay and working in matter, and of the despair that assails the higher nature at finding itself so miserably thwarted by the earthly part. Perhaps every man of genius in whatever sphere might recognize the image of his own experience in Aylmer's journal.

So deeply did these reflections affect Georgiana that she laid her face upon the open volume and burst into tears. In this situation she was found by her husband.

"It is dangerous to read in a sorcerer's books," said he with a smile, though his countenance was uneasy and displeased. "Georgiana, there are pages in that volume which I can scarcely glance over and keep my senses. Take heed lest it prove as detrimental to you."

"It has made me worship you more than ever," said she.

"Ah, wait for this one success," rejoined he, "then worship me if you will. I shall deem myself hardly unworthy of it. But come, I have sought you for the luxury of your voice. Sing to me, dearest."

So she poured out the liquid music of her voice to quench the thirst of his spirit. He then took his leave with a boyish exuberance of gayety, assuring her that her seclusion would endure but a little longer, and that the result was already certain. Scarcely had he departed when Georgiana felt irresistibly impelled to follow him. She had forgotten to inform Aylmer of a symptom which for two or three hours past had begun to excite her attention. It was a sensation in the fatal birthmark, not painful, but which induced a restlessness throughout her system. Hastening after her husband, she intruded for the first time into the laboratory.

The first thing that struck her eye was the furnace, that hot and feverish worker, with the intense glow of its fire, which by the quantities of soot clustered above it seemed to have been burning for ages. There was a distilling apparatus in full operation. Around the room were retorts, tubes, cylinders, crucibles, and other apparatus of chemical research. An electrical machine stood ready for immediate use. The atmosphere felt oppressively close, and was tainted with gaseous odors which had been tormented forth by the processes of science. The severe and homely simplicity of the apartment, with its naked walls and brick pavement, looked strange, accustomed as Georgiana had become to the fantastic elegance of her boudoir. But what chiefly, indeed almost solely, drew her attention, was the aspect of Aylmer himself.

He was pale as death, anxious and absorbed, and hung over the furnace as if it depended upon his utmost watchfulness whether the liquid which it was distilling should be the draught of immortal happiness or misery. How different from the sanguine and joyous mien that he had assumed for Georgiana's encouragement!

"Carefully now, Aminadab; carefully, thou human machine; carefully, thou man of clay!" muttered Aylmer, more to himself than his assistant. "Now, if there be a thought too much or too little, it is all over."

"Ho! ho!" mumbled Aminadab. "Look, master! look!"

Aylmer raised his eyes hastily, and at first reddened, then grew paler than ever, on beholding Georgiana. He rushed towards her and seized her arm with a gripe that left the print of his fingers upon it.

"Why do you come hither? Have you no trust in your husband?" cried he, impetuously. "Would you throw the blight of that fatal birthmark over my labors? It is not well done. Go, prying woman, go!"

"Nay, Aylmer," said Georgiana with the firmness of which she possessed no stinted endowment, "it is not you that have a right to complain. You mistrust your wife; you have concealed the anxiety with which you watch the development of this experiment. Think not so unworthily of me, my husband. Tell me all the risk we run, and fear not that I shall shrink; for my share in it is far less than your own."

"No, no. Georgiana!" said Aylmer, impatiently; "it must not be."

"I submit," replied she calmly. "And, Aylmer, I shall quaff whatever draught you bring me; but it will be on the same principle that would induce me to take a dose of poison if offered by your hand."

"My noble wife," said Aylmer, deeply moved, "I knew not the height and depth of your nature until now. Nothing shall be concealed. Know, then, that this crimson hand, superficial as it seems, has clutched its grasp into your being with a strength of which I had no previous conception. I have already administered agents powerful enough to do aught except to change your entire physical system. Only one thing remains to be tried. If that fail us we are ruined."

"Why did you hesitate to tell me this?" asked she.

"Because, Georgiana," said Aylmer, in a low voice, "there is danger."

"Danger? There is but one danger—that this horrible stigma shall be left upon my cheek!" cried Georgiana. "Remove it, remove it, whatever be the cost, or we shall both go mad!"

"Heaven knows your words are too true," said Aylmer, sadly. "And now, dearest, return to your boudoir. In a little while all will be tested."

He conducted her back and took leave of her with a solemn tenderness which spoke far more than his words how much was now at stake. After his departure Georgiana became rapt in musings. She considered the character of Aylmer, and did it completer justice than at any previous moment. Her heart exulted, while it trembled, at his honorable love—so pure and lofty that it would accept nothing less than perfection nor miserably make itself contented with an earthlier nature than he had dreamed of. She felt how much more precious was such a sentiment than the meaner kind which would have borne with the imperfection for her sake, and have been guilty of treason to holy love by degrading its perfect idea to the level of the actual; and with her whole spirit she prayed that, for a single moment, she might satisfy his highest and deepest conception. Longer than one moment she well knew it could not be; for his spirit was ever on the march, ever ascending, and each instant required something that was beyond the scope of the instant before.

The sound of her husband's footsteps aroused her. He bore a crystal goblet containing a liquor colorless as water, but bright enough to be the draught of immortality. Aylmer was pale; but it seemed rather the consequence of a highly wrought state of mind and tension of spirit than of fear or doubt.

"The concoction of the draught has been perfect," said he, in answer to Georgiana's look. "Unless all my science have deceived me, it cannot fail."

"Save on your account, my dearest Aylmer," observed his wife, "I might wish to put off this birthmark of mortality by relinquishing mortality itself in preference to any other mode. Life is but a sad possession to those who have attained precisely the degree of moral advancement at which I stand. Were I weaker and blinder it might be happiness. Were I stronger, it might be endured hopefully. But, being what I find myself, methinks I am of all mortals the most fit to die."

"You are fit for heaven without tasting death!" replied her husband. "But why do we speak of dying? The draught cannot fail. Behold its effect upon this plant."

On the window seat there stood a geranium diseased with yellow blotches, which had overspread all its leaves. Aylmer poured a small quantity of the liquid upon the soil in which it grew. In a little time, when the roots of the plant had taken up the moisture, the unsightly blotches began to be extinguished in a living verdure.

"There needed no proof," said Georgiana, quietly.

"Give me the goblet. I joyfully stake all upon your word."

"Drink, then, thou lofty creature!" exclaimed Aylmer, with fervid admiration. "There is no taint of imperfection on thy spirit. Thy sensible frame, too, shall soon be all perfect."

She quaffed the liquid and returned the goblet to his hand.

"It is grateful," said she with a placid smile. "Methinks it is like water from a heavenly fountain; for it contains I know not what of unobtrusive fragrance and deliciousness. It allays a feverish thirst that had parched me for many days. Now, dearest, let me sleep. My earthly senses are closing over my spirit like the leaves around the heart of a rose at sunset."

She spoke the last words with a gentle reluctance, as if it required almost more energy than she could command to pronounce the faint and lingering syllables. Scarcely had they loitered through her lips ere she was lost in slumber. Aylmer sat by her side, watching her aspect with the emotions proper to a man the whole value of whose existence was involved in the process now to be tested. Mingled with this mood, however, was the philosophic investigation characteristic of the man of science. Not the minutest symptom escaped him. A heightened flush of the cheek, a slight irregularity of breath, a quiver of the eyelid, a hardly perceptible tremor through the frame—such were the details which as the moments passed, he wrote down in his folio volume. Intense thought had set its stamp upon every previous page of that volume, but the thoughts of years were all concentrated upon the last.

While thus employed, he failed not to gaze often at the fatal hand, and not without a shudder. Yet once, by a strange and unaccountable impulse, he pressed it with his lips. His spirit recoiled, however, in the very act; and Georgiana, out of the midst of her deep sleep, moved uneasily and murmured as if in remonstrance. Again Aylmer resumed his watch. Nor was it without avail. The crimson hand, which at first had been strongly visible upon the marble paleness of Georgiana's cheek, now grew more faintly outlined. She remained not less pale than ever; but the birthmark, with every breath that came and went, lost somewhat of its former distinctness. Its presence had been awful; its departure was more awful still. Watch the stain of the rainbow fading out the sky, and you will know how that mysterious symbol passed away.

"By Heaven! it is well-nigh gone!" said Aylmer to himself, in almost irrepressible ecstasy. "I can scarcely trace it now. Success! success! And now it is like the faintest rose color. The lightest flush of blood across her cheek would overcome it. But she is so pale!"

He drew aside the window curtain and suffered the light of natural day to fall into the room and rest upon her cheek. At the same time he heard a gross, hoarse chuckle, which he had long known as his servant Aminadab's expression of delight.

"Ah, clod; ah, earthly mass!" cried Aylmer, laughing in a sort of frenzy, "you have served me well! Matter and spirit—earth and heaven—have both done their part in this! Laugh, thing of the senses! You have earned the right to laugh."

These exclamations broke Georgiana's sleep. She slowly unclosed her eyes and gazed into the mirror which her husband had arranged for that purpose. A faint smile flitted over her lips when she recognized how barely perceptible was now that crimson hand which had once blazed forth with such disastrous brilliancy as to scare away all their happiness. But then her eyes sought Aylmer's face with a trouble and anxiety that he could by no means account for.

"My poor Aylmer!" murmured she.

"Poor? Nay, richest, happiest, most favored!" exclaimed he. "My peerless bride, it is successful! You are perfect!"

"My poor Aylmer," she repeated, with a more than human tenderness, "you have aimed loftily; you have done nobly. Do not repent that with so high and pure a feeling, you have rejected the best the earth could offer. Aylmer, dearest Aylmer, I am dying!"

Alas! it was too true! The fatal hand had grappled with the mystery of life, and was the bond by which an angelic spirit kept itself in union with a mortal frame. As the last crimson tint of the birthmark—that sole token of human imperfection—faded from her cheek, the parting breath of the now perfect woman passed into the atmosphere, and her soul, lingering a moment near her husband, took its heavenward flight. Then a hoarse, chuckling laugh was heard again! Thus ever does the gross fatality of earth exult in its invariable triumph over the immortal essence which, in this dim sphere of half development, demands the completeness of a higher state. Yet, had Aylmer reached a profounder wisdom, he need not thus have flung away the happiness which would have woven his mortal life of the selfsame texture with the celestial. The momentary circumstance was too strong for him; he failed to look beyond the shadowy scope of time, and, living once for all in eternity, to find the perfect future in the present.

# THE CANONIZATION

## John Donne

For Godsake hold your tongue, and let me love,
   Or chide my palsie, or my gout,
My five gray haires, or ruin'd fortune flout,
     With wealth your state, your minde with Arts improve,
       Take you a course, get you a place,
       Observe his honour, or his grace,
Or the Kings reall, or his stamped face
     Contemplate, what you will, approve,
     So you will let me love.

Alas, alas, who's injur'd by my love?
   What merchants ships have my sighs drown'd?
Who saies my teares have overflow'd his ground?
     When did my colds a forward spring remove?
       When did the heats which my veines flll
       Adde one more to the plaguie Bill?
Soldiers finde warres, and Lawyers finde out still
     Litigious men, which quarrels move,
     Though she and I do love.

Call us what you will, wee are made such by love;
   Call her one, mee another flye,
We'are Tapers too, and at our owne cost die
     And wee in us finde the'Eagle and the Dove.
     The Phœnix ridle hath more wit
       By us, we two being one, are it.
So to one neutrall thing both sexes fit.
     Wee dye and rise the same, and prove
     Mysterious by this love.

Wee can dye by it, if not live by love,
    And if unfit for tombes and hearse
Our legend bee, it will be fit for verse;
      And if no peece of Chronicle wee prove,
        We'll build in sonnets pretty roomes;
        As well a well wrought urne becomes
The greatest ashes, as halfe-acre tombes,
    And by these hymnes, all shall approve
    Us *Canoniz'd* for Love:

And thus invoke us; You whom reverend love
    Made one anothers hermitage;
You, to whom love was peace, that now is rage;
      Who did the whole worlds soule contract, and drove
        Into the glasses of your eyes
        (So made such mirrors, and such spies,
That they did all to you epitomize,)
    Countries, Townes, Courts: Beg from above
    A patterne of your love!

# PRAYER
# FOR MESSIAH

## Leonard Cohen

His blood on my arm is warm as a bird
his heart in my hand is heavy as lead
his eyes through my eyes shine brighter than love
O send out the raven ahead of the dove

His life in my mouth is less than a man
his death on my breast is harder than stone
his eyes through my eyes shine brighter than love
O send out the raven ahead of the dove

O send out the raven ahead of the dove
O sing from your chains where you're chained in a cave
your eyes through my eyes shine brighter than love
your blood in my ballad collapses the grave

O sing from your chains where you're chained in a cave
your eyes through my eyes shine brighter than love
your heart in my hand is heavy as lead
your blood on my arm is warm as a bird

O break from your branches a green branch of love
after the raven has died for the dove

# THE NRACP*

## George P. Elliott

March 3

DEAR HERB,

Your first letter meant more to me than I can say, but the one I received yesterday has at last aroused me from my depression. I will try to answer both of them at once. You sensed my state of mind; I could tell it from little phrases in your letter—"open your heart, though it be only to a sunset," "try reading *Finnegans Wake;* if you ever get *into* it you won't be able to fight your way out again for months." I cherish your drolleries. They are little oases of half-light and quiet in this rasping, blinding landscape.

How I hate it! Nothing but the salary keeps me here. Nothing. I have been driven into myself in a very unhealthy way. Long hours, communal eating, the choice between a badly lighted reading room full of people and my own cell with one cot and two chairs and a table, a swim in a chlorinated pool, walks in this violent, seasonless, arid land—what is there? There seem to be only two varieties of people here: those who "have culture," and talk about the latest *New Yorker* cartoons, listen to imitation folksongs and subscribe to one of the less popular book clubs; and those who play poker, talk sports and sex, and drink too much. I prefer the latter type as people, but unfortunately I do not enjoy their activities, except drinking; and since I know the language and mores of the former type, and have more inclination toward them, I am thrown with people whom I dislike intensely. In this muddle I find myself wishing, selfishly,

* The *NRACP is the National Relocation Authority: Colored Persons. The CPR is the Colored Persons Reserve. PR is Public Relations.*

that you were here; your companionship would mean so much to me now. But you knew better than I what the CPR would mean—you were most wise to stay in Washington, most wise. You will be missing something by staying there—but I assure you it is something well worth missing.

I must mention the two universal topics of conversation. From the filing clerks to my division chief I know of no one, including myself, who does not talk absorbedly about mystery stories. A few watered-down eclectics say they haven't much preference in mysteries, but the folksongers to a man prefer the tony, phoney Dorothy Sayers-S. S. Van Dine type of pseudo-literary snobbish product, and the horsey folk prefer the Dashiell Hammett romantic cum violent realism; there is one fellow—a big-domed Irishman named O'Doone who wears those heavy-rimmed, owlish glasses that were so popular some years ago—who does nothing but read and reread Sherlock Holmes, and he has won everyone's respect, in some strange way, by this quaint loyalty. He's quite shy, in a talkative, brittle way, but I think I could grow fond of him—Yet everyone finds a strong need to read the damnable things, so strong that we prefer the absolute nausea of reading three in one day—I did it once myself, for three days on end—to not reading any. What is it actually that we prefer not to do? I can only think of Auden's lines, "The situation of our time Surrounds us like a baffling crime." Of our time, and of this job.

What are we doing here?—that is the other subject none of us can let alone. We are paid fantastic salaries—the secretary whom I share with another writer gets $325 a month, tell Mary *that* one—and for one whole month we have done nothing while on the job except to read all the provisions and addenda to the Relocation Act as interpreted by the Authority, or to browse at will in the large library of literature by and about Negroes, from sociological studies to newspaper poetry in dialect. You will know the Act generally of course; but I hope you are never for any reason subjected to this Ph.D.-candidate torture of reading to exhaustion about a subject in which you have only a general interest. But the *why* of this strange and expensive indoctrination, is totally beyond me. I thought that I was going to do much the same sort of PR work here on the spot as we had been doing in the State Department; I thought the salary differential was just a compensation for living in this hell-hole. That's what everyone here had thought too. It appears, however, that there is something more important brewing. In the whole month I have been here—I swear it— I have turned out only a couple of articles describing the physical charms of this desiccated cesspool; they appeared in Negro publications which I hope you have not heard of. And beyond that I have done nothing but bore myself to death by reading Negro novels and poetry.

They are a different tribe altogether; their primeval culture is wonderful enough to merit study—I would be the last to deny it. But not by me. I have enough trouble trying to understand the rudiments of my own culture without having this one pushed off onto me.

—I have been stifled and confused for so long that all my pent-up emotions have found their worthiest outlet in this letter to you, my dear friend. I have been vowing (as we used to vow to quit smoking, remember?) to stop reading mysteries but my vows seldom survive the day. Now I do solemnly swear and proclaim that each time I have the urge to read a mystery, I will instead write a letter to you. If these epistles become dull and repetitious, just throw them away without reading them. I'll put a mark—say an M—on the envelope of these counter-mystery letters, so you needn't even open them if you wish. I'm sure there will be a lot of them.

Does this sound silly? I suppose it does. But I am in a strange state of mind. There's too much sunlight and the countryside frightens me and I don't understand anything.

Bless you,
ANDY

March 14

Dear Herb,

It wasn't as bad as I had feared, being without mysteries. We get up at seven and go to work at eight. Between five and six in the afternoon, there's time for a couple of highballs. From seven or so, when dinner is over, till ten or eleven—that's the time to watch out for. After you have seen the movie of the week and read *Time* and *The New Yorker,* then you discover yourself, with that autonomic gesture with which one reaches for a cigarette, wandering toward the mystery shelf and trying to choose between Carter Dickson and John Dickson Carr (two names for the same writer, as I hope you don't know). On Sundays there's tennis in the early morning and bowling in the afternoon. But then those gaping rents in each tightly woven, just tolerable day remain, no matter what you do. At first I thought I should have to tell myself bedtime stories. One evening I got half-drunk in the club-rooms and absolutely potted alone in my own room afterwards. First time in my life. Another time, O'Doone and I sat up till midnight composing an "Epitaph for a Mongoose." I can't tell you how dreary some of our endeavors were; O'Doone still quotes one of mine occasionally. He's a strange fellow, I can't exactly figure him out but I like him in an oblique sort of way. We neither one fit into any of three or four possible schemes of things here and we share a good deal in general outlook. But he can amuse himself with a cerebral horseplay which only makes me uneasy. O'Doone has a French book—God knows where he got it—on Senegalese dialects so he goes around slapping stuffy people on the back and mumbling "Your grandmother on your father's side was a pig-faced gorilla" or else a phrase which in Senegalese has something to do with transplanting date trees but which in English sounds obscene, and then he laughs uproariously. In any event, he's better off than I, who am amused by almost nothing.

Now that you have been spared the threatened dejection of my counter-mystery letters, I must confess to the secret vice which I have taken up in the past week. It grows upon me too, it promises to become a habit which only age and infirmity will break. I had thought it a vice of middle age (and perhaps it is—are we not 38, Herb? When does middle age commence?). I *take walks.* I take long walks alone. If I cannot say that I enjoy them exactly, yet I look forward to them with that eagerness with which an adolescent will sometimes go to bed in order to continue the dream which waking has interrupted.

Not that my walks are in any way dreamlike. They are perfectly real. But they take place in a context so different from any of the social or intellectual contexts of the CPR day, and they afford such a strong emotional relief to it, that I think these walks may be justly compared to a continued dream. My walks, however, have a worth of their own such as dreams can never have, for instead of taking me from an ugly world to a realm of unexplained symbols, they have driven me toward two realities, about which I must confess I have had a certain ignorance: myself, and the natural world. And standing, as I feel I do, at the starting-point of high adventure, I feel the explorer's excitement and awe, and no self-pity at all.

I have recaptured—and I am not embarrassed to say it—the childhood delight in stars. That's a great thing to happen to a man, Herb—to be able to leave the smoke- and spite-laden atmosphere of bureaucracy, walk a few miles out into the huge, silent desert, and look at the stars with a delight whose purity needs no apology and whose expansiveness need find no words for description. I am astonished by the sight of a Joshua tree against the light blue twilight sky, I am entranced by the vicious innocence of one of the kinds of cactus that abound hereabouts, I enjoy these garish sunsets with a fervor that I once considered indecent. I cannot say I like this desert—certainly not enough to live in it permanently—but it has affected me, very deeply. I think that much of my trouble during my first month here was resisting the force of the desert. Now, I no longer resist it, yet I have not submitted to it; rather I have developed a largeness of spirit, a feeling of calm and magnificence. Which I am sure is in part light-headedness at having such a weight of nasty care removed all at once, but which is wonderful while it lasts.

But it's not *just* lightheadedness. Some obstruction of spirit, an obstruction of whose existence I was not even aware, has been removed within me, so that now I can and dare observe the complexities of that catalogued, indifferent, unaccountable natural world which I had always shrugged at. One saw it from train windows, one dealt with it on picnics; one admired the nasturtiums and peonies of one's more domesticated friends, one approved of lawns, and shade trees. What then? What did one know of the rigidity of nature's order or of the prodigality with which she wastes and destroys and errs? I came here furnished only with the ordinary generic names of things—snake, lizard, toad, rabbit, bug, cactus, sage-bush, flower, weed—but already I have watched a road-runner kill a rattlesnake, and I am proud that I know how rabbits drink. Do you know how rabbits drink? If you ask what difference it makes to know this, I can happily reply, "None at all, but it gives me pleasure." A pleasure which does not attempt to deny mortality, but accepts it and doesn't care—that is a true pleasure, and one worth cherishing.

11 P.M.

I owe it to you, I know, to give a somewhat less personal, less inward account of this place. But a calculated, itemized description of anything, much less of so monstrous a thing as a desert, that is beyond me. Instead I'll try to give you an idea of what effect such physical bigness can have upon one.

Our buildings are situated at the head of a very long valley—the Tehuala River Valley—which is partially arable and which, in both the upper and lower regions, is good for grazing purposes. The highway into the valley, that is, the highway that leads to the East, as well as the railroad, runs not far from our settlement. Being Public Relations, we are located just within the fence (it is a huge, barbarous fence with guards). We have had a rather surprising number of visitors already, and hundreds more are expected during the summer. Our eight buildings are flatroofed, gray, of a horizontal design, and air-conditioned. But our view of the valley is cut off by a sharp bend about four or five miles below us. The tourists, in other words, can see almost nothing of the valley, and just as little of the Reserve stretching for 800 miles to the southwest, for this is the only public entrance to the Reserve, and no airplanes are permitted over any part of it. Around the turn in the upper valley, is yet another even more barbarous, even better guarded fence, past which no one goes except certain Congressmen, the top officials (four, I believe) in the NRACP, and SSE (Special Service Employees, who, once they have gone past that gate, do not return and do not communicate with the outside world even by letter). All this secrecy—you can fill in details to suit yourself— is probably unnecessary, but it does succeed in arousing an acute sense of mystery and speculation about the Reserve. Well, being no more than human I walked the five miles to the bend, climbed a considerable hill nearby, and looked out over the main sweep of the valley for the first time. I was hot and tired when I reached the foot of the hill, so I sat down—it was around 5:30—and ate the lunch I had brought. When I reached the top of the hill the sun was about to set; the long shadows of the western hills lay over the floor of the valley and in some places they extended halfway up the hills to the east. Far, far to the west, just to the north of the setting sun, was a snow-capped mountain; and immediately in front of me, that is, a mile and a half or so away, stretched the longest building I have ever seen in my life. It had a shed roof rising away from me; there were no windows on my side of the building; nothing whatsoever broke the line of its continuous gray back; and it was at least a mile long, probably longer. Beyond it, lay dozens of buildings exactly like this one except for their length; some of them ran, as the long one did, east and west, some ran north and south, some aslant. I could not estimate to my satisfaction how large most of them were; they seemed to be roughly about the size of small factories. The effect which their planner had deliberately calculated and achieved was that of a rigidly patterned, unsymmetrical (useless?) articulation of a restricted flat area. Nothing broke the effect, and for a reason which I cannot define, these buildings in the foreground gave a focus and order to the widening scene that lay before me such that I stood for the better part of an hour experiencing a pure joy—a joy only heightened by my grateful knowledge that these Intake buildings were designed to introduce an entire people to the new and better world beyond (and I must confess I felt the better that I myself was, albeit humbly, connected with the project). The fine farms and ranches and industries and communities which would arise from these undeveloped regions took shape in the twilight scene before me, shimmering in the heat waves rising from the earth. But presently it was quite dark—the twilights are very brief here—and I was awakened from my reverie by the lights going on in one of the buildings before me. I returned to the PR settlement, and to my solitary room, in a state of exaltation which has not yet deserted me.

For an hour, the Universe and History co-extended before me; and they did not exclude me; for while I am but a grain on the shore of event, yet only within my consciousness did this co-extending take place and have any meaning. For that long moment, mine was the power.

I will write again soon.

ANDY

March 20

Dear Herb,

You complain that I didn't say anything directly about my voyage of discovery into myself, as I had promised in my last letter. And that the internal high pressures of urban life are blowing me up like a balloon in this rarefied atmosphere.

Maybe so. I'll try to explain what has been going on. But I forgot to take a cartographer on my voyage, so that my account may resemble, in crudeness, that of an Elizabethan freebooter in Caribbean waters. (If I had the energy, I'd try to synthesize these balloon-voyage metaphors; but I haven't.)

It all began when I asked myself, on one of my walks, why I was here, why I had taken this job. $8,000 a year—yes. The social importance of the project—maybe (but not my personal importance to the project). Excitement at being in on the beginning of a great experiment in planning —yes. The hope of escaping from the pressures of Washington life—yes. These are valid reasons all of them, but in the other balance—why I should want *not* to come here—are better reasons altogether. An utter absence of urban life. No friends. No chance of seeing Betty. The loss of permanent position (this one you pointed out most forcefully) in State for a better paid but temporary job here. Loss of friends. Too inadequate a knowledge of my duties, or of the whole NRACP for that matter, to permit me to have made a decision wisely. And an overpowering hatred of restrictions (never once, Herb, for three years to be allowed to leave this Reserve! I've been sweating here for seven weeks, but that is 156 weeks. Christ!). Now I had known, more or less, all these factors before I came here, all these nice rational, statistical factors. But when I asked myself the other night, in the false clarity of the desert moonlight, why I had chosen to come, why really, I still could not answer myself satisfactorily. For of one thing I was still certain, that none of the logical reasons, none of my recognized impulses, would have brought me here singly or combined.

I also, being in the mood, asked myself why I had continued to live with Clarice for five years after I had known quite consciously that I did not love her but felt a positive contempt for her. Betty accounted for part of it, and the usual fear of casting out again on one's own. But I would not have been on my own in any obvious sense: I am sure you know of my love affairs during those five years; I could have married any of three or four worthy women. And I ask myself why it was that the moment Clarice decided once and for all to divorce me—she did the deciding, not me; I don't think you knew that—from that time on I lost my taste for my current inamorata and have not had a real affair since. These questions I was unable to answer; but at least I was seriously asking them of myself. I was willing and able to face the answers.

The key to the answer came from my long-limbed, mildly pretty, efficient, but (I had originally thought) frivolous and banal secretary—Ruth. She is one of those women who, because they do not have an "intellectual" idea in their noodles, are too frequently dismissed as conveniently decorative but not very valuable. And perhaps Ruth really is that. But she has made two or three remarks recently which seem to me to display an intuitive intelligence of a considerable order. Yet they may be merely aptly chosen, conventional observations. It is hard to tell.—She interests me. She has a maxim which I resent but cannot refute: "There are those who get it and those who dish it out; I intend to be on the side of the dishers." (Is this the post-Christian golden rule? It has its own power, you know.) In any case, the other day I was sitting in my cubicle of an office, in front of which Ruth's desk is placed—she services two of us. I had my feet up on the desk in a rather indecorous fashion, and I had laid the book I was reading on my lap while I smoked a cigarette. I suppose I was daydreaming a little. Suddenly Ruth opened the door and entered. I started, picked up the book and took my feet off the table-top. Ruth cocked an eye at me and said, "You like to feel guilty, don't you? All I wanted to know was whether you could spare time for a cup of coffee." So we went to the café and had coffee, and didn't even mention her statement or its cause.

But it set me thinking; and the longer I thought about it, the better I liked it. I had always discounted wild, Dostoyevskian notions like that as being too perverse to be true. But now I am not at all sure that frivolous, red-nailed Ruth wasn't right. So long as Clarice had been there to reprove me for my infidelities, I had had them. When her censorship was removed, the infidelities, or any love affairs at all, lost their spice—the spice which was the guilt that she made me feel about them. And then, having been divorced from Clarice, I took this job. This job is a sop to my sense of guilt at being white and middle-class, that is to say, one of Ruth's "dishers," a sop because I am participating in an enterprise whose purpose is social justice; at the same time it is a punishment, because of the deprivations I am undergoing; yet the actual luxury of my life and my actual status in the bureaucracy, high but not orthodox, privileged yet not normally restricted, nourishes the guilt which supports it. What it is that causes the sense of guilt in the first place, I suppose Freud could tell me, but I am not going to bother to find out. There are certain indecencies about which one ought not to inquire unless one has to. Social guilt—that is to say, a sense of responsibility toward society—is a good thing to have, and I intend to exploit it in myself. I intend to satisfy it by doing as fine a job as I possibly can; and furthermore I intend to find a worthy European family, say Italian, who are impoverished, and to support them out of my salary. I must confess that the CARE packages we used to send to Europe after the war made me feel better than all the fine sentiments I ever gave words to.

I am grateful that I came here. I have been thrown back upon myself in a way that has only benefited me.

We begin work soon. The first trainload of Negroes arrived today, 500 of them. They are going through Intake (the buildings I described in my last letter) and our work, we are told, will commence within a few days.

Exactly what we are to do, we will be told tomorrow. I look forward to it eagerly.

ANDY

I read this letter over before putting it in the envelope. That was a mistake. All the excitement about myself which I had felt so keenly sounds rather flat as I have put it. There must be a great deal for me yet to discover. As you know, I have never spent much of my energy in intimacies, either with myself or with other people. One gets a facsimile of it when talking about the universal stereotypes of love with a woman. But this desert has thrown me back upon myself; and from your letter I take it you would find my explorations of interest. However, you must not expect many more letters in so tiresome a vein. I will seal and mail this one tonight lest I repent in the morning.

April 10

Dear Herb,

I have not known how to write this letter, though I've tried two or three times in the past week to do it. I'm going to put it in the form of a homily, with illustrations, on the text "There are those who get it and those who dish it out; I intend to be on the side of the dishers."

First, in what context did it occur? It is the motto of a charming young woman (any doubts I may have expressed about her are withdrawn as of now; she is all one could ask for) who is not malicious and does not in the least want to impose her beliefs or herself upon other people. She sends $100 a month to her mother, who is dying of cancer in a county hospital in Pennsylvania. When she told me she was sending the money, I asked her why. "Why?" said Ruth. "I'm disappointed in you to ask me such a thing." "All right, be disappointed, but tell me why." She shrugged a little in a humorous way. "She's my mother. And anyway," she added, "we're all dying, aren't we?" The important thing to note about Ruth is—she means it but she doesn't care. Just as she doesn't really care whether you like her clothes or her lovely hair; she does, and you ought to; the loss is yours if you don't. She was reared in a perfectly usual American city, and she has chosen from its unconscious culture the best in custom and attitude.

But she said it here, in the Public Relations division of the Colored Persons Reserve, here where there is as much getting and dishing out as anywhere in the world, where the most important Negro in the Reserve, the President of it, may be in a very real sense considered inferior to our window-washer. The first time O'Doone heard her say it—he had dropped by to talk awhile, and Ruth had joined us—he made the sign of the cross in the air between himself and Ruth and backed clear out of the room.

He didn't return either. I'm sure he's not religious. I don't know why he did that.

Now what does the statement imply. Primarily, it makes no judgment and does not urge to action. It is unmoral. "There is a condition such that some people must inflict pain and others must receive it; since it is impossible to be neutral in this regard and since I like neither to give nor to take injury, I shall choose the path of least resistance—ally myself with the inflictors, not because I like their side and certainly not because I dislike the other side, but only because I myself am least interfered with that way." No regret. No self-deception (*it is impossible to be neutral*). A clear conscience (*I like neither to give nor to take injury*). In other words, true resignation—this circumstance is as it is, and it will not and should not be otherwise. There is a certain intensity of joy possible after resignation of this order, greater than we frustrated hopers know. (Where do I fit into this scheme? I think I have discovered one thing about myself from contemplating Ruth's maxim: that is, I want profoundly to be a disher, but my training has been such, or perhaps I am only so weak, that I am incapable of being one with a clear conscience. Consequently I find myself in a halfway position—dishing it out, yes, but at the behest of people I have never seen, and to people I will never know.) Ruth took a job with the NRACP for the only right reason—not for any of my complicated ones nor for the general greed, but because she saw quite clearly that here was one of the very pure instances of getting it and dishing it out. She left a job as secretary to an executive in General Electric for this. I think she gets a certain pleasure from seeing her philosophy so exquisitely borne out by event. Ruth is 27. I think I am in love with her. I am sure she is not in love with me.

Tell me, Herb, does not this maxim ring a bell in you? Can you not recognize, as I do, the rightness of it? This girl has had the courage to put into deliberate words her sense of the inevitable. Do you not admire her for it? And is she not right? She is right enough. If you doubt it, let me tell you what our job here is.

The authorities consider the situation potentially explosive enough to warrant the most elaborate system of censorship I have ever heard of. To begin with, there is a rule that during his first week in the Reserve every Negro may write three letters to persons on the outside. After that period is over, only one letter a month is permitted. Now all letters leaving here during the first week are sent to PR where they are censored and typed in the correct form (on NRACP letterhead); the typed copies are sent on and the originals are filed. The reason for this elaborate system is interesting enough, and probably sound; every endeavor is to be made to discourage any leaking out of adverse reports on conditions in the CPR. There are some fourteen million Negroes in the nation, not all of whom are entirely pleased with the prospect of being relocated; and there are an indeterminate number of Caucasian sympathizers—civil liberties fanatics for the most part—who could cause trouble if any confirmation of their suspicions about the CPR should leak out. We have put out a staggering amount of data on the climatic, agricultural, power production and mining conditions of the region; and we have propagandized with every device in the book. Yet we know well enough how long it takes for propaganda to counteract prejudice, and sometimes how deceptive an apparent propaganda success can be. We are more than grateful that almost the entire news outlet system of the nation is on our side.

Well then, after the three letters of the first week have been typed and sent, the writer's job begins. Every effort is made to discourage the interned Negroes from writing to the outside. For one thing, we keep in our files all personal letters incoming during the first month. Anyone who continues to write to an internee after this month needs to be answered. The filing clerks keep track of the dates, and forward all personal letters to us. (The clerks think we send the letters on to the internees.) We then write appropriate responses to the letters, in the style of the internee as we estimate it from his three letters. We try to be as impersonal as possible, conveying the idea that everything is all right. Why do we not forward the letters to the internees to answer? First of all we do—if the internees request it. They are told that they will receive letters only from those persons whose letters they request to see, and such a request involves yards of red tape. Very few are expected to use the cumbersome mechanism at all. Then, we write the letters for them simply to save ourselves time and trouble. We would have a lot of rewriting to do anyway; this method assures us of complete control and an efficient *modus operandi*. Any outsider Negro who writes too many insistent letters will be, at our request, relocated within a month; we do not want any unnecessary unhappiness to result from the necessarily painful program. Friends and relatives are to be reunited as fast as possible. Whole communities are to be relocated together, to avoid whatever wrenches in personal relationships we can avoid.

Is not this getting it and dishing it out on a fine scale? All for very good reasons, I know. But then, is it not conceivable that there are always good reasons for the old crapperoo? Sometimes I feel absolutistic enough to say—if it's this bad, for any ultimate reason whatsoever, then to hell with it. After which sentiment, comes the gun at the head. But then reason reinstates my sense of relativity of values, and on I go writing a letter to Hector Jackson of South Carolina explaining that I've been so busy putting up a chickenhouse and plowing that I haven't had a chance to write but I hope to see you soon. (I doubt if I will.)

ANDY

I forgot to mention—I have a special job, which is to censor the letters of all the clerical personnel in PR. One of my duties is to censor any reference to the censorship! A strange state of affairs. None of them know that this job is mine; most think the censor must be some Mail Department employee. I must say you look at some people with new eyes after reading their correspondence.

I need hardly say, but if there is any doubt I will say, that this letter is absolutely confidential. How much of our system will become publicly known, I cannot guess; but naturally I don't want to jump the official gun in this regard.

April 12

Dear Herb,

Let me tell you about the strange adventure I had last evening. I am still not quite sure what to make of it.

Immediately after work I picked up a few sandwiches and a pint of whiskey, and walked out into the desert on one of my hikes. One more meal with the jabber of the café and one more of those good but always good in the same way dinners, and I felt I should come apart at the seams. (Another thing I have learned about myself—I am ill-adapted to prison life.) I had no goal in view. I intended to stroll.

But I found myself heading generally in the direction of the hill from which I had looked over the Tehuala Valley and the city of CPR Intake buildings. I came across nothing particularly interesting in a natural history way, so that by early dusk I was near to the hill; I decided to climb it again and see what I could see.

The first thing I saw, in the difficult light of dusk, was a soldier with a gun standing at the foot of the hill. I came around a large clump of cactus, and there he was, leaning on his rifle. He immediately pointed it at me, and told me to go back where I belonged. I objected that I had climbed this hill before and I could see no reason why I shouldn't do it again. He replied that he didn't see any reason either, but I couldn't just the same; they were going to put up another fence to keep people like me away. I cursed, at the whole situation; if I had dared I would have cursed him too, for he had been rude as only a guard with a gun can be. Then, before I left, I pulled out my pint and took a slug of it. The guard was a changed man.

"Christ," he said, "give me a pull."

"I should give you a pull."

"Come on," he said, "I ain't had a drop since I came to this hole. They won't even give us beer."

"All right," I replied, "if you'll tell me what the hell's going on around here."

He made me crouch behind a Joshua tree, and he himself would not look at me while he talked. I asked him why all the precautions.

"They got a searchlight up top the hill, with machine guns. They sweep the whole hill all the time. They can see plain as day in the dark. They keep an eye on us fellows down here. I know. I used to run the light."

"I haven't seen any light," I said.

He glanced at me with scorn.

"It's black," he said. "They cut down all the bushes all around the top part of that hill. Anybody comes up in the bare place—pttt! *Any*body. Even a guard."

"I still don't see any light."

"Man, it's black light. You wear glasses and shine this thing and you can see better than you can with a regular light searchlight. It's the stuff. We used to shoot rabbits with it. The little bastards never knew what hit them!"

I didn't want to appear simple, so I didn't ask any more questions about the black light. He was an irascible fellow, with a gun and a knife, and he had drunk most of the bottle already.

"Why do you let me stay at all?" I asked.

"Can't see good in the dusk. Not even them can't."

I couldn't think of anything more to say. I felt overwhelmed.

"I used to be guard on the railroad they got inside. Say, have they got a system. Trains from the outside go through an automatic gate. All the trainmen get on the engine and drive out. Then we come up through another automatic gate and hook on and drag it in. Always in the daytime. Anybody tried to hop train, inside or out, pttt! Air-conditioned box cars made out of steel. Two deep they come. Never come in at night."

"Are you married?" I asked.

"Ain't nobody married up front, huh?" I didn't answer. "There ain't, ain't there?"

"No, but there could be if anybody felt like it."

"Well, there ain't even a woman inside. Not a damn one. They let us have all the nigger women we want. Some ain't so bad. Most of them fight a lot. "

He smashed the pint bottle on a rock nearby.

"Why didn't you bring some real liquor, god damn you?" he said in a low voice full of violence. "Get the hell back home where you belong. Get out of here. It's getting dark. I'll shoot the guts out of you too. Bring me something I can use next time, huh? Get going—Stay under cover," he shouted after me. "They're likely to get you if they spot you. They can't miss if it's dark enough."

The last I heard of him he was coughing and spitting and swearing. I was as disgusted as scared, and I must confess I was scared stiff.

I walked homeward bound, slowly recovering my emotional balance, trying to understand what had happened to me with that guard, the meaning of what he had told me. For some absurd reason the tune "In the Gloaming, O, My Darling" kept running through my head in the idiotic way tunes will, so that I was unable to concentrate intelligently upon the situation. (I wonder why that tune business happens.)

I heard a sound at some distance to my left. I stopped, suddenly and inexplicably alarmed to the point of throbbing temples and clenched fists. I saw a slim figure in brown among the cactus; and then, as the figure approached, I could see it was a young woman. She did not see me, but her path brought her directly to where I was standing. I did not know whether to accost her at a distance or to let her come upon me where I stood. By the time I had decided not to accost her, I could see it was Ruth.

"Why, Ruth!" I cried, with all the emotion of relief and gratified surprise in my voice, and perhaps something more. "What are you doing here?"

She started badly, then seeing who it was she hurried up to me and to my intense surprise took my arms and put them around her body.

"Andy," she said, "I am so glad to see you. Some good angel must have put you here for me."

I squeezed her, we kissed, a friendly kiss, then she drew away and shook herself. She had almost always called me Mr. Dixon before; there was a real affection in her "Andy."

"What's the matter?" I asked her. "Where have you been?"

"I didn't know you took walks too."

"Oh, yes. It's one way to keep from going nuts."

She laughed a little, and squeezed my arm. I could not refrain from kissing her again, and this time it was not just a friendly kiss.

"Where did you go?" I asked again.

"To that hill. I went up there a couple of times before. There was a guard there wanted to lay me."

We didn't speak for a few moments.

"I think he almost shot me for giving him the brush-off. I didn't look back when I left, but I heard him click his gun. You don't know how glad I was to see you."

So we kissed again, and this time it was serious.

"Wait a minute," she said, "wait a minute."

She unlocked her arm from mine, and we continued on our way not touching.

"I had some trouble with a guard too," I said. "I wonder why they're so damned careful to keep us away."

"Mine told me they didn't want us to get any funny ideas. He said things aren't what they seem to be in there."

"Didn't you ask him what he meant?"

"Sure. That's when he said I'd better shut up and let him lay me, or else he'd shoot me. So I walked off. I'm not going to call on *him* again."

I put my arm around her—I can't tell you how fond I was of her at that moment, of her trim, poised body, her courage, her good humor, her delightful rich voice and laughter—but she only kissed me gently and withdrew.

"I want to keep my head for a while, darling," she said.

I knew what she meant. We walked on in silence, hand in hand. It was moonlight. This time if I was lightheaded I knew why.

When we were about half a mile from our buildings, we came across O'Doone also returning from a walk.

"Well," he said brightly, "it *is* a nice moon, isn't it?"

It wouldn't do to say that we had met by accident; I was embarrassed, but Ruth's fine laugh cleared the air for me.

"Nicest I ever saw," she said.

"Did you ever walk up that hill," I asked him, "where you can see out over the valley?"

"Once," he said in a surprisingly harsh voice. "I'd rather play chess."

So we went into one of the recreation rooms, and O'Doone beat me at three games of chess. Ruth sat by, knitting—a sweater for a cousin's baby. We talked little, but comfortably. It would have been a domestic scene, if it had not been for the fifty or sixty other people in the room.

Herb, what does it all mean?

ANDY

April 20

Dear Herb,

This is a *Prior* Script. If all goes well you will receive this letter from Ruth's cousin, who will be informed by O'Doone's sister to forward it to you. O'Doone's sister will also send you instructions on how to make the invisible ink visible. When I wrote the letter, I was in a self-destructive frame of mind; I was prepared to take all the certainly drastic consequences that would come from its being read by someone of authority. But O'Doone's invisible ink (what a strange fellow to have brought a quart of it here! He said he had brought it only to play mysterious lettergames with his nephew—I wonder) and Ruth's baby sweater, upon the wrapping of which I write this, combined to save me. If the authorities catch *this,* I don't care what happens. It takes so long to write lightly enough in invisible ink for no pen marks to show on the paper, that I doubt if I will have the patience to use it often. Most of my letters will be innocuous in regular ink. I may add an invisible note or two, between the lines, in the margin, at the end. O'Doone says it's not any of the ordinary kinds and if we're careful the authorities are not likely to catch us. O'Doone is strange. He refused to take this whole ink matter for anything more than a big joke—as though we were digging a tunnel under a house, O'Doone pretending we are just tunneling in a strawstack to hide our marbles, myself trying to protest (but being laughed at for my lapse in taste) that we are really undermining a house in order to blow it up. Which perhaps we are. In any event, I don't have the energy left to rewrite this letter; I'll merely copy it off, invisibly.

I cannot tell you how shocked I was to discover the familiar, black, censor's ink over five lines in your last letter. The censor censored! I had not thought of that. In my innocence I had thought that we writers in the higher brackets could be trusted to be discreet. One would think I was still a loyal subscriber to the *Nation,* I was so naïve. But no—I am trusted to censor the letters of inferiors (I suspect my censorship is sample-checked by someone), but my own letters are themselves inspected and their dangerous sentiments excised. And, irony of ironies! your own references to the fact that my letters were censored were themselves blacked out.

Who is it that does this? The head of PR here? That's a strange way to make him waste his time. One of his assistants? Then the head must censor the assistant's letters. And the chief board of the NRACP censors the head's letters? And the President theirs? And God his? And———?

Which is the more imprisoned—the jailer who thinks he is free and is not, or the prisoner who knows the precise boundaries of his liberty and accepting them explores and uses all the world he has?

I am a jailer who knows he is not free. I am a prisoner who does not know the limits of his freedom. And all this I voluntarily submitted to in the name of a higher freedom. Ever since my adolescence, when the New Deal was a faith, liberty has been one of the always repeated, never examined articles of my creed. Well, I have been examining liberty recently, and she's a pure fraud.

One thing I have learned—you don't just quietly put yourself on the side of Ruth's dishers, you become one of them yourself; and a disher *has* to dish it out, he cannot help it at all; and he pays for it. Or maybe I am only paying for my guilt-making desire to be a more important disher than I am.

Ruth was surprised at my distress upon receiving your censored letter. She only shrugged. What had I expected, after all? It was inevitable, it was a necessity. That's the key word, Herb—Necessity. Not liberty, Necessity. True liberty is what the prisoner has, because he accepts Necessity. That's the great thing, Herb, to recognize and accept Necessity.

I've slowly been working toward a realization of this. I think my decision to work in the NRACP came from recognizing the social necessity of it. The Negro problem in America was acute and was insoluble by any liberal formula; this solution gives dignity and independence to the Negroes; it staves off the Depression by the huge demand for manufactured products, for transportation, for the operations of the NRACP itself; but perhaps most important of all, it establishes irrevocably in the American people's mind the wisdom and rightness of the government; for if capitalism must go (as it must) it should be replaced peaceably by a strong and wise planned state. Such a state we are proving ourselves to be. Very well, I accepted this. But what I forgot was that *I*, I the individual, I Andrew Dixon, must personally submit to the stringencies of necessity. The relics of the New Deal faith remained to clutter up my new attitude. This experience, coming when and as it did, particularly coming when Ruth's courageous wisdom was nearby to support me, has liberated me (I hope) into the greater freedom of the Prisoner of Necessity.

Such are my pious prayers at least. I cannot say I am sure I fully understand all the strictures of necessity. I *can* say I do not enjoy those I understand. But pious I will remain.

Remember the days when we thought we could *change* Necessity? Democracy and all that? How much older I feel!

ANDY

May 1

Mary my dear,

Please let me apologize—sincerely too, Mary—for having neglected you so cruelly for the past months. Herb tells me you are quite put out, and well you might be. I can find no excuses for it, but this I will stoutly maintain—it was not a question of hostility or indifference to you, my dear. Actually I have been going through something of a crisis, as Herb may have been telling you. It has something to do with the desert, and something to do with the NRACP, and a lot to do with the charming young woman whose picture I enclose. She is Ruth Cone. We are getting married in a couple of Sundays—Mother's Day. Why Mother's Day, I really don't know. But she wants it, so there's no help. The details of our plighting troth might amuse you.

A couple of evenings ago I was playing chess in the recreation room with a man named O'Doone, my only friend here. Ruth was sitting beside us knitting some rompers for a cousin's baby. From time to time we would chat a little; it was all very comfortable and unromantic. O'Doone, between games, went to the toilet. When he had left, Ruth said to me with a twinkle in her eye, "Andy darling, don't you see what I am doing?" I replied, "Why yes, my sweet, knitting tiny garments. Is it—?" And we both laughed heartily. It was a joke, you see, a mild comfortable little joke, and no one would have thought of it a second time except that when we had finished laughing it was no longer a joke. Her face became very sober, and I am sure mine did too. I said, "Do you want children, Ruth?" "Yes," she replied. "Do you want to have *my* children?" "Yes," she said again, without looking at me. Then with the most charming conquest of modesty that you can imagine, she turned her serious little face to me, and we very lightly kissed. O'Doone had returned by then. "Well," he said in a bright way, "do I interrupt?" "Not at all," I answered; "we have just decided to get married." He burbled a little, in caricature of the over-whelmed, congratulating friend, pumped our hands, and asked us when we were marrying. "I don't know," I said. "Why not tomorrow?" "Oh no," said Ruth severely, "how can I assemble my trousseau?" At which O'Doone went off into a braying laugh, and we set up the chess pieces. "Bet you five to one," he said, "I win this game in less than sixty moves." I wouldn't take his bet. It took him about forty moves to beat me.

And thus did Dixon and Cone solemnly vow to share their fortunes.

It's the first marriage in PR. Everybody will attend. The chief promised me Monday off and temporary quarters in one of the guest suites. We are to get a two-room apartment in the new dormitory that is nearly completed. Such privacy and spaciousness will make us the envy of the whole community. I'm sure there will be a spate of marriages as soon as the dormitory is completed. We will not be married by a holy man, partly because neither of us believes in it and partly because there isn't one of any kind on the premises. (I wondered why those detailed questions about religious beliefs on our application forms.) There was a little trouble at first about who was authorized to marry people here. The PR chief, as the only person permitted to leave the place, went out and got himself authorized to do it legally. I think he rather fancies himself in the capacity of marrier. He runs to paternalism.

Ruth urges me, Mary—she assumes, quite rightly, that I have not done it already—to tell you some of the homely details of life here. Of our sleeping rooms, the less said the beter. The beds are comfortable period. We live quite communally, but very well. There's a fine gymnasium, with swimming pool and playfields attached—tennis, baseball, squash, fencing, everything but golf. There's the best library (surely the best!) in the world on American Negro affairs, and a reasonably good one of modern literature. We have comfortable working quarters—with long enough hours to be sure. There is a fine desert for us to walk around in, and I have come to need an occasional stroll in the desert for spiritual refreshment. And we eat handsomely, except for vegetables. In fact, the only complaint that I have of the cooking is the monotony of its excellence—roast, steak, chop, stew. Never or seldom, liver and kidneys and omelettes and casseroles. And always frozen vegetables. Well, probably the Negroes will be producing plenty of vegetables within a few weeks. There's lots of liquor of every kind. There is a sort of department store where one can buy everything one needs and most of the luxuries one could want in this restricted life. There's a movie a week—double-feature with news and cartoon—and bridge or poker every day. A microcosmic plenitude.

Well, as for the rest of our routine life here, I can think of nothing interesting enough to mention. We work and avoid work, backbite, confide, suspect. It's a bureaucratic existence, no doubt of that.

Will this epistle persuade you to forgive me?

Now you must write to me—soon.

Devotedly yours,

ANDY

*(In invisible ink)*

O'Doone, who sometimes gives his opinions very obliquely, came to me today with some disturbing figures. He wasn't in the least jaunty about them, and I must confess that I am not either.

According to *Time,* which seems to know more about the CPR than we do, there have been about 50,000 Negroes interned already, and these 50,000 include nearly all the wealthy and politically powerful Negroes in the nation (including an objectionable white-supremacy Senator one of whose great-great-grandmothers turns out to have been black). The leaders were interned first, reasonably enough, to provide the skeleton of government and system in the new State which they are to erect. *But,* O'Doone points out, we have yet to receive from them a request for letters from an outsider; and if any Negroes at all are going to make such requests, it must surely be these, the most important, the least afraid of red tape. (He also pointed out that not one of the entertainers or athletes of prominence has been interned. That, I'm afraid, is all too easily explained.) You see, says O'Doone, you see? But he didn't say Why? to me, and I'm glad he didn't for I can't even guess why.

Another statistic he had concerned the CPR itself. We all know that the figures on natural resources in the CPR are exaggerated. Grossly. Fourteen million people cannot possibly live well in this area, and O'Doone demonstrated that fact to me most convincingly. The Negro problem, economically, in the U.S. has been that they provided a larger cheap labor market than consumer market. Now the false stimulus of capitalizing their beginnings here will keep American industry on an even keel for years and years, but after that what? O'Doone bowed out at that point, but I think I can press the point a little further. They will provide a market for surplus commodities, great enough to keep the pressures of capitalism from blowing us sky-high, meanwhile permitting the transition to a planned State to take place. Very astute, I think, very astute indeed.

June 12

Dear Herb,

Why I have not written, you ought to be able to guess. I will not pretend to any false ardors about Ruth. She is wise and winning as a woman, and everything one could ask for as a wife. I love her dearly. She has not read very widely or profoundly, but I think she is going to do something about that, soon. We are very happy together and I think we shall continue to be happy during the difficult years to come. What more can I say?

Why are happiness and contentment and the sense of fulfillment so hard to write about? I can think of nothing to say, and besides Ruth is just coming in from tennis (it's 9:30 Sunday morning).

10 P.M.

Ruth has gone to bed, so I will continue in another vein.

I have been discovering that the wells of pity, which have lain so long locked and frozen in my eyes, are thawed in me now. I am enclosing a letter which came in from a Negress in Chicago to her lover, in the CPR, and his response. It is the first letter from inside, except for the usual three during the first week, that I have read. Apparently a few have been coming out now and then, but this is my first one, I cannot tell you how I pitied both these unhappy people. When Ruth read them, she said, "My, what a mean man! I hope he has to collect garbage all his life." I cannot agree with her. I think his little note betrays an unhappiness as great as the woman's, and even more pitiable for being unrecognized, unappreciated. Judge for yourself. I can think of nothing to add.

ANDY

*Honey dear child, why don't you write to me? Don't you even remember all those things you told me you'd do no matter what? And you're not even in jail, you just in that place where we all going to go to sooner or later. O I sure hope they take me there with you. I can't live without you. But I don't even know who to ask to go there with you. I went to the policeman and they said they didn't know nothing about it. I don't know what to do. You don't know how I ache for you honey. It's just like I got a tooth pulled out but it ain't no tooth it's worse, and there is no dentist for it neither. There's a fellow at the store keeps bothering me now and again, but I assure him I don't want him I got a man. I thought I had a man, you, but I don't hear nothing from you. Maybe you got something there, I don't see how you could do it not after those things you said, but if you have tell me so I can go off in some hole and die. I don't want this Lee Lawson, he's no good, it's you I want, sweetheart, you tell me it's all right. I got to hear from you or I'll just die.*

*Dear ——,*

*I've been so busy baby, you wouldn't believe how busy I've been. You'll be coming here pretty soon and then you'll feel better too. It's nice here. We'll get along fine then. You tell that guy to leave you be. You're my gal. Tell him I said so.*

*Yours truly,*

*(In invisible ink)*

I didn't include these letters because I thought they were in the Héloïse-Abélard class, but because I wanted to say something about them and also because they gave me more invisible space.

The man's response came to us already typed. That very much astonished me, and O'Doone, when I told him, let fly a nasty one. "I suppose," he said, "they have a couple of writers in there writing a few letters in place of the Negroes, which we then relay. Complicated, isn't it?" Not complicated, upsetting. Devastating. What if it were true? (And I must say this letter has an air more like the PR rewrite-formula than like a real letter. Then *none* of the Negroes would have even a filtered connection with the outside world. Why? Why fool even us? Is there no end to the deception and doubt of this place?

O'Doone posed another of his puzzles yesterday. He read in the current PR weekly bulletin that the CPR has been shipping whole trainloads of leather goods and canned meats to China and Europe for relief purposes, under the government's supervision of course. O'Doone came into my office at once, waving the bulletin and chortling. "How do you like it?" he cried. "Before we get a carrot out of them the Chinese get tons of meat." Then a sudden light seemed to dawn on his face. "Where did all the cattle come from?"

A strange thing happened: O'Doone's intelligent, sensitive face collapsed. The great domed forehead remained almost unwrinkled, but his features looked somehow like one of those children's rubber faces which collapse when you squeeze them. No anguish, no anxiety. Only collapse. He left without a word. I wish he had never come here with that news.

Last night I lay awake till three or four o'clock. I could hear trucks and trains rumbling occasionally throughout the night—entering and leaving the Reserve. But that guard I met at the foot of the hill told me that they only bring internees in the daytime. Are those shipments? How can it be? Sometimes I am sick at heart with doubt and uncertainty.

I dreamt last night that I was a Gulliver, lying unbound and unresisting on the ground while a thousand Lilliputians, all of them black, ate at me. I would not write the details of that dream even in invisible ink. Not even in plain water.

Dear Herb,

Hail Independence Day! Some of the overgrown kids around here are shooting off firecrackers. No one is working. It is all very pleasant. I suppose March 20 will be the Independence Day of the new Negro nation—the day when the first trainload arrived. How long ago that seems already. I do not think I have ever been through so much in so short a time. And now for the real news.

Ruth is pregnant! Amazing woman, she remains outwardly as humorous and self-contained as ever. No one else knows her condition, because she wants to avoid as much as possible of the female chatter that goes with pregnancy. She insists upon playing tennis still. Yet she is not all calmness and coolness; when we are lying in bed together before going to sleep, she croons little nonsense hymns to pregnancy in my ear, and yesterday afternoon at the office she walked into my cubicle, up to where I was sitting very solemnly, and placed my hand over her womb. Then she kissed me with a sort of unviolent passion such as I have never known before in my life. I tell you, she's a wonderful woman.

How miraculous is conception and growth! I no more understand such things than I really understand about the stars and their rushings. One event follows another, but I'm sure I don't know why. You get back to an archaic awe, if you permit yourself to, realizing that you yourself have started off a chain of miracles. I never had a sense of littleness when observing the naked heavens, of man's puniness, of my own nothingness. Perhaps it was a fear of that feeling which for so long prevented me from looking upwards at all. I mentioned my reaction to O'Doone on one of the first occasions of our meeting; he nodded and said, "But is not a man more complex than a star, and in every way but one that we know of, more valuable?" What he said remains with me yet; and when I am presented with the vastness of the stars and the forces which operate within them, I am impressed and excited enough but I am not depressed by the imagined spectacle. Their bigness does not make me little. My own complexity does not make them simple. Man is no longer the center of the universe perhaps, but neither is anything else. That I have learned.

But when I am presented with the proof of the powers that men (and myself) possess, then I still feel a little off balance. When Clarice was pregnant with Betty, I had no such feeling. I felt annoyed chiefly. But now, in this desert, in the CPR, I have been sent back at last to fundamentals, to the sources of things; and I realize fully how unaccountable is birth to life. Ruth, who never departed far from the sources, is less embarrassed in admitting her sense of mystery.

One thing I am going to teach this child, if it can be taught anything: that the humane tradition has been tried and found wanting. It's over,

finished, kaput. A new era of civilization commences. Kindness and freedom—once they were good for something, but no more. *Put yourself in
his place*—never. Rather, fight to stay where you are. I think we are entering upon an age of reason and mystery. Reason which accepts and understands the uttermost heights and depths of human power, man's depravity
and his nobility; and, understanding these, dares use them toward a great
and future goal, the goal of that stern order which is indispensable to the
fullest development of man. Mystery toward all that is not explainable,
which is a very great deal. Rationalism failed, for it asserted that everything was ultimately explainable. We know better. We know that to destroy
a man's sense of mystery is to cut him off at one of the sources of life. Awe,
acceptance, faith—these are wonderful sources of power and fulfillment. I
have discovered them. My child shall never forget them.

ANDY

(*In invisible ink*)

I have put the gun to my temple, Herb, I have pointed the knife at my
heart. But my nerve failed me. There were a few days when I was nearly
distracted. My division chief told me to stay home till I looked better, but
I dared not. I think it was only Ruth's pregnancy that saved me. My
newly awakened sense of mystery, plus my powers of reason, have saved
me. This is the third letter I have written you in a week, but I knew the
others were wild and broken, and I was not sure at all that I was physically
able to write in such a manner as to avoid detection.

It came to a head, for me, two weeks ago. O'Doone entered my office,
his face looking bright and blasted. He dropped a booklet on my desk
and left after a few comments of no importance. The booklet was an
anthropologist's preliminary report on certain taboos among American
Negroes. The fellow had been interviewing them in Intake. There was
nothing of special interest about it that I could see, except that it was
written in the past tense.

I expected O'Doone to reclaim the booklet any day. For some reason he
had always done the visiting to me, not I to him. He was very restless,
and I am slothful. But a week passed, and no O'Doone. I did not meet
him in the café nor in the recreation room. I went to his own room, but
he did not answer. The next day I went to his office, and his secretary
told me he had not shown up for two days. I returned to his room. It was
locked. The janitor unlocked it for me. When I entered I saw him lying
dead on his bed. "Well, old boy," I said to drive the janitor away, I don't
know why, "feeling poorly?" He had drunk something. There was a glass
on the table by his bed. There was no note. His face was repulsive. (That
is a mystery I have learned to respect, how hideous death is.) He was
cold, and somehow a little sticky to the touch. I covered his face with

a towel, and sat down. I knew I should call someone, but I did not want to. I knew the janitor would remember letting me in, and my staying too long. Yet I felt that there was something I must do. What it was I could not remember, something important. It took me an eternity to remember —the invisible ink. I knew where he had kept it. It was not there. I looked throughout his room, and it was simply gone. I left the room.

I still did not notify anyone of his suicide. I was not asking myself why he had done it. Or perhaps I was only shouting Where's the ink? in a loud voice to cover up the little question Why? I went to our rooms and straight to the liquor shelf. I took down the Scotch and poured myself a stiff one, and drank. It was horrible. I spat it out, cursing; then I recognized the odor. O'Doone had come over, poured out the Scotch (I hope he enjoyed it himself) and filled the bottle with the invisible ink. At that, I broke down in the most womanish way, and cried on the bed (never ask Why? Why? Why?).

Ruth found me there some time later. I told her everything that had happened, and she immediately pulled me together. She had the sense to know I had been acting more oddly than was wise. She notified the right people, and O'Doone was disposed of. No one asked me any embarassing questions, and no official mention of O'Doone's end was made anywhere.

I must continue this on a birthday card.

*(In invisible ink, on a large, plain Happy Birthday card to Mary)*
I had still not allowed myself to ask why he had done it, but Ruth put the thing in a short sentence. "He was too soft-hearted to stand it here." She was right; he was a Christian relic. He knew more than he could bear. I resolved to go that very evening again to the hill where the black search-light threatened the night.

Some sandwiches. Four half-pints of whiskey. A hunting-knife (a foolish gesture, I know). Plain drab clothes. The long walk in the still hot, late-afternoon sun. Sunset. The huge, sudden twilight. And I was within sight of a guard (not the same one I had seen before) standing by the new fence at the foot of the hill.

I crept up toward him under cover of brush and cactus, till I was close enough to toss a half-pint of whiskey in his direction. His bored, stupid face immediately became animated by the most savage emotions. He leveled his gun and pointed it in my general direction. He could not see me, however, and rather than look for me he crouched, eyes still searching the underbrush, to reach for the bottle. He drained it in five minutes.

"Throw me some more," he whispered loudly.

"Put the gun down."

I aimed my voice away from him, hoping that he would not spot me. I was lying flat beneath a large clump of sagebrush. There was a Joshua tree nearby, and several cactus plants. He pointed the gun at one of the stalks of cactus, and crept up toward it. Then he suddenly stopped, I don't know why, and walked back to his post.

"What yer want?" he asked.

I tossed out another bottle. He jumped again; then he got it and drank it.

"What's going on in there?" I asked him.

"They're fixing up the niggers," he said. "You know as much about it as I do."

He began to sing "O Susannah" in a sentimental voice. It was beginning to get too dark for my safety. I was desperate.

I tossed out another bottle, only not so far this time. When he leaned for it, I said very clearly, "You look like a butcher."

He deliberately opened the bottle and drank off half of it.

"Butcher, huh? Butcher?" he laid down his gun and took his villainous knife out. "I'm no butcher. I won't have nothing to do with the whole slimy mess. I won't eat them. No, sir, you can do that for me. But I can do a little carving, I think. No butcher, you son of a bitch. You dirty prying nigger-eating son of a bitch. I'll learn you to call me a butcher."

He was stalking the cactus again. He lunged forward at it, and with much monotonous cursing and grunting dealt with it murderously. Meanwhile I crawled out on the other side of the sagebrush and ran for it. He never shot at me. Nothing happened, except that I too ran full tilt into a cactus, and had to walk hours in agony of flesh as well as of spirit. I vomited and retched till I thought I would be unable to walk further.

I must continue this letter some other way.

ANDY

(*In invisible ink, on the papers wrapping another sweater for Ruth's cousin's baby*)

I told Ruth nothing of what I had learned. Not even *her* great sense of the inevitable could survive such a shock, I think. Yet sometimes it seems to me that she must surely know it all. I do not want to know whether she knows. Could I support it if she did?

It was more painful pulling the cactus needles out than it had been acquiring them. But she removed them all, bathed the little wounds with alcohol and put me to bed. The next morning I awoke at seven and insisted upon going to work. I sat all day in my office, eating crackers and drinking milk. I didn't accomplish a thing. It was that day my chief told me to take it easy for a while. I was in a sort of stupor for a couple of days; yet I insisted, to everyone's consternation, on going to work. I accomplished nothing, and I intended to accomplish nothing. It was just that I could not tolerate being alone. In fact, today was the first day I have been alone for more than five minutes since I returned from the walk. But today I have regained a kind of composure, or seeming of composure, which for a time I despaired of ever possessing again. And I know that by the time I have given shape enough to my thoughts to put them on this paper for you to read, I shall have gained again a peace of mind. To have you to write to, Herb, that is the great thing at this point. Without you there, I do not know what I would have done.

So much for my emotions. My thinking, my personal philosophy, has gone through at least as profound an upheaval as they.

In the chaos of my mind, in which huge invisible chunks of horror hit me unexpectedly from unexpected angles again and again, my first coherent and sensible idea came in the form of a question. "Why did they make it possible for me to find out what has been going on?" For I finally realized that it was no fluke that I had discovered it. Or O'Doone either. Or anyone with the suspicions and the courage for it. When the atom bombs were being produced, the whole vast undertaking was carried off without a single leak to the outside. Therefore, if I had been able in so simple a way to find out what had been going on in the CPR, it was only because they didn't care. They could have stopped me.

Then I thought: invisible ink is scarcely new in the history of things. Perhaps they have been reading my correspondence with you all along and will smile at this letter as they have smiled at others; or perhaps they haven't taken the trouble to read it, because they simply don't care.

Perhaps the authorities not only did not care if we gradually found out, but wanted us to.

Why should they want us to? Why, if that were true, should they have put up so formidable a system of apparent preventatives? Double fences, censorship, lies, etc., etc.?

The only answer that makes sense is this. They want the news gradually and surreptitiously to sift out to the general population—illegally, in the form of hideous rumors to which people can begin to accustom themselves. After all, everyone knew generally that something like the atom bomb was being manufactured. Hiroshima was not the profound and absolute shock in 1945 that it would have been in 1935, and a good deal of the preparation for its general acceptance was rumor. It is in the people's interest that the CPR function as it does function, and especially so that they can pretend that they have nothing to do with it. The experience of the Germans in the Jew-extermination camps demonstrated that clearly enough. It would do no good for me to go around crying out the truth about NRACP, because few would believe me in the first place and my suppression would only give strength to the rumors, which were required and planned for anyhow.

But I still had to set myself the task of answering Why? What drove them (whoever they are) to the decision to embark upon a course which was not only revolutionary but dangerous? I accepted the NRACP as inevitable, as Necessity; there remained only the task of trying to understand wherein lay the mystery of the Necessity and of adjusting myself to the situation. The individual, even the leader, has no significant choice to make in the current of event; that current is part of natural law; it is unmoral, cruel, wasteful, useless, and mysterious. The leader is he who sees and points out the course of history, that we may pursue that course with least pain. It is odd that we Americans have no such leader; what we have is committees and boards and bureau heads who collectively possess leadership and who direct our way almost impersonally. There is nothing whatsoever that I myself would like so much as to be one of those wise, courageous, anonymous planners. The wisdom I think that I possess. But in place of courage I have a set of moral scruples dating from an era when man was supposed to have a soul and when disease took care of overpopulation. The old vestigial values of Christianity must be excised in the people as they are being excised in me. The good and the lucky are assisting at the birth of a new age. The weak and unfit are perishing in the death of an old. Which shall it be for us?

For my own part, I think I am in a state of transition, from being one of the unfit to being one of the fit. I feel it. I will it. There are certain external evidences of it. For example, I was face to face with the truth at the end of April, but instead of acknowledging what I saw I turned to my love for Ruth. Yet that refusal to recognize the truth did not long survive the urgings of my sense of necessity. And I remember, when being confronted with piecemeal evidences of the truth, that I was unable to explain a number of them. You know, Herb, how accomplished a rationalizer I can be; yet this time I did not even *try* to rationalize about many of the facts.

—It is dawn outside. I cannot read this letter over, so I am not entirely sure how incoherent it is. I feel that I have said most of what I wanted to say. I am not very happy. I think I shall sleep the better for having written this. I eat nothing but bread and fruit and milk. A bird is singing outside; he is making the only sound in the world. I can see the hill which separates us from the Intake buildings. It's a pleasant hill, rather like an arm extending out from the valley sides, and I am glad it is there. I am cold now, but in three hours it will be warm and in five hours hot. I am rambling I know. But suddenly all my energy has leaked out. I walk to the door to see Ruth so happily sleeping, mysteriously replenishing life from this nightly portion of death, and I think of that baby she is bearing and will give birth to. If it were not for her and the baby, I am sure I should have gone mad. Is not that a mystery, Herb? Our child shall be fortunate; it is the first conscious generation of each new order in whom the greatest energy is released. There are splendid things ahead for our child.

It is not my fault. I did not know what I was doing. How could I have known? What can I do now?

I stare at the lightening sky, exhausted. I do not know why I do not say farewell, and go to bed. Perhaps it is because I do not want to hear that little lullaby that sings in my ears whenever I stop: I have eaten human flesh, my wife is going to have a baby; I have eaten human flesh, my wife is going to have a baby.

Remember, back in the simple days of the Spanish Civil War, when Guernica was bombed, we speculated all one evening what the worst thing in the world could be? This is the worst thing in the world, Herb. I tell you, the worst. After this, nothing.

Perhaps if I lay my head against Ruth's breast and put her hands over my ears I can go to sleep. Last night I recited Housman's "Loveliest of trees, the cherry now," over and over till I went to sleep, not because I like it particularly but because I could think of nothing else at all to recite.

My wife is going to have a baby, my wife is going to have a baby, my wife is going to have a baby.

Bless you,
ANDY

*"Indeed, whatever exists in the universe . . . . the painter has first in his mind and then in his hands."*

Leonardo da Vinci

# IV
## THE ARTIST
## AND
## HIS ART

*The Fall of Icarus* by Pieter Brueghel (Musees Royaux des Beaux-Arts de Belgique)

# MUSÉE
# DES BEAUX ARTS

## W. H. Auden

About suffering they were never wrong,
The Old Masters: how well they understood
Its human position; how it takes place
While someone else is eating or opening a window or just
    walking dully along;
How, when the aged are reverently, passionately waiting
For the miraculous birth, there always must be
Children who did not specially want it to happen, skating
On a pond at the edge of the wood:
They never forgot
That even the dreadful martyrdom must run its course
Anyhow in a corner, some untidy spot
Where the dogs go on with their doggy life and the torturer's
    horse
Scratches its innocent behind on a tree.

In Brueghel's *Icarus,* for instance: how everything turns away
Quite leisurely from the disaster; the plowman may
Have heard the splash, the forsaken cry,
But for him it was not an important failure; the sun shone
As it had to on the white legs disappearing into the green
Water; and the expensive delicate ship that must have seen
Something amazing, a boy falling out of the sky,
Had somewhere to get to and sailed calmly on.

# THE PAINTER'S HANDS

## Leonardo DaVinci

If the painter wishes to see enchanting beauties, he has the power to produce them. If he wishes to see monstrosities, whether terrifying, or ludicrous and laughable, or pitiful, he has the power and authority to create them. If he wishes to produce towns or deserts, if in the hot season he wants cool and shady places, or in the cold season warm places, he can make them. If he wants valleys, if from high mountaintops he wants to survey vast stretches of country, if beyond he wants to see the horizon on the sea, he has the power to create all this; and likewise, if from deep valleys he wants to see high mountains or from high mountains deep valleys and beaches. Indeed, whatever exists in the universe, whether in essence, in act, or in the imagination, the painter has first in his mind and then in his hands. His hands are of such excellence that they can present to our view simultaneously whatever well-proportioned harmonies real things exhibit piecemeal.

# BY WAY
# OF A PREFACE

## Arthur Rimbaud

Universal Mind has always thrown out its ideas naturally; men would pick up part of these fruits of the brain; they acted through, wrote books with them; and so things went along, since man did not work on himself, not being yet awake, or not yet in the fullness of his dream. Writers were functionaries. Author, creator, poet,—that man has never existed!

The first study for a man who wants to be a poet is the knowledge of himself, entire. He searches his soul, he inspects it, he tests it, he learns it. As soon as he knows it, he cultivates it: it seems simple: in every brain a natural development is accomplished: so many egoists proclaim themselves authors; others attribute their intellectual progress to themselves! But the soul has to be made monstrous, that's the point:—like *comprachicos,* if you like! Imagine a man planting and cultivating warts on his face.

One must, I say, be a *visionary,* make oneself a *visionary.*

The poet makes himself a *visionary* through a long, a prodigious and rational disordering of *all* the senses. Every form of love, of suffering, of madness; he searches himself, he consumes all the poisons in him, keeping only their quintessences. Ineffable torture in which he will need all his faith and superhuman strength, the great criminal, the great sickman, the accursed,— and the supreme Savant! For he arrives at the unknown! Since he has cultivated his soul—richer to begin with than any other! He arrives at the unknown; and even if, half crazed, in the end, he loses the understanding of his visions, he has seen them! Let him be destroyed in his leap by those unnamable, unutterable and innumerable things: there will come other horrible workers: they will begin at the horizons where he has succumbed.

. . .

So then, the poet is truly a thief of fire.

Humanity is his responsibility, even the animals; he must see to it that his inventions can be smelled, felt, heard. If what he brings back from beyond has form, he gives it form, if it is formless, he gives it formlessness. A language must be found; as a matter of fact, all speech being an idea, the time of a universal language will come! One has to be an academician—deader than a fossil—to finish a dictionary of any language at all. The weak-minded, beginning with the first letter of the alphabet, would soon be raving mad!

This harangue would be of the soul for the soul, summing up everything, perfumes, sounds, colors, thought grappling thought, and pulling. The poet would define the amount of unknown arising in his time in the universal soul; he would give more than the formula of his thought, more than the annotation of his march toward Progress! Enormity become norm, absorbed by every one, he would truly be the multiplier of progress!

This future, as you see, will be materialistic. Always full of *Number* and *Harmony,* these poems would be made to last. As a matter of fact it will still be Greek poetry in a way.

This eternal art will have its functions since poets are citizens. Poetry will no longer accompany action but will lead it.

These poets are going to exist! When the infinite servitude of woman shall have ended, when she will be able to live by and for herself; then, man —hitherto abominable—having given her her freedom, she too will be a poet. Woman will discover the unknown. Will her world be different from ours? She will discover strange, unfathomable things, repulsive, delicious. We shall take them, we shall understand them.

Meantime ask the poet for the new—ideas and forms. All the bright boys will imagine they have satisfied this demand: it isn't that at all!

# I WOULD BE
# A PAINTER
# MOST OF ALL

## Len Chandler

*For Peter Lafarge*
i am here again
pox marks have obscured my dimples
i smile most now when standing on my head
    (or appear to)
i think best upside out
or inside down

MY EYES WERE
once bright wholly holy eyes
    for looking out and looking in
my eyes were spying periscopes
    for peeping up and over
for looking around corners
    (most of mine and some of yours)
without exposing my head
    my neck was very short then
    and easy to keep in
    (giraffes don't need periscopes)

wide eyed and boy scout young
i stood close to the fire soon
early evening . . . campfire heat
wind smoke and cinders
narrowed eyes to slivers

Reprinted by permission of International Publishers Co., Inc. Copyright © 1969.
From *New Black Poetry*.

first to carry wood
first to fetch the tinder
first to strike the match
and fire the fire
on the inner edge of circle
staring in  .  .  .  with eyes wide open
looking at the backs of others
standing backs to fire
far from fire and ash and cinder
staring in the black of forest
caring not for log nor ember
fond of eyes and faces
and the sound of their own voices

and i with eyes unblinking
SEEING
      only fire and ash–and
HEARING
      only chorus of wind and fire–and
FEELING
      only heat and tingle—and
SMELLING
      only smoke of pine and
TASTING
      only promises of potatoes
      wrapped in leaves  .  .  .  and packed
      with mud and
TOUCHING
      all the secret places of
      fire and light and energy  .  .  .  and
KNOWING
      nothing but guessing  .  .  .  almost
      every all
riding in the open truck
      going home from summer camp
seeing still the fire consuming
log and branch and twig and tinder
as if it had seared its signal
on the back of these eyes
that i had used as whetstone
for the edge i still most hone
to cut through my unknowing
in that open truck through woods

remembering smell and all
between the senses that were cited
only as a milestone . . .
though i'd measured with micrometer
each was tangled in the total
my eyes were wide and open then
seeing clearly all the edges
i was riding facing front
the rest were looking back
i knew where i had been
i was looking at the black bird
when a low limb caught my eye
flooding chest with antiseptic tears
      red and feigning fire
       (perhaps not feigning for
       some of it was consumed)
i was nine then . . . at nineteen i got glasses
i was just the other side of ten
when first i learned
how soft the edges are
when things are just
a little out of focus
unfocus the billboard
and the ad man has no dominion
unfocus . . . and the razor edge
seems less sharp
i know it now to be
the day i started going blind
i know it now to be
the day i started going blind
the day i discovered
it was easier not to see
i let my eyes unfocus more and more
i found comfort in the haze
walking toward an almost shadow world
only really looking at what i had to

i learned to squint my ears
and to unfocus words
and reduce to tempo and pitch
      all their meaning
i learned to love abstractions young
to squint in all my senses

to shadow dream think
to drift around soft edges
to squint my skin
to feel little
to heal fast

had i held to blindness
i would have held to life
i would have been a pure musician
laying easy dot on line
in time and tempo—safe
safe—for a world of Wallace's
or l.b.j's. could see me as
no real or present danger
they might even tap their heel
(u.s. steel cleats and all)
—don't make the tyrant
tap his heel when his
foot is on your neck

had i held to blindness
i would have been a poet
surrounded by a hedge
of literary illusions
and read by those few
who have the biggest purse to pay
and reason to find comfort in
the totally obscure

but now i dare see clearly as a child
and now i even almost understand
now i would be a painter most of all
my medium would be
words and color and shape
and shape and texture
and smell and time and taste
i would press my picture
to the back of your brain
for you too have learned
to squint in all your senses
        so i must enter where i can
and hang my pictures
where you dare not even blink

## Fallen Petals Rise
Fallen petals rise
   back to the branch—I watch:
      oh . . . butterflies!


## If to the Moon
If to the moon
   one puts a handle—what
      a splendid fan!


## A Fluttering Swarm
A fluttering swarm
   of cherry petals;—and there comes,
      pursuing them, the storm!


## This Morning, How
This morning, how
   icicles drip!—Slobbering
      year of the cow!


SOKAN

From the book *An Introduction to Haiku* by Harold G. Henderson. Copyright ©
1958 by Harold G. Henderson. Reprinted by permission of Doubleday & Company,
Inc.

# LA BELLE DAME SANS MERCI

*Revised Version*

## John Keats

Ah, what can ail thee, wretched wight,
    Alone and palely loitering;
The sedge is wither'd from the lake,
    And no birds sing.

Ah, what can ail thee, wretched wight,
    So haggard and so woe-begone?
The squirrel's granary is full,
    And the harvest's done.

I see a lilly on thy brow,
    With anguish moist and fever dew;
And on thy cheek a fading rose
    Fast withereth too.

I met a Lady in the meads
    Full beautiful, a fairy's child;
Her hair was long, her foot was light,
    And her eyes were wild.

I set her on my pacing steed,
    And nothing else saw all day long;
For sideways would she lean, and sing
    A faery's song.

I made a garland for her head,
    And bracelets too, and fragrant zone;
She look'd at me as she did love,
    And made sweet moan.

She found me roots of relish sweet,
   And honey wild, and manna dew,
And sure in language strange she said,
   I love thee true.

She took me to her elfin grot,
   And there she gaz'd and sighed deep,
And there I shut her wild sad eyes—
   So kiss'd to sleep.

And there we slumber'd on the moss,
   And there I dream'd, ah woe betide
The latest dream I ever dream'd
   On the cold hill side.

I saw pale kings, and princes too,
   Pale warriors, death-pale were they all;
Who cry'd—"La belle Dame sans mercy
   Hath thee in thrall!"

I saw their starv'd lips in the gloom
   With horrid warning gaped wide,
And I awoke, and found me here
   On the cold hill side.

And this is why I sojourn here
   Alone and palely loitering,
Though the sedge is wither'd from the lake,
   And no birds sing.

# ODE ON
# A GRECIAN URN

## John Keats

### I

Thou still unravish'd bride of quietness,
   Thou foster-child of silence and slow time,
Sylvan historian, who canst thus express
   A flowery tale more sweetly than our rhyme,
What leaf-fring'd legend haunts about thy shape
    Of deities or mortals, or of both,
      In Tempe or the dales of Arcady?
    What men or gods are these? What maidens loth?
What mad pursuit? What struggle to escape?
    What pipes and timbrels? What wild ecstasy?

### II

Heard melodies are sweet, but those unheard
   Are sweeter; therefore, ye soft pipes, play on;
Not to the sensual ear, but, more endear'd,
   Pipe to the spirit ditties of no tone:
Fair youth, beneath the trees, thou canst not leave
    Thy song, nor ever can those trees be bare;
      Bold Lover, never, never canst thou kiss,
Though winning near the goal—yet, do not grieve;
      She cannot fade, though thou hast not thy bliss,
For ever wilt thou love, and she be fair!

## III

Ah, happy, happy boughs! that cannot shed
   Your leaves, nor ever bid the Spring adieu;
And, happy melodist, unwearied,
   For ever piping songs for ever new;
More happy love! more happy, happy love!
    For ever warm and still to be enjoy'd,
      For ever panting, and for ever young;
All breathing human passion far above,
    That leaves a heart high-sorrowful and cloy'd,
      A burning forehead, and a parching tongue.

## IV

Who are these coming to the sacrifice?
   To what green altar, O mysterious priest,
Lead'st thou that heifer lowing at the skies,
   And all her silken flanks with garlands drest?
What little town by river or sea shore,
    Or mountain-built with peaceful citadel,
      Is emptied of this folk, this pious morn?
And, little town, thy streets for evermore
    Will silent be; and not a soul to tell
      Why thou art desolate, can e'er return.

## V

O Attic shape! Fair attitude! with brede
   Of marble men and maidens overwrought,
With forest branches and the trodden weed;
   Thou, silent form, dost tease us out of thought
As doth eternity: Cold Pastoral!
    When old age shall this generation waste,
      Thou shalt remain, in midst of other woe
    Than ours, a friend to man, to whom thou say'st,
"Beauty is truth, truth beauty,"—that is all
    Ye know on earth, and all ye need to know.

# IN MY CRAFT
# OR SULLEN ART

## Dylan Thomas

In my craft or sullen art
Exercised in the still night
When only the moon rages
And the lovers lie abed
With all their griefs in their arms,
I labour by singing light
Not for ambition or bread
Or the strut and trade of charms
On the ivory stages
But for the common wages
Of their most secret heart.

Not for the proud man apart
From the raging moon I write
On these spindrift pages
Nor for the towering dead
With their nightingales and psalms
But for the lovers, their arms
Round the griefs of the ages,
Who pay no praise or wages
Nor heed my craft or art.

# ESSENTIALS OF SPONTANEOUS PROSE

## Jack Kerouac

SET-UP. The object is set before the mind, either in reality, as in sketching (before a landscape or teacup or old face) or is set in the memory wherein it becomes the sketching from memory of a definite image-object.

PROCEDURE. Time being of the essence in the purity of speech, sketching language is undisturbed flow from the mind of personal secret idea-words, *blowing* (as per jazz musician) on subject of image.

METHOD. No periods separating sentence-structures already arbitrarily riddled by false colons and timid usually needless commas—but the vigorous space dash separating rhetorical breathing (as jazz musician drawing breath between outblown phrases)—"measured pauses which are the essentials of our speech"—"divisions of the *sounds* we hear"—"time and how to note it down." (William Carlos Williams)

SCOPING. Not "selectivity" of expression but following free deviation (association) of mind into limitless blow-on-subject seas of thought, swimming in sea of English with no discipline other than rhythms of rhetorical exhalation and expostulated statement, like a fist coming down on a table with each complete utterance, bang! (the space dash)—Blow as deep as you want—write as deeply, fish as far down as you want, satisfy yourself first, then reader cannot fail to receive telepathic shock and meaning-excitement by same laws operating in his own human mind.

LAG IN PROCEDURE. No pause to think of proper word but the infantile pileup of scatalogical buildup words till satisfaction is gained, which will turn out to be a great appending rhythm to a thought and be in accordance with Great Law of timing.

TIMING. Nothing is muddy that *runs in time* and to laws of *time*—Shakespearian stress of dramatic need to speak now in own unalterable way or forever hold tongue—*no revisions* (except obvious rational mistakes, such as names or *calculated* insertions in act of not writing but *inserting*).

CENTER OF INTEREST. Begin not from preconceived idea of what to say about image but from jewel center of interest in subject of image at *moment* of writing, and write outwards swimming in sea of language to peripheral release and exhaustion—Do not afterthink except for poetic or P. S. reasons. Never afterthink to "improve" or defray impressions, as, the best writing is always the most painful personal wrung-out tossed from cradle warm protective mind—tap from yourself the song of yourself, *blow!*—*now!*—*your* way is your only way—"good"—or "bad"—always honest, ("ludicrous"), spontaneous, "confessional" interesting, because not "crafted." Craft *is* craft.

STRUCTURE OF WORK. Modern bizarre structures (science fiction, etc.) arise from language being dead, "different" themes give illusion of "new" life. Follow roughly outlines in outfanning movement over subject, as river rock, so mindflow over jewel-center need (run your mind over it, *once*) arriving at pivot, where what was dim formed "beginning" becomes sharp-necessitating "ending" and language shortens in race to wire of time-race of work, following laws of Deep Form, to conclusion, last words, last trickle —Night is The End.

MENTAL STATE. If possible write "without consciousness" in semi-trance (as Yeats' later "trance writing") allowing subconscious to admit in own uninhibited interesting necessary and so "modern" language what conscious art would censor, and write excitedly, swiftly, with writing-or-typing-cramps, in accordance (as from center to periphery) with laws of orgasm, Reich's "beclouding of consciousness." *Come* from within, out—to relaxed and said.

# A FEW WORDS
# OF A KIND

*Introduction to Reading His Poetry*

## Dylan Thomas

I am going to read aloud from the works of some modern British poets, and also read a few poems of my own. My own ones include some early ones, some fairly hurly-burly ones, very recent ones, reasoned, decent ones, lamenting ones and lamentable ones, together with a few comments whenever they may or may not be necessary.

I wondered what kind of words I should put down to introduce these laboriously churning poems of mine. Indeed, I thought they want from me no introduction at all. Let them stand on their own feet, the little lyrical cripples. But I felt, too, that there must be a few words of a kind before or between the ranting of the poems. A whole hour of loud and unrelieved verse-speaking is, I imagine, hell to anyone except some brash antiseptic forty-two-toothed smilingly ardent young hunters of culture with net, note-book, poison bottle, pin and label, or to the dowager hunters of small seedy lions, stalking the metropolitan bush with legs and rifles cocked, or to the infernal androgynous literary ladies with three names who produce a kind of verbal ectoplasm to order as a waiter dishes up spaghetti. But to an ordinary audience—not that there's any such thing but only, like your-selves, bushes of eccentrics—there must be a hush between poems. And how was I going to fill that hush with harmless words until the next poem came woodenly booming along like a carved bee?

I couldn't, I knew, say much if anything about what the poems might mean. In a few cases, of course, I didn't anyway know myself—though that is true, I hope, only of certain of my earliest published poems, explosive

Delivered by Dylan Thomas at the Massachusetts Institute of Technology on March 7, 1952.

bloodbursts of a boily boy in love with the shape and sound of words, death, unknown love and the shadows on his pillow. And for the rest of the poems, they are what they mean, however obscure, unsuccessful, sentimental, pretentious, ludicrous, rhetorical, wretched, ecstatic, plain bad. Or could I shove in autobiographical snippets saying where I lived and how, when I wrote this or that, indicating how I felt in heart and head at that particular time?

I could, for instance, talk about my education, which critics say I have not got. And that's true enough. But I do wish I had learned some other languages apart from English, B.B.C. Third Program and saloon. Then perhaps I could understand what some people mean when they say I have been influenced by Rimbaud.

My education was the liberty I had to read indiscriminately and all the time, with my eyes hanging out. I never could have dreamed there were such goings-on, such do's and argie-bargies, such ice blasts of words, such love and sense and terror and humbug, such and so many blinding bright lights breaking across the just awaking wits and splashing all over the pages, as they can never quite do again after the first revelation. In a million bits and pieces, all of which were words, words, words, and each of which seemed alive forever in its own delight and glory and right.

It was then, in my father's brown study before homework, usually the first botched scribblings of gauche and gawky heart-choked poems about black-bloomered nymphs, the jussive grave and the tall, improbable loves of the sardine-packed sky, poems never to be shown to anyone except on pain of death, that I began to know one kind of writing from another, one kind of badness, one kind of goodness. I wrote endless imitations, though I never at the time of writing thought them to be imitations but rather colossally original, things unheard of, like eggs laid by tigers, imitations of whatever I happened to be golloping then, Thomas Browne, Robert W. Service, Stevenson, De Quincey, Eskimo Nell, Newbolt, Blake, Marlowe, the Imagists, the boy's own paper, Keats, Poe, Burns, Dostoevsky, Anon. and Shakespeare. I tried my little trotters at every poetical form. How could I know the tricks of this trade unless I tried to do them myself? For the poets wouldn't soar from the grave and show me how their poems were done by mirrors, and I couldn't trust the critics then—or now. I learned that the bad tricks come easy and the good tricks, which help you to say what you think you wish to say in the most meaningful, moving way, naturally I am still learning—though in earnest company I must call these tricks by other, technical names. Nothing in those days was too much for me to try. If *Paradise Lost* had not already been written, I would have had a shot at it.

My early days, dear God! I never thought that one day I might be here or anywhere filling up time before, I'm afraid, a drone of poems by talking about my early days, just as though I were a man of letters. I used to think that once a writer became a man of letters, if only for ten minutes, he was done for. But I feel all right. I suppose I am suffering from one of the first pleasant injections of insidious corruption. "My early days" seems to me to suggest that I am responsible and established, that all the old doubts and worries are over. Now I need bother my head about nothing except birth, death, sex, money, politics and religion, that, jowled and wigged, aloof and branded as a bloodhound, sober as a judge in my bit of vermin, I can summon my juvenile literary delinquence before me and give it a long periodic sentence. For me to think of prefacing my poems by talking about my early days is to invite myself to indulge myself with a hundred tongue-picked, chopped and chiseled evocative shock phrases in a flamboyant rememoration of past and almost entirely fictitious peccadilloes of interest to nobody but me and my guardian angel, who was, I believe, an unsuccessful psychoanalyst in this life and who is lolloping above me now, casebook in claw, a little seedy and down at wing and heel, in the gutteral consulting room of space. I am the kind of human dredger that digs up the wordy mud of his own Dead Sea, a kind of pig that roots for unconsidered truffles in the reeky wood of his past.

But still I gladly accept the fact that I first saw the light and screamed at it in a loud lump of Wales. I'm only human, as the man says who deep inside him refuses to believe it, and of course my writing would not be what it is—always experimental and always completely unsatisfactory—if it had not been for the immortal fry of the town in which I simmered up. Naturally, my early poems and stories, two sides of an unresolved argument, came out of a person who came willy-nilly out of one particular atmosphere and environment, and are part and parcel, park and castle, lark and sea shell, dark and school bell, muck and entrail, cock, rock and bubble, accent and sea-lap, root and rhythm of them. And that, so far as I am concerned, is all there is to it. If I had been born and brought up in an igloo and lived on whales, not in it, about the same would be true, except that then it would have been extremely unlikely had I become a writer. And "Goody!" cry my justified detractors.

Or I could preface this small reading by talking about poets. I think they're pretty dull. It's a common failing to underestimate the sheer ordinariness of the lives and characters of many dead poets, and to overestimate that of living poets whom one might come across. Indeed it is not unusual for people, after they have met a more or less living poet, to wonder with hardly concealed amazement how he could ever have produced the work he has. I except certain oldish poets alive today who are made solemn and unapproachable, not so much by their poetry or their strict religious observance as by their judicial positions on the boards of eminent publishers who may even then, at one's time of meeting, be considering one's own first experimental novel of innocence lost and wisdom catastrophically gained by the age of nineteen. The same kind of amazement, the idol destroyed ("How *could* such a man have written such marvelous devotional poetry, I saw him fall downstairs yesterday in his suspenders!"), might well have occurred to us had we met many of the poets now dead. I think it was Logan Pearsall Smith who remembered how, as a small boy, he saw of all people Matthew Arnold in a restaurant, and Matthew Arnold talked and laughed much too loud.

I couldn't talk about poets, but I do wish that I was reading only the work of other modern poets now, and not my own at all. That is, I wish I were reading the work of modern poets I like, for I like to read only the poets I like. This means, of course, that I have to read a lot of poems I don't like before I find the ones I do, but when I do find the ones I do, then all I can say is, "Here they are," and read them aloud to myself or to anyone, like yourselves, voluntarily cornered. And when I read aloud the poems of modern poets I like very much, I try to make them alive from inside. I try to get across what I feel, however wrongly, to be the original impetus of the poem. I am a practicing interpreter, however much of a flannel-tongued one-night-stander.

But in my own poems I've had my say, and when I read them aloud I can only repeat it. When I read, for instance, my earliest poems aloud, my interpretation of them—though that's far too weighty a word just for reading them aloud—can't be considered as the final or original interpretation, performance or blare. I do not remember now the first impulse that pumped and drove those lines along, and that which is in them is for you more than for me, for you or for anyone, or of course for no one, to make what you or he will of them. In these poems I've had my say; now I'm only saying it again.

But what does it matter? Poetry is what in a poem makes you laugh, cry, prickle, be silent, makes your toenails twinkle, makes you want to do this or that or nothing, makes you know that you are alone and not alone in the unknown world, that your bliss and suffering is forever shared and forever all your own. All that matters about poetry is the enjoyment of it, however tragic it may be. All that matters is the eternal movement behind it, the great undercurrent of human grief, folly, pretension, exultation and ignorance, however unlofty the intention of the poem.

Now I'm going to read some poems straight, without hindrance, for this isn't a lecture at all. It isn't about trends and impacts and the influence of someone or someone else. It isn't trying to prove anything by quotations, to groove one hypothetical school of poetry oilily into another, to jigsaw all the pieces that are poems into one improbable picture and then say, "Here it is, this is modern poetry." I am no gray and tepid don smelling of water biscuits. Only posterity can see the picture of the poetry of today as a whole, and the function of posterity is to look after itself. You can tear a poem apart to see what makes it technically tick, and say to yourself when the works are laid out before you, the vowels, the consonants, the rhymes and rhythms. Yes, this is it, this is why the poem moves me so. It is because of the craftsmanship. But you're back again where you began. The best craftsmanship always leaves holes and gaps in the works of the poem so that something that is not in the poem can creep, crawl, flash or thunder in. "Everything," Yeats said, though he was talking of the highest moments of the most exalted art, "everything happens in a blaze of light." Only the printed page or the interior monologue or the private discussion can give to each separate poem the full concentrated time that the poem is justified in asking for the assessment of its success or failure to demonstrate its own hypothesis. In public all I think that can be presented is the poem itself, and all that can be experienced in public is the realization of the immediacy or lack of immediacy through which the hypothesis, the central motive of the poem, affects the reader through his ear. The printed page is the place in which to examine the works of a poem, and the platform the place on which to give the poem the works.

You won't ask me any questions afterward, will you? I don't mind answering a bit, only I can't. Even to such simple questions as, "What is the relationship of the poet to society in a hydrogenous age?" I can only cough and stammer. And some of the questions I remember from the nightmare past—"Tell me, are the young English intellectuals really psychological?" "Is it absolutely essential, do you think, to be homosexual to write love poems to women?" "I always carry Kierkegaard in my pocket. What do you carry?"

# POETRY

## Marianne Moore

I, too, dislike it: there are things that are important beyond all
   this fiddle.
   Reading it, however, with a perfect contempt for it, one dis-
      covers in
   it after all, a place for the genuine.
      Hands that can grasp, eyes
      that can dilate, hair that can rise
         if it must, these things are important not because a

high-sounding interpretation can be put upon them but because
      they are
   useful. When they become so derivative as to become un-
      intelligible,
   the same thing may be said for all of us, that we
      do not admire what
      we cannot understand: the bat
         holding on upside down or in quest of something to

eat, elephants pushing, a wild horse taking a roll, a tireless wolf
      under
   a tree, the immovable critic twitching his skin like a horse
         that feels a flea, the base-
   ball fan, the statistician—
      nor is it valid
         to discriminate against 'business documents and

school-books'; all these phenomena are important. One must
        make a distinction
   however: when dragged into prominence by half poets, the
        result is not poetry,
  nor till the poets among us can be
    'literalists of
    the imagination'—above
       insolence and triviality and can present

for inspection, imaginary gardens with real toads in them, shall
       we have
  it. In the meantime, if you demand on the one hand,
 the raw material of poetry in
   all its rawness and
   that which is on the other hand
     genuine, then you are interested in poetry.

# ANECDOTE
# OF THE JAR

## Wallace Stevens

I placed a jar in Tennessee,
And round it was, upon a hill.
It made the slovenly wilderness
Surround that hill.

The wilderness rose up to it,
And sprawled around, no longer wild.
The jar was round upon the ground
And tall and of a port in air.

It took dominion everywhere.
The jar was gray and bare.
It did not give of bird or bush,
Like nothing else in Tennessee.

## Real Words Are
### Not Vain

Real words are not vain,
Vain words not real;
And since those who argue prove nothing
A sensible man does not argue.
A sensible man is wiser than he knows,
While a fool knows more than is wise.
Therefore a sensible man does not devise resources:
The greater his use to others
The greater their use to him,
The more he yields to others
The more they yield to him.
The way of life cleaves without cutting:
Which, without need to say,
Should be man's way.

LAO TZU

Reprinted by permission of G. P. Putnam's Sons from *The Way of Life According to Lao Tzu*, translated by Witter Bynner. Copyright 1944 by Witter Bynner.

# I HAVE NOT LAIN
# WITH BEAUTY

## Lawrence Ferlinghetti

I have not lain with beauty all my life
   telling over to myself
         its most rife charms
  I have not lain with beauty all my life
        and lied with it as well
   telling over to myself
      how beauty never dies
    but lies apart
     among the aborigines
         of art
   and far above the battlefields
       of love
  It is above all that
     oh yes
  It sits upon the choicest of
      Church seats
 up there where art directors meet
to choose the things for immortality
       And they have lain with beauty
    all their lives
     And they have fed on honeydew
  and drunk the wines of Paradise
      so that they know exactly how

a thing of beauty is a joy
     forever and forever
               and how it never never
       quite can fade
                into a money-losing nothingness
   Oh no I have not lain
                on Beauty Rests like this
      afraid to rise at night
                for fear that I might somehow miss
some movement beauty might have made
   Yet I have slept with beauty
                     in my own weird way
and I have made a hungry scene or two
                     with beauty in my bed
   and so spilled out another poem or two
     and so spilled out another poem or two
                     upon the Bosch-like world

# I DIED
# FOR BEAUTY

## Emily Dickinson

I died for Beauty—but was scarce
Adjusted in the Tomb
When One who died for Truth, was lain
In an adjoining Room—

He questioned softly "Why I failed"?
"For Beauty", I replied—
"And I—for Truth—Themself are One—
We Brethren, are", He said—

And so, as Kinsmen, met a Night—
We talked between the Rooms—
Until the Moss had reached our lips—
And covered up—our names—

# THE BOUND MAN

## Ilse Aichinger

Sunlight on his face woke him, but made him shut his eyes again; it streamed unhindered down the slope, collected itself into rivulets, attracted swarms of flies, which flew low over his forehead, circled, sought to land, and were overtaken by fresh swarms. When he tried to whisk them away, he discovered that he was bound. A thick rope cut into his arms. He dropped them, opened his eyes again, and looked down at himself. His legs were tied all the way up to his thighs; a single length of rope was tied round his ankles, criss-crossed up his legs, and encircled his hips, his chest and his arms. He could not see where it was knotted. He showed no sign of fear or hurry, though he thought he was unable to move, until he discovered that the rope allowed his legs some free play and that round his body it was almost loose. His arms were tied to each other but not to his body, and had some free play too. This made him smile, and it occurred to him that perhaps children had been playing a practical joke on him.

He tried to feel for his knife, but again the rope cut softly into his flesh. He tried again, more cautiously this time, but his pocket was empty. Not only his knife, but the little money that he had on him, as well as his coat, were missing. His shoes had been pulled from his feet and taken too. When he moistened his lips he tasted blood, which had flowed from his temples down his cheeks, his chin, his neck, and under his shirt. His eyes were painful; if he kept them open for long he saw reddish stripes in the sky.

He decided to stand up. He drew his knees up as far as he could, rested his hands on the fresh grass and jerked himself to his feet. An elder branch stroked his cheek, the pain dazzled him, and the rope cut into his flesh. He collapsed to the ground again, half out of his mind with pain, and then

Reprinted by permission of Pergamon Publishing Company.

tried again. He went on trying until the blood started flowing from his hidden weals. Then he lay still again for a long while and let the sun and the flies do what they liked.

When he awoke for the second time the elder bush had cast its shadow over him, and the coolness stored in it was pouring from between its branches. He must have been hit on the head. Then they must have laid him down carefully, just as a mother lays her baby behind a bush when she goes to work in the fields.

His chances all lay in the amount of free play allowed him by the rope. He dug his elbows into the ground and tested it. As soon as the rope tautened he stopped, and tried again more cautiously. If he had been able to reach the branch over his head he could have used it to drag himself to his feet, but he could not reach it. He laid his head back on the grass, rolled over, and struggled to his knees. He tested the ground with his toes, and then managed to stand up almost without effort.

A few paces away lay the path across the plateau, and in the grass were wild pinks and thistles in bloom. He tried to lift his foot to avoid trampling on them, but the rope round his ankles prevented him. He looked down at himself.

The rope was knotted at his ankles, and ran round his legs in a kind of playful pattern. He carefully bent and tried to loosen it, but, loose though it seemed to be, he could not make it any looser. To avoid treading on the thistles with his bare feet he hopped over them like a bird.

The cracking of a twig made him stop. People in this district were very prone to laughter. He was alarmed by the thought that he was in no position to defend himself. He hopped on until he reached the path. Bright fields stretched far below. He could see no sign of the nearest village, and if he could move no faster than this, night would fall before he reached it.

He tried walking and discovered that he could put one foot before another if he lifted each foot a definite distance from the ground and then put it down again before the rope tautened. In the same way he could actually swing his arms a little.

After the first step he fell. He fell right across the path, and made the dust fly. He expected this to be a sign for the long-suppressed laughter to break out, but all remained quiet. He was alone. As soon as the dust had settled he got up and went on. He looked down and watched the rope slacken, grow taut, and then slacken again.

When the first glow-worms appeared he managed to look up. He felt in control of himself again, and his impatience to reach the nearest village faded.

Hunger made him light-headed, and he seemed to be going so fast that not even a motorcycle could have overtaken him; alternatively he felt as if he were standing still and that the earth was rushing past him, like a river flowing past a man swimming against the stream. The stream carried branches which had been bent southward by the north wind, stunted young trees, and patches of grass with bright, long-stalked flowers. It ended by submerging the bushes and the young trees, leaving only the sky and the man above water level. The moon had risen, and illuminated the bare, curved summit of the plateau, the path, which was overgrown with young grass, the bound man making his way along it with quick, measured steps, and two hares, which ran across the hill just in front of him and vanished down the slope. Though the nights were still cool at this time of the year, before midnight the bound man lay down at the edge of the escarpment and went to sleep.

In the light of morning the animal-tamer who was camping with his circus in the field outside the village saw the bound man coming down the path, gazing thoughtfully at the ground. The bound man stopped and bent down. He held out one arm to help keep his balance and with the other picked up an empty wine-bottle. Then he straightened himself and stood erect again. He moved slowly, to avoid being cut by the rope, but to the circus proprietor what he did suggested the voluntary limitation of an enormous swiftness of movement. He was enchanted by its extraordinary gracefulness, and while the bound man looked about for a stone on which to break the bottle, so that he could use the splintered neck to cut the rope, the animal-tamer walked across the field and approached him. The first leaps of a young panther had never filled him with such delight.

"Ladies and gentlemen, the bound man!" His very first movements let loose a storm of applause, which out of sheer excitement caused the blood to rush to the cheeks of the animal-tamer standing at the edge of the arena. The bound man rose to his feet. His surprise whenever he did this was like that of a four-footed animal which has managed to stand on its hind legs. He knelt, stood up, jumped, and turned cartwheels. The spectators found it as astonishing as if they had seen a bird which voluntarily remained earthbound, and confined itself to hopping.

The bound man became an enormous draw. His absurd steps and little jumps, his elementary exercises in movement, made the rope dancer superfluous. His fame grew from village to village, but the motions he went through were few and always the same; they were really quite ordinary motions, which he had continually to practice in the daytime in the half-dark tent in order to retain his shackled freedom. In that he remained entirely within the limits set by his rope he was free of it, it did not confine him, but gave him wings and endowed his leaps and jumps with purpose; just as the flights of birds of passage have purpose when they take wing in the warmth of summer and hesitantly make small circles in the sky.

All the children of the neighborhood started playing the game of "bound man." They formed rival gangs, and one day the circus people found a little girl lying bound in a ditch, with a cord tied round her neck so that she could hardly breathe. They released her, and at the end of the performance that night the bound man made a speech. He announced briefly that there was no sense in being tied up in such a way that you could not jump. After that he was regarded as a comedian.

Grass and sunlight, tent pegs driven into the ground and then pulled up again, and on to the next village. "Ladies and gentlemen, the bound man!" The summer mounted toward its climax. It bent its face deeper over the fish ponds in the hollows, taking delight in its dark reflection, skimmed the surface of the rivers, and made the plain into what it was. Everyone who could walk went to see the bound man.

Many wanted a close-up view of how he was bound. So the circus proprietor announced after each performance that anyone who wanted to satisfy himself that the knots were real and the rope not made of rubber was at liberty to do so. The bound man generally waited for the crowd in the area outside the tent. He laughed or remained serious, and held out his arms for inspection. Many took the opportunity to look him in the face, others gravely tested the rope, tried the knots on his ankles, and wanted to know exactly how the lengths compared with the length of his limbs. They asked him how he had come to be tied up like that, and he answered patiently, always saying the same thing. Yes, he had been tied up, he said, and when he awoke he found that he had been robbed as well. Those who had done it must have been pressed for time, because they had tied him up somewhat too loosely for someone who was not supposed to be able to move and somewhat too tightly for someone who was expected to be able to move. But he did move, people pointed out. Yes, he replied, what else could he do?

Before he went to bed he always sat for a time in front of the fire. When the circus proprietor asked him why he didn't make up a better story he always answered that he hadn't made up that one, and blushed. He preferred staying in the shade.

The difference between him and the other performers was that when the show was over he did not take off his rope. The result was that every movement that he made was worth seeing, and the villagers used to hang about the camp for hours, just for the sake of seeing him get up from in front of the fire and roll himself in his blanket. Sometimes the sky was beginning to lighten when he saw their shadows disappear.

The circus proprietor often remarked that there was no reason why he should not be untied after the evening performance and tied up again next day. He pointed out that the rope dancers, for instance, did not stay on their rope overnight. But no one took the idea of untying him seriously.

For the bound man's fame rested on the fact that he was always bound, that whenever he washed himself he had to wash his clothes too and vice versa, and that his only way of doing so was to jump in the river just as he was every morning when the sun came out, and that he had to be careful not to go too far out for fear of being carried away by the stream.

The proprietor was well aware that what in the last resort protected the bound man from the jealousy of the other performers was his helplessness; he deliberately left them the pleasure of watching him groping painfully from stone to stone on the river bank every morning with his wet clothes clinging to him. When the proprietor's wife pointed out that even the best clothes would not stand up indefinitely to such treatment (and the bound man's clothes were by no means of the best), he replied curtly that it was not going to last forever. That was his answer to all objections—it was for the summer season only. But when he said this he was not being serious; he was talking like a gambler who has no intention of giving up his vice. In reality he would have been prepared cheerfully to sacrifice his lions and his rope dancers for the bound man.

He proved this on the night when the rope dancers jumped over the fire. Afterward he was convinced that they did it, not because it was midsummer's day, but because of the bound man, who as usual was lying and watching them with that peculiar smile that might have been real or might have been only the effect of the glow on his face. In any case no one knew anything about him because he never talked about anything that had happened to him before he emerged from the wood that day.

But that evening two of the performers suddenly picked him up by the arms and legs, carried him to the edge of the fire and started playfully swinging him to and fro, while two others held out their arms to catch him on the other side. In the end they threw him, but too short. The two men on the other side drew back—they explained afterward that they did so the better to take the shock. The result was that the bound man landed at the very edge of the flames and would have been burned if the circus proprietor had not seized his arms and quickly dragged him away to save the rope which was starting to get singed. He was certain that the object had been to burn the rope. He sacked the four men on the spot.

A few nights later the proprietor's wife was awakened by the sound of footsteps on the grass, and went outside just in time to prevent the clown from playing his last practical joke. He was carrying a pair of scissors. When he was asked for an explanation he insisted that he had had no intention of taking the bound man's life, but only wanted to cut his rope because he felt sorry for him. He was sacked too.

These antics amused the bound man because he could have freed himself if he had wanted to whenever he liked, but perhaps he wanted to learn a few new jumps first. The children's rhyme: "We travel with the circus, we travel with the circus" sometimes occurred to him while he lay awake at night. He could hear the voices of spectators on the opposite bank who had been driven too far downstream on the way home. He could see the river gleaming in the moonlight, and the young shoots growing out of the thick tops of the willow trees, and did not think about autumn yet.

The circus proprietor dreaded the danger that sleep involved for the bound man. Attempts were continually made to release him while he slept. The chief culprits were sacked rope dancers, or children who were bribed for the purpose. But measures could be taken to safeguard against these. A much bigger danger was that which he represented to himself. In his dreams he forgot his rope, and was surprised by it when he woke in the darkness of morning. He would angrily try to get up, but lose his balance and fall back again. The previous evening's applause was forgotten, sleep was still too near, his head and neck too free. He was just the opposite of a hanged man—his neck was the only part of him that was free. You had to make sure that at such moments no knife was within his reach. In the early hours of the morning the circus proprietor sometimes sent his wife to see whether the bound man was all right. If he was asleep she would bend over him and feel the rope. It had grown hard from dirt and damp. She would test the amount of free play it allowed him, and touch his tender wrists and ankles.

The most varied rumors circulated about the bound man. Some said he had tied himself up and invented the story of having been robbed, and toward the end of the summer that was the general opinion. Others maintained that he had been tied up at his own request, perhaps in league with the circus proprietor. The hesitant way in which he told his story, his habit of breaking off when the talk got round to the attack on him, contributed greatly to these rumors. Those who still believed in the robbery-with-violence story were laughed at. Nobody knew what difficulties the circus proprietor had in keeping the bound man, and how often he said he had had enough and wanted to clear off, for too much of the summer had passed.

Later, however, he stopped talking about clearing off. When the proprietor's wife brought him his food by the river and asked him how long he proposed to remain with them, he did not answer. She thought he had got used, not to being tied up, but to remembering every moment that he was tied up—the only thing that anyone in his position could get used to. She asked him whether he did not think it ridiculous to be tied up all the time, but he answered that he did not. Such a variety of people—clowns, freaks, and comics, to say nothing of elephants and tigers—traveled with circuses that he did not see why a bound man should not travel with a circus too. He told her about the movements he was practicing, the new ones he had discovered, and about a new trick that had occurred to him while he was whisking flies from the animals' eyes. He described to her how he always anticipated the effect of the rope and always restrained his movements in such a way as to prevent it from ever tautening; and she knew that there were days when he was hardly aware of the rope, when he jumped down from the wagon and slapped the flanks of the horses in the morning as if he were moving in a dream. She watched him vault over the bars almost without touching them, and saw the sun on his face, and he told her that sometimes he felt as if he were not tied up at all. She answered that if he were prepared to be untied, there would never be any need for him to feel tied up. He agreed that he could be untied whenever he felt like it.

The woman ended by not knowing whether she was more concerned with the man or with the rope that tied him. She told him that he could go on traveling with the circus without his rope, but she did not believe it. For what would be the point of his antics without his rope, and what would he amount to without it? Without his rope he would leave them, and the happy days would be over. She would no longer be able to sit beside him on the stones by the river without arousing suspicion, and she knew that his continued presence, and her conversations with him, of which the rope was the only subject, depended on it. Whenever she agreed that the rope had its advantages, he would start talking about how troublesome it was, and whenever he started talking about its advantages, she would urge him to get rid of it. All this seemed as endless as the summer itself.

At other times she worried at the thought that she was herself hastening the end by her talk. Sometimes she would get up in the middle of the night and run across the grass to where he slept. She wanted to shake him, wake him up and ask him to keep the rope. But then she would see him lying there; he had thrown off his blanket, and there he lay like a corpse, with his legs outstretched and his arms close together, with the rope tied round them. His clothes had suffered from the heat and the water, but the rope had grown no thinner. She felt that he would go on traveling with the circus until the flesh fell from him and exposed the joints. Next morning she would plead with him more ardently than ever to get rid of his rope.

The increasing coolness of the weather gave her hope. Autumn was coming, and he would not be able to go on jumping into the river with his clothes on much longer. But the thought of losing his rope, about which he had felt indifferent earlier in the season, now depressed him.

The songs of harvesters filled him with foreboding. "Summer has gone, summer has gone." But he realized that soon he would have to change his clothes, and he was certain that when he had been untied it would be impossible to tie him up again in exactly the same way. About this time the proprietor started talking about traveling south that year.

The heat changed without transition into quiet, dry cold, and the fire was kept going all day long. When the bound man jumped down from the wagon he felt the coldness of the grass under his feet. The stalks were bent with ripeness. The horses dreamed on their feet and the wild animals, crouching to leap even in their sleep, seemed to be collecting gloom under their skins which would break out later.

On one of these days a young wolf escaped. The circus proprietor kept quiet about it, to avoid spreading alarm, but the wolf soon started raiding cattle in the neighborhood. People at first believed that the wolf had been driven to these parts by the prospect of a severe winter, but the circus soon became suspect. The proprietor could not conceal the loss of the animal from his own employees, so the truth was bound to come out before long. The circus people offered the burgomasters of the neighboring villages their aid in tracking down the beast, but all their efforts were in vain. Eventually the circus was openly blamed for the damage and the danger, and spectators stayed away.

The bound man went on performing before half-empty seats without losing anything of his amazing freedom of movement. During the day he wandered among the surrounding hills under the thin-beaten silver of the autumn sky, and, whenever he could, lay down where the sun shone longest. Soon he found a place which the twilight reached last of all, and when at last it reached him he got up most unwillingly from the withered grass. In coming down the hill he had to pass through a little wood on its southern slope, and one evening he saw the gleam of two little green lights. He knew that they came from no church window, and was not for a moment under any illusion about what they were.

He stopped. The animal came toward him through the thinning foliage. He could make out its shape, the slant of its neck, its tail which swept the ground, and its receding head. If he had not been bound, perhaps he would have tried to run away, but as it was he did not even feel fear. He stood calmly with dangling arms and looked down at the wolf's bristling coat under which the muscles played like his own underneath the rope. He thought the evening wind was still between him and the wolf when the beast sprang. The man took care to obey his rope.

Moving with the deliberate care that he had so often put to the test, he seized the wolf by the throat. Tenderness for a fellow creature arose in him, tenderness for the upright being concealed in the four-footed. In a movement that resembled the drive of a great bird (he felt a sudden awareness that flying would be possible only if one were tied up in a special way) he flung himself at the animal and brought it to the ground. He felt a slight elation at having lost the fatal advantage of free limbs which causes men to be worsted.

The freedom he enjoyed in this struggle was having to adapt every movement of his limbs to the rope that tied him—the freedom of panthers, wolves, and the wild flowers that sway in the evening breeze. He ended up lying obliquely down the slope, clasping the animal's hind legs between his own bare feet and its head between his hands. He felt the gentleness of the faded foliage stroking the backs of his hands, and he felt his own grip almost effortlessly reaching its maximum, and he felt too how he was in no way hampered by the rope.

As he left the wood light rain began to fall and obscured the setting sun. He stopped for a while under the trees at the edge of the wood. Beyond the camp and the river he saw the fields where the cattle grazed, and the places where they crossed. Perhaps he would travel south with the circus after all. He laughed softly. It was against all reason. Even if he continued to put up with the sores that covered his joints and opened and bled when he made certain movements, his clothes would not stand up much longer to the friction of the rope.

The circus proprietor's wife tried to persuade her husband to announce the death of the wolf without mentioning that it had been killed by the bound man. She said that even at the time of his greatest popularity people would have refused to believe him capable of it, and in their present angry mood, with the nights getting cooler, they would be more incredulous than ever. The wolf had attacked a group of children at play that day, and nobody would believe that it had really been killed; for the circus proprietor had many wolves, and it was easy enough for him to hang a skin on the rail and allow free entry. But he was not to be dissuaded. He thought that the announcement of the bound man's act would revive the triumphs of the summer.

That evening the bound man's movements were uncertain. He stumbled in one of his jumps, and fell. Before he managed to get up he heard some low whistles and catcalls, rather like birds calling at dawn. He tried to get up too quickly, as he had done once or twice during the summer, with the result that he tautened the rope and fell back again. He lay still to regain his calm, and listened to the boos and catcalls growing into an uproar. "Well, bound man, and how did you kill the wolf?" they shouted, and: "Are you the man who killed the wolf?" If he had been one of them, he would not have believed it himself. He thought they had a perfect right to be angry: a circus at this time of year, a bound man, an escaped wolf, and all ending up with this. Some groups of spectators started arguing with others, but the greater part of the audience thought the whole thing a bad joke. By the time he had got to his feet there was such a hubbub that he was barely able to make out individual words.

He saw people surging up all round him, like faded leaves raised by a whirlwind in a circular valley at the center of which all was yet still. He thought of the golden sunsets of the last few days; and the sepulchral light which lay over the blight of all that he had built up during so many nights, the gold frame which the pious hang round dark, old pictures; this sudden collapse of everything, filled him with anger.

They wanted him to repeat his battle with the wolf. He said that such a thing had no place in a circus performance, and the proprietor declared that he did not keep animals to have them slaughtered in front of an audience. But the mob stormed the ring and forced them toward the cages. The proprietor's wife made her way between the seats to the exit and managed to get round to the cages from the other side. She pushed aside the attendant whom the crowd had forced to open a cage door, but the spectators dragged her back and prevented the door from being shut.

"Aren't you the woman who used to lie with him by the river in the summer?" they called out. "How does he hold you in his arms?" She shouted back at them that they needn't believe in the bound man if they didn't want to, they had never deserved him. Painted clowns were good enough for them.

The bound man felt as if the bursts of laughter were what he had been expecting ever since early May. What had smelt so sweet all through the summer now stank. But, if they insisted, he was ready to take on all the animals in the circus. He had never felt so much at one with his rope.

Gently he pushed the woman aside. Perhaps he would travel south with them after all. He stood in the open doorway of the cage, and he saw the wolf, a strong young animal, rise to its feet, and he heard the proprietor grumbling again about the loss of his exhibits. He clapped his hands to attract the animal's attention, and when it was near enough he turned to slam the cage door. He looked the woman in the face. Suddenly he remembered the proprietor's warning to suspect of murderous intentions anyone near him who had a sharp instrument in his hand. At the same moment he felt the blade on his wrists, as cool as the water of the river in autumn, which during the last few weeks he had been barely able to stand. The rope curled up in a tangle beside him while he struggled free. He pushed the woman back, but there was no point in anything he did now. Had he been insufficiently on his guard against those who wanted to release him, against the sympathy in which they wanted to lull him? Had he lain too long on the river bank? If she had cut the cord at any other moment it would have been better than this.

He stood in the middle of the cage, and rid himself of the rope like a snake discarding its skin. It amused him to see the spectators shrinking back. Did they realize that he had no choice now? Or that fighting the wolf now would prove nothing whatever? At the same time he felt all his blood rush to his feet. He felt suddenly weak.

The rope, which fell at its feet like a snare, angered the wolf more than the entry of a stranger into its cage. It crouched to spring. The man reeled, and grabbed the pistol that hung ready at the side of the cage. Then, before anyone could stop him, he shot the wolf between the eyes. The animal reared, and touched him in falling.

On the way to the river he heard the footsteps of his pursuers—spectators, the rope dancers, the circus proprietor, and the proprietor's wife, who persisted in the chase longer than anyone else. He hid in a clump of bushes and listened to them hurrying past, and later on streaming in the opposite direction back to the camp. The moon shone on the meadow; in that light its color was both of growth and of death.

When he came to the river his anger died away. At dawn it seemed to him as if lumps of ice were floating in the water, and as if snow had fallen, obliterating memory.

# EARLY MORNIN' BLUES

## "Leadbelly"
## Huddie Ledbetter

Now this is the blues:
There was a white man had the blues
Caused nothin' to worry 'bout.
Now you lay around at night
Y' roll from one side of the bed to the other
All night long y' can't sleep.
What's matter? The blues has got you.
Y' get up's an' y' sit on the side o yer bed
In the mornin'.
Y' may have a sister, a brother, a mother, a father around
But you doan want no talk out of 'em.
What's the matter?
The blues has got you.
Well y' go an' put yer feet under that table
And look down at yer plate.
Got everythin' y' want to eat
But you shake your head and you get up
And you say, "Lord, I can't sleep and I can't eat,
Want to talk to you."
What's the matter? The blues got you.
Here's what you got to tell 'em:
"Good Mornin', Blues.
Good Lord, how do you do?
Good Mornin', Blues.
Good Lord, how do you do?"
"I'm doin' alright.
Good Mornin', how are you?"

"I lay down last night
Turnin' from side to side
Oh turnin' from side to side.
I was not sick, but I was just dissatisfied.
When I got up this mornin'
With the Blues walkin' 'round my bed,
Oh, with the Blues walkin' 'round my bed,
I went to eat my breakfast
The Blues all in my bread.
Good Mornin', Blues.
Good Lord, how do you do?"
"I'm doin alright.
Good Mornin'. How are you?"
"Oh, I got a woman
Make a moon-eyed man go blind
Oh, she would make a moon-eyed man go blind
And a just her lovin'
Make you take yer time.
Good Mornin' Blues.
How do you do you do?
Good Lord, how do you do?"
"I do alright,
Good Mornin', how are you?"

# TODAY IS A DAY OF GREAT JOY

## Victor Hernandez Cruz

when they stop poems
in the mail & clap
their hands & dance to
them
when women become pregnant
by the side of poems
the strongest sounds     making
the river go along

it is a great day

as poems fall down to
movie crowds     in restaurants
in bars

when poems start to
knock down walls     to
choke politicians
when poems scream &
begin to break the air

this is the time of
true poets        that is
the time of greatness

a true poet    aiming
poems & watching things
fall to the ground

it is a great day.

*"pity this busy monster manunkind,
    not"*

                        *E. E. Cummings*

# V

# ART AS
# SOCIAL
# COMMENTARY

*Que hay que hacer mas?* from *The Disasters of War* by Francisco José de Goya
y Lucientes (The Metropolitan Museum of Art, Schiff Fund, 1922)

# THE UNKNOWN CITIZEN

## W. H. Auden

*(To JS/07/M/378*
*This Marble Monument*
*Is Erected by the State)*

He was found by the Bureau of Statistics to be
One against whom there was no official complaint,
And all the reports on his conduct agree
That, in the modern sense of an old-fashioned word, he was a saint,
For in everything he did he served the Greater Community.
Except for the War till the day he retired
He worked in a factory and never got fired,
But satisfied his employers, Fudge Motors Inc.
Yet he wasn't a scab or odd in his views,
For his Union reports that he paid his dues,
(Our report on his Union shows it was sound)
And our Social Psychology workers found
That he was popular with his mates and liked a drink.
The Press are convinced that he bought a paper every day
And that his reactions to advertisements were normal in every way.
Policies taken out in his name prove that he was fully insured,
And his Health-card shows he was once in hospital but left
   it cured.
Both Producers Research and High-Grade Living declare

He was fully sensible to the advantages of the Instalment Plan
And had everything necessary to the Modern Man,
A phonograph, a radio, a car and a frigidaire.
Our researchers into Public Opinion are content
That he held the proper opinions for the time of year;
When there was peace, he was for peace; when there was war, he went.
He was married and added five children to the population,
Which our Eugenist says was the right number for a parent of his generation,
And our teachers report that he never interfered with their education.
Was he free? Was he happy? The question is absurd:
Had anything been wrong, we should certainly have heard.

*The Flag In Dog We Truck* by Raymond Keller

*Pollution* by Raymond Keller

*The Natural Revolution* by Jill Dunner and Jill Bohlander

*The Opiate* by Raymond Keller

# PITY
# THIS BUSY MONSTER,
# MANUNKIND

## E. E. Cummings

pity this busy monster,manunkind,

not.    Progress is a comfortable disease:
your victim(death and life safely beyond)

plays with the bigness of his littleness
—electrons deify one razorblade
into a mountainrange;lenses extend

unwish through curving wherewhen till unwish
returns on its unself.
                          A world of made
is not a world of born—pity poor flesh

and trees,poor stars and stones,but never this
fine specimen of hypermagical

ultraomnipotence.    We doctors know

a hopeless case if—listen:there's a hell
of a good universe next door;let's go

# NEXT TO OF COURSE
# GOD AMERICA I

## E. E. Cummings

"next to of course god america i
love you land of the pilgrims' and so forth oh
say can you see by the dawn's early my
country 'tis of centuries come and go
and are no more what of it we should worry
in every language even deafanddumb
thy sons acclaim your glorious name by gorry
by jingo by gee by gosh by gum
why talk of beauty what could be more beautiful than these heroic happy dead
who rushed like lions to the roaring slaughter
they did not stop to think they died instead
then shall the voices of liberty be mute?"

He spoke. And drank rapidly a glass of water

# SOUL

## Austin Black

from ivory towers they come
for poetry music art & food
no homosapien peers for you
grand delusion's soul supreme
funky soul brothers keeping the faith
gleaned from squalid shambles of life
    400 years of crass illusion
great soul erotic soul happy soul
your splashed canvas expensive now!
preserved cans to tickle the palate
    stored bottled crated you see
pressed in wax in sharps & flats
    hours days seasons & years
soul the pain of misery amassed!
depriving altars of physical joys
    philosophy of being in the void
for soul is where its really been
    faded thin hand-me-downs
just simply take a look inside
    eating funky souled ghoulash
from disconcerted spiritual void
    the individual striving suicide
    wisdom of age is not facade!!!

# MERRY-GO-ROUND

## Langston Hughes

*Colored child*
*at carnival*

Where is the Jim Crow section
On this merry-go-round,
Mister, cause I want to ride?
Down South where I come from
White and colored
Can't sit side by side.
Down South on the train
There's a Jim Crow car.
On the bus we're put in the back—
But there ain't no back
To a merry-go-round!
Where's the horse
For a kid that's black?

# THIRD DEGREE

## Langston Hughes

Hit me! Jab me!
Make me say I did it.
Blood on my sport shirt
And my tan suede shoes.

Faces like jack-o'-lanterns
In gray slouch hats.

Slug me! Beat me!
Scream jumps out
Like blowtorch.
Three kicks between the legs
That kill the kids
I'd make tomorrow.

Bars and floor skyrocket
And burst like Roman candles.

When you throw
Cold water on me,
I'll sign the
Paper . . .

# CHRIST
# IN ALABAMA

## Langston Hughes

Christ is a nigger,
Beaten and black:
Oh, bare your back!

Mary is His mother:
Mammy of the South,
Silence your mouth.

God is His father:
White Master above
Grant Him your love.

Most holy bastard
Of the bleeding mouth,
 Nigger Christ
 On the cross
 Of the South.

# THE MALEFIC RETURN

## Ramón López Velarde

Better not to go back to the village,
to the ruined Eden lying silent
in the devastation of the shrapnel.

Even to the mutilated ash-trees,
dignitaries of the swelling dome,
the lamentations must be borne of
the tower riddled in the slinging winds.

And on the chalk of all
the ghostly hamlct's walls
the fusillade engraved
black and baneful maps,
whereon the prodigal son might trace,
returning to his threshold,
in a malefic nightfall,
by a wick's petrol light,
his hopes destroyed.

When the clumsy mildewed key
turns the creaking lock,
in the ancient
cloistered porch
the two chaste gyps
medallions will unseal narcotic lids,
look at each other and say: "Who is that?"

Reprinted by permission of Indiana University Press from *An Anthology of Mexican Poetry,* edited by Octavio Paz, translated by Samuel Beckett. Copyright © 1958 by Indiana University Press.

And I shall enter on intruding feet,
reach the fatidic court
where a well-curb broods
with a skin pail dripping
its categoric drop
like a sad refrain.

If the tonic, gay, inexorable sun
makes the catechumen fountains boil
in which my chronic dream was wont to bathe;
if the ants toil;
if on the roof the crawy call resounds
and grows aweary of the turtle-doves
and in the cobwebs murmurs on and on;
my thirst to love will then be like a ring
imbedded in the slabstone of a tomb.

The new swallows, renewing
with their new potter beaks
the early nests;
beneath the signal opal
of monachal eventides
the cry of calves newly calved
for the forbidden exuberant udder
of the cud-chewing Pharaonic cow
who awes her young;
belfry of new-aspiring peal;
renovated altars;
loving love
of well-paired pairs;
bethrothals of young
humble girls, like humble kales;
some young lady
singing on some piano
some old song;
the policeman's whistle  . . .
    . . . and a profound reactionary sorrow.

# THE ROCKING-HORSE WINNER

## D. H. Lawrence

There was a woman who was beautiful, who started with all the advantages, yet she had no luck. She married for love, and the love turned to dust. She had bonny children, yet she felt they had been thrust upon her, and she could not love them. They looked at her coldly, as if they were finding fault with her. And hurriedly she felt she must cover up some fault in herself. Yet what it was that she must cover up she never knew. Nevertheless, when her children were present, she always felt the centre of her heart go hard. This troubled her, and in her manner she was all the more gentle and anxious for her children, as if she loved them very much. Only she herself knew that at the centre of her heart was a hard little place that could not feel love, no, not for anybody. Everybody else said of her: "She is such a good mother. She adores her children." Only she herself, and her children themselves, knew it was not so. They read it in each other's eyes.

There were a boy and two little girls. They lived in a pleasant house, with a garden, and they had discreet servants, and felt themselves superior to anyone in the neighbourhood.

Although they lived in style, they felt always an anxiety in the house. There was never enough money. The mother had a small income, and the father had a small income, but not nearly enough for the social position which they had to keep up. The father went in to town to some office. But though he had good prospects, these prospects never materialized.

There was always the grinding sense of the shortage of money, though the style was always kept up.

At last the mother said: "I will see if *I* can't make something." But she did not know where to begin. She racked her brains, and tried this thing and the other, but could not find anything successful. The failure made deep lines come into her face. Her children were growing up, they would have to go to school. There must be more money, there must be more money. The father, who was always very handsome and expensive in his tastes, seemed as if he never *would* be able to do anything worth doing. And the mother, who had a great belief in herself, did not succeed any better, and her tastes were just as expensive.

And so the house came to be haunted by the unspoken phrase: *There must be more money! There must be more money!* The children could hear it all the time, though nobody said it aloud. They heard it at Christmas, when the expensive and splendid toys filled the nursery. Behind the shining modern rocking-horse, behind the smart doll's-house, a voice would start whispering: "There *must* be more money! There *must* be more money!" And the children would stop playing, to listen for a moment. They would look into each other's eyes, to see if they had all heard. And each one saw in the eyes of the other two that they too had heard. "There *must* be more money! There *must* be more money!"

It came whispering from the springs of the still-swaying rocking-horse, and even the horse, bending his wooden, champing head, heard it. The big doll, sitting so pink and smirking in her new pram, could hear it quite plainly, and seemed to be smirking all the more self-consciously because of it. The foolish puppy, too, that took the place of the teddy-bear, he was looking so extraordinarily foolish for no other reason but that he heard the secret whisper all over the house: "There *must* be more money!"

Yet nobody ever said it aloud. The whisper was everywhere, and therefore no one spoke it. Just as no one ever says: "We are breathing!" in spite of the fact that breath is coming and going all the time.

"Mother," said the boy Paul one day, "why don't we keep a car of our own? Why do we always use uncle's, or else a taxi?"

"Because we're the poor members of the family," said the mother.

"But why *are* we, mother?"

"Well—I suppose," she said slowly and bitterly, "it's because your father has no luck."

The boy was silent for some time.

"Is luck money, mother?" he asked rather timidly.

"No, Paul. Not quite. It's what causes you to have money."

"Oh!" said Paul vaguely. "I thought when Uncle Oscar said *filthy lucker,* it meant money."

"*Filthy lucre* does mean money," said the mother. "But it's lucre, not luck."

"Oh!" said the boy. "Then what *is* luck, mother?"

"It's what causes you to have money. If you're lucky you have money. That's why it's better to be born lucky than rich. If you're rich, you may lose your money. But if you're lucky, you will always get more money."

"Oh! Will you? And is father not lucky?"

"Very unlucky, I should say," she said bitterly.

The boy watched her with unsure eyes.

"Why?" he asked.

"I don't know. Nobody ever knows why one person is lucky and another unlucky."

"Don't they? Nobody at all? Does *nobody* know?"

"Perhaps God. But He never tells."

"He ought to, then. And aren't you lucky either, mother?"

"I can't be, if I married an unlucky husband."

"But by yourself, aren't you?"

"I used to think I was, before I married. Now I think I am very unlucky indeed."

"Why?"

"Well—never mind! Perhaps I'm not really," she said.

The child looked at her, to see if she meant it. But he saw, by the lines of her mouth, that she was only trying to hide something from him.

"Well, anyhow," he said stoutly, "I'm a lucky person."

"Why?" said his mother, with a sudden laugh.

He stared at her. He didn't even know why he had said it.

"God told me," he asserted, brazening it out.

"I hope He did, dear!" she said, again with a laugh, but rather bitter.

"He did, mother!"

"Excellent!" said the mother, using one of her husband's exclamations.

The boy saw she did not believe him; or, rather, that she paid no attention to his assertion. This angered him somewhat, and made him want to compel her attention.

He went off by himself, vaguely, in a childish way, seeking for the clue to "luck." Absorbed, taking no heed of other people, he went about with a sort of stealth, seeking inwardly for luck. He wanted luck, he wanted it, he wanted it. When the two girls were playing dolls in the nursery, he would sit on his big rocking-horse, charging madly into space, with a frenzy that made the little girls peer at him uneasily. Wildly the horse careered, the waving dark hair of the boy tossed, his eyes had a strange glare in them. The little girls dared not speak to him.

When he had ridden to the end of his mad little journey, he climbed down and stood in front of his rocking-horse, staring fixedly into its lowered face. Its red mouth was slightly open, its big eye was wide and glassy-bright.

"Now!" he would silently command the snorting steed. "Now, take me to where there is luck! Now take me!"

And he would slash the horse on the neck with the little whip he had asked Uncle Oscar for. He *knew* the horse could take him to where there was luck, if only he forced it. So he would mount again, and start on his furious ride, hoping at last to get there. He knew he could get there.

"You'll break your horse, Paul!" said the nurse.

"He's always riding like that! I wish he'd leave off!" said his elder sister Joan.

But he only glared down on them in silence. Nurse gave him up. She could make nothing of him. Anyhow he was growing beyond her.

One day his mother and his Uncle Oscar came in when he was on one of his furious rides. He did not speak to them.

"Hallo, you young jockey! Riding a winner?" said his uncle.

"Aren't you growing too big for a rocking-horse? You're not a very little boy any longer, you know," said his mother.

But Paul only gave a blue glare from his big, rather close-set eyes. He would speak to nobody when he was in full tilt. His mother watched him with an anxious expression on her face.

At last he suddenly stopped forcing his horse into the mechanical gallop, and slid down.

"Well, I got there!" he announced fiercely, his blue eyes still flaring, and his sturdy long legs straddling apart.

"Where did you get to?" asked his mother.

"Where I wanted to go," he flared back at her.

"That's right, son!" said Uncle Oscar. "Don't you stop till you get there. What's the horse's name?"

"He doesn't have a name," said the boy.

"Gets on without all right?" asked the uncle.

"Well, he has different names. He was called Sansovino last week."

"Sansovino, eh? Won the Ascot. How did you know his name?"

"He always talks about horse-races with Bassett," said Joan.

The uncle was delighted to find that his small nephew was posted with all the racing news. Bassett, the young gardener, who had been wounded in the left foot in the war and had got his present job through Oscar Cresswell, whose batman he had been, was a perfect blade of the "turf." He lived in the racing events, and the small boy lived with him.

Oscar Cresswell got it all from Bassett.

"Master Paul comes and asks me, so I can't do more than tell him, sir," said Bassett, his face terribly serious, as if he were speaking of religious matters.

"And does he ever put anything on a horse he fancies?"

"Well—I don't want to give him away—he's a young sport, a fine sport, sir. Would you mind asking him himself? He sort of takes a pleasure in it, and perhaps he'd feel I was giving him away, sir, if you don't mind."

Basset was serious as a church.

The uncle went back to his nephew and took him off for a ride in the car.

"Say, Paul, old man, do you ever put anything on a horse?" the uncle asked.

The boy watched the handsome man closely.

"Why, do you think I oughtn't to?" he parried.

"Not a bit of it! I thought perhaps you might give me a tip for the Lincoln."

The car sped on into the country, going down to Uncle Oscar's place in Hampshire.

"Honour bright?" said the nephew.

"Honour bright, son!" said the uncle.

"Well, then, Daffodil."

"Daffodil! I doubt it, sonny. What about Mirza?"

"I only know the winner," said the boy. "That's Daffodil."

"Daffodil, eh?"

There was a pause. Daffodil was an obscure horse comparatively.

"Uncle!"

"Yes, son?"

"You won't let it go any further, will you? I promised Bassett."

"Bassett be damned, old man! What's he got to do with it?"

"We're partners. We've been partners from the first. Uncle, he lent me my first five shillings, which I lost. I promised him, honour bright, it was only between me and him; only you gave me that ten-shilling note I started winning with, so I thought you were lucky. You won't let it go any further, will you?"

The boy gazed at his uncle from those big, hot, blue eyes, set rather close together. The uncle stirred and laughed uneasily.

"Right you are, son! I'll keep your tip private. Daffodil, eh? How much are you putting on him?"

"All except twenty pounds," said the boy. "I keep that in reserve."

The uncle thought it a good joke.

"You keep twenty pounds in reserve, do you, you young romancer? What are you betting, then?"

"I'm betting three hundred," said the boy gravely. "But it's between you and me, Uncle Oscar! Honour bright?"

The uncle burst into a roar of laughter.

"It's between you and me all right, you young Nat Gould," he said, laughing. "But where's your three hundred?"

"Bassett keeps it for me. We're partners."

"You are, are you! And what is Bassett putting on Daffodil?"

"He won't go quite as high as I do, I expect. Perhaps he'll go a hundred and fifty."

"What, pennies?" laughed the uncle.

"Pounds," said the child, with a surprised look at his uncle. "Bassett keeps a bigger reserve than I do."

Between wonder and amusement Uncle Oscar was silent. He pursued the matter no further, but he determined to take his nephew with him to the Lincoln races.

"Now, son," he said, "I'm putting twenty on Mirza, and I'll put five for you on any horse you fancy. What's your pick?"

"Daffodil, uncle."

"No, not the fiver on Daffodil!"

"I should if it was my own fiver," said the child.

"Good! Good! Right you are! A fiver for me and a fiver for you on Daffodil."

The child had never been to a race-meeting before, and his eyes were blue fire. He pursed his mouth tight, and watched. A Frenchman just in front had put his money on Lancelot. Wild with excitement, he flayed his arms up and down, yelling *"Lancelot! Lancelot!"* in his French accent.

Daffodil came in first, Lancelot second, Mirza third. The child, flushed and with eyes blazing, was curiously serene. His uncle brought him four five-pound notes, four to one.

"What am I to do with these?" he cried, waving them before the boy's eyes.

"I suppose we'll talk to Bassett," said the boy. "I expect I have fifteen hundred now; and twenty in reserve; and this twenty."

His uncle studied him for some moments.

"Look here, son!" he said. "You're not serious about Bassett and that fifteen hundred, are you?"

"Yes, I am. But it's between you and me, uncle. Honour bright!"

"Honour bright all right, son! But I must talk to Bassett."

"If you'd like to be a partner, uncle, with Bassett and me, we could all be partners. Only, you'd have to promise, honour bright, uncle, not to let it go beyond us three. Bassett and I are lucky, and you must be lucky, because it was your ten shillings I started winning with. . . ."

Uncle Oscar took both Bassett and Paul into Richmond Park for an afternoon, and there they talked.

"It's like this, you see, sir," Bassett said. "Master Paul would get me talking about racing events, spinning yarns, you know, sir. And he was always keen on knowing if I'd made or if I'd lost. It's about a year since, now, that I put five shilling on Blush of Dawn for him—and we lost. Then the luck turned, with that ten shillings he had from you, that we put on Singhalese. And since that time, It's been pretty steady, all things considering. What do you say, Master Paul?"

"We're all right when we're sure," said Paul. "It's when we're not quite sure that we go down."

"Oh, but we're careful then," said Bassett.

"But when are you *sure?*" smiled Uncle Oscar.

"It's Master Paul, sir," said Bassett, in a secret, religious voice. "It's as if he had it from heaven. Like Daffodil, now, for the Lincoln. That was as sure as eggs."

"Did you put anything on Daffodil?" asked Oscar Cresswell.

"Yes, sir. I made my bit."

"And my nephew?"

Bassett was obstinately silent, looking at Paul.

"I made twelve hundred, didn't I, Bassett? I told uncle I was putting three hundred on Daffodil."

"That's right," said Bassett, nodding.

"But where's the money?" asked the uncle.

"I keep it safe locked up, sir. Master Paul he can have it any minute he likes to ask for it."

"What, fifteen hundred pounds?"

"And twenty! And *forty,* that is, with the twenty he made on the course."

"It's amazing!" said the uncle.

"If Master Paul offers you to be partners, sir, I would, if I were you; if you'll excuse me," said Bassett.

Oscar Cresswell thought about it.

"I'll see the money," he said.

They drove home again, and sure enough, Bassett came round to the garden-house with fifteen hundred pounds in notes. The twenty pounds reserve was left with Joe Glee, in the Turf Commission deposit.

"You see, it's all right, uncle, when I'm *sure!* Then we go strong, for all we're worth. Don't we, Bassett?"

"We do that, Master Paul."

"And when are you sure?" said the uncle, laughing.

"Oh, well, sometimes I'm *absolutely* sure, like about Daffodil," said the boy, "and sometimes I have an idea; and sometimes I haven't even an idea, have I, Bassett? Then we're careful, because we mostly go down."

"You do, do you! And when you're sure, like about Daffodil, what makes you sure, sonny?"

"Oh, well, I don't know," said the boy uneasily. "I'm sure, you know, uncle; that's all."

"It's as if he had it from heaven, sir," Bassett reiterated.

"I should say so!" said the uncle.

But he became a partner. And when the Leger was coming on, Paul was "sure" about Lively Spark, which was a quite inconsiderable horse. The boy insisted on putting a thousand on the horse, Bassett went for five hundred, and Oscar Cresswell two hundred. Lively Spark came in first, and the betting had been ten to one against him. Paul had made ten thousand.

"You see," he said, "I was absolutely sure of him."

Even Oscar Cresswell had cleared two thousand.

"Look here, son," he said, "this sort of thing makes me nervous."

"It needn't, uncle! Perhaps I shan't be sure again for a long time."

"But what are you going to do with your money?" asked the uncle.

"Of course," said the boy, "I started it for mother. She said she had no luck, because father is unlucky, so I thought if *I* was lucky, it might stop whispering."

"What might stop whispering?"

"Our house. I *hate* our house for whispering."

"What does it whisper?"

"Why—why"—the boy fidgeted—"why, I don't know. But it's always short of money, you know, uncle."

"I know it, son, I know it."

"You know people send mother writs, don't you, uncle?"

"I'm afraid I do," said the uncle.

"And then the house whispers, like people laughing at you behind your back. It's awful, that is! I thought if I was lucky  . . ."

"You might stop it," added the uncle.

The boy watched him with big blue eyes, that had an uncanny cold fire in them, and he said never a word.

"Well, then!" said the uncle. "What are we doing?"

"I shouldn't like mother to know I was lucky," said the boy.

"Why not, son?"

"She'd stop me."

"I don't think she would."

"Oh!"—and the boy writhed in an odd way—"I *don't* want her to know, uncle."

"All right, son! We'll manage it without her knowing."

They managed it very easily. Paul, at the other's suggestion, handed over five thousand pounds to his uncle, who deposited it with the family lawyer, who was then to inform Paul's mother that a relative had put five thousand pounds into his hands, which sum was to be paid out a thousand pounds at a time, on the mother's birthday, for the next five years.

"So she'll have a birthday present of a thousand pounds for five successive years," said Uncle Oscar. "I hope it won't make it all the harder for her later."

Paul's mother had her birthday in November. The house had been "whispering" worse than ever lately, and, even in spite of his luck, Paul could not bear up against it. He was very anxious to see the effect of the birthday letter, telling his mother about the thousand pounds.

When there were no visitors, Paul now took his meals with his parents, as he was beyond nursery control. His mother went into town nearly every day. She had discovered that she had an odd knack of sketching furs and dress materials, so she worked secretly in the studio of a friend who was the chief "artist" for the leading drapers. She drew the figures of ladies in furs and ladies in silk and sequins for the newspaper advertisements. This young woman artist earned several thousand pounds a year, but Paul's mother only made several hundreds, and she was again dissatisfied. She so wanted to be first in something, and she did not succeed, even in making sketches for drapery advertisements.

She was down to breakfast on the morning of her birthday. Paul watched her face as she read her letters. He knew the lawyer's letter. As his mother read it, her face hardened and became more expressionless. Then a cold, determined look came on her mouth. She hid the letter under the pile of others, and said not a word about it.

"Didn't you have anything nice in the post for your birthday, mother?" said Paul.

"Quite moderately nice," she said, her voice cold and absent.

She went away to town without saying more.

But in the afternoon Uncle Oscar appeared. He said Paul's mother had had a long interview with the lawyer, asking if the whole five thousand could not be advanced at once, as she was in debt.

"What do you think, uncle?" said the boy.

"I leave it to you, son."

"Oh, let her have it, then! We can get some more with the other," said the boy.

"A bird in the hand is worth two in the bush, laddie!" said Uncle Oscar.

"But I'm sure to *know* for the Grand National; or the Lincolnshire; or else the Derby. I'm sure to know for *one* of them," said Paul.

So Uncle Oscar signed the agreement, and Paul's mother touched the whole five thousand. Then something very curious happened. The voices in the house suddenly went mad, like a chorus of frogs on a spring evening. There were certain new furnishings, and Paul had a tutor. He was *really* going to Eton, his father's school, in the following autumn. There were flowers in the winter, and a blossoming of the luxury Paul's mother had been used to. And yet the voices in the house, behind the sprays of mimosa and almond blossom, and from under the piles of iridescent cushions, simply trilled and screamed in a sort of ecstasy: "There *must* be more money! Oh-h-h; there *must* be more money. Oh, now, now-w! Now-w-w— there *must* be more money!—more than ever! More than ever!"

It frightened Paul terribly. He studied away at his Latin and Greek with his tutors. But his intense hours were spent with Bassett. The Grand National had gone by: he had not "known," and had lost a hundred pounds. Summer was at hand. He was in agony for the Lincoln. But even for the Lincoln he didn't "know," and he lost fifty pounds. He became wild-eyed and strange, as if something were going to explode in him.

"Let it alone, son! Don't you bother about it!" urged Uncle Oscar. But it was as if the boy couldn't really hear what his uncle was saying.

"I've got to know for the Derby! I've got to know for the Derby!" the child reiterated, his big blue eyes blazing with a sort of madness.

His mother noticed how overwrought he was.

"You'd better go to the seaside. Wouldn't you like to go now to the seaside, instead of waiting? I think you'd better," she said, looking down at him anxiously, her heart curiously heavy because of him.

But the child lifted his uncanny blue eyes.

"I couldn't possibly go before the Derby, mother!" he said. "I couldn't possibly!"

"Why not?" she said, her voice becoming heavy when she was opposed. "Why not? You can still go from the seaside to see the Derby with your Uncle Oscar, if that's what you wish. No need for you to wait here. Besides, I think you care too much about these races. It's a bad sign. My family has been a gambling family, and you won't know till you grow up how much damage it has done. But it has done damage. I shall have to send Bassett away, and ask Uncle Oscar not to talk racing to you, unless you promise to be reasonable about it; go away to the seaside and forget it. You're all nerves!"

"I'll do what you like, mother, so long as you don't send me away till after the Derby," the boy said.

"Send you away from where? Just from this house?"

"Yes," he said, gazing at her.

"Why, you curious child, what makes you care about this house so much, suddenly? I never knew you loved it."

He gazed at her without speaking. He had a secret within a secret, something he had not divulged, even to Bassett or to his Uncle Oscar.

But his mother, after standing undecided and a little bit sullen for some moments, said:

"Very well, then! Don't go to the seaside till after the Derby, if you don't wish it. But promise me you won't let your nerves go to pieces. Promise you won't think so much about horse-racing and *events,* as you call them!"

"Oh, no," said the boy casually. "I won't think much about them, mother. You needn't worry. I wouldn't worry, mother, if I were you."

"If you were me and I were you," said his mother, "I wonder what we *should* do!"

"But you know you needn't worry, mother, don't you?" the boy repeated.

"I should be awfully glad to know it," she said wearily.

"Oh, well, you *can,* you know. I mean, you *ought* to know you needn't worry," he insisted.

"Ought I? Then I'll see about it," she said.

Paul's secret of secrets was his wooden horse, that which had no name. Since he was emancipated from a nurse and a nursery-governess, he had had his rocking-horse removed to his own bedroom at the top of the house.

"Surely, you're too big for a rocking-horse!" his mother had remonstrated.

"Well, you see, mother, till I can have a *real* horse, I like to have *some* sort of animal about," had been his quaint answer.

"Do you feel he keeps you company?" she laughed.

"Oh, yes! He's very good, he always keeps me company, when I'm there," said Paul.

So the horse, rather shabby, stood in an arrested prance in the boy's bedroom.

The Derby was drawing near, and the boy grew more and more tense. He hardly heard what was spoken to him, he was very frail, and his eyes were really uncanny. His mother had sudden strange seizures of uneasiness about him. Sometimes, for half-an-hour, she would feel a sudden anxiety about him that was almost anguish. She wanted to rush to him at once, and know he was safe.

Two nights before the Derby, she was at a big party in town, when one of her rushes of anxiety about her boy, her first-born, gripped her heart till she could hardly speak. She fought with the feeling, might and main, for she believed in common-sense. But it was too strong. She had to leave the dance and go downstairs to telephone to the country. The children's nursery-governess was terribly surprised and startled at being rung up in the night.

"Are the children all right, Miss Wilmot?"

"Oh, yes, they are quite all right."

"Master Paul? Is he all right?"

"He went to bed as right as a trivet. Shall I run up and look at him?"

"No," said Paul's mother reluctantly. "No! Don't trouble. It's all right. Don't sit up. We shall be home fairly soon." She did not want her son's privacy intruded upon.

"Very good," said the governess.

It was about one o'clock when Paul's mother and father drove up to their house. All was still. Paul's mother went to her room and slipped off her white fur cloak. She had told her maid not to wait up for her. She heard her husband downstairs, mixing a whisky-and-soda.

And then, because of the strange anxiety at her heart, she stole upstairs to her son's room. Noiselessly she went along the upper corridor. Was there a faint noise? What was it?

She stood, with arrested muscles, outside his door, listening. There was a strange, heavy, and yet not loud noise. Her heart stood still. It was a soundless noise, yet rushing and powerful. Something huge, in violent, hushed motion. What was it? What in God's name was it? She ought to know. She felt that she knew the noise. She knew what it was.

Yet she could not place it. She couldn't say what it was. And on and on it went, like a madness.

Softly, frozen with anxiety and fear, she turned the door-handle.

The room was dark. Yet in the space near the window, she heard and saw something plunging to and fro. She gazed in fear and amazement.

Then suddenly she switched on the light, and saw her son, in his green pyjamas, madly surging on the rocking-horse. The blaze of light suddenly lit him up, as he urged the wooden horse, and lit her up, as she stood, blonde, in her dress of pale green and crystal, in the doorway.

"Paul!" she cried. "Whatever are you doing?"

"It's Malabar!" he screamed, in a powerful, strange voice. "It's Malabar!"

His eyes blazed at her for one strange and senseless second, as he ceased urging his wooden horse. Then he fell with a crash to the ground, and she, all her tormented motherhood flooding upon her, rushed to gather him up.

But he was unconscious, and unconscious he remained, with some brain-fever. He talked and tossed, and his mother sat stonily by his side.

"Malabar! It's Malabar! Bassett. Bassett, I *know!* It's Malabar!"

So the child cried, trying to get up and urge the rocking-horse that gave him his inspiration.

"What does he mean by Malabar?" asked the heart-frozen mother.

"I don't know," said the father stonily.

"What does he mean by Malabar?" she asked her brother Oscar.

"It's one of the horses running for the Derby," was the answer.

And, in spite of himself, Oscar Cresswell spoke to Bassett, and himself put a thousand on Malabar: at fourteen to one.

The third day of the illness was critical: they were waiting for a change. The boy, with his rather long, curly hair, was tossing ceaselessly on the pillow. He neither slept nor regained consciousness, and his eyes were like blue stones. His mother sat, feeling her heart had gone, turned actually into a stone.

In the evening, Oscar Cresswell did not come, but Bassett sent a message, saying could he come up for one moment, just one moment? Paul's mother was very angry at the intrusion, but on second thought she agreed. The boy was the same. Perhaps Bassett might bring him to consciousness.

The gardener, a shortish fellow with a little brown moustache, and sharp little brown eyes, tip-toed into the room, touched his imaginary cap to Paul's mother, and stole to the bedside, staring with glittering, smallish eyes, at the tossing, dying child.

"Master Paul!" he whispered. "Master Paul! Malabar came in first all right, a clean win. I did as you told me. You've made over seventy thousand pounds, you have; you've got over eighty thousand. Malabar came in all right, Master Paul."

"Malabar! Malabar! Did I say Malabar, mother? Did I say Malabar? Do you think I'm lucky, mother? I knew Malabar, didn't I? Over eighty thousand pounds! I call that lucky, don't you, mother? Over eighty thousand pounds! I knew, didn't I know I knew? Malabar came in all right. If I ride my horse till I'm sure, then I tell you, Bassett, you can go as high as you like. Did you go for all you were worth, Bassett?"

"I went a thousand on it, Master Paul."

"I never told you, mother, that if I can ride my horse, and *get there,* then I'm absolutely sure—oh, absolutely! Mother, did I ever tell you? I *am* lucky!"

"No, you never did," said the mother.

But the boy died in the night.

And even as he lay dead, his mother heard her brother's voice saying to her: "My God, Hester, you're eighty-odd thousand to the good, and a poor devil of a son to the bad. But, poor devil, poor devil, he's best gone out of a life where he rides his rocking-horse to find a winner."

# POWER AND RACISM

## Stokley Carmichael

One of the tragedies of the struggle against racism is that up to now there has been no national organization which could speak to the growing militancy of young black people in the urban ghetto. There has been only a civil rights movement, whose tone of voice was adapted to an audience of liberal whites. It served as a sort of buffer zone between them and angry young blacks. None of its so-called leaders could go into a rioting community and be listened to. In a sense, I blame ourselves—together with the mass media—for what has happened in Watts, Harlem, Chicago, Cleveland, Omaha. Each time the people in those cities saw Martin Luther King get slapped, they became angry; when they saw four little black girls bombed to death, they were angrier; and when nothing happened, they were steaming. We had nothing to offer that they could see, except to go out and be beaten again. We helped to build their frustration.

For too many years, black Americans marched and had their heads broken and got shot. They were saying to the country, "Look, you guys are supposed to be nice guys and we are only going to do what we are supposed to do—why do you beat us up, why don't you give us what we ask, why don't you straighten yourselves out?" After years of this, we are at almost the same point—because we demonstrated from a position of weakness. We cannot be expected any longer to march and have our heads broken in order to say to whites: come on, you're nice guys. For you are not nice guys. We have found you out.

An organization which claims to speak for the needs of a community—as does the Student Nonviolent Coordinating Committee—must speak in the tone of that community, not as somebody else's buffer zone. This is the significance of black power as a slogan. For once, black people are going to use the words they want to use—not just the words whites want to hear. And they will do this no matter how often the press tries to stop the use of the slogan by equating it with racism or separatism.

An organization which claims to be working for the needs of a community—as SNCC does—must work to provide that community with a position of strength from which to make its voice heard. This is the significance of black power beyond the slogan.

Black power can be clearly defined for those who do not attach the fears of white America to their questions about it. We should begin with the basic fact that black Americans have two problems: they are poor and they are black. All other problems arise from this two-sided reality: lack of education, the so called apathy of black men. Any program to end racism must address itself to that double reality.

Almost from its beginning, SNCC sought to address itself to both conditions with a program aimed at winning political power for impoverished Southern blacks. We had to begin with politics because black Americans are a propertyless people in a country where property is valued above all. We had to work for power, because this country does not function by morality, love, and nonviolence, but by power. Thus we determined to win political power, with the idea of moving on from there into activity that would have economic effects. With power, the masses could *make or participate in making* the decisions which govern their destinies, and thus create basic change in their day-to-day lives.

But if political power seemed to be the key to self-determination, it was also obvious that the key had been thrown down a deep well many years earlier. Disenfranchisement, maintained by racist terror, made it impossible to talk about organizing for political power in 1960. The right to vote had to be won, and SNCC workers devoted their energies to this from 1961 to 1965. They set up voter registration drives in the Deep South. They created pressure for the vote by holding mock elections in Mississippi in 1963 and by helping to establish the Mississippi Freedom Democratic Party (MFDP) in 1964. That struggle was eased, though not won, with the passage of the 1965 Voting Rights Act. SNCC workers could then address themselves to the question: "Who can we vote for, to have our needs met—how do we make our vote meaningful?"

SNCC had already gone to Atlantic City for recognition of the Mississippi Freedom Democratic Party by the Democratic convention and been rejected; it had gone with the MFDP to Washington for recognition by Congress and been rejected. In Arkansas, SNCC helped thirty Negroes to run for School Board elections; all but one were defeated, and there was evidence of fraud and intimidation sufficient to cause their defeat. In

Atlanta, Julian Bond ran for the state legislature and was elected—twice—and unseated—twice. In several states, black farmers ran in elections for agricultural committees which make crucial decisions concerning land use, loans, etc. Although they won places on a number of committees, they never gained the majorities needed to control them.

All of the efforts were attempts to win black power. Then, in Alabama, the opportunity came to see how blacks could be organized on an independent party basis. An unusual Alabama law provides that any group of citizens can nominate candidates for county office and, if they win 20 per cent of the vote, may be recognized as a county political party. The same then applies on a state level. SNCC went to organize in several counties such as Lowndes, where black people—who form 80 per cent of the population and have an average annual income of $943—felt they could accomplish nothing within the framework of the Alabama Democratic Party because of its racism and because the qualifying fee for this year's elections was raised from $50 to $500 in order to prevent most Negroes from becoming candidates. On May 3, five new county "freedom organizations" convened and nominated candidates for the offices of sheriff, tax assessor, members of the school boards. These men and women are up for election in November—if they live until then. Their ballot symbol is the black panther: a bold, beautiful animal, representing the strength and dignity of black demands today. A man needs a black panther on his side when he and his family must endure—as hundreds of Alabamians have endured—loss of job, eviction, starvation, and sometimes death, for political activity. He may also need a gun and SNCC reaffirms the right of black men everywhere to defend themselves when threatened or attacked. As for initiating the use of violence, we hope that such programs as ours will make that unnecessary; but it is not for us to tell black communities whether they can or cannot use any particular form of action to resolve their problems. Responsibility for the use of violence by black men, whether in self-defense or initiated by them, lies with the white community.

This is the specific historical experience from which SNCC's call for "black power" emerged on the Mississippi march last July. But the concept of "black power" is not a recent or isolated phenomenon: It has grown out of the ferment of agitation and activity by different people and organizations in many black communities over the years. Our last year of work in Alabama added a new concrete possibility. In Lowndes county, for example, black power will mean that if a Negro is elected sheriff, he can end police brutality. If a black man is elected tax assessor, he can collect and channel funds for the building of better roads and schools serving black people—thus advancing the move from political power into the economic arena. In such areas as Lowndes, where black men have a majority, they will attempt to use it to exercise control. This is what they seek: control. Where Negroes lack a majority, black power means proper representation and sharing of control. It means the creation of power bases from which black people can work to change statewide or nationwide patterns of oppression through pressure from strength—instead of weakness. Politically, black power means what it has always meant to SNCC: the coming-together of black people to elect representatives and *to force those representatives to speak to their needs*. It does not mean merely putting black faces into office. A man or woman who is black and from the slums cannot be automatically expected to speak to the needs of black people. Most of the black politicians we see around the country today are not what SNCC means by black power. The power must be that of a community, and emanate from there.

SNCC today is working in both North and South on programs of voter registration and independent political organizing. In some places, such as Alabama, Los Angeles, New York, Philadelphia, and New Jersey, independent organizing under the black panther symbol is in progress. The creation of a national "black panther party" must come about; it will take time to build, and it is much too early to predict its success. We have no infallible master plan and we make no claim to exclusive knowledge of how to end racism; different groups will work in their own different ways. SNCC cannot spell out the full logistics of self-determination but it can address itself to the problem by helping black communities define their needs, realize their strength, and go into action along a variety of lines which they must choose for themselves. Without knowing all the answers, it can address itself to the basic problem of poverty; to the fact that in Lowndes County, 86 white families own 90 per cent of the land. What are black people in that county going to do for jobs, where are they going to get money? There must be reallocation of land, of money.

Ultimately, the economic foundations of this country must be shaken if black people are to control their lives. The colonies of the United States— and this includes the black ghettoes within its borders, north and south— must be liberated. For a century this nation has been like an octopus of exploitation, its tentacles stretching from Mississippi and Harlem to South America, the Middle East, southern Africa, and Vietnam; the form of exploitation varies from area to area but the essential result has been the same—a powerful few have been maintained and enriched at the expense of the poor and voiceless colored masses. This pattern must be broken. As its grip loosens here and there around the world, the hopes of black Americans become more realistic. For racism to die, a totally different America must be born.

This is what the white society does not wish to face; this is why that society prefers to talk about integration. But integration speaks not at all to the problem of poverty, only to the problem of blackness. Integration today means the man who "makes it," leaving his black brothers behind in the ghetto as fast as his new sports car will take him. It has no relevance to the Harlem wino or to the cottonpicker making three dollars a day. As a lady I know in Alabama once said, "the food that Ralph Bunche eats doesn't fill my stomach."

Integration, moreover, speaks to the problem of blackness in a despicable way. As a goal, it has been based on complete acceptance of the fact that in *order to have* a decent house or education, blacks must move into a white neighborhood or send their children to a white school. This reinforces, among both black and white, the idea that "white" is automatically better and "black" is by definition inferior. This is why integration is a subterfuge for the maintenance of white supremacy. It allows the nation to focus on a handful of Southern children who get into white schools, at great price, and to ignore the 94 per cent who are left behind in unimproved all-black schools. Such situations will not change until black people have power—to control their own school boards, in this case. Then Negroes become equal in a way that means something, and integration ceases to be a one-way street. Then integration doesn't mean draining skills and energies from the ghetto into white neighborhoods; then it can mean white people moving from Beverly Hills into Watts, white people joining the Lowndes County Freedom Organization. Then integration becomes relevant.

Last April, before the furor over black power, Christopher Jencks wrote in a *New Republic* article on white Mississippi's manipulation of the anti-poverty program:

> The war on poverty has been predicated on the notion that there is such a thing as *a community* which can be defined geographically and mobilized for a collective effort to help the poor. This theory has no relationship to reality in the Deep South. In every Mississippi county there are *two* communities. Despite all the pious platitudes of the moderates on both sides, these two communities habitually see their interest in terms of conflict rather than cooperation. Only when the Negro community can muster enough political, economic and professional strength to compete on somewhat equal terms, will Negroes believe in the possibility of true cooperation and whites accept its necessity. En route to integration, the Negro community needs to develop greater independence—a chance to run its own affairs and not cave in whenever "the man" barks. . . . Or so it seems to me, and to most of the knowledgeable people with whom I talked in Mississippi. To OEO, this judgment may sound like black nationalism. . . .

Mr. Jencks, a white reporter, perceived the reason why America's anti-poverty program has been a sick farce in both North and South. In the South, it is clearly racism which prevents the poor from running their own programs; in the North, it more often seems to be politicking and bureaucracy. But the results are not so different: In the North, non-whites make up 42 per cent of all families in metropolitan "poverty areas" and only 6 per cent of families in areas classified as not poor. SNCC has been working with local residents in Arkansas, Alabama, and Mississippi to achieve control by the poor of the program and its funds; it has also been working with groups in the North, and the struggle is no less difficult. Behind it all is a federal government which cares far more about winning the war on the Vietnamese than the war on poverty; which has put the poverty program in the hands of self-serving politicians and bureaucrats rather than the poor themselves; which is unwilling to curb the misuse of white power but quick to condemn black power.

To most whites, black power seems to mean that the Mau Mau are coming to the suburbs at night. The Mau Mau are coming, and whites must stop them. Articles appear about plots to "get Whitey," creating an atmosphere in which "law and order must be maintained." Once again, responsibility is shifted from the oppressor to the oppressed. Other whites chide, "Don't forget—you're only 10 per cent of the population; if you get too smart, we'll wipe you out." If they are liberals, they complain, "what about me?—don't you want my help any more?" These are people supposedly concerned about black Americans, but today they think first of themselves, of their feelings of rejection. Or they admonish, "you can't get anywhere without coalitions," without considering the problems of coalition with whom?; on what terms? (coalescing from weakness can mean absorption, betrayal); when? Or they accuse us of "polarizing the races" by our calls for black unity, when the true responsibility for polarization lies with whites who will not accept their responsibility as the majority power for making the democratic process work.

White America will not face the problem of color, the reality of it. The well-intended say: "We're all human, everybody is really decent, we must forget color." But color cannot be "forgotten" until its weight is recognized and dealt with. White America will not acknowledge that the ways in which this country sees itself are contradicted by being black—and always have been. Whereas most of the people who settled this country came here for freedom or for economic opportunity, blacks were brought here to be slaves. When the Lowndes County Freedom Organization chose the black panther as its symbol, it was christened by the press "the Black Panther Party"—but the Alabama Democratic Party, whose symbol is a rooster, has never been called the White Cock Party. No one ever talked about "white power" because power in this country is white. All this adds up to more than merely identifying a group phenomenon by some catchy name or adjective. The furor over that black panther reveals the problems that white America has with color and sex; the furor over "black power" reveals how deep racism runs and the great fear which is attached to it.

Whites will not see that I, for example, as a person oppressed because of my blackness, have common cause with other blacks who are oppressed because of blackness. This is not to say that there are no white people who see things as I do, but that it is black people I must speak to first. It must be the oppressed to whom SNCC addresses itself primarily, not to friends from the oppressing group.

From birth, black people are told a set of lies about themselves. We are told that we are lazy—yet I drive through the Delta area of Mississippi and watch black people picking cotton in the hot sun for fourteen hours. We are told, "if you work hard you'll succeed"—but if that were true, black people would own this country. We are oppressed because we are black—not because we are ignorant, not because we are lazy, not because we're stupid (and got good rhythm), but because we're black.

I remember that when I was a boy, I used to go to see Tarzan movies on Saturday. White Tarzan used to beat up the black natives. I would sit there yelling, "Kill the beasts, kill the savages, kill 'em!" I was saying: Kill *me*. It was as if a Jewish boy watched Nazis taking Jews off to concentration camps and cheered them on. Today, I want the chief to beat hell out of Tarzan and send him back to Europe. But it takes time to become free of the lies and their shaming effect on black minds. It takes time to reject the most important lie: that black people inherently can't do the same things white people can do, unless white people help them.

The need for psychological equality is the reason why SNCC today believes that blacks must organize in the black community. Only black people can convey the revolutionary idea that black people are able to do things themselves. Only they can help create in the community an aroused and continuing black consciousness that will provide the basis for political strength. In the past, white allies have furthered white supremacy without the whites involved realizing it—or wanting it, I think. Black people must do things for themselves; they must get poverty money they will control and spend themselves, they must conduct tutorial programs themselves so that black children can identify with black people. This is one reason Africa has such importance: The reality of black men ruling their own nations gives blacks elsewhere a sense of possibility, of power, which they do not now have.

This does not mean we don't welcome help, or friends. But we want the right to decide whether anyone is, in fact, our friend. In the past, black Americans have been almost the only people whom everybody and his momma could jump up and call their friends. We have been tokens, symbols, objects—as I was in high school to many young whites, who liked having "a Negro friend." We want to decide who is our friend, and we will not accept someone who comes to us and says: "If you do X, Y, and Z, then I'll help you." We will not be told whom we should choose as allies. We will not be isolated from any group or nation except by our own choice. We cannot have the oppressors telling the oppressed how to rid themselves of the oppressor.

I have said that most liberal whites react to "black power" with the question, What about me?, rather than saying: Tell me what you want me to do and I'll see if I can do it. There are answers to the right question. One of the most disturbing things about almost all white supporters of the movement has been that they are afraid to go into their own communities—which is where the racism exists—and work to get rid of it. They want to run from Berkeley to tell us what to do in Mississippi; let them look instead at Berkeley. They admonish blacks to be nonviolent; let them preach nonviolence in the white community. They come to teach me Negro history; let them go to the suburbs and open up freedom schools for whites. Let them work to stop America's racist foreign policy; let them press this government to cease supporting the economy of South Africa.

There is a vital job to be done among poor whites. We hope to see, eventually, a coalition between poor blacks and poor whites. That is the only coalition which seems acceptable to us, and we see such a coalition as the major internal instrument of change in American society. SNCC has tried several times to organize poor whites; we are trying again now, with an initial training program in Tennessee. It is purely academic today to talk about bringing poor blacks and whites together, but the job of creating a poor-white power bloc must be attempted. The main responsibility for it falls upon whites. Black and white can work together in the white community where possible; it is not possible, however, to go into a poor Southern town and talk about integration. Poor whites everywhere are becoming more hostile—not less—partly because they see the nation's attention focused on black poverty and nobody coming to them. Too many young middle-class Americans, like some sort of Pepsi generation, have wanted to come alive through the black community; they've wanted to be where the action is—and the action has been in the black community.

Black people do not want to "take over" this country. They don't want to "get whitey"; they just want to get him off their backs, as the saying goes. It was for example the exploitation by Jewish landlords and merchants which first created black resentment toward Jews—not Judaism. The white man is irrelevant to blacks, except as an oppressive force. Blacks want to be in his place, yes, but not in order to terrorize and lynch and starve him. They want to be in his place because that is where a decent life can be had.

But our vision is not merely of a society in which all black men have enough to buy the good things of life. When we urge that black money go into black pockets, we mean the communal pocket. We want to see money go back into the community and used to benefit it. We want to see the cooperative concept applied in business and banking. We want to see black ghetto residents demand that an exploiting landlord or store-keeper sell them, at minimal cost, a building or a shop that they will own and improve cooperatively; they can back their demand with a rent strike, or a boycott, and a community so unified behind them that no one else will move into the building or buy at the store. The society we seek to build among black people, then, is not a capitalist one. It is a society in which the spirit of community and humanistic love prevail. The word love is suspect; black expectations of what it might produce have been betrayed too often. But those were expectations of a response from the white community, which failed us. The love we seek to encourage is within the black community, the only American community where men call each other "brother" when they meet. We can build a community of love only where we have the ability and power to do so: among blacks.

As for white America, perhaps it can stop crying out against "black supremacy," "black nationalism," "racism in reverse," and begin facing reality. The reality is that this nation, from top to bottom, is racist; that racism is not primarily a problem of "human relations" but of an exploi-tation maintained—either actively or through silence—by the society as a whole. Camus and Sartre have asked, can a man condemn himself? Can whites, particularly liberal whites, condemn themselves? Can they stop blaming us, and blame their own system? Are they capable of the shame which might become a revolutionary emotion?

We have found that they usually cannot condemn themselves, and so we have done it. But the rebuilding of this society, if at all possible, is basically the responsibility of whites—not blacks. We won't fight to save the present society, in Vietnam or anywhere else. We are just going to work, in the way *we* see fit, and on goals *we* define, not for civil rights but for all our human rights.

*Christ Carrying the Cross, Ghent* (detail) by Hieronymous Bosch (Musée Royaux des Beaux-Arts de Beligique)

# MANCHILD IN
# THE PROMISED LAND

## Claude Brown

"Run!"

Where?

Oh, hell! Let's get out of here!

"Turk! Turk! I'm shot!"

I could hear Turk's voice calling from a far distance, telling me not to go into the fish-and-chips joint. I heard, but I didn't understand. The only thing I knew was that I was going to die.

I ran. There was a bullet in me trying to take my life, all thirteen years of it.

I climbed up on the bar yelling, "Walsh, I'm shot. I'm shot." I could feel the blood running down my leg. Walsh, the fellow who operated the fish-and-chips joint, pushed me off the bar and onto the floor. I couldn't move now, but I was still completely conscious.

Walsh was saying, "Git outta here, kid. I ain't got no time to play."

A woman was screaming, mumbling something about the Lord, and saying, "Somebody done shot that poor child."

Mama ran in. She jumped up and down, screaming like a crazy woman. I began to think about dying. The worst part of dying was thinking about the things and the people that I'd never see again. As I lay there trying to imagine what being dead was like, the policeman who had been trying to control Mama gave up and bent over me. He asked who had shot me. Before I could answer, he was asking me if I could hear him. I told him that I didn't know who had shot me and would he please tell Mama to stop jumping up and down. Every time Mama came down on that shabby floor, the bullet lodged in my stomach felt like a hot poker.

Another policeman had come in and was struggling to keep the crowd outside. I could see Turk in the front of the crowd. Before the cops came, he asked me if I was going to tell them that he was with me. I never answered. I looked at him and wondered if he saw who shot me. Then his question began to ring in my head: "Sonny, you gonna tell 'em I was with you?" I was bleeding on a dirty floor in a fish-and-chips joint, and Turk was standing there in the doorway hoping that I would die before I could tell the cops that he was with me. Not once did Turk ask me how I felt.

Hell, yeah, I thought, I'm gonna tell 'em.

It seemed like hours had passed before the ambulance finally arrived. Mama wanted to go to the hospital with me, but the ambulance attendant said she was too excited. On the way to Harlem Hospital, the cop who was riding with us asked Dad what he had to say. His answer was typical: "I told him about hanging out with those bad-ass boys." The cop was a little surprised. This must be a rookie, I thought.

The next day, Mama was at my bedside telling me that she had prayed and the Lord had told her that I was going to live. Mama said that many of my friends wanted to donate some blood for me, but the hospital would not accept it from narcotics users.

This was one of the worst situations I had ever been in. There was a tube in my nose that went all the way to the pit of my stomach. I was being fed intravenously, and there was a drain in my side. Everybody came to visit me, mainly out of curiosity. The girls were all anxious to know where I had gotten shot. They had heard all kinds of tales about where the bullet struck. The bolder ones wouldn't even bother to ask: they just snatched the cover off me and looked for themselves. In a few days, the word got around that I was in one piece.

On my fourth day in the hospital, I was awakened by a male nurse at about 3 A.M. When he said hello in a very ladyish voice, I thought that he had come to the wrong bed by mistake. After identifying himself, he told me that he had helped Dr. Freeman save my life. The next thing he said, which I didn't understand, had something to do with the hours he had put in working that day. He went on mumbling something about how tired he was and ended up asking me to rub his back. I had already told him that I was grateful to him for helping the doctor save my life. While I rubbed his back above the beltline, he kept pushing my hand down and saying, "Lower, like you are really grateful to me." I told him that I was sleepy from the needle a nurse had given me. He asked me to pat his behind. After I had done this, he left.

The next day when the fellows came to visit me, I told them about my early-morning visitor. Dunny said he would like to meet him. Tito joked about being able to get a dose of clap in the hospital. The guy with the tired back never showed up again, so the fellows never got a chance to meet him. Some of them were disappointed.

After I had been in the hospital for about a week, I was visited by another character. I had noticed a woman visiting one of the patients on the far side of the ward. She was around fifty-five years old, short and fat, and she was wearing old-lady shoes. While I wondered who this woman was, she started across the room in my direction. After she had introduced herself, she told me that she was visiting her son. Her son had been stabbed in the chest with an ice pick by his wife. She said that his left lung had been punctured, but he was doing fine now, and that Jesus was so-o-o good.

Her name was Mrs. Ganey, and she lived on 145th Street. She said my getting shot when I did "was the work of the Lord." My gang had been stealing sheets and bedspreads off clotheslines for months before I had gotten shot. I asked this godly woman why she thought it was the work of the Lord or Jesus or whoever. She began in a sermonlike tone, saying, "Son, people was gitting tired-a y'all stealing all dey sheets and spreads," She said that on the night that I had gotten shot, she baited her clothesline with two brand-new bedspreads, turned out all the lights in the apartment, and sat at the kitchen window waiting for us to show.

She waited with a double-barreled shotgun.

The godly woman said that most of our victims thought that we were winos or dope fiends and that most of them had vowed to kill us, At the end of the sermon, the godly woman said, "Thank the Lord I didn't shoot nobody's child." When the godly woman had finally departed, I thought, Thank the Lord for taking her away from my bed.

Later on that night, I was feeling a lot of pain and couldn't get to sleep. A nurse who had heard me moaning and groaning came over and gave me a shot of morphine. Less than twenty minutes later, I was deep into a nightmare.

I was back in the fish-and-chips joint, lying on the floor dying. Only, now I was in more pain than before, and there were dozens of Mamas around me jumping up and screaming. I could feel myself dying in a rising pool of blood. The higher the blood rose the more I died.

I dreamt about the boy who Rock and big Stoop had thrown off that roof on 149th Street. None of us had stayed around to see him hit the ground, but I just knew that he died in a pool of blood too. I wished that he would stop screaming, and I wished that Mama would stop screaming. I wished they would let me die quietly.

. . .

I dreamt about waking up in the middle of the night seven years before and thinking that the Germans or the Japs had come and that the loud noises I heard were bombs falling. Running into Mama's room, I squeezed in between her and Dad at the front window. Thinking that we were watching an air raid, I asked Dad where the sirens were and why the street lights were on. He said, "This ain't no air raid—just a whole lotta niggers gone fool. And git the hell back in that bed!" I went back to bed, but I couldn't go to sleep. The loud screams in the street and the crashing sound of falling plate-glass windows kept me awake for hours. While I listened to the noise, I imagined bombs falling and people running through the streets screaming. I could see mothers running with babies in their arms, grown men running over women and children to save their own lives, and the Japs stabbing babies with bayonets, just like in the movies. I thought, Boy, I sure wish I was out there. I bet the Stinky brothers are out there. Danny and Butch are probably out there having all the fun in the world.

The next day, I was running out of the house without underwear or socks on, I could hear Mama yelling, "Boy, come back here and put a hat or something on your head!" When I reached the stoop, I was knocked back into the hall by a big man carrying a ham under his coat. While I looked up at him, wondering what was going on, he reached down with one hand and snatched me up, still holding the ham under his coat with his other hand. He stood me up against a wall and ran into the hall with his ham. Before I had a chance to move, other men came running through the hall carrying cases of whiskey, sacks of flour, and cartons of cigarettes. Just as I unglued myself from the wall and started out the door for the second time, I was bowled over again. This time by a cop with a gun in his hand. He never stopped, but after he had gone a couple of yards into the hall, I heard him say, "Look out, kid." On the third try, I got out of the building. But I wasn't sure that this was my street. None of the stores had any windows left, and glass was everywhere. It seemed that all the cops in the world were on 145th Street and Eighth Avenue that day. The cops were telling everybody to move on, and everybody was talking about the riot. I went over to a cop and asked him what a riot was. He told me to go on home. The next cop I asked told me that a riot was what had happened the night before. Putting two and two together I decided that a riot was "a whole lotta niggers gone fool."

I went around the corner to Butch's house. After I convinced him that I was alone, he opened the door. He said that Kid and Danny were in the kitchen. I saw Kid sitting on the floor with his hand stuck way down in a gallon jar of pickled pigs' ears. Danny was cooking some bacon at the stove, and Butch was busy hiding stuff. It looked as though these guys had stolen a whole grocery store. While I joined the feast, they took turns telling me about the riot. Danny and Kid hadn't gone home the night before; they were out following the crowds and looting.

My only regret was that I had missed the excitement. I said, "Why don't we have another riot tonight? Then Butch and me can get in it."

Danny said that there were too many cops around to have a riot now. Butch said that they had eaten up all the bread and that he was going to steal some more. I asked if I could come along with him, and he said that I could if I promised to do nothing but watch. I promised, but we both knew that I was lying.

When we got to the street, Butch said he wanted to go across the street and look at the pawnshop. I tagged along. Like many of the stores where the rioters had been, the pawnshop had been set afire. The firemen had torn down a sidewall getting at the fire. So Butch and I just walked in where the wall used to be. Everything I picked up was broken or burned or both. My feet kept sinking into the wet furs that had been burned and drenched. The whole place smelled of smoke and was as dirty as a Harlem gutter on a rainy day. The cop out front yelled to us to get out of there. He only had to say it once.

After stopping by the seafood joint and stealing some shrimp and oysters, we went to what was left of Mr. Gordon's grocery store. Butch just walked in, picked up a loaf of bread, and walked out. He told me to come on, but I ignored him and went into the grocery store instead. I picked up two loaves of bread and walked out. When I got outside, a cop looked at me, and I ran into a building and through the backyard to Butch's house. Running through the backyard, I lost all the oysters that I had; when I reached Butch's house, I had only two loaves of bread and two shrimp in my pocket.

Danny, who was doing most of the cooking, went into the street to steal something to drink. Danny, Butch, and Kid were ten years old, four years older than I. Butch was busy making sandwiches on the floor, and Kid was trying to slice up a loaf of bologna. I had never eaten shrimp, but nobody seemed to care, because they refused to cook it for me. I told Butch that I was going to cook it myself. He said that there was no more lard in the house and that I would need some grease.

I looked around the house until I came up with some Vaseline hair pomade. I put the shrimp in the frying pan with the hair grease, waited until they had gotten black and were smoking, then took them out and made a sandwich. A few years later, I found out that shrimp were supposed to be shelled before cooking. I ate half of the sandwich and hated shrimp for years afterward.

The soft hand tapping on my face to wake me up was Jackie's. She and Della had been to a New Year's Eve party. Jackie wanted to come by the hospital and kiss me at midnight. This was the only time in my life that I ever admitted being glad to see Jackie. I asked them about the party, hoping that they would stay and talk to me for a while. I was afraid that if I went back to sleep, I would have another bad dream.

The next thing I knew, a nurse was waking me up for breakfast. I didn't recall saying good night to Jackie and Della, so I must have fallen asleep while they were talking to me. I thought about Sugar, how nice she was, and how she was a real friend. I knew she wanted to be my girl friend, and I liked her a lot. But what would everybody say if I had a buck-toothed girl friend. I remembered Knoxie asking me how I kissed her. That question led to the first fight I'd had with Knoxie in years. No, I couldn't let Sugar be my girl. It was hard enough having her as a friend.

The next day, I asked the nurse why she hadn't changed my bed linen, and she said because they were evicting me. I had been in the hospital for eleven days, but I wasn't ready to go home. I left the hospital on January 2 and went to a convalescent home in Valhalla, New York. After I had been there for three weeks, the activity director took me aside and told me that I was going to New York City to see a judge and that I might be coming back. The following morning, I left to see that judge, but I never got back to Valhalla.

I stood there before Judge Pankin looking solemn and lying like a professional. I thought that he looked too nice to be a judge. A half hour after I had walked into the courtroom, Judge Pankin was telling me that he was sending me to the New York State Training School for Boys. The judge said that he thought I was a chronic liar and that he hoped I would be a better boy when I came out. I asked him if he wanted me to thank him. Mama stopped crying just long enough to say, "Hush your mouth, boy."

Mama tried to change the judge's mind by telling him that I had already been to Wiltwyck School for Boys for two and a half years. And before that, I had been ordered out of the state for at least one year. She said that I had been away from my family too much; that was why I was always getting into trouble.

The judge told Mama that he knew what he was doing and that one day she would be grateful to him for doing it.

I had been sent away before, but this was the first time I was ever afraid to go. When Mama came up to the detention room in Children's Court, I tried to act as though I wasn't afraid. After I told her that Warwick and where I was going were one and the same, Mama began to cry, and so did I.

Most of the guys I knew had been to Warwick and were too old to go back. I knew that there were many guys up there I had mistreated. The Stinky brothers were up there. They thought that I was one of the guys who had pulled a train on their sister in the park the summer before. Bumpy from 144th Street was up there. I had shot him in the leg with a zip gun in a rumble only a few months earlier. There were many guys up there I used to bully on the streets and at Wiltwyck, guys I had sold tea leaves to as pot. There were rival gang members up there who just hated my name. All of these guys were waiting for me to show. The word was out that I couldn't fight any more—that I had slowed down since I was shot and that a good punch to the stomach would put my name in the undertaker's book.

When I got to the Youth House, I tried to find out who was up at Warwick that I might know. Nobody knew any of the names I asked about. I knew that if I went up to Warwick in my condition, I'd never live to get out. I had a reputation for being a rugged little guy. This meant that I would have at least a half-dozen fights in the first week of my stay up there.

It seemed the best thing for me to do was to cop out on the nut. For the next two nights, I woke up screaming and banging on the walls. On the third day, I was sent to Bellevue for observation. This meant that I wouldn't be going to Warwick for at least twenty-eight days.

While I was in Bellevue, the fellows would come down and pass notes to me through the doors. Tito and Turk said they would get bagged and sent to Warwick by the time I got there. They were both bagged a week later for smoking pot in front of the police station. They were both sent to Bellevue. Two weeks after they showed, I went home. The judge still wanted to send me to Warwick, but Warwick had a full house, so he sent me home for two weeks.

The day before I went back into court, I ran into Turk, who had just gotten out of Bellevue. Tito had been sent to Warwick, but Turk had gotten a walk because his sheet wasn't too bad. I told him I would probably be sent to Warwick the next day. Turk said he had run into Bucky in Bellevue. He told me that he and Tito had voted Bucky out of the clique. I told him that I wasn't going for it because Bucky was my man from short-pants days. Turk said he liked him too, but what else could he do after Bucky had let a white boy beat him in the nutbox? When I heard this, there was nothing I could do but agree with Turk. Bucky had to go. That kind of news spread fast, and who wanted to be in a clique with a stud who let a paddy boy beat him?

# LATE AT THE BEACH

## G. W.

Look out of yourselves,
Men of this world,
Look out into the sun.

There you will see
What idea of Eden
and of Eden lost, tossed
against an eternity of
Sea-Mountains, means.

There into the late evening sun
You will see
All Bodies the Black
Against the Sun,
and your petty distinctions,
setting one against one,
Will dis-appear
against the setting of the Sun.

# OLD MYTHS
# AND
# NEW REALITIES

## Senator J. William Fulbright

## CONCLUSION

Of all the myths that have troubled the lives of modern nations the most pervading have been those associated with the nation itself. Nationalism, which is pre-eminently a state of mind rather than a state of nature, has become a dominant and universal state of mind in the twentieth century.[1] Designating the sovereign nation-state as the ultimate object of individual loyalty and obligation, the idea of nationalism prevails in every region of the world, in rich nations as well as poor nations, in democracies as well as dictatorships. Nationalism, I believe, is the most powerful single force in the world politics of the twentieth century, more powerful than communism or democracy or any other system of ideas about social organization.

It is also the most dangerous. Dividing communities against one another, it has become a universal force at precisely the time in history when technology has made the world a single unit in the physical sense—interdependent for economic, political, and cultural purposes and profoundly interdependent for survival in the nuclear age. Having for many centuries represented a broadening of human loyalties from their family and tribal origins—as indeed it does even today in certain African countries which are still emerging from tribalism—the nation has now become a barrier to the historical process by which men have associated themselves in ever larger political and economic communities. In the face of a compelling need for broader associations, nationalism sets both great and small na-

[1] *See* Hans Kohn, *The Idea of Nationalism* (New York: Macmillan, 1944).

tions against one another, to their vast peril and at an enormous price in the welfare and happiness of their people.

"How," asked a seventeenth-century French historian, "does it serve the people and add to their happiness if their ruler extends his empire by annexing the provinces of his enemies; . . . how does it help me or my countrymen that my sovereign be successful and covered with glory, that my country be powerful and dreaded, if, sad and worried, I live in oppression and poverty?" [2]

The question, phrased somewhat differently, is how and why it happens that the groups into which men organize themselves come to be regarded as ends in themselves, as living organisms with needs and preferences of their own which are separate from and superior to those of individuals, warranting, when necessary, the sacrifice of the hopes and pleasures of individual men. One of the paradoxes of politics is that so great a part of our organized efforts as societies is directed toward abstract and mystic goals—towards spreading a faith or ideology, toward enhancing the pride and power and self-respect of the nation, as if the nation had a "self" and a "soul" apart from the individuals who compose it, and as if the wishes of individual men, for life and happiness and prosperity, were selfish and dishonorable and unworthy of our best creative efforts.

Throughout history men have contested causes that had little to do with their own needs and preferences, but until quite recently this tendency, though irrational, has been less than irreparably destructive. Since the invention of nuclear weapons, it has become possible that the great struggles of international politics will bring about the destruction not merely of cities and nations but of much or all of human civilization. This great change has made international politics dangerous as it has never been before, confronting us with the need to ask ourselves whether there are not other causes to be served than the struggle for prestige and power, causes which are closer to human needs and far less likely to lead to nuclear incineration.

Science has radically changed the conditions of human life on earth. It has expanded our knowledge and our power but not our capacity to use them with wisdom. Somehow, if we are to save ourselves, we must find this capacity. We must find in ourselves the judgment and the will to alter the focus of international politics in ways which are at once less dangerous to mankind and more beneficial to individual men. Without deceiving ourselves as to the difficulty of the task, we must try to develop a new capacity for creative political action.

[2] Jean de la Bruyère, *"Du Souverain ou de la République,"* in *Oeuvres Complètes,* Julian Benda, Ed., Bibliothèque de la Pléiade (Paris: Librairie Gallimard, 1951), Vol. 23, pp. 302–303.

"If to do were as easy to know what were good to do," wrote Shakespeare, "chapels had been churches, and poor men's cottages princes' palaces." [3] The task of altering the character of international politics is of course infinitely more difficult than acknowledging the need to do so, and that is difficult enough. But if we are very clear about the difficulties of change, about how change occurs in human affairs and how it does not occur, then perhaps we can begin to alter the passions and prejudices that lead nations into wars as well as the weapons with which they fight them. We must recognize, first of all, that the ultimate source of war and peace lies in human nature and that nothing is more difficult to change than the human mind. "Even given the freest scope by their institutions," wrote Ruth Benedict, "men are never inventive enough to make more than minute changes. From the point of view of an outsider the most radical innovations in any culture amount to no more than a minor revision." [4]

To recognize the difficulty of change is to recognize its possibility as well. Those who are sanguine about the power of reason to reshape human attitudes are soon disillusioned and driven to a pessimism which is no less erroneous than the false optimism with which they began. The beginning of wisdom, I think, is to understand that, difficult as it is, it is yet possible to alter human attitudes, and that to do so, to however slight a degree, is to shape the course of human events.

Some years ago a group of eight distinguished psychologists and social scientists issued a statement on the causes of nationalistic aggression and the conditions necessary for international understanding. They stated in part:

> To the best of our knowledge, there is no evidence to indicate that wars are necessary and inevitable consequences of 'human nature' as such. While men vary greatly in their capacities and temperaments, we believe there are vital needs common to all men which must be fulfilled in order to establish and maintain peace: men everywhere want to be free from hunger and disease, from insecurity and fear; men everywhere want fellowship and the respect of their fellow men; the chance for personal growth and development. [5]

If conflict and war are not indigenous to our nature, why, we may ask, are they so prevalent? "The crux of the matter," writes social psychologist Gordon Allport, "lies in the fact that while most people deplore war, they nonetheless *expect* it to continue. *And what people expect determines their behavior. . . .* the indispensable condition of war," says Professor All-

---

[3] Portia in *The Merchant of Venice,* Act I, Scene ii.

[4] Ruth Benedict, *Patterns of Culture* (New York: Penguin Books, 1946), p. 76.

[5] Hadley Cantril, Ed., *Tensions That Cause Wars* (Urbana: University of Illinois Press, 1950), pp. 17–18.

port, "is that people must *expect* war and must prepare for war, before, under warminded leadership, they make war. It is in this sense that 'wars begin in the minds of men.' " [6]

This being so, there can be no "normal equivalent of war"—that is to say, a harmless outlet for aggression—because men are not endowed with a fixed reservoir of aggression which can be released through some "safety valve" and thus expended. Aggression is rather a habit, which feeds upon itself by building the expectancy that, once tried successfully, it will solve other problems as well. "If wars were simply a relief from tension," writes Professor Allport, "they might conceivably have their justification. But experience shows that not only does one war engender another, but it brings fierce domestic postwar strain and conflict into the *nation itself*." [7]

This is precisely what has happened in the twentieth century. Crisis has fed upon crisis and each conflict has generated the *expectancy* of another. Meanwhile, the development of nuclear weapons and rockets has created the technological means of destroying, or virtually destroying, civilization. It follows quite obviously that the alteration of deeply rooted human attitudes, that is to say, the reshaping of the fatal expectancy of war, is the foremost requirement of statesmanship in the twentieth century.

We must generate expectancies of peace as powerful and self-generating as the expectancy of war. We must learn to deal with our adversaries in terms of the *needs* and *hopes* of both sides rather than the demands of one side upon the other. We must remove stridency and bad manners from our diplomacy, because the language of the ultimatum is the language of conflict, because there is no way more certain to turn tension into open conflict than to strike at an adversary's pride and self-respect.

We must strive, in the face of unprecedented need, toward unprecedented acts of political creativity. In one direction, we must move toward broadening forms of association more nearly appropriate to the interdependence of the world than the sovereign nation-state—and as we progress toward a broader world community, we must be prepared to encounter more than a few "unthinkable thoughts." In the other direction, we must turn a substantially greater proportion of our collective energies to the welfare of individuals—to the education and employment of our citizens, to creating societies in which the individual is encouraged and assisted in his striving for personal fulfillment.

It is the nation, or more exactly the pervading force of nationalism, that now obstructs our progress in both of these directions. Posing barriers between communities and exacting heavy sacrifices from its citizens to pursue the quarrels which these barriers engender, the sovereign nation itself is

---

[6] Gordon W. Allport, "The Role of Expectancy," *ibid.,* pp. 43, 48.
[7] *Ibid.,* p. 52.

the most pervasive of the old myths that blind us to the realities of our time. Only when we have broken out of the constraints of nationalist mythology will the way be open to the only possible security in the nuclear age—the security of an international community in which men will be free of the terror of the bomb and free at last to pursue the satisfactions of personal fulfillment in civilized societies. We must broaden the frontiers of our loyalties, never forgetting as we do so that it is the human individual, and not the state or any other community, in whom ultimate sovereignty is vested.

# ALL ALONG
# THE WATCH TOWER

## Bob Dylan

"There must be some way out of here,"
Said the Joker to the Thief.
"There's too much confusion
I can't get no relief.

"Businessmen they drink my wine
Plowmen dig my earth.
None of them along the line
Know what any of it is worth."

"No reason to get excited,"
The Thief he kindly spoke.
"There are many here among us
Who feel that life is but a joke.

"But you and I, we've been through that
And this is not our fate.
So let us not talk falsely now
The hour is getting late."

All along the Watch Tower
Princes kept the view
While all the women came and went,
Barefoot servants too.

Outside in the distance
A wild cat did growl;
Two riders were approaching;
The wind began to howl.

# THE SECOND COMING

## William Butler Yeats

Turning and turning in the widening gyre
The falcon cannot hear the falconer;
Things fall apart; the centre cannot hold;
Mere anarchy is loosed upon the world,
The blood-dimmed tide is loosed, and everywhere
The ceremony of innocence is drowned;
The best lack all conviction, while the worst
Are full of passionate intensity.

Surely some revelation is at hand;
Surely the Second Coming is at hand.
The Second Coming! Hardly are those words out
When a vast image out of *Spiritus Mundi*
Troubles my sight: somewhere in sands of the desert
A shape with lion body and the head of a man,
A gaze blank and pitiless as the sun,
Is moving its slow thighs, while all about it
Reel shadows of the indignant desert birds.
The darkness drops again; but now I know
That twenty centuries of stony sleep
Were vexed to nightmare by a rocking cradle,
And what rough beast, its hour come round at last,
Slouches toward Bethlehem to be born?

*"There he hath lain for
ages, and will lie
Battening upon huge sea
worms in his sleep."*

*Alfred, Lord Tennyson*

# VI
# THE
# NECESSITY
# OF MYTH

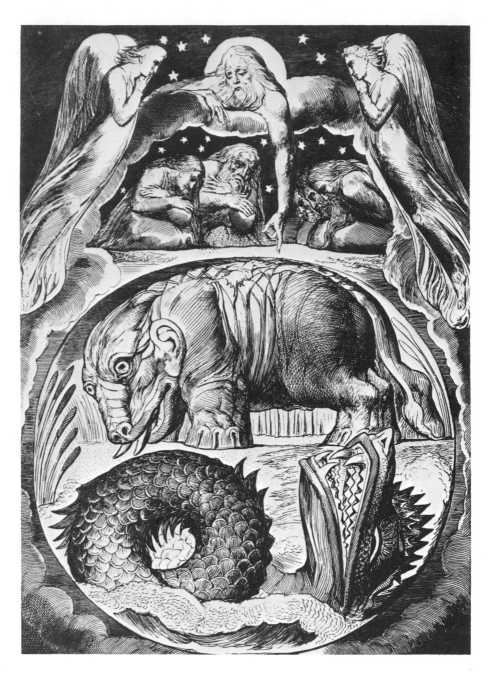

*Behold Now Behemoth* by William Blake (By permission of The Huntington Library, San Marino, California)

# MYTH

## William Flint Thrall
## and Addison Hibbard

MYTH. Anonymous stories having their roots in the primitive folk-beliefs of races or nations and presenting supernatural episodes as a means of interpreting natural events in an effort to make concrete and particular a special perception of man or a cosmic view. *Myths* differ from LEGENDS in that they have less of historical background and more of the supernatural; they differ from the FABLE in that they are less concerned with moral didacticism and are the product of a racial group rather than the creation of an individual. Every country and literature has its mythology; the best known to English readers being the Greek, Roman, and Norse. But the mythology of all groups takes shape around certain common themes; they all attempt to explain the creation, divinity, and religion, to guess at the meaning of existence and death, to account for natural phenomena, and to chronicle the adventures of racial heroes.

They also have a startlingly similar group of MOTIFS, characters, and actions, as a number of students of *myth* and religion, particularly Sir James Frazer, have pointed out. Although there was a time when *myth* was a virtual synonym for error, notably in the NEO-CLASSIC PERIOD, the tendency today is to see *myths* as dramatic or narrative embodiments of a people's perception of the deepest truths. Various modern writers have insisted on the necessity of *myth* as a material with which the artist works, and in varying ways and degrees have appropriated the old *myths* or created new ones as necessary substances to give order and a frame of meaning to their personal perceptions and images; notable among such

Reprinted from William Flint Thrall and Addison Hibbard, *A Handbook to Literature,* revised and enlarged by C. Hugh Holman, by permission of The Odyssey Press, Inc.

"mythmakers" have been William Blake, W. B. Yeats, T. S. Eliot (particularly in *The Waste Land*), James Joyce, and Wallace Stevens.

Since the introduction of Jung's concept of the "racial unconscious" and of Ernst Cassirer's theories of language and *myth,* contemporary critics have found in the *myth* a useful device for examining literature. There is a type of imagination, Philip Wheelwright insists, that can properly be called "the Archetypal Imagination, which sees the particular object as embodying and adumbrating suggestions of universality." The possessors of such imagination arrange their works in archetypal patterns, and present us with narratives which stir us as "something at once familiar and strange." They thus give concrete expression to something deep and primitive in us all. Thus those critics—and they are many—who approach literature as *myth* see in it vestiges of primordial ritual and ceremony, or the repository of racial memories, or a structure of unconsciously held value systems, or an expression of the general beliefs of a race, social class or nation, or a unique embodiment of a cosmic view. One significant difference should be noted, however; *myth* in its traditional sense is an anonymous, nonliterary, essentially religious formulation of the cosmic view of a people who approach its formulations not as representations of truth but as truth itself; *myth* in the sophisticated literary sense in which it is currently used is the intelligible and often self-conscious use of such primitive methods to express something deeply felt by the individual artist which will, he hopes, prove to have universal responses. The MYTHOPOEIC poet attempts to return to the role of the prophet-seer, by creating a *myth* which strikes resonant points in the minds of his readers and speaks with something of the authority of the old *myths.*

# THE KRAKEN

## Alfred, Lord Tennyson

Below the thunders of the upper deep,
Far, far beneath in the abysmal sea,
His ancient, dreamless, uninvaded sleep
The Kraken sleepeth: faintest sunlights flee
About his shadowy sides; above him swell
Huge sponges of millennial growth and height;
And far away into the sickly light,
From many a wondrous grot and secret cell
Unnumber'd and enormous polypi
Winnow with giant arms the slumbering green.
There hath he lain for ages, and will lie
Battening upon huge sea-worms in his sleep,
Until the latter fire shall heat the deep;
Then once by man and angels to be seen,
In roaring he shall rise and on the surface die.

# from AION

## Carl G. Jung

### III. THE SYZYGY:[1] ANIMA AND ANIMUS

What, then, is this projection-making factor? The East calls it the "Spinning Woman"—Maya, who creates illusion by her dancing. Had we not long since known it from the symbolism of dreams, this hint from the Orient would put us on the right track: the enveloping, embracing, and devouring element points unmistakably to the mother,[2] that is, to the son's relation to the real mother, to her imago, and to the woman who is to become a mother for him. His Eros is passive like a child's; he hopes to be caught, sucked in, enveloped, and devoured. He seeks, as it were, the protecting, nourishing, charmed circle of the mother, the condition of the infant released from every care, in which the outside world bends over him and even forces happiness upon him. No wonder the real world vanishes from sight!

If this situation is dramatized, as the unconscious usually dramatizes it, then there appears before you on the psychological stage a man living regressively, seeking his childhood and his mother, fleeing from a cold cruel world which denies him understanding. Not infrequently a mother appears beside him who apparently shows not the slightest concern that her little son should become a man, but who, with tireless and self-immolating effort, neglects nothing that might hinder him from growing up and marrying. You

From *The Collected Works of C. G. Jung,* ed. by G. Adler, M. Fordham, and H. Read, trans. by R.F.C. Hull, Bollingen Series XX, vol. 911, *Aion* (copyright © 1959 by Princeton University Press), pp. 11–14, 23–24, 30–38. Reprinted by permission of Princeton University Press.

[1] Syzygy; syzygia: a joining together, conjunction.

[2] Here and in what follows, the word "mother" is not meant in the literal sense but as a symbol of everything that functions as a mother.

behold the secret conspiracy between mother and son, and how each helps the other to betray life.

Where does the guilt lie? With the mother, or with the son? Probably with both. The unsatisfied longing of the son for life and the world ought to be taken seriously. There is in him a desire to touch reality, to embrace the earth and fructify the field of the world. But he makes no more than a series of impatient beginnings, for his initiative as well as his staying power are crippled by the secret memory that the world and happiness may be had as a gift—from the mother. It makes demands on the masculinity of a man, on his ardor, above all on his courage and resolution, when it comes to throwing his whole being into the scales. For this he would need a faithless Eros, one capable of forgetting the mother and of hurting himself by deserting the first love of his life. The mother, foreseeing this danger, has carefully inculcated into him the virtues of faithfulness, devotion, loyalty, so as to protect him from the moral disruption which is the risk of every life adventure. He has learned these lessons only too well, and remains true to his mother, perhaps causing her the deepest anxiety (when, in her honor, he turns out to be a homosexual, for example) and at the same time affords her an unconscious satisfaction of a mythological nature, for in the relationship now reigning between them, there is consummated the immemorial and most sacred archetype of the marriage of mother and son.

At this level of the myth, which probably illustrates the nature of the collective unconscious better than any other, the mother is both old and young, Demeter and Persephone, and the son is spouse and sleeping infant all in one. The imperfections of real life, with its laborious adaptations and manifold disappointments, naturally cannot compete with such a state of indescribable fulfillment.

. . .

The projection-making factor is the anima, or rather the unconscious as represented by the anima. Whenever she appears, in dreams, visions, and fantasies, she takes on personified form, thus demonstrating that the factor she embodies possesses all the outstanding characteristics of a feminine being. She is not an invention of the conscious mind, but a spontaneous production of the unconscious. Nor is she a substitute figure for the mother. On the contrary, there is every likelihood that the numinous qualities which make the mother imago so dangerously powerful stem from the collective archetype of the anima, which is incarnated anew in every male child.

Since the anima is an archetype that is manifest in men, it is reasonable to suppose that an equivalent archetype must be present in women; for just as the man is compensated by a feminine element, so woman is compensated by a masculine one. I do not, however, wish this argument to give the impression that these compensatory relationships were arrived at by deduction. On the contrary, long and varied experience was needed in order to grasp the nature of anima and animus empirically. Whatever we have to say about these archetypes, therefore, is either directly verifiable or at least rendered probable by the facts. At the same time, I am fully aware that we are discussing pioneer work which by its very nature can only be provisional.

Just as the mother seems to be the first carrier of the projection-making factor for the son, so is the father for the daughter. Practical experience of these relationships is made up of many individual cases presenting all kinds of variations on the same basic theme. A concise description of them can, therefore, be no more than schematic.

Woman is compensated by a masculine element and therefore her unconscious has, so to speak, a masculine imprint.

.   .   .

## IV.   THE SELF

We shall now turn to the question of whether the increase in self-knowledge resulting from the withdrawal of impersonal projections—in other words, the integration of the contents of the collective unconscious—exerts a specific influence on the ego personality. To the extent that the integrated contents are *parts of the self,* we can expect this influence to be considerable. Their assimilation augments not only the area of the field of consciousness but also the importance of the ego, especially when, as usually happens, the ego lacks any critical approach to the unconscious. In that case it is easily overpowered and becomes identical with the contents that have been assimilated. In this way, for instance, a masculine consciousness comes under the influence of the anima and can even be possessed by her.

I have discussed the wider effects of the integration of unconscious contents elsewhere and can therefore omit going into details here. I should only like to mention that the more numerous and the more significant the unconscious contents which are assimilated to the ego, the closer the approximation of the ego to the self, even though this approximation must be a never-ending process. This inevitably produces an inflation of the *ego,* unless a critical line of demarcation is drawn between it and the unconscious figures. But this act of discrimination yields practical results only if it succeeds in fixing reasonable boundaries to the ego and in granting the figures of the unconscious—the self, anima, animus, and shadow—relative autonomy and reality (of a psychic nature). To psychologize this reality out of existence either is ineffectual or else merely increases the inflation of the ego. One cannot dispose of facts by declaring them unreal. The projection-making factor, for instance, has undeniable reality. Anyone who insists on denying it becomes identical with it, which is not only dubious in itself but a positive danger to the well-being of the individual. Everyone who has dealings with such cases knows how perilous an inflation can be. No more than a flight of steps or a smooth floor is needed to precipitate a fatal fall. Besides the "pride goeth before a fall" motif, there are other factors of a no less disagreeable psychosomatic and psychic nature which serve to reduce inflation. This condition should not be interpreted as one of conscious self-aggrandizement. Such is far from being the rule. In general we are not directly conscious of this condition at all, but can at best infer its existence indirectly from the symptoms. These include the reactions of our immediate environment. Inflation magnifies the blind spot in the eye, and the more we are assimilated by the projection-making factor, the greater becomes the tendency to identify with it. A clear symptom of this is our growing disinclination to take note of the reactions of the environment and pay heed to them.

It must be reckoned a psychic catastrophe when the *ego is assimilated by the self*. The image of wholeness then remains in the unconscious, so that on the one hand it shares the archaic nature of the unconscious and on the other finds itself in the psychically relative space-time continuum that is characteristic of the unconscious as such. Both these qualities are numinous and hence have an unlimited determining effect on ego consciousness, which is differentiated, i.e., separated, from the unconscious and moreover exists in an absolute space and an absolute time. It is a vital necessity that this should be so. If, therefore, the ego falls for any length of time under the control of an unconscious factor, its adaptation is disturbed and the way opened for all sorts of possible accidents.

. . . a content can only be integrated when its double aspect has become conscious and when it is grasped not merely intellectually but understood according to its feeling value. Intellect and feeling, however, are difficult to put into one harness—they conflict with one another by definition. Whoever identifies with an intellectual standpoint will occasionally find his feeling confronting him like an enemy in the guise of the anima; conversely, an intellectual animus will make violent attacks on the feeling standpoint. Therefore, if one wants to bring off the trick not only intellectually but realize the feeling value as well, one must for better or worse come to grips with the anima-animus problem in order to open the way for a higher union, a *coniunctio oppositorum*. This is an indispensable prerequisite for wholeness.

Although "wholeness" seems at first sight to be nothing but an abstract idea (like anima and animus), it is nevertheless empirical in so far as it is anticipated by the psyche in the form of spontaneous or autonomous symbols. These are the quaternity or *mandāla* symbols, which occur not only in the dreams of moderns who have never heard of them, but are widely disseminated in the historical records of many peoples and many epochs. Their significance as *symbols of unity and totality* is amply confirmed by history as well as by empirical psychology. What at first looks like an abstract idea stands in reality for something that exists and can be experienced, that demonstrates its a priori presence spontaneously. Wholeness is thus an objective factor that confronts the subject independently of him, like anima or animus; and just as the latter have a higher position in the hierarchy than the shadow, so wholeness lays claim to a position and a value superior to those of the syzygy. The syzygy seems to be at least an essential part of it, or like the two halves of the totality represented by the royal brother-sister pair, and hence the tension of opposites from which the divine child is born as the symbol of unity.

Unity and totality stand at the highest point on the scale of objective values because their symbols can no longer be distinguished from the *imago Dei*. Hence all statements about the God-image apply also to the empirical symbols of totality. Experience shows that individual *mandālas* are symbols of *order,* and that they occur in patients chiefly during times of psychic disorientation or reorientation. As magic circles they bind and subdue the lawless powers belonging to the world of darkness, and depict or create an order that transforms the chaos into a cosmos. To the conscious mind the *mandāla* appears at first as an unimpressive point or dot, and a great deal of hard and painstaking work as well as the integration of many projections are generally required before the full range of the symbol can be anything like completely understood. If this insight were purely intellectual it could be achieved without much difficulty, for the all-embracing pronouncements about the God within us and above us, about Christ and the *corpus mysticum,* the personal and suprapersonal *atman,* etc., are all formulations that can easily be mastered by the philosophic intellect. This is the common source of the illusion that one is then in possession of the thing itself. But actually one has acquired nothing more than its name, despite the age-old prejudice that the name magically represents the thing, and that it is sufficient to pronounce the name in order to posit the thing's existence In. the course of the millennia the reasoning mind has been given every opportunity to see through the futility of this conceit, though that has done nothing to prevent the intellectual mastery of a thing from being accepted at its face value. It is precisely our experiences in psychology which demonstrate as plainly as could be wished that the intellectual "grasp" of a psychological fact produces no more than a concept of it, and that a concept is no more than a name, a *flatus vocis*. These intellectual counters can be bandied about easily enough. They pass lightly from hand to hand, for they have no weight or substance. They sound full but are hollow; and though purporting to designate a heavy task and obligation, they commit us to nothing. The intellect is undeniably useful in its own field, but is a great cheat and illusionist outside of it whenever it tries to manipulate values.

It would seem that one can pursue any science with the intellect alone except psychology, whose subject—the psyche—has more than the two aspects mediated by sense perception and thinking. The function of value— feeling—is an integral part of our conscious orientation and ought not to be missing in a psychological judgment of any scope; otherwise the model we are trying to build of the real process will be incomplete. Every psychic process has a value quality attached to it, namely, its feeling-tone. This indicates the degree to which the subject is *affected* by the process, or how much it means to him (in so far as the process reaches consciousness at all). It is through the "affect" that the subject becomes involved and so comes to feel the whole weight of reality. The difference amounts roughly to that between a severe illness which one reads about in a textbook and the real illness which one has. In psychology one possesses nothing unless one has experienced it in reality. Hence a purely intellectual insight is not enough, because one knows only the words and not the substance of the thing from inside.

There are far more people who are afraid of the unconscious than one would expect. They are even afraid of their own shadow. And when it comes to the anima and animus, this fear turns to panic. For the syzygy does indeed represent the psychic contents that irrupt into consciousness in a psychosis (most clearly of all in the paranoid forms of schizophenia). The overcoming of this fear is often a moral achievement of unusual magnitude, and yet it is not the only condition that must be fulfilled on the way to a real experience of the self.

The shadow, the syzygy, and the self are psychic factors of which an adequate picture can be formed only on the basis of a fairly thorough experience of them. Just as these concepts arose out of an experience of reality, so they can be elucidated only by further experience. Philosophical criticism will find everything to object to in them unless it begins by recognizing that they are concerned with *facts,* and that the "concept" is simply an abbreviated description or definition of these facts. Such criticism has as little effect on the object as zoological criticism on a duckbill platypus. It is not the concept that matters; the concept is only a word, a counter, and it has meaning and use only because it stands for a certain sum of experience. Unfortunately I cannot pass on this experience to my public. I have tried in a number of publications, with the help of case material, to present the nature of these experiences and also the method of obtaining them. Wherever my methods were really applied the facts I give have been confirmed. One could see the moons of Jupiter even in Galileo's day if one took the trouble to use his telescope.

Outside the narrower field of professional psychology these figures meet with understanding from all who have any knowledge of comparative mythology. They have no difficulty in recognizing the shadow as the adverse representative of the dark chthonic world, a figure whose characteristics are

universal. The syzygy is immediately comprehensible as the psychic proto-
type of all divine couples. Finally the self, on account of its empirical
peculiarities, proves to be the *eidos* behind the supreme ideas of unity and
totality that are inherent in all monotheistic and monistic systems.

I regard these parallels as important because it is possible, through them,
to relate so-called *metaphysical* concepts, which have lost their root connection with natural experience, to living, universal psychic processes, so
that they can recover their true and original meaning. In this way the
connection is reestablished between the ego and projected contents now
formulated as "metaphysical" ideas. Unfortunately, as already said, the fact
that metaphysical ideas exist and are believed in does nothing to prove the
actual existence of their content or of the object they refer to, although the
coincidence of idea and reality in the form of a special psychic state, a state
of grace, should not be deemed impossible, even if the subject cannot bring
it about by an act of will. Once metaphysical ideas have lost their capacity
to recall and evoke the original experience, they have not only become useless but prove to be actual impediments on the road to wider development.
One clings to possessions that have once meant wealth; and the more inef-
fective, incomprehensible, and lifeless they become the more obstinately
people cling to them. (Naturally it is only sterile ideas that they cling to;
living ideas have content and riches enough, so there is no need to cling to-
them.) Thus in the course of time the meaningful turns into the meaningless. This is unfortunately the fate of metaphysical ideas.

Today it is a real problem what on earth such ideas can mean. The
world—so far as it has not completely turned its back on tradition—has
long ago stopped wanting to hear a "message"; it would rather be told
what the message means. The words that resound from the pulpit are
incomprehensible and cry for an explanation. How has the death of Christ
brought us redemption when no one feels redeemed? In what way is Jesus
a God-man and what is such a being? What is the Trinity about, and the
parthenogenesis, the eating of the body and the drinking of the blood, and
all the rest of it? How hopeless is a relationship between the world of such
concepts and the everyday world, whose material reality is the concern of
natural science on the widest possible scale? At least sixteen hours out of
twenty-four we live exclusively in this everyday world, and the remaining
eight we spend preferably in an unconscious condition. Where and when
does anything take place to remind us even remotely of phenomena like
angels, miraculous feedings, benedictions, the resurrection of the dead, etc.?
It was therefore something of a discovery to find that during the unconscious state of sleep intervals occur, called "dreams," which occasionally
contain scenes having a not inconsiderable resemblance to the motifs of
mythology. For myths are miracle tales and treat of all those things which,
very often, are also objects of belief.

In the everyday world of consciousness such things hardly exist; that is to say, until 1933 only lunatics would have been found in possession of living fragments of mythology. After this date the world of heroes and monsters spread like a devastating fire over whole nations, proving that the strange world of myth had suffered no loss of vitality during the centuries of reason and enlightenment. If metaphysical ideas no longer have such a fascinating effect as before, this is certainly not due to any lack of primitivity in the European psyche, but simply and solely to the fact that the erstwhile symbols no longer express what is now welling up from the unconscious as the end result of the development of Christian consciousness through the centuries. This end result is a true *antimimon pneuma,* a false spirit of arrogance, hysteria, woolly-mindedness, criminal amorality, and doctrinaire fanaticism, a purveyor of shoddy spiritual goods, spurious art, philosophical stutterings, and Utopian humbug, fit only to be fed wholesale to the mass man of today. That is what the post-Christian spirit looks like.

## V.  CHRIST, A SYMBOL OF THE SELF

The de-Christianization of our world, the Luciferian development of science and technology, and the frightful material and moral destruction left behind by the Second World War have been compared more than once with the *eschatological* events foretold in the New Testament. These, as we know, are concerned with the coming of the Antichrist: "This is Antichrist, who denieth the Father and the Son." [3] The Apocalypse is full of expectations of terrible things that will take place at the end of time, before the marriage of the Lamb. This shows plainly that the *anima christiana* has a sure knowledge not only of the existence of an adversary but also of his future usurpation of power.

Why—my reader will ask—do I discourse here upon Christ and his adversary, the Antichrist? Our discourse necessarily brings us to Christ, because he is the still living myth of our culture. He is our culture hero, who, regardless of his historical existence, embodies the myth of the divine Primordial Man, the mystic Adam. It is he who occupies the center of the Christian *mandāla,* who is the Lord of the Tetramorph, i.e., the four symbols of the evangelists, which are like the four columns of his throne. He is in us and we in him. His kingdom is the pearl of great price, the treasure buried in the field, the grain of mustard seed which will become a great tree, and the heavenly city. As Christ is in us, so also is his heavenly kingdom.

These few familiar references should be sufficient to make the psychological position of the Christ symbol quite clear. *Christ exemplifies the archetype of the self.* He represents a totality of a divine or heavenly kind,

[3] Epistles of St. John I: 2:22(D.V.).

a glorified man, a son of God *sine macula peccati,* unspotted by sin. As Adam *secundus* he corresponds to the first Adam before the Fall, when the latter was still a pure image of God, of which Tertullian says: "And this therefore is to be considered as the image of God in man, that the human spirit has the same motions and senses as God has, though not in the same way as God has them." Origin is very much more explicit: The *imago Dei* imprinted on the soul, not on the body, is an image of an image, "for my soul is not directly the image of God, but is made after the likeness of the former image." Christ, on the other hand, is the true image of God, after whose likeness our inner man is made, invisible, incorporeal, incorrupt, and immortal. The God-image in us reveals itself through *"prudentia, iustitia, moderatio, virtus, sapientia et disciplina."*

St. Augustine distinguishes between the God-image which is Christ and the image which is implanted in man as a means or possibility of becoming like God. The God-image is not in the corporeal man, but in the *anima rationalis,* the possession of which distinguishes man from animals. "The God-image is within, not in the body. . . . Where the understanding is, where the mind is, where the power of investigating truth is, there God has his image." Therefore we should remind ourselves, says Augustine, that we are fashioned after the image of God nowhere save in the understanding. "But where man knows himself to be made after the image of God, there he knows there is something more in him than is given to the beasts." From this it is clear that the God-image is, so to speak, identical with the *anima rationalis.* The latter is the higher spiritual man, the *homo coelestis* of St. Paul.[4] Like Adam before the Fall, Christ is an embodiment of the God-image, whose totality is specially emphasized by St. Augustine. "The Word," he says, "took on complete manhood, as it were in its fullness: the soul and body of a man. And if you would have me put it more exactly—since even a beast of the field has a "soul" and a body—when I say a human soul and human flesh, I mean he took upon him a complete human soul."

---

[4] I Cor. 15:47.

# BLACK ELK SPEAKS

## John G. Niehardt

My friend, I am going to tell you the story of my life, as you wish; and if it were only the story of my life I think I would not tell it; for what is one man that he should make much of his winters, even when they bend him like a heavy snow? So many other men have lived and shall live that story, to be grass upon the hills.

It is the story of all life that is holy and is good to tell, and of us two-leggeds sharing in it with the four-leggeds and the wings of the air and all green things; for these are children of one mother and their father is one Spirit.

This, then, is not the tale of a great hunter or of a great warrior, or of a great traveler, although I have made much meat in my time and fought for my people both as boy and man, and have gone far and seen strange lands and men. So also have many others done, and better than I. These things I shall remember by the way, and often they may seem to be the very tale itself, as when I was living them in happiness and sorrow. But now that I can see it all as from a lonely hilltop, I know it was the story of a mighty vision given to a man too weak to use it; of a holy tree that should have flourished in a people's heart with flowers and singing birds, and now is withered; and of a people's dream that died in bloody snow.

But if the vision was true and mighty, as I know, it is true and mighty yet; for such things are of the spirit, and it is in the darkness of their eyes that men get lost.

## THE GREAT VISION

What happened after that until the summer I was nine years old is not a story. There were winters and summers, and they were good; for the Wasichus had made their iron road [1] along the Platte and traveled there. This had cut the bison herd in two, but those that stayed in our country with us were more than could be counted, and we wandered without trouble in our land.

Now and then the voices would come back when I was out alone, like someone calling me, but what they wanted me to do I did not know. This did not happen very often, and when it did not happen, I forgot about it; for I was growing taller and was riding horses now and could shoot prairie chickens and rabbits with my bow. The boys of my people began very young to learn the ways of men, and no one taught us; we just learned by doing what we saw, and we were warriors at a time when boys now are like girls.

It was the summer when I was nine years old, and our people were moving slowly towards the Rocky Mountains. We camped one evening in a valley beside a little creek just before it ran into the Greasy Grass,[2] and there was a man by the name of Man Hip who liked me and asked me to eat with him in the tepee.

While I was eating, a voice came and said: "It is time; now they are calling you." The voice was so loud and clear that I believed it, and I thought I would just go where it wanted me to go. So I got right up and started. As I came out of the tepee, both my thighs began to hurt me, and suddenly it was like waking from a dream, and there wasn't any voice. So I went back into the tepee, but I didn't want to eat. Man Hip looked at me in a strange way and asked me what was wrong. I told him that my legs were hurting me.

The next morning the camp moved again, and I was riding with some boys. We stopped to get a drink from a creek, and when I got off my horse, my legs crumpled under me and I could not walk. So the boys helped me up and put me on my horse; and when we camped again that evening, I was sick. The next day the camp moved on to where the different bands of our people were coming together, and I rode in a pony drag, for I was very sick. Both my legs and both my arms were swollen badly and my face was all puffed up.

When we had camped again, I was lying in our tepee and my mother and father were sitting beside me. I could see out through the opening, and there two men were coming from the clouds, head-first like arrows slanting down, and I knew they were the same that I had seen before.

[1] The Union Pacific Railway.
[2] The Little Big Horn River.

Each now carried a long spear, and from the points of these a jagged lightning flashed. They came clear down to the ground this time and stood a little way off and looked at me and said: "Hurry! Come! Your Grandfathers are calling you!"

Then they turned and left the ground like arrows slanting upward from the bow. When I got up to follow, my legs did not hurt me any more and I was very light. I went outside the tepee, and yonder where the men with flaming spears were going, a little cloud was coming very fast. It came and stooped and took me and turned back to where it came from, flying fast. And when I looked down I could see my mother and my father yonder, and I felt sorry to be leaving them.

Then there was nothing but the air and the swiftness of the little cloud that bore me and those two men still leading up to where white clouds were piled like mountains on a wide blue plain, and in them thunder beings lived and leaped and flashed.

Now suddenly there was nothing but a world of cloud, and we three were there alone in the middle of a great white plain with snowy hills and mountains staring at us; and it was very still; but there were whispers.

Then the two men spoke together and they said: "Behold him, the being with four legs!"

I looked and saw a bay horse standing there, and he began to speak: "Behold me!" he said, "My life-history you shall see." Then he wheeled about to where the sun goes down, and said: "Behold them! Their history you shall know."

I looked, and there were twelve black horses yonder all abreast with necklaces of bison hoofs, and they were beautiful, but I was frightened, because their manes were lightning and there was thunder in their nostrils.

Then the bay horse wheeled to where the great white giant lives (the north) and said: "Behold!" And yonder there were twelve white horses all abreast. Their manes were flowing like a blizzard wind and from their noses came a roaring, and all about them white geese soared and circled.

Then the bay wheeled round to where the sun shines continually (the east) and bade me look; and there twelve sorrel horses, with necklaces of elk's teeth, stood abreast with eyes that glimmered like the day-break star and manes of morning light.

Then the bay wheeled once again to look upon the place where you are always facing (the south), and yonder stood twelve buckskins all abreast with horns upon their heads and manes that lived and grew like trees and grasses.

And when I had seen all these, the bay horse said: "Your Grandfathers are having a council. These shall take you; so have courage."

Then all the horses went into formation, four abreast—the blacks, the whites, the sorrels, and the buckskins—and stood behind the bay, who turned now to the west and neighed; and wonder suddenly the sky was terrible with a storm of plunging horses in all colors that shook the world with thunder, neighing back.

Now turning to the north the bay horse whinnied, and yonder all the sky roared with a mighty wind of running horses in all colors, neighing back.

And when he whinnied to the east, there too the sky was filled with glowing clouds of manes and tails of horses in all colors singing back. Then to the south he called, and it was crowded with many colored, happy horses, nickering.

Then the bay horse spoke to me again and said: "See how your horses all come dancing!" I looked, and there were horses, horses everywhere—a whole skyful of horses dancing round me.

"Make haste!" the bay horse said; and we walked together side by side, while the blacks, the whites, the sorrels, and the buckskins followed, marching four by four.

I looked about me once again, and suddenly the dancing horses without number changed into animals of every kind and into all the fowls that are, and these fled back to the four quarters of the world from whence the horses came, and vanished.

Then as we walked, there was a heaped up cloud ahead that changed into a tepee, and a rainbow was the open door of it; and through the door I saw six old men sitting in a row.

The two men with the spears now stood beside me, one on either hand, and the horses took their places in their quarters, looking inward, four by four. And the oldest of the Grandfathers spoke with a kind voice and said: "Come right in and do not fear." And as he spoke, all the horses of the four quarters neighed to cheer me. So I went in and stood before the six, and they looked older than men can ever be—old like hills, like stars.

The oldest spoke again: "Your Grandfathers all over the world are having a council, and they have called you here to teach you." His voice was very kind, but I shook all over with fear now, for I knew that these were not old men, but the Powers of the World. And the first was the Power of the West; the second, of the North; the third, of the East; the fourth, of the South; the fifth, of the Sky; the sixth, of the Earth. I knew this, and was afraid, until the first Grandfather spoke again: "Behold them yonder where the sun goes down, the thunder beings! You shall see, and have from them my power; and they shall take you to the high and lonely center of the earth that you may see; even to the place where the sun continually shines, they shall take you there to understand."

And as he spoke of understanding, I looked up and saw the rainbow leap with flames of many colors over me.

Now there was a wooden cup in his hand and it was full of water and in the water was the sky.

"Take this," he said. "It is the power to make live, and it is yours."

Now he had a bow in his hands. "Take this," he said. "It is the power to destroy, and it is yours."

Then he pointed to himself and said: "Look close at him who is your spirit now, for you are his body and his name is Eagle Wing Stretches."

And saying this, he got up very tall and started running toward where the sun goes down; and suddenly he was a black horse that stopped and turned and looked at me, and the horse was very poor and sick; his ribs stood out.

Then the second Grandfather, he of the North, arose with a herb of power in his hand, and said: "Take this and hurry." I took and held it toward the black horse yonder. He fattened and was happy and came prancing to his place again and was the first Grandfather sitting there.

The second Grandfather, he of the North, spoke again: "Take courage, younger brother," he said; "on earth a nation you shall make live, for yours shall be the power of the white giant's wing, the cleansing wind." Then he got up very tall and started running toward the north; and when he turned toward me, it was a white goose wheeling. I looked about me now, and the horses in the west were thunders and the horses of the north were geese. And the second Grandfather sang two songs that were like this:

> They are appearing, may you behold!
> They are appearing, may you behold!
> The thunder nation is appearing, behold!

> They are appearing, may you behold!
> They are appearing, may you behold!
> The white geese nation is appearing, behold!

And now it was the third Grandfather who spoke, he of where the sun shines continually. "Take courage, younger brother," he said, "for across the earth they shall take you!" Then he pointed to where the daybreak star was shining, and beneath the star two men were flying. "From them you shall have power," he said, "from them who have awakened all the beings of the earth with roots and legs and wings." And as he said this, he held in his hand a peace pipe which had a spotted eagle outstretched upon the stem; and this eagle seemed alive, for it was poised there, fluttering, and its eyes were looking at me. "With this pipe," the Grandfather said, "you shall walk upon the earth, and whatever sickens there you shall make well." Then he pointed to a man who was bright red all over, the color of good and of plenty, and as he pointed, the red man lay down and rolled and changed into a bison that got up and galloped toward the sorrel horses of the east, and they too turned to bison, fat and many.

And now the fourth Grandfather spoke, he of the place where you are always facing (the south), whence comes the power to grow. "Younger brother," he said, "with the powers of the four quarters you shall walk, a relative. Behold, the living center of a nation I shall give you, and with it many you shall save." And I saw that he was holding in his hand a bright red stick that was alive, and as I looked it sprouted at the top and sent forth branches, and on the branches many leaves came out and murmured and in the leaves the birds began to sing. And then for just a little while I thought I saw beneath it in the shade the circled villages of people and every living thing with roots or legs or wings, and all were happy. "It shall stand in the center of the nation's circle," said the Grandfather, "a cane to walk with and a people's heart; and by your powers you shall make it blossom."

Then when he had been still a little while to hear the birds sing, he spoke again: "Behold the earth!" So I looked down and saw it lying yonder like a hoop of peoples, and in the center bloomed the holy stick that was a tree, and where it stood there crossed two roads, a red one and a black. "From where the giant lives (the north) to where you always face (the south) the red road goes, the road of good," the Grandfather said, "and on it shall your nation walk. The black road goes from where the thunder beings live (the west) to where the sun continually shines (the east), a fearful road, a road of troubles and of war. On this also you shall walk, and from it you shall have the power to destroy a people's foes. In four ascents you shall walk the earth with power."

I think he meant that I should see four generations, counting me, and now I am seeing the third.

Then he rose very tall and started running toward the south, and was an elk; and as he stood among the buckskins yonder, they too were elks.

Now the fifth Grandfather spoke, the oldest of them all, the Spirit of the Sky. "My boy," he said, "I have sent for you and you have come. My power you shall see!" He stretched his arms and turned into a spotted eagle hovering. "Behold," he said, "all the wings of the air shall come to you, and they and the winds and the stars shall be like relatives. You shall go across the earth with my power." Then the eagle soared above my head and fluttered there; and suddenly the sky was full of friendly wings all coming toward me.

Now I knew the sixth Grandfather was about to speak, he who was the Spirit of the Earth, and I saw that he was very old, but more as men are old. His hair was long and white, his face was all in wrinkles and his eyes were deep and dim. I stared at him, for it seemed I knew him somehow; and as I stared, he slowly changed, for he was growing backwards into youth, and when he had become a boy, I knew that he was myself with all the years that would be mine at last. When he was old again, he said: "My boy, have courage, for my power shall be yours, and you shall need it, for your nation on the earth will have great troubles. Come."

He rose and tottered out through the rainbow door, and as I followed I was riding on the bay horse who had talked to me at first and led me to that place.

Then the bay horse stopped and faced the black horses of the west, and a voice said: "They have given you the cup of water to make live the greening day, and also the bow and arrow to destroy." The bay neighed, and the twelve black horses came and stood behind me, four abreast.

The bay faced the sorrels of the east, and I saw that they had morning stars upon their foreheads and they were very bright. And the voice said: "They have given you the sacred pipe and the power that is peace, and the good red day." The bay neighed, and the twelve sorrels stood behind me, four abreast.

My horse now faced the buckskins of the south, and a voice said: "They have given you the sacred stick and your nation's hoop, and the yellow day; and in the center of the hoop you shall set the stick and make it grow into a shielding tree, and bloom." The bay neighed, and the twelve buckskins came and stood behind me, four abreast.

Then I knew that there were riders on all the horses there behind me, and a voice said: "Now you shall walk the black road with these; and as you walk, all the nations that have roots or legs or wings shall fear you."

So I started, riding toward the east down the fearful road, and behind me came the horsebacks four abreast—the blacks, the whites, the sorrels, and the buckskins—and far away above the fearful road the daybreak star was rising very dim.

I looked below me where the earth was silent in a sick green light, and saw the hills look up afraid and the grasses on the hills and all the animals; and everywhere about me were the cries of frightened birds and sounds of fleeing wings. I was the chief of all the heavens riding there, and when I looked behind me, all the twelve black horses reared and plunged and thundered and their manes and tails were whirling hail and their nostrils snorted lightning. And when I looked below again, I saw the slant hail falling and the long, sharp rain, and where we passed, the trees bowed low and all the hills were dim.

Now the earth was bright again as we rode. I could see the hills and valleys and the creeks and rivers passing under. We came above a place where three streams made a big one—a source of mighty waters[3]—and something terrible was there. Flames were rising from the waters and in the flames a blue man lived. The dust was floating all about him in the air,

---

[3] Black Elk thinks this was the Three Forks of the Missouri.

the grass was short and withered, the trees were wilting, two-legged and four-legged beings lay there thin and panting, and wings too weak to fly.

Then the black horse riders shouted "Hoka hey!" and charged down upon the blue man, but were driven back. And the white troop shouted, charging, and was beaten; then the red troop and the yellow.

And when each had failed, they all cried together: "Eagle Wing Stretches, hurry!" And all the world was filled with voices of all kinds that cheered me, so I charged. I had the cup of water in one hand and in the other was the bow that turned into a spear as the bay and I swooped down, and the spear's head was sharp lightning. It stabbed the blue man's heart, and as it struck I could hear the thunder rolling and many voices that cried "Un-hee," meaning I had killed. The flames died. The trees and grasses were not withered any more and murmured happily together, and every living being cried in gladness with whatever voice it had. Then the four troops of horsemen charged down and struck the dead body of the blue man, counting coup; and suddenly it was only a harmless turtle.

You see, I had been riding with the storm clouds, and had come to earth as rain, and it was drouth that I had killed with the power that the Six Grandfathers gave me. So we were riding on the earth now down along the river flowing full from the sources of waters, and soon I saw ahead the circled village of a people in the valley. And a Voice said: "Behold a nation; it is yours. Make haste, Eagle Wing Stretches!"

I entered the village, riding, with the four horse troops behind me—the blacks, the whites, the sorrels, and the buckskins; and the place was filled with moaning and with mourning for the dead. The wind was blowing from the south like fever, and when I looked around I saw that in nearly every tepee the women and the children and the men lay dying with the dead.

So I rode around the circle of the village, looking in upon the sick and dead, and I felt like crying as I rode. But when I looked behind me, all the women and the children and the men were getting up and coming forth with happy faces.

And a Voice said: "Behold, they have given you the center of the nation's hoop to make it live."

So I rode to the center of the village, with the horse troops in their quarters round about me, and there the people gathered. And the Voice said: "Give them now the flowering stick that they may flourish, and the sacred pipe that they may know the power that is peace, and the wing of the white giant that they may have endurance and face all winds with courage."

So I took the bright red stick and at the center of the nation's hoop I thrust it in the earth. As it touched the earth it leaped mightily in my hand

and was a waga chun, the rustling tree,[4] very tall and full of leafy branches and of all birds singing. And beneath it all the animals were mingling with the people like relatives and making happy cries. The women raised their tremolo of joy, and the men shouted all together: "Here we shall raise our children and be as little chickens under the mother sheo's[5] wing."

Then I heard the white wind blowing gently through the tree and singing there, and from the east the sacred pipe came flying on its eagle wings, and stopped before me there beneath the tree, spreading deep peace around it.

Then the daybreak star was rising, and a Voice said: "It shall be a relative to them; and who shall see it, shall see much more, for thence comes wisdom; and those who do not see it shall be dark." And all the people raised their faces to the east, and the star's light fell upon them, and all the dogs barked loudly and the horses whinnied.

Then when the many little voices ceased, the great Voice said: "Behold the circle of the nation's hoop, for it is holy, being endless, and thus all powers shall be one power in the people without end. Now they shall break camp and go forth upon the red road, and your Grandfathers shall walk with them." So the people broke camp and took the good road with the white wing on their faces, and the order of their going was like this:

First, the black horse riders with the cup of water; and the white horse riders with the white wing and the sacred herb; and the sorrel riders with the holy pipe; and the buckskins with the flowering stick. And after these the little children and the youths and maidens followed in a band.

Second, came the tribe's four chieftains, and their band was all young men and women.

Third, the nation's four advisers leading men and women neither young nor old.

Fourth, the old men hobbling with their canes and looking to the earth.

Fifth, old women hobbling with their canes and looking to the earth.

Sixth, myself all alone upon the bay with the bow and arrows that the First Grandfather gave me. But I was not the last; for when I looked behind me there were ghosts of people like a trailing fog as far as I could see—grandfathers of grandfathers and grandmothers of grandmothers without number. And over these a great Voice—the Voice that was the South—lived, and I could feel it silent.

And as we went the Voice behind me said: "Behold a good nation walking in a sacred manner in a good land!"

Then I looked up and saw that there were four ascents ahead, and these

---

[4] The cottonwood.
[5] Prairie hen.

were generations I should know. Now we were on the first ascent, and all the land was green. And as the long line climbed, all the old men and women raised their hands, palms forward, to the far sky yonder and began to croon a song together, and the sky ahead was filled with clouds of baby faces.

When we came to the end of the first ascent we camped in the sacred circle as before, and in the center stood the holy tree, and still the land about us was all green.

Then we started on the second ascent, marching as before, and still the land was green, but it was getting steeper. And as I looked ahead, the people changed into elks and bison and all four-footed beings and even into fowls, all walking in a sacred manner on the good red road together. And I myself was a spotted eagle soaring over them. But just before we stopped to camp at the end of that ascent, all the marching animals grew restless and afraid that they were not what they had been, and began sending forth voices of trouble, calling to their chiefs. And when they camped at the end of that ascent, I looked down and saw that leaves were falling from the holy tree.

And the Voice said: "Behold your nation, and remember what your Six Grandfathers gave you, for thenceforth your people walk in difficulties."

Then the people broke camp again, and saw the black road before them towards where the sun goes down, and black clouds coming yonder; and they did not want to go but could not stay. And as they walked the third ascent, all the animals and fowls that were the people ran here and there, for each one seemed to have his own little vision that he followed and his own rules; and all over the universe I could hear the winds at war like wild beasts fighting.[6]

And when we reached the summit of the third ascent and camped, the nation's hoop was broken like a ring of smoke that spreads and scatters and the holy tree seemed dying and all its birds were gone. And when I looked ahead I saw that the fourth ascent would be terrible.

Then when the people were getting ready to begin the fourth ascent, the Voice spoke like some one weeping, and it said: "Look there upon your nation." And when I looked down, the people were all changed back to human, and they were thin, their faces sharp, for they were starving. Their ponies were only hide and bones, and the holy tree was gone.

And as I looked and wept, I saw that there stood on the north side of the starving camp a sacred man who was painted red all over his body, and he held a spear as he walked into the center of the people, and there he lay down and rolled. And when he got up, it was a fat bison standing there,

---

[6] At this point Black Elk remarked: "I think we are near that place now, and I am afraid something very bad is going to happen all over the world." He cannot read and knows nothing of world affairs.

and where the bison stood a sacred herb sprang up right where the tree had been in the center of the nation's hoop. The herb grew and bore four blossoms on a single stem while I was looking—a blue,[7] a white, a scarlet, and a yellow—and the bright rays of these flashed to the heavens.

I know now what this meant, that the bison were the gift of a good spirit and were our strength, but we should lose them, and from the same good spirit we must find another strength. For the people all seemed better when the herb had grown and bloomed, and the horses raised their tails and neighed and pranced around, and I could see a light breeze going from the north among the people like a ghost; and suddenly the flowering tree was there again at the center of the nation's hoop where the four-rayed herb had blossomed.

I was still the spotted eagle floating, and I could see that I was already in the fourth ascent and the people were camping yonder at the top of the third long rise. It was dark and terrible about me, for all the winds of the world were fighting. It was like rapid gun-fire and like whirling smoke, and like women and children wailing and like horses screaming all over the world.

I could see my people yonder running about, setting the smoke-flap poles and fastening down their tepees against the wind, for the storm cloud was coming on them very fast and black, and there were frightened swallows without number fleeing before the cloud.

Then a song of power came to me and I sang it there in the midst of that terrible place where I was. It went like this:

A good nation I will make live.
This the nation above has said.
They have given me the power to make over.

And when I had sung this, a Voice said: "To the four quarters you shall run for help, and nothing shall be strong before you. Behold him!"

Now I was on my bay horse again, because the horse is of the earth, and it was there my power would be used. And as I obeyed the Voice and looked, there was a horse all skin and bones yonder in the west, a faded brownish black. And a Voice there said: "Take this and make him over; and it was the four-rayed herb that I was holding in my hand. So I rode above the poor horse in a circle, and as I did this I could hear the people yonder calling for spirit power, "A-hey! a-hey! a-hey! a-hey!" Then the poor horse neighed and rolled and got up, and he was a big, shiny, black stallion with dapples all over him and his mane about him like a cloud. He was the chief of all the horses; and when he snorted, it was a flash of lightning and his eyes were like the sunset star. He dashed to the west and

[7] Blue as well as black may be used to represent the power of the west.

neighed, and the west was filled with a dust of hoofs, and horses without number, shiny black, came plunging from the dust. Then he dashed toward the north and neighed, and to the east and to the south, and the dust clouds answered, giving forth their plunging horses without number—whites and sorrels and buckskins, fat, shiny, rejoicing in their fleetness and their strength. It was beautiful, but it was also terrible.

Then they all stopped short, rearing, and were standing in a great hoop about their black chief at the center, and were still. And as they stood, four virgins, more beautiful than women of the earth can be, came through the circle, dressed in scarlet, one from each of the four quarters, and stood about the great black stallion in their places; and one held the wooden cup of water, and one the white wing, and one the pipe, and one the nation's hoop. All the universe was silent, listening; and then the great black stallion raised his voice and sang. The song he sang was this:

> My horses, prancing they are coming.
> My horses, neighing they are coming;
> Prancing, they are coming.
> All over the universe they come.
> They will dance; may you behold them.
>
> (4 times)
>
> A horse nation, they will dance. May you behold them.
>
> (4 times)

His voice was not loud, but it went all over the universe and filled it. There was nothing that did not hear, and it was more beautiful than anything can be. It was so beautiful that nothing anywhere could keep from dancing. The virgins danced, and all the circled horses. The leaves on the trees, the grasses on the hills and in the valleys, the waters in the creeks and in the rivers and the lakes, the four-legged and the two-legged and the wings of the air—all danced together to the music of the stallion's song.

And when I looked down upon my people yonder, the cloud passed over, blessing them with friendly rain, and stood in the east with a flaming rainbow over it.

Then all the horses went singing back to their places beyond the summit of the fourth ascent, and all things sang along with them as they walked.

And a Voice said: "All over the universe they have finished a day of happiness." And looking down I saw that the whole wide circle of the day was beautiful and green, with all fruits growing and all things kind and happy.

Then a Voice said: "Behold this day, for it is yours to make. Now you shall stand upon the center of the earth to see, for there they are taking you."

I was still on my bay horse, and once more I felt the riders of the west, the north, the east, the south, behind me in formation, as before, and we

were going east. I looked ahead and saw the mountains there with rocks
and forests on them, and from the mountains flashed all colors upward to
the heavens. Then I was standing on the highest mountain of them all,
and round about beneath me was the whole hoop of the world.[8] And while
I stood there I saw more than I can tell and I understood more than I saw;
for I was seeing in a sacred manner the shapes of all things in the spirit,
and the shape of all shapes as they must live together like one being. And I
saw that the sacred hoop of my people was one of many hoops that made
one circle, wide as daylight and as starlight, and in the center grew one
mighty flowering tree to shelter all the children of one mother and one
father. And I saw that it was holy.

Then as I stood there, two men were coming from the east, head first
like arrows flying, and between them rose the day-break star. They came
and gave a herb to me and said: "With this on earth you shall undertake
anything and do it." It was the day-break-star herb, the herb of understanding, and they told me to drop it on the earth. I saw it falling far, and
when it struck the earth it rooted and grew and flowered, four blossoms on
one stem, a blue, a white, a scarlet, and a yellow; and the rays from these
streamed upward to the heavens so that all creatures saw it and in no place
was there darkness.

Then the Voice said: "Your Six Grandfathers—now you shall go back
to them."

I had not noticed how I was dressed until now, and I saw that I was
painted red all over, and my joints were painted black, with white stripes
between the joints. My bay had lightning stripes all over him, and his mane
was cloud. And when I breathed, my breath was lightning.

Now two men were leading me, head first like arrows slanting upward—
the two that brought me from the earth. And as I followed on the bay, they
turned into four flocks of geese that flew in circles, one above each quarter,
sending forth a sacred voice as they flew: Br-r-r-p, br-r-r-p, br-r-r-p,
br-r-r-p!

Then I saw ahead the rainbow flaming above the tepee of the Six
Grandfathers, built and roofed with cloud and sewed with thongs of
lightning; and underneath it were all the wings of the air and under them
the animals and men. All these were rejoicing, and thunder was like happy
laughter.

As I rode in through the rainbow door, there were cheering voices from
all over the universe, and I saw the Six Grandfathers sitting in a row, with
their arms held toward me and their hands, palms out; and behind them in
the cloud were faces thronging, without number, of the people yet to be.

---

[8] Black Elk said the mountain he stood upon in his vision was Harney Peak in the
Black Hills. "But anywhere is the center of the world," he added.

"He has triumphed!" cried the six together, making thunder. And as I passed before them there, each gave again the gift that he had given me before—the cup of water and the bow and arrows, the power to make live and to destroy; the white wing of cleansing and the healing herb; the sacred pipe; the flowering stick. And each one spoke in turn from west to south, explaining what he gave as he had done before, and as each one spoke he melted down into the earth and rose again; and as each did this, I felt nearer to the earth.

Then the oldest of them all said: "Grandson, all over the universe you have seen. Now you shall go back with power to the place from whence you came, and it shall happen yonder that hundreds shall be sacred, hundreds shall be flames! Behold!"

I looked below and saw my people there, and all were well and happy except one, and he was lying like the dead—and that one was myself. Then the oldest Grandfather sang, and his song was like this:

> There is someone lying on earth in a sacred manner.
> There is someone—on earth he lies.
> In a sacred manner I have made him to walk.

Now the tepee, built and roofed with cloud, began to sway back and forth as in a wind, and the flaming rainbow door was growing dimmer. I could hear voices of all kinds crying from outside: "Eagle Wing Stretches is coming forth! Behold him!"

When I went through the door, the face of the day of earth was appearing with the day-break star upon its forehead; and the sun leaped up and looked upon me, and I was going forth alone.

And as I walked alone, I heard the sun singing as it arose, and it sang like this:

> With visible face I am appearing.
> In a sacred manner I appear.
> For the greening earth a pleasantness I make.
> The center of the nation's hoop I have made pleasant.
> With visible face, behold me!
> The four-leggeds and two-leggeds, I have made them to walk;
> The wings of the air, I have made them to fly.
> With visible face I appear.
> My day, I have made it holy.

When the singing stopped, I was feeling lost and very lonely. Then a Voice above me said: "Look back!" It was a spotted eagle that was hovering over me and spoke. I looked, and where the flaming rainbow tepee, built and roofed with cloud, had been, I saw only the tall rock mountain at the center of the world.

I was all alone on a broad plain now with my feet upon the earth, alone but for the spotted eagle guarding me. I could see my people's village far ahead, and I walked very fast, for I was homesick now. Then I saw my own tepee, and inside I saw my mother and my father bending over a sick boy that was myself. And as I entered the tepee, some one was saying: "The boy is coming to; you had better give him some water."

Then I was sitting up; and I was sad because my mother and my father didn't seem to know I had been so far away.

. . .

And so it was all over.

I did not know then how much was ended. When I look back now from this high hill of my old age, I can still see the butchered women and children lying heaped and scattered all along the crooked gulch as plain as when I saw them with eyes still young. And I can see that something else died there in the bloody mud, and was buried in the blizzard. A people's dream died there. It was a beautiful dream.

And I, to whom so great a vision was given in my youth,—you see me now a pitiful old man who has done nothing, for the nation's hoop is broken and scattered. There is no center any longer, and the sacred tree is dead.

# THE BOOK

## Alan Watts

Irrevocable commitment to any religion is not only intellectual suicide; it is positive unfaith because it closes the mind to any new vision of the world. Faith is, above all, open-ness—an act of trust in the unknown.

An ardent Jehovah's Witness once tried to convince me that if there were a God of love, he would certainly provide mankind with a reliable and infallible textbook for the guidance of conduct. I replied that no considerate God would destroy the human mind by making it so rigid and unadaptable as to depend upon one book, the Bible, for all the answers. For the use of words, and thus of a book, is to point beyond themselves to a world of life and experience that is not mere words or even ideas. Just as money is not real, consumable wealth, books are not life. To idolize scriptures is like eating paper currency.

Therefore The Book that I would like to slip to my children would itself be slippery. It would slip them into a new domain, not of ideas alone, but of experience and feeling. It would be a temporary medicine, not a diet; a point of departure, not a perpetual point of reference. They would read it and be done with it, for if it were well and clearly written they would not have to go back to it again and again for hidden meanings or for clarification of obscure doctrines.

We do not need a new religion or a new bible. We need a new experience —a new feeling of what it is to be "I." The lowdown (which is, of course, the secret and profound view) on life is that our normal sensation of self is a hoax or, at best, a temporary role that we are playing, or have been conned into playing— with our own tacit consent, just as every hypnotized person is basically willing to be hypnotized. The most strongly enforced of all known taboos is the taboo against knowing who or what you really are behind the mask of your apparently separate, independent, and isolated ego. I am not thinking of Freud's barbarous Id or Unconscious as the actual reality behind the façade of personality. Freud, as we shall see, was under the influence of a nineteenth-century fashion called "reductionism," a curious need to put down human culture and intelligence by calling it a fluky by-product of blind and irrational forces. They worked very hard, then, to prove that grapes can grow on thornbushes.

As is so often the way, what we have suppressed and overlooked is something startlingly obvious. The difficulty is that it is *so* obvious and basic that one can hardly find the words for it. The Germans call it a *Hintergendanke,* an apprehension lying tacitly in the back of our minds which we cannot easily admit, even to ourselves. The sensation of "I" as a lonely and isolated center of being is so powerful and commonsensical, and so fundamental to our modes of speech and thought, to our laws and social institutions, that we cannot experience selfhood except as something superficial in the scheme of the universe. I seem to be a brief light that flashes but once in all the aeons of time—a rare, complicated, and all-too-delicate organism on the fringe of biological evolution, where the wave of life bursts into individual, sparkling, and multicolored drops that gleam for a moment only to vanish forever. Under such conditioning it seems impossible and even absurd to realize that myself does not reside in the drop alone, but in the whole surge of energy which ranges from the galaxies to the nuclear fields in my body. At this level of existence "I" am immeasurably old; my forms are infinite and their comings and goings are simply the pulses or vibrations of a single and eternal flow of energy.

The difficulty in realizing this to be so is that conceptual thinking cannot grasp it. It is as if the eyes were trying to look at themselves directly, or as if one were trying to describe the color of a mirror in terms of colors reflected in the mirror. Just as sight is something more than all things seen, the foundation or "ground" of our existence and our awareness cannot be understood in terms of things that are known. We are forced, therefore, to speak of it through myth—that is, through special metaphors, analogies, and images which say what it is *like* as distinct from what it *is*. At one extreme of its meaning, "myth" is fable, falsehood, or superstition. But at another, "myth" is a useful and fruitful image by which we make sense of life in somewhat the same way that we can explain electrical forces by comparing them with the behavior of water or air. Yet "myth," in this second sense, is not to be taken literally, just as electricity is not to be confused with air or water. Thus in using myth one must take care not to confuse image with fact, which would be like climbing up the signpost instead of following the road.

Myth, then, is the form in which I try to answer when children ask me those fundamental metaphysical questions which come so readily to their minds: "Where did the world come from?" "Why did God make the world?" "Where was I before I was born?" "Where do people go when they die?" Again and again I have found that they seem to be satisfied with a simple and very ancient story, which goes something like this:

"There was never a time when the world began, because it goes round and round like a circle, and there is no place on a circle where it begins. Look at my watch, which tells the time; it goes round, and so the world repeats itself again and again. But just as the hour-hand of the watch goes up to twelve and down to six, so, too, there is day and night, waking and sleeping, living and dying, summer and winter. You can't have any one of these without the other, because you wouldn't be able to know what black is unless you had seen it side-by-side with white, or white unless side-by-side with black.

"In the same way, there are times when the world is, and times when it isn't, for if the world went on and on without rest for ever and ever, it would get horribly tired of itself. It comes and it goes. Now you see it; now you don't. So because it doesn't get tired of itself, it always comes back again after it disappears. It's like your breath: it goes in and out, in and out, and if you try to hold it in all the time you feel terrible. It's also like the game of hide-and-seek, because it's always fun to find new ways of hiding, and to seek for someone who doesn't always hide in the same place.

"God also likes to play hide-and-seek, but because there is nothing outside God, he has no one but himself to play with. But he gets over this difficulty by pretending that he is not himself. This is his way of hiding from himself. He pretends that he is you and I and all the people in the world, all the animals, all the plants, all the rocks, and all the stars. In this way he has strange and wonderful adventures, some of which are terrible and frightening. But these are just like bad dreams, for when he wakes up they will disappear.

"Now when God plays hide and pretends that he is you and I, he does it so well that it takes him a long time to remember where and how he hid himself. But that's the whole fun of it—just what he wanted to do. He doesn't want to find himself too quickly, for that would spoil the game. That is why it is so difficult for you and me to find out that we are God in disguise, pretending not to be himself. But when the game has gone on long enough, all of us will wake up, stop pretending, and remember that we are all one single Self—the God who is all that there is and who lives for ever and ever.

"Of course, you must remember that God isn't shaped like a person. People have skins and there is always something outside our skins. If there weren't, we wouldn't know the difference between what is inside and outside our bodies. But God has no skin and no shape because there isn't any outside to him. [With a sufficiently intelligent child, I illustrate this with a Mobius strip—a ring of paper tape twisted once in such a way that it has only one side and one edge.] The inside and the outside of God are the same. And though I have been talking about God as 'he' and not 'she,' God isn't a man or a woman. I didn't say 'it' because we usually say 'it' for things that aren't alive.

"God is the Self of the world, but you can't see God for the same reason that, without a mirror, you can't see your own eyes, and you certainly can't bite your own teeth or look inside your head. Your self is that cleverly hidden because it is God hiding.

"You may ask why God sometimes hides in the form of horrible people, or pretends to be people who suffer great disease and pain. Remember, first, that he isn't really doing this to anyone but himself. Remember, too, that in almost all the stories you enjoy there have to be bad people as well as good people, for the thrill of the tale is to find out how the good people will get the better of the bad. It's the same as when we play cards. At the beginning of the game we shuffle them all into a mess, which is like the bad things in the world, but the point of the game is to put the mess into good order, and the one who does it best is the winner. Then we shuffle the cards once more and play again, and so it goes with the world."

This story, obviously mythical in form, is not given as a *scientific* description of the way things are. Based on the analogies of games and the drama, and using that much worn-out word "God" for the Player, the story claims only to be *like* the way things are. I use it just as astronomers use the image of inflating a black balloon with white spots on it for the galaxies, to explain the expanding universe. But to most children, and many adults, the myth is at once intelligible, simple, and fascinating. By contrast, so many other mythical explanations of the world are crude, tortuous, and unintelligible. But many people think that believing in the unintelligible propositions and symbols of their religions is the test of true faith. "I believe," said Tertullian of Christianity, "because it is absurd."

People who think for themselves do not accept ideas on this kind of authority. They don't feel commanded to believe in miracles or strange doctrines as Abraham felt commanded by God to sacrifice his son Isaac. As T. George Harris put it:

The social hierarchies of the past, where some boss above you always punished any error, conditioned men to feel a chain of harsh authority reaching all the way "up there." We don't feel this bond in today's egalitarian freedom. We don't even have, since Dr. Spock, many Jehovah-like fathers in the human family. So the average unconscious no longer learns to seek forgiveness from a wrathful God above.

But, he continues—

> Our generation knows a cold hell, solitary confinement in this life, without
> a God to damn or save it. Until man figures out the trap and hunts . . . "the
> Ultimate Ground of Being," he has no reason at all for his existence. Empty,
> finite, he knows only that he will soon die. Since this life has no meaning,
> and he sees no future life, he is not really a person but a victim of self-
> extinction.[1]

"The Ultimate Ground of Being" is Paul Tillich's decontaminated term
for "God" and would also do for "the Self of the world" as I put it in my
story for children. But the secret which my story slips over to the child is
that the Ultimate Ground of Being is *you*. Not, of course, the everyday
you which the Ground is assuming, or "pretending" to be, but that inmost
Self which escapes inspection because it's always the inspector. This, then,
is the taboo of taboos: you're IT!

Yet in our culture this is the touchstone of insanity, the blackest of
blasphemies, and the wildest of delusions. This, we believe, is the ultimate
in megalomania—an inflation of the ego to complete absurdity. For though
we cultivate the ego with one hand, we knock it down wih the other. From
generation to generation we kick the stuffing out of our children to teach
them to "know their place" and to behave, think, and feel with proper
modesty as befits one little ego among many. As my mother used to say,
"You're not the only pebble on the beach!" Anyone in his right mind who
believes that he is God should be crucified or burned at the stake, though
now we take the more charitable view that no one in his right mind could
believe such nonsense. Only a poor idiot could conceive himself as the
omnipotent ruler of the world, and expect everyone else to fall down and
worship.

But this is because we think of God as the King of the Universe, the
Absolute Technocrat who personally and consciously controls every detail
of his cosmos—and that is not the kind of God in my story. In fact, it isn't
*my* story at all, for any student of the history of religions will know that it
comes from ancient India, and is the mythical way of explaining the
Vedanta philosophy. Vedanta is the teaching of the *Upanishads,* a collection
of dialogues, stories, and poems, most of which go back to at least 800 B.C.
Sophisticated Hindus do not think of God as a special and separate super-
person who *rules* the world from above, like a monarch. Their God is
"underneath" rather than "above" everything, and he (or it) *plays* the
world from inside. One might say that if religion is the opium of the people,
the Hindus have the inside dope. What is more, no Hindu can realize that
he is God in disguise without seeing at the same time that this is true of

---

[1] A discussion of the views of theologian Paul Tillich in "The Battle of the Bible,"
*Look,* Vol. XIX, No. 15. July 27, 1965, p. 19.

everyone and everything else. In the Vedanta philosophy, nothing exists except God. There *seem* to be other things than God, but only because he is dreaming them up and making them his disguises to play hide-and-seek with himself. The universe of seemingly separate things is therefore real only for a while, not eternally real, for it comes and goes as the Self hides and seeks itself.

But Vedanta is much more than the idea or the belief that this is so. It is centrally and above all the *experience,* the immediate knowledge of its being so, and for this reason such a complete subversion of our ordinary way of seeing things. It turns the world inside out and outside in. Likewise, a saying attributed to Jesus runs:

> When you make the two one, and
> when you make the inner as the outer
> and the outer as the inner and the above
> as the below . . .
> then shall you enter [the Kingdom]. . . .
> I am the Light that is above
> them all, I am the All,
> the All came forth from Me and the All
> attained to Me. Cleave a [piece of] wood, I
> am there; lift up the stone and you will
> find Me there.[2]

Today the Vedanta discipline comes down to us after centuries of involvement with all the forms, attitudes, and symbols of Hindu culture in its flowering and slow demise over nearly 2,800 years, sorely wounded by Islamic fanaticism and corrupted by British puritanism. As often set forth, Vedanta rings no bell in the West, and attracts mostly the fastidiously spiritual and diaphanous kind of people for whom incarnation in a physical body is just too disgusting to be borne.[3] But it is possible to state its essentials in a present-day idiom, and when this is done without exotic trappings, Sanskrit terminology, and excessive postures of spirituality, the message is not only clear to people with no special interest in "Oriental religions"; it is also the very jolt that we need to kick ourselves out of our isolated sensation of self .

But this must not be confused with our usual ideas of the practice of "unselfishness," which is the effort to identify with others and their needs while still under the strong illusion of being no more than a skin-contained

---

[2] A. Guillaumont and others (trs.) *The Gospel According to Thomas.* Harper & Row, New York, 1959. pp. 17–18, 43. A recently discovered Coptic manuscript, possibly translated from a Greek version as old as A.D. 140. The "I" and the "Me" are obvious references to the disguised Self.

[3] I said "mostly" because I am aware of some very special exceptions both here and in India.

ego. Such "unselfishness" is apt to be a highly refined egotism, comparable to the in-group which plays the game of "we're-more-tolerant-than-you." The Vedanta was not originally moralistic; it did not urge people to ape the saints without sharing their real motivations, or to ape motivations without sharing the knowledge which sparks them.

For this reason The Book I would pass to my children would contain no sermons, no shoulds and oughts. Genuine love comes from knowledge, not from a sense of duty or guilt. How would you like to be an invalid mother with a daughter who can't marry because she feels she ought to look after you, and therefore hates you? My wish would be to tell, not how things ought to be, but how they are, and how and why we ignore them as they are. You cannot teach an ego to be anything but egotistic, even though egos have the subtlest ways of pretending to be reformed. The basic thing is therefore to dispel, by experiment and experience, the illusion of oneself as a separate ego. The consequences may not be behavior along the lines of *conventional* morality. It may well be as the squares said of Jesus, "Look at him! A glutton and a drinker, a friend of tax-gatherers and sinners!"

Furthermore, on seeing through the illusion of the ego, it is impossible to think of oneself as better than, or superior to, others for having done so. In every direction there is just the one Self playing its myriad games of hide-and-seek. Birds are not *better* than the eggs from which they have broken. Indeed, it could be said that a bird is one egg's way of becoming other eggs. Egg is ego, and bird is the liberated Self. There is a Hindu myth of the Self as a divine swan which laid the egg from which the world was hatched. Thus I am not even saying that you *ought* to break out of your shell. Sometime, somehow, you (the real you, the Self) will do it anyhow, but it is not impossible that the play of the Self will be to remain un-awakened in most of its human disguises, and so bring the drama of life on earth to its close in a vast explosion. Another Hindu myth says that as time goes on, life in the world gets worse and worse, until at last the de-structive aspect of the Self, the god Shiva, dances a terrible dance which consumes everything in fire. There follow, says the myth, 4,320,000 years of total peace during which the Self is just itself and does not play hide. And then the game begins again, starting off as a universe of perfect splendor which begins to deteriorate only after 1,728,000 years, and every round of the game is so designed that the forces of darkness present them-selves for only one third of the time, enjoying at the end a brief but quite illusory triumph.

# BADGER TELLS WART

## T. H. White

"So Merlyn sent you to me," said the badger, "to finish your education. Well, I can only teach you two things—to dig, and love your home. These are the true end of philosophy."

"Would you show me your home?"

"Certainly," said the badger, "though, of course, I don't use it all. It is a rambling old place, much too big for a single man. I suppose some parts of it may be a thousand years old. There are about four families of us in it, here and there, take it by and large from cellar to attics, and sometimes we don't meet for months. A crazy old place, I suppose it must seem to you modern people—but there, it's cosy."

He went ambling down the corridors of the enchanted sett, rolling from leg to leg with the queer badger paddle, his white mask with its black stripes looking ghostly in the gloom.

"It's along that passage," he said, "if you want to wash your hands."

Badgers are not like foxes. They have a special midden where they put out their used bones and rubbish, proper earth closets, and bedrooms whose bedding they turn out frequently, to keep it clean. The Wart was charmed with what he saw. He admired the Great Hall most, for this was the central room of the tumulus—it was difficult to know whether to think of it as a college or as a castle—and the various suites and bolt holes radiated outward from it. It was a bit cobwebby, owing to being a sort of common-room instead of being looked after by one particular family, but it was decidedly solemn. Badger called it the Combination Room. All round the panelled walls there were ancient paintings of departed badgers, famous in their day for scholarship or godliness, lit from above by shaded glow-worms. There were stately chairs with the badger arms stamped in gold on their Spanish leather seats—the leather was coming off—and a portrait of the Founder over the fireplace. The chairs were arranged in a semi-circle round the fire, and there were mahogany fans with which everybody could shield their faces from the flames, and a kind of tilting board by means of which the decanters could be slid back from the bottom of the semi-circle to the top. Some black gowns hung in the passage outside, and all was extremely ancient.

"I am a bachelor at the moment," said the badger apologetically, when they got back to his own snug room with the flowered wallpaper, "so I am afraid there is only one chair. You will have to sit on the bed. Make yourself at home, my dear, while I brew some punch, and tell me how things are going in the wide world."

"Oh, they go on much the same. Merlyn is well, and Kay is to be made a knight next week."

"An interesting ceremony."

"What enormous arms you have," remarked the Wart, watching him stir the spirits with a spoon. "So have I, for that matter." And he looked down at his own bandy-legged muscles. He was mainly a tight chest holding together a pair of forearms, mighty as thighs.

"It is to dig with," said the learned creature complacently. "Mole and I, I suppose you would have to dig pretty quick to match with us."

"I met a hedgehog outside."

"Did you now? They say nowadays that hedgehogs can carry swine fever and foot-and-mouth disease."

"I thought he was rather nice."

"They do have a sort of pathetic appeal," said the badger sadly, "but I'm afraid I generally just munch them up. There is something irresistible about pork crackling.

"The Egyptians," he added, and by this he meant the gypsies, "are fond of them for eating, too."

"Mine would not uncurl."

"You should have pushed him into some water, and then he'd have shown you his poor legs quick enough. Come, the punch is ready. Sit down by the fire and take your ease."

"It is nice to sit here with the snow and wind outside."

"It is nice. Let us drink good luck to Kay in his knighthood."

"Good luck to Kay, then."

"Good luck."

"Well," said the badger, setting down his glass again with a sigh. "Now what could have possessed Merlyn to send you to me?"

"He was talking about learning," said the Wart.

"Ah, well, if it is learning you are after, you have come to the right shop. But don't you find it rather dull?"

"Sometimes I do," said the Wart, "and sometimes I don't. On the whole I can bear a good deal of learning if it is about natural history."

"I am writing a treatise just now," said the badger, coughing diffidently to show that he was absolutely set on explaining it, "which is to point out why Man has become the master of the animals. Perhaps you would like to hear it?

"It's for my doctor's degree, you know," he added hastily, before the Wart could protest. He got few chances of reading his treatises to anybody, so he could not bear to let the opportunity slip by.

"Thank you very much," said the Wart.

"It will be good for you, dear boy. It is just the thing to top off an education. Study birds and fish and animals: then finish off with Man. How fortunate that you came! Now where the devil did I put that manuscript?"

The old gentleman scratched about with his great claws until he had turned up a dirty bundle of papers, one corner of which had been used for lighting something. Then he sat down in his leather armchair, which had a deep depression in the middle of it; put on his velvet smoking-cap with the tassel; and produced a pair of tarantula spectacles, which he balanced on the end of his nose.

"Hem," said the badger.

He immediately became paralysed with shyness, and sat blushing at his papers, unable to begin.

"Go on," said the Wart.

"It is not very good," he explained coyly. "It is just a rough draft, you know. I shall alter a lot before I send it in."

"I am sure it must be interesting."

"Oh no, it is not a bit interesting. It is just an odd thing I threw off in an odd half-hour, just to pass the time. But still, this is how it begins.

"Hem!" said the badger. Then he put on an impossibly high falsetto voice and began to read as fast as possible.

"People often ask, as an idle question, whether the process of evolution began with the chicken or the egg. Was there an egg out of which the first chicken came, or did a chicken lay the first egg? I am in a position to say that the first thing created was the egg.

"When God had manufactured all the eggs out of which the fishes and the serpents and the birds and the mammals and even the duck-billed platypus would eventually emerge, he called the embryos before Him, and saw that they were good.

"Perhaps I ought to explain," added the badger, lowering his papers nervously and looking at the Wart over the top of them, *"that all embryos look very much the same.* They are what you are before you are born—and, whether you are going to be a tadpole or a peacock or a cameleopard or a man, when you are an embryo you just look like a peculiarly repulsive and helpless human being. I continue as follows:

"The embryos stood in front of God, with their feeble hands clasped politely over their stomachs and their heavy heads hanging down respectfully, and God addressed them.

"He said: 'Now, you embryos, here you are, all looking exactly the same, and We are going to give you the choice of what you want to be. When you grow up you will get bigger anyway, but We are pleased to grant you another gift as well. You may alter any parts of yourselves into anything which you think would be useful to you in later life. For instance, at the moment you cannot dig. Anybody who would like to turn his hands into a pair of spades or garden forks is allowed to do so. Or, to put it another way, at present you can only use your mouths for eating. Anybody who would like to use his mouth as an offensive weapon, can change it by asking, and be a corkindrill or a sabre-toothed tiger. Now then, step up and choose your tools, but remember that what you choose you will grow into, and will have to stick to.'

"All the embryos thought the matter over politely, and then, one by one, they stepped up before the eternal throne. They were allowed two or three specializations, so that some chose to use their arms as flying machines and their mouths as weapons, or crackers, or drillers, or spoons, while others selected to use their bodies as boats and their hands as oars. We badgers thought very hard and decided to ask three boons. We wanted to change our skins for shields, our mouths for weapons, and our arms for garden forks. These boons were granted. Everybody specialized in one way or another, and some of us in very queer ones. For instance, one of the desert lizards decided to swap his whole body for blotting-paper, and one of the toads who lived in the drouthy antipodes decided simply to be a water-bottle.

"The asking and granting took up two long days—they were the fifth and sixth, so far as I remember—and at the very end of the sixth day, just before it was time to knock off for Sunday, they had got through all the little embryos except one. This embryo was Man.

" 'Well, Our little man,' said God. 'You have waited till the last, and slept on your decision, and We are sure you have been thinking hard all the time. What can We do for you?"

" 'Please God,' said the embryo, 'I think that You made me in the shape which I now have for reasons best known to Yourselves, and that it would be rude to change. If I am to have my choice I will stay as I am. I will not alter any of the parts which You gave me, for other and doubtless inferior tools, and I will stay a defenceless embryo all my life, doing my best to make myself a few feeble implements out of the wood, iron and the other materials which You have seen fit to put before me. If I want a boat I will try to construct it out of trees, and if I want to fly, I will put together a chariot to do it for me. Probably I have been very silly in refusing to take advantage of Your kind offer, but I have done my very best to think it over carefully, and now hope that the feeble decision of this small innocent will find favour with Yourselves.'

" 'Well done,' exclaimed the Creator in delighted tones. 'Here, all you embryos, come here with your beaks and whatnots to look upon Our first Man. He is the only one who has guessed Our riddle, out of all of you, and We have great pleasure in conferring upon him the Order of Dominion over the Fowls of the Air, and the Beasts of the Earth, and the Fishes of the Sea. Now let the rest of you get along, and love and multiply, for it is time to knock off for the week-end. As for you, Man, you will be a naked tool all your life, though a user of tools. You will look like an embryo till they bury you, but all the others will be embryos before your might. Eternally undeveloped, you will always remain potential in Our image, able to see some of Our sorrows and to feel some of Our joys. We are partly sorry for you, Man, but partly hopeful. Run along then, and do your best. And listen, Man, before you go . . .'

" 'Well?' asked Adam, turning back from his dismissal.

" 'We were only going to say,' said God shyly, twisting Their hands together. 'Well, We were just going to say, God bless you.' "

"It's a good story," said the Wart doubtfully.

# THE BLACKFOOT GENESIS

## George Bird Grinnell

All animals of the Plains at one time heard and knew him, and all birds of the air heard and knew him. All things that he had made understood him, when he spoke to them,—the birds, the animals and the people.

Old Man was travelling about, south of here, making the people. He came from the south, travelling north, making animals and birds as he passed along. He made the mountains, prairies, timber, and brush first. So he went along, travelling northward, making things as he went, putting rivers here and there, and falls on them, putting red paint here and there in the ground,—fixing up the world as we see it today. He made the Milk River (the Teton) and crossed it, and, being tired, went up on a little hill and lay down to rest. As he lay on his back, stretched out on the ground, with arms extended, he marked himself out with stones,—the shape of his body, head, legs, arms, and everything. There you can see those rocks to-day. After he had rested, he went on northward, and stumbled over a knoll and fell down on his knees. Then he said, "You are a bad thing to be stumbling against"; so he raised up two large buttes there, and named them the Knees, and they are called so to this day. He went on further north, and with some of the rocks he carried with him he built the Sweet Grass Hills.

Old Man covered the plains with grass for the animals to feed on. He marked off a piece of ground, and in it he made to grow all kinds of roots and berries,—camas, wild carrots, wild turnips, sweet-root, bitter-root, sarvis berries, bull berries, cherries, plums, and rosebuds. He put trees in the ground. He put all kinds of animals on the ground. When he made the bighorn with its big head and horns, he made it out on the prairie. It

"The Blackfoot Genesis" is reprinted by permission of Charles Scribner's Sons from *Blackfoot Lodge Tales* by George Bird Grinnell.

did not seem to travel easily on the prairie; it was awkward and could not go fast. So he took it by one of its horns, and led it up into the mountains, and turned it loose; and it skipped about among the rocks, and went up fearful places with ease. So he said, "This is the place that suits you; this is what you are fitted for, the rocks and the mountains." While he was in the mountains, he made the antelope out of dirt, and turned it loose, to see how it would go. It ran so fast that it fell over some rocks and hurt itself. He saw that this would not do, and took the antelope down on the prairie, and turned it loose; and it ran away fast and gracefully, and he said, "This is what you are suited to."

One day Old Man determined that he would make a woman and a child; so he formed them both—the woman and the child, her son—of clay. After he had moulded the clay in human shape, he said to the clay, "You must be people," and then he covered it up and left it, and went away. The next morning he went to the place and took the covering off, and saw that the clay shapes had changed a little. The second morning there was still more change, and the third still more. The fourth morning he went to the place, took the covering off, looked at the images, and told them to rise and walk; and they did so. They walked down to the river with their Maker, and then he told them that his name was *Na' pi,* Old Man.

As they were standing by the river, the woman said to him, "How is it? will we always live, will there be no end to it?" He said: "I have never thought of that. We will have to decide it. I will take this buffalo chip and throw it in the river. If it floats, when people die, in four days they will become alive again; they will die for only four days. But if it sinks, there will be an end to them." He threw the chip into the river, and it floated. The woman turned and picked up a stone, and said: "No, I will throw this stone in the river; if it floats we will always live, if it sinks people must die, that they may always be sorry for each other." The woman threw the stone into the water, and it sank. "There," said Old Man, "you have chosen. There will be an end to them."

It was not many nights after, that the woman's child died, and she cried a great deal for it. She said to Old Man: "Let us change this. The law that you first made, let that be a law." He said: "Not so. What is made law must be law. We will undo nothing that we have done. The child is dead, but it cannot be changed. People will have to die."

That is how we came to be people. It is he who made us.

The first people were poor and naked, and did not know how to get a living. Old Man showed them the roots and berries, and told them that they could eat them; that in a certain month of the year they could peel the bark off some trees and eat it, that it was good. He told the people that the animals should be their food, and gave them to the people, saying, "These are your herds." He said: "All these little animals that live in the ground—rats, squirrels, skunks, beavers—are good to eat. You need not fear to eat of their flesh." He made all the birds that fly, and told the people that there was no harm in their flesh, that it could be eaten. The first people that he created he used to take about through the timber and swamps and over the prairies, and show them the different plants. Of a certain plant he would say, "the root of this plant, if gathered in a certain month of the year, is good for a certain sickness." So they learned the power of all herbs.

In those days there were buffalo. Now the people had no arms, but those black animals with long beards were armed; and once, as the people were moving about, the buffalo saw them, and ran after them, and hooked them, and killed and ate them. One day, as the Maker of the people was travelling over the country, he saw some of his children, that he had made, lying dead, torn to pieces and partly eaten by the buffalo. When he saw this he was very sad. He said: "This will not do. I will change this. The people shall eat the buffalo."

He went to some of the people who were left, and said to them, "How is it that you people do nothing to these animals that are killing you?" The people said: "What can we do? We have no way to kill these animals, while they are armed and can kill us." Then said the Maker: "That is not hard. I will make you a weapon that will kill these animals." So he went out, and cut some sarvis berry shoots, and brought them in, and peeled the bark off them. He took a larger piece of wood, and flattened it, and tied a string to it, and made a bow. Now, as he was the master of all birds and could do with them as he wished, he went out and caught one, and took feathers from its wing, and split them, and tied them to the shaft of wood. He tied four feathers along the shaft, and tried the arrow at a mark, and found that it did not fly well. He took these feathers off, and put on three; and when he tried it again, he found that it was good. He went out and began to break sharp pieces off the stones. He tried them, and found that the black flint stones made the best arrow points, and some white flints. Then he taught the people how to use these things.

Then he said: "The next time you go out, take these things with you, and use them as I tell you, and do not run from these animals. When they run at you, as soon as they get pretty close, shoot the arrows at them, as I have taught you; and you will see that they will run from you or will run in a circle around you."

Now, as people became plenty, one day three men went out on to the plain to see the buffalo, but they had no arms. They saw the animals, but when the buffalo saw the men, they ran after them and killed two of them, but one got away. One day after this, the people went on a little hill to look about, and the buffalo saw them, and said, *"Saiyah,* there is some more of our food," and they rushed on them. This time the people did not run. They began to shoot at the buffalo with the bows and arrows *Na' pi* had given them, and the buffalo began to fall; but in the fight a person was killed.

At this time these people had flint knives given them, and they cut up the bodies of the dead buffalo. It is not healthful to eat the meat raw, so Old Man gathered soft dry rotten driftwood and made punk of it, and then got a piece of hard wood, and drilled a hole in it with an arrow point, and gave them a pointed piece of hard wood, and taught them how to make a fire with fire sticks, and to cook the flesh of these animals and eat it.

They got a kind of stone that was in the land, and then took another harder stone and worked one upon the other, and hollowed out the softer one, and made a kettle of it. This was the fashion of their dishes.

Also Old Man said to the people: "Now, if you are overcome, you may go and sleep, and get power. Something will come to you in your dream, that will help you. Whatever these animals tell you to do, you must obey them, as they appear to you in your sleep. Be guided by them. If anybody wants help, if you are alone and travelling, and cry aloud for help, your prayer will be answered. It may be by the eagles, perhaps by the buffalo, or by the bears. Whatever animal answers your prayer, you must listen to him."

That was how the first people got through the world, by the power of their dreams.

After this, Old Man kept on, travelling north. Many of the animals that he had made followed him as he went. The animals understood him when he spoke to them, and he used them as his servants. When he got to the north point of the Porcupine Mountains, there he made some more mud images of people, and blew breath upon them, and they became people. He made men and women. They asked him, "What are we to eat?" He made many images of clay, in the form of buffalo. Then he blew breath on these, and they stood up; and when he made signs to them, they started to run. Then he said to the people, "Those are your food." They said to him, "Well, now, we have those animals; how are we to kill them?" "I will show you," he said. He took them to the cliff, and made them build rock piles like this, > ; and he made the people hide behind these piles of rock, and said, "When I lead the buffalo this way, as I bring them opposite to you, rise up."

After he had told them how to act, he started on toward a herd of buffalo. He began to call them, and the buffalo started to run toward him, and they followed him until they were inside the lines. Then he dropped back; and as the people rose up, the buffalo ran in a straight line and jumped over the cliff. He told the people to go and take the flesh of those animals. They tried to tear the limbs apart, but they could not. They tried to bite pieces out, and could not. So Old Man went to the edge of the cliff, and broke some pieces of stone with sharp edges, and told them to cut the flesh with these. When they had taken the skins from these animals, they set up some poles and put the hides on them, and so made a shelter to sleep under. There were some of these buffalo that went over the cliff that were not dead. Their legs were broken, but they were still alive. The people cut strips of green hide, and tied stones in the middle, and made large mauls, and broke in the skulls of the buffalo, and killed them.

After he had taught those people these things, he started off again, travelling north, until he came to where Bow and Elbow rivers meet. There he made some more people, and taught them the same things. From here he again went on northward. When he had come nearly to the Red Deer's River, he reached the hill where the Old Man sleeps. There he lay down and rested himself. The form of his body is to be seen there yet.

When he awoke from his sleep, he travelled further northward and came to a fine high hill. He climbed to the top of it, and there sat down to rest. He looked over the country below him, and it pleased him. Before him the hill was steep, and he said to himself, "Well, this is a fine place for sliding; I will have some fun," and he began to slide down the hill. The marks where he slid down are to be seen yet, and the place is known to all people as the "Old Man's Sliding Ground."

This is as far as the Blackfeet followed Old Man. The Crees know what he did further north.

In later times once, *Na' pi* said, "Here I will mark you off a piece of ground," and he did so. Then he said: "There is your land, and it is full of all kinds of animals, and many things grow in this land. Let no other people come into it. This is for you five tribes (Blackfeet, Bloods, Piegans, Gros Ventres, Sarcees). When people come to cross the line, take your bows and arrows, your lances and your battle axes, and give them battle and keep them out. If they gain a footing, trouble will come to you."

Our forefathers gave battle to all people who came to cross these lines, and kept them out. Of late years we have let our friends, the white people, come in, and you know the result. We, his children, have failed to obey his laws.

# GENESIS

## CHAPTER 1

In the beginning God created the heaven and the earth.

2 And the earth was without form, and void; and darkness *was* upon the face of the deep. And the Spirit of God moved upon the face of the waters.

3 And God said, Let there be light: and there was light.

4 And God saw the light, that *it was* good: and God divided the light from the darkness.

5 And God called the light Day, and the darkness he called Night. And the evening and the morning were the first day.

6 And God said, Let there be a firmament in the midst of the waters, and let it divide the waters from the waters.

7 And God made the firmament, and divided the waters which *were* under the firmament from the waters which *were* above the firmament: and it was so.

8 And God called the firmament Heaven. And the evening and the morning were the second day.

9 And God said, Let the waters under the heaven be gathered together unto one place, and let the dry *land* appear: and it was so.

10 And God called the dry *land* Earth; and the gathering together of the waters called he Seas: and God saw that *it was* good.

11 And God said, Let the earth bring forth grass, the herb yielding seed, *and* the fruit tree yielding fruit after his kind, whose seed *is* in itself, upon the earth: and it was so.

From the King James Version of the Bible.

12 And the earth brought forth grass, *and* herb yielding seed after his kind, and the tree yielding fruit, whose seed *was* in itself, after his kind: and God saw that *it was* good.

13 And the evening and the morning were the third day.

14 And God said, Let there be lights in the firmament of the heaven to divide the day from the night; and let them be for signs, and for seasons, and for days, and years:

15 And let them be for lights in the firmament of the heaven to give light upon the earth: and it was so.

16 And God made two great lights; the greater light to rule the day, and the lesser light to rule the night: *he made* the stars also.

17 And God set them in the firmament of the heaven to give light upon the earth,

18 And to rule over the day and over the night, and to divide the light from the darkness: and God saw that *it was* good.

19 And the evening and the morning were the fourth day.

20 And God said, Let the waters bring forth abundantly the moving creature that hath life, and fowl *that* may fly above the earth in the open firmament of heaven.

21 And God created great whales, and every living creature that moveth, which the waters brought forth abundantly, after their kind, and every winged fowl after his kind: and God saw that *it was* good.

22 And God blessed them, saying, Be fruitful, and multiply, and fill the waters in the seas, and let fowl multiply in the earth.

23 And the evening and the morning were the fifth day.

24 And God said, Let the earth bring forth the living creature after his kind, cattle, and creeping thing, and beast of the earth after his kind: and it was so.

25 And God made the beast of the earth after his kind, and cattle after their kind, and every thing that creepeth upon the earth after his kind: and God saw that *it was* good.

26 And God said, Let us make man in our image, after our likeness: and let them have dominion over the fish of the sea, and over the fowl of the air, and over the cattle, and over all the earth, and over every creeping thing that creepeth upon the earth.

27 So God created man in his *own* image, in the image of God created he him; male and female created he them.

28 And God blessed them, and God said unto them, Be fruitful, and multiply, and replenish the earth, and subdue it: and have dominion over the fish of the sea, and over the fowl of the air, and over every living thing that moveth upon the earth.

29 And God said, Behold, I have given you every herb bearing seed, which *is* upon the face of all the earth, and every tree, in the which *is* the fruit of a tree yielding seed; to you it shall be for meat.

30 And to every beast of the earth, and to every fowl of the air, and to every thing that creepeth upon the earth, wherein *there is* life, *I have given* every green herb for meat: and it was so.

31 And God saw every thing that he had made, and, behold, *it was* very good. And the evening and the morning were the sixth day.

## CHAPTER 2

Thus the heavens and the earth were finished, and all the host of them.

2 And on the seventh day God ended his work which he had made; and he rested on the seventh day from all his work which he had made.

3 And God blessed the seventh day, and sanctified it: because that in it he had rested from all his work which God created and made.

4 These *are* the generations of the heavens and of the earth when they were created, in the day that the LORD God made the earth and the heavens,

5 And every plant of the field before it was in the earth, and every herb of the field before it grew: for the LORD God had not caused it to rain upon the earth, and *there was* not a man to till the ground.

6 But there went up a mist from the earth, and watered the whole face of the ground.

7 And the LORD God formed man *of* the dust of the ground, and breathed into his nostrils the breath of life; and man became a living soul.

8 And the LORD God planted a garden eastward in Eden; and there he put the man whom he had formed.

9 And out of the ground made the LORD God to grow every tree that is pleasant to the sight, and good for food; the tree of life also in the midst of the garden, and the tree of knowledge of good and evil.

10 And a river went out of Eden to water the garden; and from thence it was parted, and became into four heads.

11 The name of the first *is* Pison: that *is* it which compasseth the whole land of Havilah, where *there* is gold;

12 And the gold of that land *is* good: there *is* bdellium and the onyx stone.

13 And the name of the second river *is* Gihon: the same *is* it that compasseth the whole land of Ethiopia.

14 And the name of the third river *is* Hiddekel: that *is* it which goeth toward the east of Assyria. And the fourth river *is* Euphrates.

15 And the LORD God took the man, and put him into the garden of Eden to dress it and to keep it.

16 And the LORD God commanded the man, saying, Of every tree of the garden thou mayest freely eat:

17 But of the tree of the knowledge of good and evil, thou shalt not eat of it: for in the day that thou eatest thereof thou shalt surely die.

18 And the LORD God said, *It is* not good that the man should be alone; I will make him a help meet for him.

19 And out of the ground the LORD God formed every beast of the field, and every fowl of the air; and brought *them* unto Adam to see what he would call them: and whatsoever Adam called every living creature, that *was* the name thereof.

20 And Adam gave names to all cattle, and to the fowl of the air, and to every beast of the field; but for Adam there was not found a help meet for him.

21 And the LORD God caused a deep sleep to fall upon Adam, and he slept; and he took one of his ribs, and closed up the flesh instead thereof.

22 And the rib, which the LORD God had taken from man, made he a woman, and brought her unto the man.

23 And Adam said, This *is* now bone of my bones, and flesh of my flesh: she shall be called Woman, because she was taken out of man.

24 Therefore shall a man leave his father and his mother, and shall cleave unto his wife: and they shall be one flesh.

25 And they were both naked, the man and his wife, and were not ashamed.

## CHAPTER 3

Now the serpent was more subtile than any beast of the field which the LORD God had made. And he said unto the woman, Yea, hath God said, Ye shall not eat of every tree of the garden?

2 And the woman said unto the serpent, We may eat of the fruit of the trees of the garden:

3 But of the fruit of the tree which *is* in the midst of the garden, God hath said, Ye shall not eat of it, neither shall ye touch it, lest ye die.

4 And the serpent said unto the woman, Ye shall not surely die:

5 For God doth know that in the day ye eat thereof, then your eyes shall be opened, and ye shall be as gods, knowing good and evil.

6 And when the woman saw that the tree *was* good for food, and that it *was* pleasant to the eyes, and a tree to be desired to make *one* wise, she took of the fruit thereof, and did eat, and gave also unto her husband with her; and he did eat.

7 And the eyes of them both were opened, and they knew that they *were* naked; and they sewed fig leaves together, and made themselves aprons.

8 And they heard the voice of the Lord God walking in the garden in the cool of the day: and Adam and his wife hid themselves from the presence of the Lord God amongst the trees of the garden.

9 And the Lord God called unto Adam, and said unto him, Where *art* thou?

10 And he said, I heard thy voice in the garden, and I was afraid, because I *was* naked; and I hid myself.

11 And he said, Who told thee that thou *wast* naked? Hast thou eaten of the tree, whereof I commanded thee that thou shouldest not eat?

12 And the man said, The woman whom thou gavest *to be* with me, she gave me of the tree, and I did eat.

13 And the Lord God said unto the woman, What *is* this *that* thou hast done? And the woman said, The serpent beguiled me and I did eat.

14 And the Lord God said unto the serpent, Because thou hast done this, thou *art* cursed above all cattle, and above every beast of the field; upon thy belly shalt thou go, and dust shalt thou eat all the days of thy life:

15 And I will put enmity between thee and the woman, and between thy seed and her seed; it shall bruise thy head, and thou shalt bruise his heel.

16 Unto the woman he said, I will greatly multiply thy sorrow and thy conception; in sorrow thou shalt bring forth children; and thy desire *shall be* to thy husband, and he shall rule over thee.

17 And unto Adam he said, Because thou hast hearkened unto the voice of thy wife, and hast eaten of the tree, of which I commanded thee, saying, Thou shalt not eat of it: cursed *is* the ground for thy sake; in sorrow shalt thou eat *of* it all the days of thy life;

18 Thorns also and thistles shall it bring forth to thee; and thou shalt eat the herb of the field:

19 In the sweat of thy face shalt thou eat bread, till thou return unto the ground; for out of it wast thou taken: for dust thou *art,* and unto dust shalt thou return.

20 And Adam called his wife's name Eve; because she was the mother of all living.

21 Unto Adam also and to his wife did the Lord God make coats of skins, and clothed them.

22 And the Lord God said, Behold, the man is become as one of us, to know good and evil: and now, lest he put forth his hand, and take also of the tree of life, and eat, and live for ever:

23 Therefore the Lord God sent him forth from the garden of Eden, to till the ground from whence he was taken.

24 So he drove out the man: and he placed at the east of the garden of Eden cherubim, and a flaming sword which turned every way, to keep the way of the tree of life.

## CHAPTER 4

And Adam knew Eve his wife; and she conceived, and bare Cain, and said, I have gotten a man from the LORD.

2 And she again bare his brother Abel. And Abel was a keeper of sheep, but Cain was a tiller of the ground.

3 And in process of time it came to pass, that Cain brought of the fruit of the ground an offering unto the LORD.

4 And Abel, he also brought of the firstlings of his flock and of the fat thereof. And the LORD had respect unto Abel and to his offering:

5 But unto Cain and to his offering he had not respect. And Cain was very wroth, and his countenance fell.

6 And the LORD said unto Cain, Why art thou wroth? and why is thy countenance fallen?

7 If thou doest well, shalt thou not be accepted? and if thou doest not well, sin lieth at the door: and unto thee *shall be* his desire, and thou shalt rule over him.

8 And Cain talked with Abel his brother: and it came to pass, when they were in the field, that Cain rose up against Abel his brother, and slew him.

9 And the LORD said unto Cain, Where *is* Abel thy brother? And he said, I know not: *Am* I my brother's keeper?

10 And he said, What hast thou done? the voice of thy brother's blood crieth unto me from the ground.

11 And now *art* thou cursed from the earth, which hath opened her mouth to receive thy brother's blood from thy hand.

12 When thou tillest the ground, it shall not henceforth yield unto thee her strength; a fugitive and a vagabond shalt thou be in the earth.

13 And Cain said unto the LORD, My punishment *is* greater than I can bear.

14 Behold, thou hast driven me out this day from the face of the earth; and from thy face shall I be hid; and I shall be a fugitive and a vagabond in the earth; and it shall come to pass, *that* every one that findeth me shall slay me.

15 And the LORD said unto him, Therefore whosoever slayeth Cain, vengeance shall be taken on him sevenfold. And the LORD set a mark upon Cain, lest any finding him should kill him.

16 And Cain went out from the presence of the LORD, and dwelt in the land of Nod, on the east of Eden.

# PROMETHEUS-PANDORA

## Compiled by Hope Blacker

In the beginning was chaos and nothingness. Chaos, however, was not for the Greeks turmoil. It simply meant yawning. Out of this nothingness there emerged Nyx, Night, and Erebos, the place of death. There then arose from Nyx and Erebos, Aither, heaven's light, and Hermera, the day. Then arose Eros, love. These were powers in the universe and were not seen as anthropomorphic images. Then there emerged from Chaos Gaia, the earth herself. She bore a son named Uranus. Fertilizing her with rainstorms, he brought forth plants and trees and filled in the seas and rivers. From the union of mother and son came hundred-headed monsters; later came the Cyclops or one-eyed monsters whose names represented thunder and lightning. Finally a group of divine beings called Titans were born. Uranus banished his sons, the Cyclops, and the other monsters to the nether world. In revenge Gaia incited the Titans, under the leadership of one named Chronos to rebel against their father. Armed with a sickle which his mother had given him, Chronos castrated his father. Where the blood fell upon the earth the Erinnes, or furies, who avenge crimes, arose, and in yet other places wood nymphs came into being. The members of the father fell upon the waves, and the goddess Aphrodite arose from the bloodied foam.

Chronos married his sister Rhea and by her fathered children, the Olympian gods: Hestia, goddess of the hearth; Demeter, the corn goddess; Hera, special goddess of women; Hades, lord of the dead; and Posiedon, god of the sea. At this time, however, these gods had not assumed their rule. As it had been foretold by his wife Rhea that one of his own sons would overthrow his rule, Chronos devoured each of his children in turn. Enraged by his lust for power, Rhea retired to Mount Lycaem in Arcadia, where she bore her last child, a son called Zeus. He was the child who would rebel against his father and rule the gods and men from Olympus.

Rhea took the child to her mother, Gaia, who gave the boy to wood nymphs to be raised. With his mother's help, Zeus became cup-bearer to his father. The position offered him the opportunity to feed his father an emetic. Chronos vomited his other children as well as the stone given him by Rhea as a substitute for Zeus. There ensued a frightful battle for supremacy which absorbed the entire cosmos. Zeus released from the realm of the dead the hundred-headed monsters so that they might aid him. The wisest of the Titans, Prometheus, also came to his aid. With these powerful forces Zeus was able to dethrone and destroy Chronos and establish his reign. He then banished the monsters and destroyed the Titans, that the earth might be a peaceful place, all except Prometheus and his brother. Not only the monsters and the misshapen had been banished but the formlessness which they represented gave way to order and peace. The ordered cosmos stood as a witness to the truth of this story.

The sun moved in his chariot across the heavens by day, and his sister, the moon, strode across the skies in her chariot by night. The earth flowered, but mortal man had not yet been created. Later Greeks, called Orphics, said that man was created from the pieces into which the Titans had been hacked after their defeat. Thus they explained the nature of man as both divine and mortal.

Most Greeks believed that Zeus himself created man after many experiments; many, however, believed that the wise Prometheus created man out of the clay. Prometheus, it was believed, taught men how to sow and reap the grains. But men still lacked fire. He could not cook his food, warm his house or smelt metal for tools. Prometheus because he loved his creation stole fire, igniting a torch from the sparks which flew from the wheels of the sun chariot.

In punishment, Zeus chained Prometheus to a rock, where his liver, which was immortal, was torn out day after day by a vulture. The rebellion of the Titan was avenged. Zeus, in spite of his anger toward man, created woman, Pandora. She was given a box and told never to open it. Her curiosity compelled her to open the box, and from it flew greed, jealousy, and a host of plagues. Among all these only one disease remained. Finally it too flew from the box; it was hope. This sole comfort of man was indeed his worst plague, for it sustained his life in a world beset by evil.

# THE CURSE
# ON THE HOUSE
# OF ATREUS

## Compiled by Hope Blacker

Heinrich Schleimann, who discovered Troy, also discovered, in Greece, the citadel of Mycenae, with its gargantuan stone walls and beehive shaped tombs full of gold masks, rings, flagons and armor. Although he made many errors in identification, the treasure and the megalithic palaces which he found there led to more intensive excavation at Mycenae and later at other places in Greece identified with those mentioned in the works of Homer. We now have a picture of a wealthy and powerful confederacy of states whose trade routes extended north to Ireland and across the Baltic for gold and amber, south throughout the Mediterranean, through Egypt to Nubia. This civilization, with its great ports and citadels of palaces and comfortable two-story homes for the nobility, was overrun by barbarians, perhaps from what we today call Hungary. We may visualize this invasion as similar to the fall of the civilized and opulent Rome.

Mycenae and the other states of Hellas fell in the twelfth century before Christ. In the dark ages that followed, when Greece was a nation of shepherds and fishermen, men remembered that there was a time when mighty kings ruled Hellas. One of these kings had mobilized all of Hellas for a great war. His name was Agamemnon, and his brother was Menelaus.

What do we know about Agamemnon, and what stories were told of him and of his family, the acurséd House of Atreus?

The cycle begins three generations back from Agamemnon with Tantalus. Tantalus was the son of the god Zeus, and he was honored by the gods as no mortal had ever been honored. But he rebelled against his privileged position. He murdered his son, Pelops, roasted the boy's flesh, and dared to serve it as a dish for a banquet which he had prepared for the gods. The crime which he committed was that of pride, *hybris*.

The Olympians were not to be so tricked. They recognized his infamy and restored the boy, sending the father to a place in the nether world where he was to stand, chained forever in a pool of water which receeded as he thirstily bent to drink. Above him was luscious fruit which the wind eternally kept from his grasp. Thus our word "tantalize."

This act was the infamous founding of the royal house. The boy, Pelops, nevertheless prospered and came into his kingdom. He had two sons, Atreus, the father of Agamemnon and Menelaus, and Thyestes, father of Aegisthus. Having murdered a certain Chryssipos, the princes were forced to flee to the city of Midea, near Mycenae. The Greek nobility were not killed or jailed for crimes but, like Oedipus, forced to leave their cities and endure their fate. The ballots which the Greek citizens used to exile a man were called *ostraka;* the man was ostrasized. He could not participate in sacred feasts in his own city, and he could not speak before a group of his fellow citizens. The banished man could, however, reside elsewhere in comfort; and we can imagine the brothers, Atreus and Thyestes, living as gentlemen farmers in Midea.

Atreus had vowed to sacrifice his finest head of cattle to the goddess Artemis, who had a very important local cult. Unexpectedly, one of his shepherds brought him a wonderful lamb with a golden fleece. This lamb was unquestionably the most fitting sacrifice. In his greed, however, Atreus was unwilling to sacrifice the animal, and, sacrificing only the innards, he locked the marvelous fleece in a chest.

At this time his wife, Aerope, was secretly having an affair with her husband's brother, Thyestes. She stole the fleece from the chest and brought it to her lover, unknown to anyone save themselves.

The people of Mycenae, whose royal house had died off, received word from an oracle that they should choose one of the sons of Pelops to be king. When the people had assembled to choose one of the brothers, Thyestes confidently proposed that the man who could sacrifice a golden fleece should rule; and Atreus, unaware of the deception, agreed with equal confidence. The sacred quality of any city where men lived was preserved through ritual. Frequently, it was a guardian of the city that the king sacrificed to the god, reaffirming his own link to the divine powers. Thus the sacrifice not only symbolized the king's secular role, as our President affirms his role by throwing the first baseball of the season, but the act renewed the king's sacred role. Most cultures retain traces of such divine fertility rites. Some African tribes have, for thousands of years, sacrificed the old king to the new, first through the old king's death and then through the new king's defeat of a male lion who is symbolically believed to house the remaining vitality of the old king. In Hebrew culture is the ram, the scapegoat, Isaac. In Christianity there is the spring crucifixion and the communion ritual which symbolically suggests the need to eat the godhead to regenerate the vitality of the spirit. The sacrifice of a golden fleece was a fitting test of royal perogative.

Thyestes treacherously produced the fleece. Zeus himself set his mark upon Atreus, for he caused the forces of the sun to turn around in their path. When the people of Mycenae saw the day change its course, they were horrified and realized they had erred in accepting Thyestes and asked Atreus to become king.

Atreus assumed the kingship, but, perhaps because he was insecure in his position, perhaps because he was enraged at having been cuckolded and deceived, he decided to pollute his brother. Atreus slew Thyestes' three young sons and served them, boiled and roasted, as had his grandfather Tantalus earlier, to their father, Thyestes. Thyestes ate of the flesh of his sons, but when he realized what had happened, he vomited and cursed his brother's house.

Atreus continued in his rule and had two sons, Agamemnon and Menelaus. In time Atreus grew old, and Agamemnon assumed the throne of Mycenae.

The kingdom of Sparta was ruled by King Tyndareus. His presumed daughter, Helen of Troy, was considered the most beautiful woman in Greece. Legend had it that Zeus, in the form of a swan, had ravaged Helen's mother, Leda, and that Helen had been born from an egg. Others claimed that it was her lovely but less devastatingly beautiful sister, Clytemnestra, who had been born of the union of Leda and Zeus. Still others said that it was the half-men—half-horse twin brothers, Castor and Pollux (whom Zeus was later to raise into the heavens as a constellation), who were born from the double egg. The twin egg, however, was for Greece The Annunciation. Mary's vision of giving birth to a god's child through a dove seems similar, even if some would contend it was somehow more "immaculate."

King Tyndareus, Leda's husband, had promised his kingdom of Sparta to the man who would marry the beautiful Helen, and he was afraid that if he were to give her to one or another of the Achaens, the others would break into battle over her, for all the lords of Hellas had assembled to court the woman. He asked Odysseus, who, although still young, was already known for his cunning, to advise him. Odysseus told him to have all the suitors swear that they would support whoever was chosen as Helen's husband.

Tyndareus did this and awarded Helen and the throne of Sparta to the wealthy prince Menelaus of Mycenae. He gave his other daughter, Clytemnestra, to Agamemnon, and out of gratitude for the wise advice, Tyndareus gave the less affluent Odysseus his niece Penelope.

Helen had two children, Hermione and Nicostratus; and Clytemnestra had three, a son, Orestes, and two daughters, Iphigenia and Electra. Penelope bore a son called Telemachus. So it stood with the royal households of Hellas when Paris, son of Priam the King of Troy, came from the Trojan citadel which lay across the straits from today's Constantinople, to visit the home of Menelaus. He seduced Helen and took her with him. Historically, it is believed Paris did not return to Troy at all.

Agamemnon called together the Achaen kings to avenge the outrage to his brother's hearth and position. A thousand ships set sail for Troy. At Aulis the ships were becalmed. After consulting an oracle, the Greeks learned that it would be necessary for Agamemnon to sacrifice his eldest daughter, Iphigenia, to the goddess Artemis before the winds would rise. Accordingly, Agamemnon sent for the maiden and sacrificed her that the fleet might sail to Troy. She was magically stolen from the sacrificial knife by the goddess and transported to the kingdom of the Tauri, where she grew up. This was not known to Agamemnon nor to her hysterical mother, who believed her dead.

The winds rose and the ships sailed to Troy. Homer, in his *Iliad,* told of a war so important in the formation of the Greek nation that the gods themselves took sides and entered the battle. When the later Greeks wrote of their civil war, they did not speak of the gods aiding either victor or defeated. The myth, obviously transcends historical import.

As we know, great princes on both sides, like Achilles and his friend Patroclus and Priam's son, Hector, were killed. After ten years of bloodletting, the Greeks won Troy through the ruse of a wooden horse.

The victorious Greeks burned "the topless towers of Illium" and dashed the children of princes from the burning walls of the city. The Romans believed that one prince, Aeneas, fleeing the burning city with his aged father on his back, came to found their city. English kings have also claimed descent from the House of Troy.

The wives and daughters of the royal house the Achaens took for themselves. The young princess Polyxena was killed at the grave of Achilles that she might satisfy him in Elysium. Hector's widow was given to Achilles' son. Agamemnon himself took for his bed the visionary princess Cassandra. As a young woman Cassandra had attracted the attention of the god Apollo. In the course of their affair, he gave her the gift of prophecy, but when she spurned him, he cursed her so that none of her prophecies would be believed; she would be considered mad. Like the Priest Laocoön, she had recognized the ominous nature of the wooden horse. Lest someone listen to his warning, Athena destroyed him and his two sons. The earth opened, and they were strangled by the serpents which emerged. Cassandra was scorned; the depth of her tragedy is revealed by Aeschylus.

The general of the victorious army, Agamemnon, took Cassandra and sailed home. He had been gone for many years and had left a wife incensed over the sacrifice of a daughter. In Clytemnestra's mind the murder of their child nullified their marriage, and she had taken for a lover Agamemnon's cousin, Aegisthus, a man who had not gone to war. As the son of Thyestes, Aegisthus was to avenge his dead brothers and fulfill his father's curse upon the House of Atreus.

Together they had planned Agamemnon's death. When the king returned, Clytemnestra welcomed him warmly, bade him relax, and led him to the bath. She had convinced him to commit the crime of *hybris* by exalting his ego with the grandeur of his victory over the greatest of kings, Priam. Agamemnon walked upon the crimson carpet into the bath. There Clytemnestra and Aegisthus threw a net over his head and stabbed him violently to death. Clytemnestra and her consort Aegisthus undertook to rule Mycenae, but the people were restless.

A nurse had taken the royal son, Orestes, away, fearing that the queen might harm him. The girl, Electra, grew up and was given in marriage to a shepherd. The act was symbolic; she was not to be considered of the royal household. Humiliated, she carried out her daily duties as a shepherd's wife and dreamed of the return of her brother, Orestes, who would help her to avenge her father's death and the insult of her marriage.

Orestes returned secretly and the two children killed their mother and her lover, Aegisthus. Orestes was forced to flee once again, driven by the furies, demons of vengeance. Finally intervention of the goddess Athena released him from his guilt and purified him and his seed. The curse of the tyrant revenge was made impotent by love.

# LEDA AND THE SWAN

## William Butler Yeats

A sudden blow : the great wings beating still
Above the staggering girl, her thighs caressed
By the dark webs, her nape caught in his bill,
He holds her helpless breast upon his breast.
How can those terrified vague fingers push
The feathered glory from her loosening thighs?
And how can body, laid in that white rush,
But feel the strange heart beating where it lies?

A shudder in the loins engenders there
The broken wall, the burning roof and tower
And Agamemnon dead.
                  Being so caught up,
So mastered by the brute blood of the air,
Did she put on his knowledge with his power
Before the indifferent beak could let her drop?

*Leda* after Michelangelo Buonarroti (By permission of the Royal Academy of Arts, London)

*Leda and the Swan* by Raphael, copy of a drawing by Leonardo da Vinci (University of London, Courtauld Institute of Art)

# THE MARRIAGE
# OF HEAVEN AND HELL

## William Blake

**Plate 2**

### THE ARGUMENT

Rintrah roars & shakes his fires in the burden'd air;
Hungry clouds swag on the deep.

Once meek, and in a perilous path,
The just man kept his course along
The vale of death.
Roses are planted where thorns grow,
And on the barren heath
Sing the honey bees.

Then the perilous path was planted,
And a river and a spring
On every cliff and tomb,
And on the bleached bones
Red clay brought forth;

Till the villain left the paths of ease,
To walk in perilous paths, and drive
The just man into barren climes.

Now the sneaking serpent walks
In mild humility,
And the just man rages in the wilds
Where lions roam.

Rintrah roars & shakes his fires in the burden'd air;
Hungry clouds swag on the deep.

## Plate 3

As a new heaven is begun, and it is now thirty-three years since its advent, the Eternal Hell revives. And lo! Swedenborg is the Angel sitting at the tomb: his writings are the linen clothes folded up. Now is the dominion of Edom, & the return of Adam into Paradise; see Isaiah xxxiv & xxxv Chap.

Without Contraries is no progression. Attraction and Repulsion, Reason and Energy, Love and Hate, are necessary to Human existence.

From these contraries spring what the religious call Good & Evil. Good is the passive that obeys Reason. Evil is the active springing from Energy.

Good is Heaven. Evil is Hell.

## Plate 4

### THE VOICE OF THE DEVIL

All Bibles or sacred codes have been the causes of the following Errors:

1. That Man has two real existing principles: Viz: a Body & a Soul.
2. That Energy, call'd Evil, is alone from the Body; & that Reason, call'd Good, is alone from the Soul.
3. That God will torment Man in Eternity for following his Energies.

But the following Contraries to these are True:

1. Man has no Body distinct from his Soul; for that call'd Body is a portion of Soul discern'd by the five Senses, the chief inlets of Soul in this age.
2. Energy is the only life, and is from the Body; and Reason is the bound or outward circumference of Energy.
3. Energy is Eternal Delight.

## Plates 5–6

Those who restrain desire, do so because theirs is weak enough to be restrained; and the restrainer or reason usurps its place & governs the unwilling.

And being restrain'd, it by degrees becomes passive, till it is only the shadow of desire.

The history of this is written in Paradise Lost, & the Governor or Reason is call'd Messiah.

And the original Archangel, or possessor of the command of the heavenly host, is call'd the Devil or Satan, and his children are call'd Sin & Death.

But in the Book of Job, Milton's Messiah is call'd Satan.

For this history has been adopted by both parties.

It indeed appear'd to Reason as if Desire was cast out; but the Devil's account is, that the Messiah fell, & formed a heaven of what he stole from the Abyss.

This is shewn in the Gospel, where he prays to the Father to send the comforter, or Desire, that Reason may have Ideas to build on; the Jehovah of the Bible being no other than he who dwells in flaming fire.

Know that after Christ's death, he became Jehovah.

But in Milton, the Father is Destiny, the Son a Ratio of the five senses, & the Holy-ghost Vacuum!

Note: The reason Milton wrote in fetters when he wrote of Angels & God, and at liberty when of Devils & Hell, is because he was a true Poet and of the Devil's party without knowing it.

## Plates 6–7
### A MEMORABLE FANCY

As I was walking among the fires of hell, delighted with the enjoyments of Genius, which to Angels look like torment and insanity, I collected some of their Proverbs; thinking that as the sayings used in a nation mark its character, so the Proverbs of Hell show the nature of Infernal wisdom better than any description of buildings or garments.

When I came home: on the abyss of the five senses, where a flat sided steep frowns over the present world, I saw a mighty Devil folded in black clouds, hovering on the sides of the rock: with corroding fires he wrote the following sentence now percieved by the minds of men, & read by them on earth:

> How do you know but ev'ry Bird that cuts the airy way,
> Is an immense world of delight, clos'd by your senses five?

## Plate 7
### PROVERBS OF HELL

In seed time learn, in harvest teach, in winter enjoy.
Drive your cart and your plow over the bones of the dead.
The road of excess leads to the palace of wisdom.
Prudence is a rich, ugly old maid courted by Incapacity.
He who desires but acts not, breeds pestilence.
The cut worm forgives the plow.
Dip him in the river who loves water.
A fool sees not the same tree that a wise man sees.
He whose face gives no light, shall never become a star.
Eternity is in love with the productions of time.
The busy bee has no time for sorrow.
The hours of folly are measur'd by the clock; but of wisdom, no clock can measure.
All wholesom food is caught without a net or a trap.

Bring out number, weight & measure in a year of dearth.

No bird soars too high, if he soars with his own wings.

A dead body revenges not injuries.

The most sublime act is to set another before you.

If the fool would persist in his folly he would become wise.

Folly is the cloke of knavery.

Shame is Pride's cloke.

## Plate  8

Prisons are built with stones of Law, Brothels with bricks of Religion.

The pride of the peacock is the glory of God.

The lust of the goat is the bounty of God.

The wrath of the lion is the wisdom of God.

The nakedness of woman is the work of God.

Excess of sorrow laughs. Excess of joy weeps.

The roaring of lions, the howling of wolves, the raging of the stormy sea, and the destructive sword, are portions of eternity, too great for the eye of man.

The fox condemns the trap, not himself.

Joys impregnate. Sorrows bring forth.

Let man wear the fell of the lion, woman the fleece of the sheep.

The bird a nest, the spider a web, man friendship.

The selfish, smiling fool, & the sullen, frowning fool shall be both thought wise, that they may be a rod.

What is now proved was once only imagin'd.

The rat, the mouse, the fox, the rabbet watch the roots; the lion, the tyger, the horse, the elephant watch the fruits.

The cistern contains: the fountain overflows.

One thought fills immensity.

Always be ready to speak your mind, and a base man will avoid you.

Every thing possible to be believ'd is an image of truth.

The eagle never lost so much time as when he submitted to learn of the crow.

## Plate  9

The fox provides for himself, but God provides for the lion.

Think in the morning. Act in the noon. Eat in the evening. Sleep in the night.

He who has suffer'd you to impose on him, knows you.

As the plow follows words, so God rewards prayers.

The tygers of wrath are wiser than the horses of instruction.

Expect poison from the standing water.

You never know what is enough unless you know what is more than enough.

Listen to the fool's reproach! it is a kingly title!

The eyes of fire, the nostrils of air, the mouth of water, the beard of earth.

The weak in courage is strong in cunning.

The apple tree never asks the beech how he shall grow; nor the lion, the horse, how he shall take his prey.

The thankful reciever bears a plentiful harvest.

If others had not been foolish, we should be so.

The soul of sweet delight can never be defil'd.

When thou seest an Eagle, thou seest a portion of Genius; lift up thy head!

As the catterpiller chooses the fairest leaves to lay her eggs on, so the priest lays his curse on the fairest joys.

To create a little flower is the labour of ages.

Damn braces: Bless relaxes.

The best wine is the oldest, the best water the newest.

Prayers plow not; Praises reap not!

Joys laugh not! Sorrows weep not!

## Plate 10

The head Sublime, the heart Pathos, the genitals Beauty, the hands & feet Proportion.

As the air to a bird or the sea to a fish, so is contempt to the contemptible.

The crow wish'd every thing was black, the owl that every thing was white.

Exuberance is Beauty.

If the lion was advised by the fox, he would be cunning.

Improve[me]nt makes strait roads; but the crooked roads without Improvement are roads of Genius.

Sooner murder an infant in its cradle than nurse unacted desires.

Where man is not, nature is barren.

Truth can never be told so as to be understood, and not be believ'd.

Enough! or Too much.

## Plate 11

The ancient Poets animated all sensible objects with Gods or Geniuses, calling them by the names and adorning them with the properties of woods, rivers, mountains, lakes, cities, nations, and whatever their enlarged & numerous senses could percieve.

And particularly they studied the genius of each city & country, placing it under its mental deity;

Till a system was formed, which some took advantage of, & enslav'd the vulgar by attempting to realize or abstract the mental deities from their objects: thus began Priesthood;

Choosing forms of worship from poetic tales.

And at length they pronounc'd that the Gods had order'd such things.

Thus men forgot that All deities reside in the human breast.

# AFTER THE DELUGE

## Arthur Rimbaud

As soon as the idea of the Deluge had subsided,

A hare stopped in the clover and swaying flowerbells, and said a prayer to the rainbow, through the spider's web.

Oh! the precious stones that began to hide,—and the flowers that already looked around.

In the dirty main street, stalls were set up and boats were hauled toward the sea, high tiered as in old prints.

Blood flowed at Blue Beard's,—through slaughterhouses, in circuses, where the windows were blanched by God's seal. Blood and milk flowed.

Beavers built. "Mazagrans" smoked in the little bars.

In the big glass house, still dripping, children in mourning looked at the marvelous pictures.

A door banged; and in the village square the little boy waved his arms, understood by weather vanes and cocks on steeples everywhere, in the bursting shower.

Madame*** installed a piano in the Alps. Mass and first communions were celebrated at the hundred thousand altars of the cathedral.

Caravans set out. And Hotel Splendid was built in the chaos of ice and the polar night.

Ever after the moon heard jackals howling across the deserts of thyme, and eclogues in wooden shoes growling in the orchard. Then in the violet and budding forest, Eucharis told me it was spring.

Gush, pond,—Foam, roll on the bridge and over the woods;—black

Arthur Rimbaud, *Illuminations,* translated by Louise Varèse. Copyright 1946, © 1957 by New Directions Publishing Corporation. Reprinted by permission of New Directions Publishing Corporation.

palls and organs, lightning and thunder, rise and roll;—waters and sorrows rise and launch the Floods again.

For since they have been dissipated—oh! the precious stones being buried and the opened flowers!—it's unbearable! and the Queen, the Witch who lights her fire in the earthen pot will never tell us what she knows, and what we do not know.

# A GOD IN WRATH

## Stephen Crane

A god in wrath
Was beating a man;
He cuffed him loudly
With thunderous blows
That rang and rolled over the earth.
All people came running.
The man screamed and struggled,
And bit madly at the feet of the god.
The people cried,
"Ah, what a wicked man!"
And—
"Ah, what a redoubtable god!"

# I SAW
# A MAN PURSUING

## Stephen Crane

I saw a man pursuing the horizon;
Round and round they sped.
I was disturbed at this;
I accosted the man.
"It is futile," I said,
"You can never——"

"You lie," he cried,
And ran on.

# A SPIRIT SPED

## Stephen Crane

A spirit sped
Through spaces of night;
And as he sped, he called,
"God! God!"
He went through valleys
Of black death-slime,
Ever calling,
"God! God!"
Their echoes
From crevice and cavern
Mocked him:
"God! God! God!"
Fleetly into the plains of space
He went, ever calling,
"God! God!"
Eventually, then, he screamed,
Mad in denial,
"Ah, there is no God!"

A swift hand,
A sword from the sky,
Smote him,
And he was dead.

# PIED BEAUTY

## Gerard Manley Hopkins

Glory be to God for dappled things—
    For skies of couple-colour as a brinded cow;
      For rose-moles all in stipple upon trout that swim;
Fresh-firecoal chestnut-falls; finches' wings;
    Landscape plotted and pieced—fold, fallow, and plough;
      And áll trádes, their gear and tackle and trim.

All things counter, original, spare, strange;
    Whatever is fickle, freckled (who knows how?)
      With swift, slow; sweet, sour; adazzle, dim;
He fathers-forth whose beauty is past change:
                  Praise him.

# GOD'S GRANDEUR

## Gerard Manley Hopkins

The world is charged with the grandeur of God.
    It will flame out, like shining from shook foil;
    It gathers to a greatness, like the ooze of oil
Crushed. Why do men then now not reck his rod?
Generations have trod, have trod, have trod;
    And all is seared with trade; bleared, smeared with toil;
    And wears man's smudge and shares man's smell: the soil
Is bare now, nor can foot feel, being shod.

And for all this, nature is never spent;
    There lives the dearest freshness deep down things;
And though the last lights off the black West went
    Oh, morning, at the brown brink eastward, springs—
Because the Holy Ghost over the bent
    World broods with warm breast and with ah! bright wings.

# THE WINDHOVER

*To Christ our Lord*

## Gerard Manley Hopkins

I caught this morning morning's minion, king-
    dom of daylight's dauphin, dapple-dawn-drawn Falcon, in
      his riding
Of the rolling level underneath him steady air, and striding
High there, how he rung upon the rein of a wimpling wing
In his ecstasy! then off, off forth on swing,
    As a skate's heel sweeps smooth on a bow-bend: the hurl and
      gliding
Rebuffed the big wind. My heart in hiding
Stirred for a bird,—the achieve of, the mastery of the thing!

Brute beauty and valour and act, oh, air, pride, plume, here
    Buckle! AND the fire that breaks from thee then, a billion
Times told lovelier, more dangerous, O my chevalier!

    No wonder of it: shéer plód makes plough down sillion
Shine, and blue-bleak embers, ah my dear,
    Fall, gall themselves, and gash gold-vermilion.

*Crucifixion* (detail) by Hieronymous Bosch (Musee Royaux des Beaux-Arts de Belgique)

# THE VOICE OF THE ANCIENT BARD

*from Songs of Innocence*

## William Blake

Youth of delight, come hither,
And see the opening morn,
Image of truth new born.
Doubt is fled, & clouds of reason,
Dark disputes & artful teazing.
Folly is an endless maze,
Tangled roots perplex her ways.
How many have fallen there!
They stumble all night over bones of the dead,
And feel they know not what but care,
And wish to lead others, when they should be led.

# INTRODUCTION

*from Songs of Experience*

## William Blake

Hear the voice of the Bard!
Who Present, Past, & Future sees
Whose ears have heard,
The Holy Word,
That walk'd among the ancient trees.

Calling the lapsed Soul
And weeping in the evening dew:
That might controll
The starry pole:
And fallen fallen light renew!

O Earth O Earth return!
Arise from out the dewy grass;
Night is worn,
And the morn
Rises from the slumberous mass.

Turn away no more:
Why wilt thou turn away
The starry floor
The watry shore
Is giv'n thee till the break of day.

# THE HUMAN ABSTRACT

## William Blake

Pity would be no more,
If we did not make somebody Poor:
And Mercy no more could be,
If all were as happy as we:

And mutual fear brings peace:
Till the selfish loves increase.
Then Cruelty knits a snare,
And spreads his baits with care.

He sits down with holy fears,
And waters the ground with tears:
Then Humility takes its root
Underneath his foot.

Soon spreads the dismal shade
Of Mystery over his head;
And the Catterpiller and Fly,
Feed on the Mystery.

And it bears the fruit of Deceit,
Ruddy and sweet to eat:
And the Raven his nest has made
In its thickest shade.

The Gods of the earth and sea,
Sought thro' Nature to find this Tree
But their search was all in vain;
There grows one in the Human Brain

# THE DIVINE IMAGE

## William Blake

To Mercy Pity Peace and Love,
All pray in their distress:
And to these virtues of delight
Return their thankfulness.

For Mercy Pity Peace and Love,
Is God our father dear:
And Mercy Pity Peace and Love,
Is Man his child and care.

For Mercy has a human heart
Pity, a human face:
And Love, the human form divine,
And Peace, the human dress.

Then every man of every clime,
That prays in his distress,
Prays to the human form divine
Love Mercy Pity Peace.

And all must love the human form,
In heathen, turk or jew.
Where Mercy, Love & Pity dwell,
There God is dwelling too.

# A DIVINE IMAGE

## William Blake

Cruelty has a Human Heart
And Jealousy a Human Face
Terror, the Human Form Divine
And Secrecy, the Human Dress

The Human Dress, is forged Iron
The Human Form, a fiery Forge.
The Human Face, a Furnace seal'd
The Human Heart, its hungry Gorge.

# DIRECTIVE

## Robert Frost

Back out of all this now too much for us,
Back in a time made simple by the loss
Of detail, burned, dissolved, and broken off
Like graveyard marble sculpture in the weather,
There is a house that is no more a house
Upon a farm that is no more a farm
And in a town that is no more a town.
The road there, if you'll let a guide direct you
Who only has at heart your getting lost,
May seem as if it should have been a quarry—
Great monolithic knees the former town
Long since gave up pretense of keeping covered.
And there's a story in a book about it:
Besides the wear of iron wagon wheels
The ledges show lines ruled southeast-northwest,
The chisel work of an enormous Glacier
That braced his feet against the Arctic Pole.
You must not mind a certain coolness from him
Still said to haunt this side of Panther Mountain.
Nor need you mind the serial ordeal
Of being watched from forty cellar holes
As if by eye pairs out of forty firkins.
As for the woods' excitement over you
That sends light rustle rushes to their leaves,

Charge that to upstart inexperience.
Where were they all not twenty years ago?
They think too much of having shaded out
A few old pecker-fretted apple trees.
Make yourself up a cheering song of how
Someone's road home from work this once was,
Who may be just ahead of you on foot
Or creaking with a buggy load of grain.
The height of the adventure is the height
Of country where two village cultures faded
Into each other. Both of them are lost.
And if you're lost enough to find yourself
By now, pull in your ladder road behind you
And put a sign up CLOSED to all but me.
Then make yourself at home. The only field
Now left's no bigger than a harness gall.
First there's the children's house of make-believe,
Some shattered dishes underneath a pine,
The playthings in the playhouse of the children.
Weep for what little things could make them glad.
Then for the house that is no more a house,
But only a belilaced cellar hole,
Now slowly closing like a dent in dough.
This was no playhouse but a house in earnest.
Your destination and your destiny's
A brook that was the water of the house,
Cold as a spring as yet so near its source,
Too lofty and original to rage.
(We know the valley streams that when aroused
Will leave their tatters hung on barb and thorn.)
I have kept hidden in the instep arch
Of an old cedar at the waterside
A broken drinking goblet like the Grail
Under a spell so the wrong ones can't find it,
So can't get saved, as Saint Mark says they mustn't.
(I stole the goblet from the children's playhouse.)
Here are your waters and your watering place.
Drink and be whole again beyond confusion.

# FRAU BAUMAN, FRAU SCHMIDT, AND FRAU SCHWARTZE

## Theodore Roethke

Gone the three ancient ladies
Who creaked on the greenhouse ladders,
Reaching up white strings
To wind, to wind
The sweet-pea tendrils, the smilax,
Nasturtiums, the climbing
Roses, to straighten
Carnations, red
Chrysanthemums; the stiff
Stems, jointed like corn,
They tied and tucked,—
These nurses of nobody else.
Quicker than birds, they dipped
Up and sifted the dirt;
They sprinkled and shook;
They stood astride pipes,
Their skirts billowing out wide into tents,
Their hands twinkling with wet;
Like witches they flew along rows
Keeping creation at ease;
With a tendril for needle
They sewed up the air with a stem;
They teased out the seed that the cold kept asleep,—
All the coils, loops, and whorls.

They trellised the sun; they plotted for more than themselves.

I remember how they picked me up, a spindly kid,
Pinching and poking my thin ribs
Till I lay in their laps, laughing,
Weak as a whiffet;
Now, when I'm alone and cold in my bed,
They still hover over me,
Those ancient leathery crones,
With their bandannas stiffened with sweat,
And their thorn-bitten wrists,
And their snuff-laden breath blowing lightly over me in my first sleep.

# THE WAREHOUSE

## Isaac Bashevis Singer

In a warehouse in heaven, a number of naked souls stood around waiting for the issuance of their new bodies. Bagdial, the angel in charge of such goods, was a trifle late that morning. To be precise, Bagdial handed out a card entitling the spirit to receive a body but did not hand out the body itself. In heaven there is as much red tape as on earth, the dignitaries finding it necessary to make work to keep unemployed angels busy. But angels who have got used to an easy life resent having to do anything too strenuous.

It was now ten o'clock in the morning. The angelic choirs had long since finished chanting their lauds. The righteous in paradise had already had their second helping of leviathan. The wicked, lying on their fiery beds in hell, had just been turned onto their other side. But in the commissariat not a single card had been issued. Finally Bagdial, a corpulent angel whose wings were not sufficiently large to conceal either his massive legs or his navel, entered and, without even bothering to say good morning, shouted, "Cut out that shoving. There are enough bodies for all. The day's still young. When your number is called, step forward. In the meantime, shut up." Bagdial headed for his private office. "I'll be back in a minute."

"The morning's almost over, but he must see to his private business," an impatient soul muttered. "According to regulations, work is supposed to begin promptly with the cock's crow."

"Stop that grumbling. If you don't like what goes on here, report me to the Lord Malbushial. You keep your right of appeal until your departure."

"No, Bagdial, we're more than satisfied," a number of humble souls called out.

"I will return soon."

As Bagdial shut the door of his office, one of the souls remarked, "An absolutely worthless caterpillar. In the old days that sort of angel was kicked out of heaven and exiled to earth to consort with the daughters of Adam. Some were changed into devils and imps. Now, since they have organized, they do as they please. It almost seems that God Himself is afraid of them."

"How can God be afraid of one of His own creations?"

The soul of one who had once been a philosopher tugged at its spiritual beard. "That's one of the ancient problems. My opinion is that though God is very powerful, He is not omnipotent. He can destroy a world or two if He has a tantrum, but not the entire cosmos. Omnipotence would mean He could destroy Himself and leave the universe godless, an obvious contradiction. Although I've roasted in Gehenna for a full year, it's made me no wiser. I still concur with Aristotle that the world had no beginning. The notion that the world was created from nothing is repugnant to reason."

"I am no scholar, just an ordinary woman," another soul said, "but it's obvious to me that there's no order here. Thirty-one years ago I was exiled to earth from the Throne of Glory, where I used to polish one of the legs, and imprisoned in a beautiful body. Why they sent me to earth I did not understand until today. People say it's men who are the lecherous ones; my lust was more powerful than that of any ten men. My mother baked delicious pretzels with caraway seeds which the yeshiva boys loved, but they liked me even better. She warned me against men, but already when I was nine I could think of nothing else. I saw two dogs coupling once and after that. . . ."

"All right, we catch on. You became a whore."

"Not right away."

"How long did you fry in Gehenna?"

"An entire year."

"Well, you got off easy. There are lots of whores that they sling into the desert. When they get to Gehenna, they think it's paradise. What did they do to you?"

"The usual. I was hung by my breasts, hurled from fire into ice, and from ice into fire, and so on, except, of course, Sabbaths and holidays."

"You were lucky not to have to remain in the vale of tears longer," another soul remarked. "I lived there for eighty-nine years three months five days two hours and eight minutes."

"Were you also a whore?"

"No, a man."

"That's what I'd like to be. If I have to be dressed in blood and flesh, let it be male."

"What's so wonderful about being a man?"

"You are not a female."

"So I became a miser. A woman of pleasure has at least some pleasure. My sack of bones could do nothing but gather money. I got married but never gave my wife enough for the household and accused her of being a spendthrift. You don't need me to tell you that women hate a tightwad. All females are wasteful. My wife was always cooking twice the porridge we could eat. There was always a pot of spoiling food in our larder. We had so much schmaltz it turned rancid. Our flour became moldy. The Angel of Good pleaded with me: 'Let her have her will. She enjoys it. Why quarrel?' But my bag of money obsessed me."

"Was she any good in bed?"

"Even there I was stingy. Those who hoard money hoard everything. The upshot of it was that she ran off with a shoemaker."

"I would have done it, too."

"After that happened, I was afraid to take another wife. For all I knew, the woman I got would be crazy about marzipan. I got so bad I broke my teeth on stale bread because it cost a half cent a loaf less than the fresh. The moment I entered my house, I took off my gaberdine and, forgive my expression, even my underwear to keep them from wearing. I even saved snuff."

"How did you do that?"

"I would stretch out my hand when I saw someone taking a pinch and ask him for some. Instead of using it, I hid it in a bag."

"Did you save much?"

"Two sacks full."

"How long did it take you to do that?"

"More than forty years."

"If I become a man, I won't stint my wife. I'll give her anything she wants. If you ever become a woman, you'll find out what pleases women."

"If you become a man, you'll forget all this feminine nonsense."

"What do you want to be?" the whore asked.

"I don't want to be anyone," the miser answered.

"Perhaps they will make you a woman."

"For all I care, they can make me a flea."

"It could be that you'll be stillborn."

"The stiller the better."

"I don't care what you say, I would like the taste of being a man."

"You won't be consulted. You'll be handed a body whether it fits or not. I know. I've been here now for more than thirty years. For ten years I worked sorting bodies. The whole thing's just one enormous mess. A woman's torso is given a man's head. Just a short time ago, a man's body turned up with a pair of breasts of a wet nurse. They even get mixed up on who gets what genitals. You know about hermaphrodites, don't you? That Bagdial is both lazy and incompetent. If he weren't Malbushial's second cousin, he would have been scrapped long ago."

"What about God?"

"Does anyone believe in God here? Here in the lowest heaven we have only atheists. He is supposed to dwell in the seventh heaven, which is an infinity away. One thing we can be sure of, He's not here."

"Be quiet. Here comes Bagdial."


## 2

Bagdial scratched his left buttock with his right wing. "I'm not deaf, miser. If Malbushial knew of your barkings, he'd give you the body of a dog. No, we're not atheists here. But when you've hung around here some 689,000 years and been continually told about a boss who never shows up, you begin to have your doubts. Why does He sit there forever in His seventh heaven? Oughtn't He to come down here occasionally and see what's going on? Souls are shipped in this direction and that, wearing this or that body.

"You think that we warehouse people are negligent, but can we do anything if the manufacturers and the cutters send us poor products? We almost never receive a well-lathed nose. The noses we get are almost all either long as a ram's horn or short as a bean. Our suppliers have been in the nose business since the time of Methuselah, but they don't know their trade. The lips we're sent are either too thin or too thick. Almost none of the ears has decent proportions. The angel in charge of procreation is supposed to adjust the genitals of the sexes to fit correctly, and he's the worst bungler of all. He is capable of mating an elephant to a mouse.

"All of you clamor for beautiful bodies, but if you get one, what use do you make of it? It's destroyed, either by drinking or by lechery or by sloth. A short time ago we did a splendid job; soul and body fitted perfectly. Once a millennium we do such a good job. But that pampered little body started eating as if it had been given a bottomless stomach. It ate for forty years and returned round as a barrel, a mere heap of repulsive flesh. Miser, if you continue your blasphemies, I will. . . ."

"I didn't blaspheme. Honest, I didn't. What style body am I to get?"

"A eunuch."

"Why a eunuch? I was just saying that for all I cared I could be turned into a flea."

"I heard you. We have one eunuch-style body on hand which will fit you perfectly. You'll never be in a position to support a wife. And you certainly don't deserve to have someone else support you."

"What sort of temptations does a eunuch have?"

"Money."

"Will I be rich?"

"The wealthiest inmate in the poorhouse of Pinchev."

"What do I have to correct?"

"You'll return all the tobacco you stole to its rightful owners. The snuff was given to you to use, not to hoard."

"Where will I get so much snuff?"

"That's your problem. Hey there, whore."

"What style have I been given?"

"A woman."

"Again?"

"Exactly."

"Why not a man this time?"

"Don't bargain with me. I distribute the cards, not the bodies. We don't have our full quota of males in this batch. Eighty male bodies were ruined in the factory yesterday. This year we've over-produced women. But we'll get rid of them all because Rabbi Gershom's edict against polygamy is about to be repealed. Every schlemiel dreams of having a harem. Even tailor's assistants want to become King Solomons. If you ask me, it's better to be a mortar than a pestle."

"I would like to be a man just once."

"We all have unfulfilled desires. I would have preferred to have been a seraph and sit in paradise between Bathsheba and Abigail. Instead, I have to come here six days a week and hand out cards for defective bodies. Everyone haggles with me as though I had the power of Metatron. I don't know what it's like in the other heavens; here in the warehouse it's chaos. At times I even envy the miserable creatures who are sent down to earth. At least there are temptations in the lower world. If you try hard you can achieve sainthood and receive your reward in paradise. What do I have? Nothing. No one tempts me and I'm fed with sour moon milk. I'm slandered disgracefully. I'm begrudged even a little stardust. Evil tongues make me feel that if I weren't Malbushial's second cousin I'd be nowhere."

"Maybe you could do me a small favor?"

"What sort of a favor, whore? Take your card and leave. You were a wanton for eighteen years; you'll be chaste now for exactly the same amount of time. If not, you'll return again, a double hunchback, one in the front and one in the rear."

"Have you already had a look at my body?"

"I caught a glimpse of it."

"What does it look like?"

"What's the use telling you? Once you get to earth, you'll forget that the body is only a garment. Down there they think the body is everything. All around you, people will be saying that there isn't a soul."

"What will I look like?"

"Since you must correct the errors you made in your former existence, you will not be exactly a beauty. The body you receive will make your task easier."

"Ugly, eh?"

"Men will not care for you, nor will you care for men. You have been given nine measures of shyness, which is exactly what is required to create a spinster."

"You dirty scoundrel."

Another soul flew over.

"Who are you?" Bagdial asked. "I don't recognize you."

"Liebke the thief."

"Well, no more stealing for you. You'll be robbed by others. Everything will be taken from you—your money, your wife, even the pillow you rest your head on. You'll hide your money in your boot tops, go to the steam bath, and leave your boots behind you. You'll swear never to hide anything in your boots again and yet not be able to resist the urge to do so. Every body is made with its own particular obsession.

"Once we had a gambler here. Do you know what he'd done? He was playing draw poker and threw his wife into the pot. Can you imagine what he had? A pair of jacks. He was a big bluffer, only you can't bluff a man who has four aces. When his wife came back to him three months later, she was pregnant. He swallowed a ladle in an attempt to kill himself!"

"Did he get it down?"

"It stuck in his throat. Was there any sense to it? But you know how people are. The angels are no wiser. Who are you?"

"Hayim the coachman."

"Since you had a beautiful wife and in addition fornicated with a Gentile, what did you need the mare for?"

"I don't know."

"Hadn't you ever heard that horses kick?"

"It just slipped my mind."

"Those down below are always forgetting. Is it their fault? The most defective of all the organs is the portion of the brain containing the memory. They put on two pairs of underwear in the winter and only take off one when they go to the outhouse. The only things they never forget are the injuries done them. Two sisters in Frampol quarreled over the tail of a herring for sixty years. When the older died, the younger urinated on her grave. You,

Hayim, will be the horse this time. You'll pull freight from Izbitza to Krasnistaw."

"Has that road been fixed?"

"It's as muddy as it was, but a little bumpier."

"If that's so, there is no God."

"And suppose there isn't. Will that make pulling the wagon any easier? Anyway, you'll only last three years. Zelig the Red will whip you to death."

"Is that murderer still around?"

"He has a score to settle. He hasn't forgotten that you sold him a lame stallion."

"That happened thirty years ago. I was swindled myself. I got the horse from a gypsy."

"We know that. It's all on record here. The gypsy is now a stallion, and the stallion a gypsy. But the whip remains what it was and still has seven knots. Hey, who are you?"

"Shiffra the cook."

"You're not supposed to spit into your employer's porridge, even though he did spit in your face."

"What will I become?"

"Your employer's spittoon."

"Will I feel his spit?"

"Everything knows and feels. Your employer suffers from consumption and will spit out his last piece of lung into you. Both of you will be back in three quarters of a year."

"Together?"

"You will be married. You will be his footstool in the antechamber of paradise."

"I'd rather be a pisspot in Gehenna."

"Little fool, that amorous ass loved you. That's how men are. What they can't have, they spit at."

Bagdial scratched the nape of his neck with one of his lower wings and brooded in silence. "Is it much better in heaven?" he finally asked. "I stay here all day surrounded by rabble and listen to their needling. Other angels sing hymns three times a day and that's the end of it. Some can't even sing, only bellow. The higher your position, the less work you do. He created the world in six short winter days and has been resting ever since. There are those who are of the opinion that He didn't even work that hard."

"Do you mean by that that He wasn't the First Cause?" the philosopher demanded.

"Who else is the First Cause? He is a jealous God. He would never delegate such power. But being the cause and keeping order are different things altogether."

# SAILING TO BYZANTIUM

## William Butler Yeats

**I**

That is no country for old men. The young
In one another's arms, birds in the trees,
—Those dying generations—at their song,
The salmon-falls, the mackerel-crowded seas,
Fish, flesh, or fowl, commend all summer long
Whatever is begotten, born, and dies.
Caught in that sensual music all neglect
Monuments of unageing intellect.

**II**

An aged man is but a paltry thing,
A tattered coat upon a stick, unless
Soul clap its hands and sing, and louder sing
For every tatter in its mortal dress,
Nor is there singing school but studying
Monuments of its own magnificence;
And therefore I have sailed the seas and come
To the holy city of Byzantium.

**III**

O sages standing in God's holy fire
As in the gold mosaic of a wall,

Come from the holy fire, perne in a gyre,
And be the singing-masters of my soul.
Consume my heart away; sick with desire
And fastened to a dying animal
It knows not what it is; and gather me
Into the artifice of eternity.

## IV

Once out of nature I shall never take
My bodily form from any natural thing,
But such a form as Grecian goldsmiths make
Of hammered gold and gold enamelling
To keep a drowsy Emperor awake;
Or set upon a golden bough to sing
To lords and ladies of Byzantium
Of what is past, or passing, or to come.

*Existence, by*
*Nothing Bred*
Existence, by nothing bred,
Breeds everything.
Parents of the universe,
It smooths rough edges,
Unties hard knots,
Tempers the sharp sun,
Lays blowing dust,
Its image in the wellspring never fails.
But how was it conceived?—this image
Of no other sire.


Lao Tzu

Reprinted by permission of G. P. Putnam's Sons from *The Way of Life According to Lao Tzu,* translated by Witter Bynner. Copyright 1944 by Witter Bynner.

*"Let others complain that times are
bad; I complain that they are petty
because they lack passion. . . . Men's
thoughts are too petty to be sinful.
A worm might consider such thoughts
to be sinful, but not a man created
in the image of God. Their pleasures
are circumspect and boring; their
passions sleep."*

Soren Kierkegaard

# VII
# THE SENSE
# OF EVIL

# THE TWA CORBIES

## Anonymous

As I was walking all alane,
I heard twa corbies making a mane;
The tane unto t' other say,
"Where sall we gang and dine to-day?"

"In behint yon auld fail dyke,
I wot there lies a new slain knight;
And naebody kens that he lies there,
But his hawk, his hound, and lady fair.

"His hound is to the hunting gane,
His hawk to fetch the wild-fowl hame,
His lady's ta'en another mate,
So we may mak our dinner sweet.

"Ye'll sit on his white hause-bane,
And I'll pike out his bonny blue een;
Wi ae lock o his gowden hair
We'll theek our nest when it grows bare.

"Mony a one for him makes mane,
But nane sall ken where he is gane;
Oer his white banes, when they are bare,
The wind sall blaw for evermair."

# SIR PATRICK SPENS

## Anonymous

The king sits in Dumferline town,
    Drinking the blude-reid° wine:         *blood-red*
"O whar will I get a guid sailor
    To sail this ship of mine?"

Up and spak an eldern° knicht,           *ancient*
    Sat at the king's richt knee:
"Sir Patrick Spens is the best sailor
    That sails upon the sea."

The king has written a braid° letter     *broad*
    And signed it wi' his hand,
And sent it to Sir Patrick Spens,
    Was walking on the sand.

The first line that Sir Patrick read,
    A loud lauch° lauched he;           *laugh*
The next line that Sir Patrick read,
    The tear blinded his ee.°           *eye*

"O wha° is this has done this deed,    *who*
    This ill deed done to me,
To send me out this time o' the year,
    To sail upon the sea?

"Make haste, make haste, my mirry men all,
          Our guid ship sails the morn."
"O say na° sae,° my master dear,          *not/so*
   For I fear a deadly storm.

"Late late yestre'en I saw the new moon
   Wi' the auld° moon in her arm,       *old*
And I fear, I fear, my dear master,
   That we will come to harm."

O our Scots nobles were richt laith°     *loath*
   To weet° their cork-heeled shoon,°  *wet/shoes*
But lang owre° a' the play were played  *before*
   Their hats they swam aboon.°     *above*

O lang, lang their ladies sit,
   Wi' their fans into their hand,
Or e'er they see Sir Patrick Spens
   Come sailing to the land.

O lang, lang may the ladies stand,
   Wi' their gold kembs° in their hair,  *combs*
Waiting for their ain° dear lords,     *own*
   For they'll see thame na mair.°   *more*

Half o'er, half o'er to Aberdour
   It's fifty fadom° deep,         *fathom*
And there lies guid Sir Patrick Spens,
   Wi' the Scots lords at his feet.

# THE LABORATORY

*Ancien Régime*

## Robert Browning

Now that I, tying thy glass mask tightly,
May gaze through these faint smokes curling whitely,
As thou pliest thy trade in this devil's-smithy—
Which is the poison to poison her, prithee?

He is with her, and they know that I know
Where they are, what they do : they believe my tears flow
While they laugh, laugh at me, at me fled to the drear
Empty church, to pray God in, for them!—I am here.

Grind away, moisten and mash up thy paste,
Pound at thy powder—I am not in haste!
Better sit thus, and observe thy strange things,
Than go where men wait me and dance at the King's.

That in the mortar—you call it a gum?
Ah, the brave tree whence such gold oozings come!
And yonder soft phial, the exquisite blue,
Sure to taste sweetly,—is that poison too?

Had I but all of them, thee and thy treasures,
What a wild crowd of invisible pleasures!
To carry pure death in an earring, a casket,
A signet, a fan-mount, a filigree basket!

Soon, at the King's, a mere lozenge to give,
And Pauline should have just thirty minutes to live!
But to light a pastile, and Elsie, with her head
And her breast and her arms and her hands, should drop dead!

Quick—is it finished? The color's too grim!
Why not soft like the phial's, enticing and dim?
Let it brighten her drink, let her turn it and stir,
And try it and taste, ere she fix and prefer!

What a drop! She's not little, no minion like me!
That's why she ensnared him: this never will free
The soul from those masculine eyes,—say, "no!"
To that pulse's magnificent come-and-go.

For only last night, as they whispered, I brought
My own eyes to bear on her so, that I thought
Could I keep them one half minute fixed, she would fall
Shrivelled; she fell not; yet this does it all!

Not that I bid you spare her the pain;
Let death be felt and the proof remain:
Brand, burn up, bite into its grace—
He is sure to remember her dying face!

Is it done? Take my mask off! Nay, be not morose;
It kills her, and this prevents seeing it close:
The delicate droplet, my whole fortune's fee!
If it hurts her, beside, can it ever hurt me?

Now, take all my jewels, gorge gold to your fill,
You may kiss me, old man, on my mouth if you will!
But brush this dust off me, lest horror it brings
Ere I know it—next moment I dance at the King's!

# RASHOMON [1]

## Ryunosuke Akutagawa

It was a chilly evening. A servant of a samurai stood under the Rashōmon, waiting for a break in the rain.

No one else was under the wide gate. On the thick column, its crimson lacquer rubbed off here and there, perched a cricket. Since the Rashōmon stands on Sujaku Avenue, a few other people at least, in sedge hat or nobleman's headgear, might have been expected to be waiting there for a break in the rain storm. But no one was near except this man.

For the past few years the city of Kyōto had been visited by a series of calamities, earthquakes, whirlwinds, and fires, and Kyōto had been greatly devastated. Old chronicles say that broken pieces of Buddhist images and other Buddhist objects, with their lacquer, gold, or silver leaf worn off, were heaped up on roadsides to be sold as firewood. Such being the state of affairs in Kyōto, the repair of the Rashōmon was out of the question. Taking advantage of the devastation, foxes and other wild animals made their dens in the ruins of the gate, and thieves and robbers found a home there too. Eventually it became customary to bring unclaimed corpses to this gate and abandon them. After dark it was so ghostly that no one dared approach.

Flocks of crows flew in from somewhere. During the daytime these cawing birds circled around the ridgepole of the gate. When the sky overhead

From *Rashomon & Other Stories by Ryunosuke Akutagawa,* permission of Liveright, Publisher, New York. Copyright © 1952 Liveright Publishing Corporation.

[1] The "Rashōmon" was the largest gate in Kyoto, the ancient capital of Japan. It was 106 feet wide and 26 feet deep, and was topped with a ridge-pole; its stone-wall rose 75 feet high. This gate was constructed in 789 when the then capital of Japan was transferred to Kyoto. With the decline of West Kyoto, the gate fell into bad repair, cracking and crumbling in many places, and became a hide-out for thieves and robbers and a place for abandoning unclaimed corpses.

turned red in the afterlight of the departed sun, they looked like so many grains of seasame flung across the gate. But on that day not a crow was to be seen, perhaps because of the lateness of the hour. Here and there the stone steps, beginning to crumble, and with rank grass growing in their crevices, were dotted with the white droppings of crows. The servant, in a worn blue kimono, sat on the seventh and highest step, vacantly watching the rain. His attention was drawn to a large pimple irritating his right cheek.

As has been said, the servant was waiting for a break in the rain. But he had no particular idea of what to do after the rain stopped. Ordinarily, of course, he would have returned to his master's house, but he had been discharged just before. The prosperity of the city of Kyōto had been rapidly declining, and he had been dismissed by his master, whom he had served many years, because of the effects of this decline. Thus, confined by the rain, he was at a loss to know where to go. And the weather had not a little to do with his depressed mood. The rain seemed unlikely to stop. He was lost in thoughts of how to make his living tomorrow, helpless incoherent thoughts protesting an inexorable fate. Aimlessly he had been listening to the pattering of the rain on the Sujaku Avenue.

The rain, enveloping the Rashōmon, gathered strength and came down with a pelting sound that could be heard far away. Looking up, he saw a fat black cloud impale itself on the tips of the tiles jutting out from the roof of the gate.

He had little choice of means, whether fair or foul, because of his helpless circumstances. If he chose honest means, he would undoubtedly starve to death beside the wall or in the Sujaku gutter. He would be brought to this gate and thrown away like a stray dog. If he decided to steal . . . His mind, after making the same detour time and again, came finally to the conclusion that he would be a thief.

But doubts returned many times. Though determined that he had no choice, he was still unable to muster enough courage to justify the conclusion that he must become a thief.

After a loud fit of sneezing he got up slowly. The evening chill of Kyōto made him long for the warmth of a brazier. The wind in the evening dusk howled through the columns of the gate. The cricket which had been perched on the crimson-lacquered column was already gone.

Ducking his neck, he looked around the gate, and drew up the shoulders of the blue kimono which he wore over his thin underwear. He decided to spend the night there, if he could find a secluded corner sheltered from wind and rain. He found a broad lacquered stairway leading to the tower over the gate. No one would be there, except the dead, if there were any. So, taking care that the sword at his side did not slip out of the scabbard, he set foot on the lowest step of the stairs.

A few seconds later, halfway up the stairs, he saw a movement above.

Holding his breath and huddling cat-like in the middle of the broad stairs leading to the tower, he watched and waited. A light coming from the upper part of the tower shone faintly upon his right cheek. It was the cheek with the red, festering pimple visible under his stubbly whiskers. He had expected only dead people inside the tower, but he had only gone up a few steps before he noticed a fire above, about which someone was moving. He saw a dull, yellow, flickering light which made the cobwebs hanging from the ceiling glow in a ghostly way. What sort of person would be making a light in the Rashōmon . . . and in a storm? The unknown, the evil terrified him.

As quietly as a lizard, the servant crept up to the top of the steep stairs. Crouching on all fours, and stretching his neck as far as possible, he timidly peeped into the tower.

As rumor had said, he found several corpses strewn carelessly about the floor. Since the glow of the light was feeble, he could not count the number. He could only see that some were naked and others clothed. Some of them were women, and all were lolling on the floor with their mouths open or their arms outstretched showing no more signs of life than so many clay dolls. One would doubt that they had ever been alive, so eternally silent they were. Their shoulders, breasts, and torsos stood out in the dim light; other parts vanished in shadow. The offensive smell of these decomposed corpses brought his hand to his nose.

The next moment his hand dropped and he stared. He caught sight of a ghoulish form bent over a corpse. It seemed to be an old woman, gaunt, gray-haired, and nunnish in appearance. With a pine torch in her right hand, she was peeping into the face of a corpse which had long black hair.

Seized more with horror than curiosity, he even forgot to breathe for a time. He felt the hair of his head and body stand on end. As he watched, terrified, she wedged the torch between two floor boards and, laying hands on the head of the corpse, began to pull out the long hairs one by one, as a monkey kills the lice of her young. The hair came out smoothly with the movement of her hands.

As the hair came out, fear faded from his heart, and his hatred toward the old woman mounted. It grew beyond hatred, becoming a consuming antipathy against all evil. At this instant if anyone had brought up the question of whether he would starve to death or become a thief—the question which had occurred to him a little while ago—he would not have hesitated to choose death. His hatred toward evil flared up like the piece of pine wood which the old woman had stuck in the floor.

He did not know why she pulled out the hair of the dead. Accordingly, he did not know whether her case was to be put down as good or bad. But in his eyes, pulling out the hair of the dead in the Rashōmon on this stormy night was an unpardonable crime. Of course it never entered his mind that a little while ago he had thought of becoming a thief.

Then, summoning strength into his legs, he rose from the stairs and strode, hand on sword, right in front of the old creature. The hag turned, terror in her eyes, and sprang up from the floor, trembling. For a small moment she paused, poised there, then lunged for the stairs with a shriek.

"Wretch! Where are you going?" he shouted, barring the way of the trembling hag who tried to scurry past him. Still she attempted to claw her way by. He pushed her back to prevent her . . . they struggled, fell among the corpses, and grappled there. The issue was never in doubt. In a moment he had her by the arm, twisted it, and forced her down to the floor. Her arms were all skin and bones, and there was no more flesh on them than on the shanks of a chicken. No sooner was she on the floor than he drew his sword and thrust the silver-white blade before her very nose. She was silent. She trembled as if in a fit, and her eyes were open so wide that they were almost out of their sockets, and her breath come in hoarse gasps. The life of this wretch was his now. This thought cooled his boiling anger and brought a calm pride and satisfaction. He looked down at her, and said in a somewhat calmer voice:

"Look here, I'm not an officer of the High Police Commissioner. I'm a stranger who happened to pass by this gate. I won't bind you or do anything against you, but you must tell me what you're doing up here."

Then the old woman opened her eyes still wider, and gazed at his face intently with the sharp red eyes of a bird of prey. She moved her lips, which were wrinkled into her nose, as though she were chewing something. Her pointed Adam's apple moved in her thin throat. Then a panting sound like the cawing of a crow came from her throat:

"I pull the hair . . . I pull out the hair . . . to make a wig."

Her answer banished all unknown from their encounter and brought disappointment. Suddenly she was only a trembling old woman there at his feet. A ghoul no longer: only a hag who makes wigs from the hair of the dead—to sell, for scraps of food. A cold contempt seized him. Fear left his heart, and his former hatred entered. These feelings must have been sensed by the other. The old creature, still clutching the hair she had pulled off the corpse, mumbled out these words in her harsh broken voice:

"Indeed, making wigs out of the hair of the dead may seem a great evil to you, but these that are here deserve no better. This woman, whose beautiful black hair I was pulling, used to sell cut and dried snake flesh at the guard barracks, saying that it was dried fish. If she hadn't died of the plague, she'd be selling it now. The guards liked to buy from her, and used to say her fish was tasty. What she did couldn't be wrong, because if she hadn't, she would have starved to death. There was no other choice. If she knew I had to do this in order to live, she probably wouldn't care."

He sheathed his sword, and, with his left hand on its hilt, he listened to her meditatively. His right hand touched the big pimple on his cheek. As he listened, a certain courage was born in his heart—the courage which he had not had when he sat under the gate a little while ago. A strange power was driving him in the opposite direction of the courage which he had had when he seized the old woman. No longer did he wonder whether he should starve to death or become a thief. Starvation was so far from his mind that it was the last thing that would have entered it.

"Are you sure?" he asked in a mocking tone, when she finished talking. He took his right hand from his pimple, and, bending forward, seized her by the neck and said sharply:

"Then it's right if I rob you. I'd starve if I didn't."

He tore her clothes from her body and kicked her roughly down on the corpses as she struggled and tried to clutch his leg. Five steps, and he was at the top of the stairs. The yellow clothes he had wrested off were under his arm, and in a twinkling he had rushed down the steep stairs into the abyss of night. The thunder of his descending steps pounded in the hollow tower, and then it was quiet.

Shortly after that the hag raised up her body from the corpses. Grumbling and groaning, she crawled to the top stair by the still flickering torchlight, and through the gray hair which hung over her face, she peered down to the last stair in the torch light.

Beyond this was only darkness . . . unknowing and unknown.

# SONG

from *Death's Jest-Book*

## Thomas L. Beddoes

Old Adam, the carrion crow,
   The old crow of Cairo;
He sat in the shower, and let it flow
   Under his tail and over his crest;
     And through every feather
     Leaked the wet weather;
   And the bough swung under his nest;
For his beak it was heavy with marrow.
     Is that the wind dying? O no;
     Its only two devils, that blow
     Through a murderer's bones, to and fro,
      In the ghosts' moonshine.

Ho! Eve, my grey carrion wife,
   When we have supped on kings' marrow,
Where shall we drink and make merry our life?
   Our nest it is queen Cleopatra's skull,
     'Tis cloven and cracked,
     And battered and hacked,
   But with tears of blue eyes it is full:
Let us drink then, my raven of Cairo.
     Is that the wind dying? O no;
     It's only two devils, that blow
     Through a murderer's bones, to and fro,
      In the ghosts' moonshine.

# THE QUEEN OF AIR AND DARKNESS

## T. H. White

When shall I be dead and rid
Of the wrong my father did?
How long, how long, till spade and hearse
Put to sleep my mother's curse?

There was a round tower with a weather-cock on it. The weather-cock was a carrion crow, with an arrow in its beak to point to the wind.

There was a circular room at the top of the tower, curiously uncomfortable. It was draughty. There was a closet on the east side which had a hole in the floor. This hole commanded the outer doors of the tower, of which there were two, and people could drop stones through it when they were besieged. Unfortunately the wind used to come up through the hole and go pouring out of the unglazed shot-windows or up the chimney—unless it happened to be blowing the other way, in which case it went downward. It was like a wind tunnel. A second nuisance was that the room was full of peat-smoke, not from its own fire but from the fire in the room below. The complicated system of draughts sucked the smoke down the chimney. The stone walls sweated in damp weather. The furniture itself was uncomfortable. It consisted solely of heaps of stones—which were handy for throwing down the hole—together with a few rusty Genoese cross-bows with their bolts and a pile of turfs for the unlit fire. The four children had no bed. If it had been a square room, they might have had a cupboard bed, but, as it was, they had to sleep on the floor—where they covered themselves with straw and plaids as best they could.

The children had erected an amateur tent over their heads, out of the plaids, and under this they were lying close together, telling a story. They could hear their mother stoking the fire in the room below, which made them whisper for fear that she could hear. It was not exactly that they were afraid of being beaten if she came up. They adored her dumbly and uncritically, because her character was stronger than theirs. Nor had they been forbidden to talk after bedtime. It was more as if she had brought them up—perhaps through indifference or through laziness or even through some kind of possessive cruelty—with an imperfect sense of right and wrong. It was as if they could never know when they were being bad.

They were whispering in Gaelic. Or rather, they were whispering in a strange mixture of Gaelic and of the Old Language of chivalry—which had been taught to them because they would need it when they were grown. They had little English. In later years, when they became famous knights at the court of the great king, they were to speak English perfectly—all of them except Gawaine, who, as the head of the clan, was to cling to a Scots accent on purpose, to show that he was not ashamed of his birth.

Gawaine was telling the story, because he was the eldest. They lay together, like thin, strange, secret frogs, their bodies well-boned and ready to fill out into toughness as soon as they might be given decent nourishment. They were fairhaired. Gawaine's was bright red and Gareth's whiter than hay. The ranged from ten years old to fourteen, and Gareth was the youngest of the four. Gaheris was a stolid child. Agravaine, the next after Gawaine, was the bully of the family—he was shifty, inclined to cry, and frightened of pain. It was because he had a good imagination and used his head more than the others.

"Long time past, my heroes," Gawaine was saying, "before ourselves were born or thought of, there was a beautiful grandmother at us, called Igraine."

"She is the Countess of Cornwall," said Agravaine.

"Our grandmother is the Countess of Cornwall," agreed Gawaine, "and the bloody King of England fell in love with her."

"His name was Uther Pendragon," said Agravaine.

"Who is at telling this story?" asked Gareth angrily. "Close your mouth."

"King Uther Pendragon," continued Gawaine, "let send for the Earl and Countess of Cornwall——"

"Our Grandfather and Granny," said Gaheris.

"——and he proclaimed to them that they must stay with him at his house in the Tower of London. Then, when they were at staying with him therein, he asked our Granny that she would become the wife of himself, instead of being with our Grandfather at all. But the chaste and beautiful Countess of Cornwall——'

"Granny," said Gaheris.

Gareth exclaimed: "Sorrow take it, will you give us peace?" There was a muffled argument, punctuated by squeaks, bumps and complaining remarks.

"The chaste and beautiful Countess of Cornwall," resumed Gawaine, "spurned the advances of King Uther Pendragon, and she told our Grandfather about it. She said: 'I suppose we were sent for that I should be dishonoured. Wherefore, husband, I counsel you that we depart from hence suddenly, that we may ride all night to our own castle.' So they went out of the King's rath in the middle night——'

"At dead of night," Gareth corrected.

"——when all the people of the house had gone on sleep, and there they saddled their prancing, fire-eyed, swift-footed, symmetrical, large-lipped, small-headed, vehement steeds, by the light of a dark lantern, and they rode away into Cornwall, as fast as they could go."

"It was a terrible ride," said Gaheris.

"They killed the horses underneath them," said Agravaine.

"So they did not, then," said Gareth. "Our Grandfather and Granny would not have ridden any horses to kill them."

"Did they?" asked Gaheris.

"No, they did not," said Gawaine, after considering. "But they nearly did so."

He went on with the story.

"When King Uther Pendragon learned what had happened in the morning, he was wonderly wroth."

"Wood wroth," suggested Gareth.

"Wonderly wroth," said Gawaine. "King Uther Pendragon was wonderly wroth. He said, 'I will have that Earl of Cornwall's head in a pie-dish, by my halidome!' So he sent our Grandfather a letter which bid him to stuff him and garnish him, for within forty days he would fetch him out of the strongest castle that he had!"

"There were two castles at him," said Agravaine haughtily. "They were the Castle Tintagil and the Castle Terrabil."

"So the Earl of Cornwall put our Granny in Tintagil, and he himself went into Terrabil, and King Uther Pendragon came to lay them siege."

"And there," cried Gareth, unable to contain himself, "the king pight many pavilions, and there was great war made on both parties, and much people slain!"

"A thousand?" suggested Gaheris.

"Two thousand at least," said Agravaine. "We of the Gael would not have slain less than two thousand. In truth, it was a million probably."

"So when our Grandfather and Granny were winning the sieges, and it looked as if King Uther would be utterly defeated, there came along a wicked magician called Merlyn——'

"A nigromancer," said Gareth.

"And this nigromancer, would you believe it, by means of his infernal arts, succeeded in putting the treacherous Uther Pendragon inside our Granny's Castle. Granda immediately made a sortie out of Terrabil, but he was slain in the battle——"

"Treacherously."

"And the poor Countess of Cornwall——"

"The chaste and beautiful Igraine——'

"Our Granny——"

"——was captured prisoner by the blackhearted, southron, faithless King of the Dragon, and then, in spite of it that she had three beautiful daughters already whatever——'

"The lovely Cornwall Sisters."

"Aunt Elaine."

"Aunt Morgan."

"And Mammy."

"And if she had these lovely daughters, she was forced into marrying the King of England—the man who had slain her husband!"

They considered the enormous English wickedness in silence, overwhelmed by its *dénouement*. It was their mother's favourite story, on the rare occasions when she troubled to tell them one, and they had learned it by heart. Finally Agravaine quoted a Gaelic proverb, which she had also taught them.

"Four things," he whispered, "that a Lothian cannot trust—a cow's horn, a horse's hoof, a dog's snarl, and an Englishman's laugh."

They moved in the straw uneasily, listening to some secret movements in the room below.

The room underneath the story-tellers was lit by a single candle and by the saffron light of its peat fire. It was a poor room for a royal one, but at least it had a bed in it—the great four-poster which was used as a throne during the daytime. An iron cauldron with three legs was boiling over the fire. The candle stood in front of a sheet of polished brass, which served as a mirror. There were two living beings in the chamber, a Queen and a cat. Both of them had black hair and blue eyes.

The black cat lay on its side in the firelight as if it were dead. This was because its legs were tied together, like the legs of a roe deer which is to be carried home from the hunt. It had given up struggling and now lay gazing into the fire with slit eyes and heaving sides, curiously resigned. Or else it was exhausted—for animals know when they have come to the end. Most of them have a dignity about dying, denied to human beings. This cat, with the small flames dancing in its oblique eyes, was perhaps seeing the pageant of its past eight lives, reviewing them with an animal's stoicism, beyond hope or fear.

The Queen picked up the cat. She was trying a well-known piseog to amuse herself, or at any rate to pass the time while the men were away at the war. It was a method of becoming invisible. She was not a serious witch like her sister Morgan le Fay—for her head was too empty to take any great art seriously, even if it were the black one. She was doing it because the little magics ran in her blood—as they did with all the women of her race.

In the boiling water, the cat gave some horrible convulsions and a dreadful cry. Its wet fur bobbed in the steam, gleaming like the side of a speared whale, as it tried to leap or to swim with its bound feet. Its mouth opened hideously, showing the whole of its pink gullet, and the sharp, white cat-teeth, like thorns. After the first shriek it was not able to articulate, but only to stretch its jaws. Later it was dead.

Queen Morgause of Lothian and Orkney sat beside the cauldron and waited. Occasionally she stirred the cat with a wooden spoon. The stench of boiling fur began to fill the room. A watcher would have seen, in the flattering peat light, what an exquisite creature she was tonight: her deep, big eyes, her hair glinting with dark lustre, her full body, and her faint air of watchfulness as she listened for the whispering in the room above.

Gawaine said: "Revenge!"
"They had done no harm to King Pendragon."
"They had only asked to be left in peace."
It was the unfairness of the rape of their Cornish grandmother which was hurting Gareth—the picture of weak and innocent people victimized by a resistless tyranny—the old tyranny of the Gall—which was felt like a personal wrong by every crofter of the Islands. Gareth was a generous boy. He hated the idea of strength against weakness. It made his heart swell, as if he were going to suffocate. Gawaine, on the other hand, was angry because it had been against his family. He did not think it was wrong for strength to have its way, but only that it was intensely wrong for anything to succeed against his own clan. He was neither clever nor sensitive, but he was loyal—stubbornly sometimes, and even annoyingly and stupidly so in later life. For him it was then as it was always to be: Up Orkney, Right or Wrong. The third brother, Agravaine, was moved because it was a matter which concerned his mother. He had curious feelings about her, which he kept to himself. As for Gaheris, he did and felt what the others did.

The cat had come to pieces. The long boiling had shredded its meat away until there was nothing in the cauldron except a deep scum of hair and grease and gobbets. Underneath, the white bones revolved in the eddies of the water, the heavy ones lying still and the airy membranes lifting gracefully, like leaves in an autumn wind. The Queen, wrinkling her nose slightly in the thick stench of unsalted broth, strained the liquid into a second pot.

On top of the flannel strainer there was left a sediment of cat, a sodden mass of matted hair and meat shreds and the delicate bone. She blew on the sediment and began turning it over with the handle of the spoon, prodding it to let the heat out. Later, she was able to sort it with her fingers.

The Queen knew that every pure black cat had a certain bone in it, which, if it were held in the mouth after boiling the cat alive, was able to make you invisible. But nobody knew precisely, even in those days, which the bone was. This was why the magic had to be done in front of a mirror, so that the right one could be found by practice.

It was not that Morgause courted invisibility—indeed, she would have detested it, because she was beautiful. But the men were away. It was something to do, an easy and well-known charm. Besides, it was an excuse for lingering with the mirror.

The Queen scraped the remains of her cat into two heaps, one of them a neat pile of warm bones, the other a miscellaneous lump which softly steamed. Then she chose one of the bones and lifted it to her red lips, cocking the little finger. She held it between her teeth and stood in front of the polished brass, looking at herself with sleepy pleasure. She threw the bone into the fire and fetched another.

There was nobody to see her. It was strange, in these circumstances, the way in which she turned and turned, from mirror to bone-pile, always putting a bone in her mouth, and looking at herself to see if she had vanished, as if she were dancing, as if there really was somebody to see her, or as if it were enough that she should see herself.

Finally, but before she had tested all the bones, she lost interest. She threw the last ones down impatiently and tipped the mess out of the window, not caring where it fell. Then she smoored the fire, stretched herself on the big bed with a strange motion, and lay there in the darkness for a long time without sleeping—her body moving discontentedly.

"And this, my heroes," concluded Gawaine, "is the reason why we of Cornwall and Orkney must be against the Kings of England ever more, and most of all against the clan Mac Pendragon."

"It is why our Da has gone away to fight against King Arthur whatever, for Arthur is a Pendragon. Our Mammy said so."

"And we must keep the feud living forever," said Agravaine, "because Mammy is a Cornwall. Dame Igraine is our Granny."

"We must avenge our family."

"Because our Mammy is the most beautiful woman in the high-ridged, extensive, ponderous, pleasantly-turning world."

"And because we love her."

Indeed, they did love her. Perhaps we all give the best of our hearts uncritically—to those who hardly think about us in return.

# THE MINISTER'S BLACK VEIL

*A Parable*[1]

# Nathaniel Hawthorne

The sexton stood in the porch of Milford meeting-house, pulling busily at the bell-rope. The old people of the village came stooping along the street. Children, with bright faces, tripped merrily beside their parents, or mimicked a graver gait, in the conscious dignity of their Sunday clothes. Spruce bachelors looked sidelong at the pretty maidens, and fancied that the Sabbath sunshine made them prettier than on week days. When the throng had mostly streamed into the porch, the sexton began to toll the bell, keeping his eye on the Reverend Mr. Hooper's door. The first glimpse of the clergyman's figure was the signal for the bell to cease its summons.

"But what has good Parson Hooper got upon his face?" cried the sexton in astonishment.

All within hearing immediately turned about, and beheld the semblance of Mr. Hooper, pacing slowly his meditative way towards the meeting-house. With one-accord they started, expressing more wonder than if some strange minister were coming to dust the cushions of Mr. Hooper's pulpit.

"Are you sure it is our parson?" inquired Goodman Gray of the sexton.

"Of a certainty it is good Mr. Hooper," replied the sexton. "He was to have exchanged pulpits with Parson Shute, of Westbury; but Parson Shute sent to excuse himself yesterday, being to preach a funeral sermon."

The cause of so much amazement may appear sufficiently slight. Mr. Hooper, a gentlemanly person, of about thirty, though still a bachelor, was dressed with due clerical neatness, as if a careful wife had starched his band,

[1] Another clergyman in New England, Mr. Joseph Moody, of York, Maine, who died about eighty years since, made himself remarkable by the same eccentricity that is here related of the Reverend Mr. Hooper. In his case, however, the symbol had a different import. In early life he had accidentally killed a beloved friend; and from that day till the hour of his own death, he hid his face from men.

and brushed the weekly dust from his Sunday's garb. There was but one thing remarkable in his appearance. Swathed about his forehead, and hanging down over his face, so low as to be shaken by his breath, Mr. Hooper had on a black veil. On a nearer view it seemed to consist of two folds of crape, which entirely concealed his features, except the mouth and chin, but probably did not intercept his sight, further than to give a darkened aspect to all living and inanimate things. With this gloomy shade before him, good Mr. Hooper walked onward, at a slow and quiet pace, stooping somewhat, and looking on the ground, as is customary with abstracted men, yet nodding kindly to those of his parishioners who still waited on the meeting-house steps. But so wonder-struck were they that his greeting hardly met with a return.

"I can't really feel as if good Mr. Hooper's face was behind that piece of crape," said the sexton.

"I don't like it," muttered an old woman, as she hobbled into the meeting-house. "He has changed himself into something awful, only by hiding his face.'"

"Our parson has gone mad!" cried Goodman Gray, following him across the threshold.

A rumor of some unaccountable phenomenon had preceded Mr. Hooper into the meeting-house, and set all the congregation astir. Few could refrain from twisting their heads towards the door; many stood upright, and turned directly about; while several little boys clambered upon the seats, and came down again with a terrible racket. There was a general bustle, a rustling of the women's gowns and shuffling of the men's feet, greatly at variance with that hushed repose which should attend the entrance of the minister. But Mr. Hooper appeared not to notice the perturbation of his people. He entered with an almost noiseless step, bent his head mildly to the pews on each side, and bowed as he passed his oldest parishioner, a white-haired great grandsire, who occupied an arm-chair in the centre of the aisle. It was strange to observe how slowly this venerable man became conscious of something singular in the appearance of his pastor. He seemed not fully to partake of the prevailing wonder, till Mr. Hooper had ascended the stairs, and showed himself in the pulpit, face to face with his congregation, except for the black veil. That mysterious emblem was never once withdrawn. It shook with his measured breath, as he gave out the psalm; it threw its obscurity between him and the holy page, as he read the Scriptures; and while he prayed, the veil lay heavily on his uplifted countenance. Did he seek to hide it from the dread Being whom he was addressing?

Such was the effect of this simple piece of crape, that more than one woman of delicate nerves was forced to leave the meeting-house. Yet perhaps the pale-faced congregation was almost as fearful a sight to the minister, as his black veil to them.

Mr. Hooper had the reputation of a good preacher, but not an energetic one: he strove to win his people heavenward by mild, persuasive influences, rather than to drive them thither by the thunders of the Word. The sermon which he now delivered was marked by the same characteristics of style and manner as the general series of his pulpit oratory. But there was something, either in the sentiment of the discourse itself, or in the imagination of the auditors, which made it greatly the most powerful effort that they had ever heard from their pastor's lips. It was tinged, rather more darkly than usual, with the gentle gloom of Mr. Hooper's temperament. The subject had reference to secret sin, and those sad mysteries which we hide from our nearest and dearest, and would fain conceal from our own consciousness, even forgetting that the Omniscient can detect them. A subtle power was breathed into his words. Each member of the congregation, the most innocent girl, and the man of hardened breast, felt as if the preacher had crept upon them, behind his awful veil, and discovered their hoarded iniquity of deed or thought. Many spread their clasped hands on their bosoms. There was nothing terrible in what Mr. Hooper said, at least, no violence; and yet, with every tremor of his melancholy voice, the hearers quaked. An unsought pathos came hand in hand with awe. So sensible were the audience of some unwonted attribute in their minister, that they longed for a breath of wind to blow aside the veil, almost believing that a stranger's visage would be discovered, though the form, gesture, and voice were those of Mr. Hooper.

At the close of the services, the people hurried out with indecorous confusion, eager to communicate their pent-up amazement, and conscious of lighter spirits the moment they lost sight of the black veil. Some gathered in little circles, huddled closely together, with their mouths all whispering in the centre; some went homeward alone, wrapt in silent meditation; some talked loudly, and profaned the Sabbath day with ostentatious laughter. A few shook their sagacious heads, intimating that they could penetrate the mystery; while one or two affirmed that there was no mystery at all but only that Mr. Hooper's eyes were so weakened by the midnight lamp, as to require a shade. After a brief interval, forth came good Mr. Hooper also, in the rear of this flock. Turning his veiled face from one group to another, he paid due reverence to the hoary heads, saluted the middle aged with kind dignity as their friend and spiritual guide, greeted the young with mingled authority and love, and laid his hands on the little children's heads to bless them. Such was always his custom on the Sabbath day. Strange and bewildered looks repaid him for his courtesy. None, as on former occasions, aspired to the honor of walking by their pastor's side. Old Squire Saunders, doubtless by an accidental lapse of memory, neglected to invite Mr. Hooper to his table, where the good clergyman had been wont to bless the food, almost every Sunday since his settlement. He returned, therefore, to the parsonage, and, at the moment of closing the door, was observed to look back upon the people, all of whom had their eyes fixed upon the minister. A sad smile gleamed faintly from beneath the black veil, and flickered about his mouth, glimmering as he disappeared.

"How strange," said a lady, "that a simple black veil, such as any woman might wear on her bonnet, should become such a terrible thing on Mr. Hooper's face!"

"Something must surely be amiss with Mr. Hooper's intellects," observed her husband, the physician of the village. "But the strangest part of the affair is the effect of this vagary, even on a sober-minded man like myself. The black veil, though it covers only our pastor's face, throws its influence over his whole person, and makes him ghostlike from head to foot. Do you not feel it so?"

"Truly do I," replied the lady; "and I would not be alone with him for the world. I wonder he is not afraid to be alone with himself!"

"Men sometimes are so," said her husband.

The afternoon service was attended with similar circumstances. At its conclusion, the bell tolled for the funeral of a young lady. The relatives and friends were assembled in the house, and the more distant acquaintances stood about the door, speaking of the good qualities of the deceased, when their talk was interrupted by the appearance of Mr. Hooper, still covered with his black veil. It was now an appropriate emblem. The clergyman stepped into the room where the corpse was laid, and bent over the coffin, to take a last farewell of his deceased parishioner. As he stooped, the veil hung straight down from his forehead, so that, if her eyelids had not been closed forever, the dead maiden might have seen his face. Could Mr. Hooper be fearful of her glance, that he so hastily caught back the black veil? A person who watched the interview between the dead and living, scrupled not to affirm, that, at the instant when the clergyman's features were disclosed, the corpse had slightly shuddered, rustling the shroud and muslin cap, though the countenance retained the composure of death. A superstitious old woman was the only witness of this prodigy. From the coffin Mr. Hooper passed into the chamber of the mourners, and thence to the head of the staircase, to make the funeral prayer. It was a tender and heart-dissolving prayer, full of sorrow, yet so imbued with celestial hopes, that the music of a heavenly harp, swept by the fingers of the dead, seemed faintly to be heard among the saddest accents of the minister. The people trembled, though they but darkly understood him when he prayed that they, and himself, and all of mortal race, might be ready, as he trusted this young maiden had been, for the dreadful hour that should snatch the veil from their faces. The bearers went heavily forth, and the mourners followed, saddening all the street, with the dead before them, and Mr. Hooper in his black veil behind.

"Why do you look back?" said one in the procession to his partner.

"I had a fancy," replied she, "that the minister and the maiden's spirit were walking hand in hand.

"And so had I, at the same moment," said the other.

That night, the handsomest couple in Milford village were to be joined in wedlock. Though reckoned a melancholy man, Mr. Hooper had a placid cheerfulness for such occasions, which often excited a sympathetic smile where livelier merriment would have been thrown away. There was no quality of his disposition which made him more beloved than this. The company at the wedding awaited his arrival with impatience, trusting that the strange awe, which had gathered over him throughout the day, would now be dispelled. But such was not the result. When Mr. Hooper came, the first thing that their eyes rested on was the same horrible black veil, which had added deeper gloom to the funeral, and could portend nothing but evil to the wedding. Such was its immediate effect on the guests that a cloud seemed to have rolled duskily from beneath the black crape, and dimmed the light of the candles. The bridal pair stood up before the minister. But the bride's cold fingers quivered in the tremulous hand of the bridegroom, and her deathlike paleness caused a whisper that the maiden who had been buried a few hours before was come from her grave to be married. If ever another wedding were so dismal, it was that famous one where they tolled the wedding knell. After performing the ceremony, Mr. Hooper raised a glass of wine to his lips, wishing happiness to the new-married couple in a strain of mild pleasantry that ought to have brightened the features of the guests, like a cheerful gleam from the hearth. At that instant, catching a glimpse of his figure in the looking-glass, the black veil involved his own spirit in the horror with which it overwhelmed all others. His frame shuddered, his lips grew white, he spilt the untasted wine upon the carpet, and rushed forth into the darkness. For the Earth, too, had on her Black Veil.

The next day, the whole village of Milford talked of little else than Parson Hooper's black veil. That, and the mystery concealed benid it, supplied a topic for discussion between acquaintances meeting in the street, and good women gossiping at their open windows. It was the first item of news that the tavern-keeper told to his guests. The children babbled of it on their way to school. One imitative little imp covered his face with an old black handkerchief, thereby so affrighting his playmates that the panic seized himself, and he well-nigh lost his wits by his own waggery.

It was remarkable that all of the busybodies and impertinent people in the parish, not one ventured to put the plain question to Mr. Hooper, wherefore he did this thing. Hitherto, whenever there appeared the slightest call for such interference, he had never lacked advisers, nor shown himself averse to be guided by their judgment. If he erred at all, it was by so painful a degree of self-distrust, that even the mildest censure would lead him to consider an indifferent action as a crime. Yet, though so well acquainted with this amiable weakness, no individual among his parishioners chose to make the black veil a subject of friendly remonstrance. There was a feeling of dread, neither plainly confessed nor carefully concealed, which caused each to shift the responsibility upon another, till at length it was found expedient to send a deputation of the church, in order to deal with Mr. Hooper about the mystery, before it should grow into a scandal. Never did an embassy so ill discharge its duties. The minister received them with friendly courtesy, but became silent, after they were seated, leaving to his visitors the whole burden of introducing their important business. The topic, it might be supposed, was obvious enough. There was the black veil swathed round Mr. Hooper's forehead, and concealing every feature above his placid mouth, on which, at times, they could perceive the glimmering of a melancholy smile. But that piece of crape, to their imagination, seemed to hang down before his heart, the symbol of a fearful secret between him and them. Were the veil but cast aside, they might speak freely of it, but not till then. Thus they sat a considerable time, speechless, confused, and shrinking uneasily from Mr. Hooper's eye, which they felt to be fixed upon them with an invisible glance. Finally, the deputies returned abashed to their constituents, pronouncing the matter too weighty to be handled, except by a council of the churches, if, indeed, it might not require a general synod.

But there was one person in the village unappalled by the awe with which the black veil had impressed all beside herself. When the deputies returned without an explanation, or even venturing to demand one, she, with the calm energy of her character, determined to chase away the strange cloud that appeared to be settling round Mr. Hooper, every moment more darkly than before. As his plighted wife, it should be her privilege to know what the black veil concealed. At the minister's first visit, therefore, she entered upon the subject with a direct simplicity, which made the task easier both for him and her. After he had seated himself, she fixed her eyes steadfastly upon the veil, but could discern nothing of the dreadful gloom that had so overawed the multitude: it was but a double fold of crape, hanging down from his forehead to his mouth, and slightly stirring with his breath.

"No," said she aloud, and smiling, "there is nothing terrible in this piece of crape, except that it hides a face which I am always glad to look upon. Come, good sir, let the sun shine from behind the cloud. First lay aside your black veil: then tell me why you put it on."

Mr. Hooper's smile glimmered faintly.

"There is an hour to come," said he, "when all of us shall cast aside our veils. Take it not amiss, beloved friend, if I wear this piece of crape till then."

"Your words are a mystery, too," returned the young lady. "Take away the veil from them, at least."

"Elizabeth, I will," said he, "so far as my vow may suffer me. Know, then, this veil is a type and a symbol, and I am bound to wear it ever, both in light and darkness, in solitude and before the gaze of multitudes, and as with strangers, so with my familiar friends. No mortal eye will see it withdrawn. This dismal shade must separate me from the world: even you, Elizabeth, can never come behind it!"

"What grievous affliction hath befallen you," she earnestly inquired, "that you should thus darken your eyes forever?"

"If it be a sign of mourning," replied Mr. Hooper, "I, perhaps, like most other mortals, have sorrows dark enough to be typified by a black veil."

"But what if the world will not believe that it is the type of an innocent sorrow?" urged Elizabeth. "Beloved and respected as you are, there may be whispers that you hide your face under the consciousness of secret sin. For the sake of your holy office, do away this scandal!"

The color rose into her cheeks as she intimated the nature of the rumors that were already abroad in the village. But Mr. Hooper's mildness did not forsake him. He even smiled again—that same sad smile, which always appeared like a faint glimmering of light, proceeding from the obscurity beneath the veil.

"If I hide my face for sorrow, there is cause enough," he merely replied; "and if I cover it for secret sin, what mortal might not do the same?"

And with this gentle, but unconquerable obstinacy did he resist all her entreaties. At length Elizabeth sat silent. For a few moments she appeared lost in thought, considering, probably, what new methods might be tried to withdraw her lover from so dark a fantasy, which, if it had no other meaning, was perhaps a symptom of mental disease. Though of a firmer character than his own, the tears rolled down her cheeks. But, in an instant, as it were, a new feeling took the place of sorrow: her eyes were fixed insensibly on the black veil, when, like a sudden twilight in the air, its terrors fell around her. She arose, and stood trembling before him.

"And do you feel it then, at last?" said he mournfully.

She made no reply, but covered her eyes with her hand, and turned to leave the room. He rushed forward and caught her arm.

"Have patience with me, Elizabeth!" cried he, passionately. "Do not desert me, though this veil must be between us here on earth. Be mine, and hereafter there shall be no veil over my face, no darkness between our souls! It is but a mortal veil—it is not for eternity! O! you know not how lonely I am, and how frightened, to be alone behind my black veil. Do not leave me in this miserable obscurity forever!"

"Lift the veil but once, and look me in the face," said she.

"Never! It cannot be!" replied Mr. Hooper.

"Then farewell!" said Elizabeth.

She withdrew her arm from his grasp, and slowly departed, pausing at the door, to give one long shuddering gaze, that seemed almost to penetrate the mystery of the black veil. But, even amid his grief, Mr. Hooper smiled to think that only a material emblem had separated him from happiness, though the horrors, which it shadowed forth, must be drawn darkly between the fondest of lovers.

From that time no attempts were made to remove Mr. Hooper's black veil, or, by a direct appeal, to discover the secret which it was supposed to hide. By persons who claimed a superiority to popular prejudice, it was reckoned merely an eccentric whim, such as often mingles with the sober actions of men otherwise rational, and tinges them all with its own semblance of insanity. But with the multitude, good Mr. Hooper was irreparbly a bugbear. He could not walk the street with any peace of mind, so conscious was he that the gentle and timid would turn aside to avoid him, and that others would make it a point of hardihood to throw themselves in his way. The impertinence of the latter class compelled him to give up his customary walk at sunset to the burial ground; for when he leaned pensively over the gate, there would always be faces behind the gravestones, peeping at his black veil. A fable went the round that the stare of the dead people drove him thence. It grieved him, to the very depth of his kind heart, to observe how the children fled from his approach, breaking up their merriest sports, while his melancholy figure was yet afar off. Their instinctive dread caused him to feel more strongly than aught else, that a preternatural horror was interwoven with the threads of the black crape. In truth, his own antipathy to the veil was known to be so great, that he never willingly passed before a mirror, nor stooped to drink at a still fountain, lest, in its peaceful bosom, he should be affrighted by himself. This was what gave plausibility to the whispers, that Mr. Hooper's conscience tortured him for some great crime too horrible to be entirely concealed, or otherwise than so obscurely intimated. Thus, from beneath the black veil, there rolled a cloud into the sunshine, an ambiguity of sin or sorrow, which enveloped the poor minister, so that love or sympathy could never reach him. It was said that ghost and fiend consorted with him there. With self-shudderings and outward terrors, he walked continually in its shadow, groping darkly within his own soul, or gazing through a medium that saddened the whole world. Even the lawless wind, it was believed, respected his dreadful secret, and never blew aside the veil. But still good Mr. Hooper sadly smiled at the pale visages of the worldly throng as he passed by.

Among all its bad influences, the black veil had the one desirable effect, of making its wearer a very efficient clergyman. By the aid of his mysterious emblem—for there was no other apparent cause—he became a man of awful power over souls that were in agony for sin. His converts always regarded him with a dread peculiar to themselves, affirming, though but figuratively, that, before he brought them to celestial light, they had been with him behind the black veil. Its gloom, indeed, enabled him to sympathize with all dark affections. Dying sinners cried aloud for Mr. Hooper, and would not yield their breath till he appeared; though ever, as he stooped to whisper consolation, they shuddered at the veiled face so near their own. Such were the terrors of the black veil, even when Death had bared his visage! Strangers came long distances to attend service at his church, with the mere idle purpose of gazing at his figure, because it was forbidden them to behold his face. But many were made to quake ere they departed! Once, during Governor Belcher's administration, Mr. Hooper was appointed to preach the election sermon. Covered with his black veil, he stood before the chief magistrate, the council, and the representatives, and wrought so deep an impression, that the legislative measures of that year were characterized by all the gloom and piety of our earliest ancestral sway.

In this manner Mr. Hooper spent a long life, irreproachable in outward act, yet shrouded in dismal suspicions; kind and loving, though unloved, and dimly feared; a man apart from men, shunned in their health and joy, but ever summoned to their aid in mortal anguish. As years wore on, shedding their snows above his sable veil, he acquired a name throughout the New England churches, and they called him Father Hooper. Nearly all his parishioners, who were of mature age when he was settled, had been borne away by many a funeral: he had one congregation in the church, and a more crowded one in the churchyard; and having wrought so late into the evening, and done his work so well, it was now good Father Hooper's turn to rest.

Several persons were visible by the shaded candlelight, in the death chamber of the old clergyman. Natural connections he had none. But there was the decorously grave, though unmoved physician, seeking only to mitigate the last pangs of the patient whom he could not save. There were the deacons, and other eminently pious members of his church. There, also, was the Reverend Mr. Clark, of Westbury, a young and zealous divine, who had ridden in haste to pray by the bedside of the expiring minister. There was the nurse, no hired handmaiden of death, but one whose calm affection had endured thus long in secrecy, in solitude, amid the chill of age, and would not perish, even at the dying hour. Who, but Elizabeth! And there lay the hoary head of good Father Hooper upon the death pillow, with the black veil still swathed about his brow, and reaching down over his face, so that each more difficult gasp of his faint breath caused it to stir. All through life that piece of crape had hung between him and the world: it had separated him from cheerful brotherhood and woman's love, and kept him in that saddest of all prisons, his own heart; and still it lay upon his face, as if to deepen the gloom of his darksome chamber, and shade him from the sunshine of eternity.

For some time previous, his mind had been confused, wavering doubtfully between the past and the present, and hovering forward, as it were, at intervals, into the indistinctness of the world to come. There had been feverish turns, which tossed him from side to side, and wore away what little strength he had. But in his most convulsive struggles, and in the wildest vagaries of his intellect, when no other thought retained its sober influence, he still showed an awful solicitude lest the black veil should slip aside. Even if his bewildered soul could have forgotten, there was a faithful woman at his pillow, who, with averted eyes, would have covered that aged face, which she had last beheld in the comeliness of manhood. At length the death-stricken old man lay quietly in the torpor of mental and bodily exhaustion, with an imperceptible pulse, and breath that grew fainter and fainter, except when a long, deep, and irregular inspiration seemed to prelude the flight of his spirit.

The minister of Westbury approached the bedside.

"Venerable Father Hooper," said he, "the moment of your release is at hand. Are you ready for the lifting of the veil that shuts in time from eternity?"

Father Hooper at first replied merely by a feeble motion of his head: then, apprehensive, perhaps, that his meaning might be doubted, he exerted himself to speak.

"Yea," said he, in faint accents, "my soul hath a patient weariness until that veil be lifted."

"And is it fitting," resumed the Reverend Mr. Clark, "that a man so given to prayer, of such a blameless example, holy in deed and thought, so far as mortal judgment may pronounce; is it fitting that a father in the church should leave a shadow on his memory, that may seem to blacken a life so pure? I pray you, my venerable brother, let not this thing be! Suffer us to be gladdened by your triumphant aspect as you go to your reward. Before the evil of eternity be lifted, let me cast aside this black veil from your face!"

And thus speaking, the Reverend Mr. Clark bent forward to reveal the mystery of so many years. But, exerting a sudden energy, that made all the beholders stand aghast, Father Hooper snatched both his hands from beneath the bedclothes, and pressed them strongly on the black veil, resolute to struggle, if the minister of Westbury would contend with a dying man.

"Never!" cried the veiled clergyman. "On earth, never!"

"Dark old man!" exclaimed the affrighted minister, "with what horrible crime upon your soul are you now passing to the judgment?"

Father Hooper's breath heaved; it rattled in his throat; but, with a mighty effort, grasping forward with his hands, he caught hold of life, and held it back till he should speak. He even raised himself in bed; and there he sat, shivering with the arms of death around him, while the black veil hung down, awful, at that last moment, in the gathered terrors of a lifetime. And yet the faint, sad smile, so often there, now seemed to glimmer from its obscurity, and linger on Father Hooper's lips.

"Why do you tremble at me alone?" cried he, turning his veiled face round the circle of pale spectators. "Tremble also at each other! Have men avoided me, and women shown no pity, and children screamed and fled, only for my black veil? What, but the mystery which it obscurely typifies, has made this piece of crape so awful? When the friend shows his inmost heart to his friend; the lover to his best beloved; when man does not vainly shrink from the eye of his Creator, loathsomely treasuring up the secret of his sin; then deem me a monster, for the symbol beneath which I have lived, and die! I look around me, and lo! on every visage a Black Veil!"

While his auditors shrank from one another, in mutual affright, Father Hooper fell back upon his pillow, a veiled corpse, with a faint smile lingering on the lips. Still veiled, they laid him in his coffin, and a veiled corpse they bore him to the grave. The grass of many years has sprung up and withered on that grave, the burial stone is moss-grown, and good Mr. Hooper's face is dust; but awful is still the thought that it mouldered beneath the Black Veil!

# SINNERS
# IN THE HANDS
# OF AN ANGRY GOD

## Jonathan Edwards

6. There are in the souls of wicked men those hellish *principles* reigning, that would presently kindle and flame out into hell fire, if it were not for God's restraints. There is laid in the very nature of carnal men a foundation for the torments of Hell: there are those corrupt principles, in reigning power in them, and in full possession of them, that are seeds of hell fire. These principles are active and powerful, and exceeding violent in their nature, and if it were not for the restraining hand of God upon them, they would soon break out, they would flame out after the same manner as the same corruptions, the same enmity does in the hearts of damned souls, and would beget the same torments in 'em as they do in them. The souls of the wicked are in Scripture compared to the troubled sea, Isai. lvii. 20. For the present God restrains their wickedness by his mighty power, as he does the raging waves of the troubled sea, saying, *Hitherto shalt thou come, and no further;* but if God should withdraw that restraining power, it would soon carry all afore it. Sin is the ruin and misery of the soul; it is destructive in its nature; and if God should leave it without restraint, there would need nothing else to make the soul perfectly miserable. The corruption of the heart of man is a thing that is immoderate and boundless in its fury; and while wicked men live here, it is like fire pent up by God's restraints, whenas if it were let loose it would set on fire the course of nature; and as the heart is now a sink of sin, so, if sin was not restrained, it would immediately turn the soul into a fiery oven, or a furnace of fire and brimstone.

7. It is no security to wicked men for one moment, that there are no *visible means* of *death* at hand. 'Tis no security to a natural man, that he is now in health, and that he don't see which way he should now immediately go out of the world by any accident, and that there is no visible danger in any respect in his circumstances. The manifold and continual experience of

the world in all ages, shews that this is no evidence that a man is not on the very brink of eternity, and that the next step won't be into another world. The unseen, unthought of ways and means of persons going suddenly out of the world are innumerable and inconceivable. Unconverted men walk over the pit of Hell on a rotten covering, and there are innumerable places in this covering so weak that they won't bear their weight, and these places are not seen. The arrows of death fly unseen at noon-day; the sharpest sight can't discern them. God has so many different unsearchable ways of taking wicked men out of the world and sending 'em to Hell, that there is nothing to make it appear that God had need to be at the expence of a miracle, or go out of the ordinary course of his Providence, to destroy any wicked man, at any moment. All the means that there are of sinners going out of the world, are so in God's hands, and so universally absolutely subject to his power and determination, that it don't depend at all less on the mere will of God, whether sinners shall at any moment go to Hell, than if means were never made use of, or at all concerned in the case.

8. Natural men's *prudence* and *care* to preserve their own *lives,* or the care of others to preserve them, don't secure 'em a moment. This divine Providence and universal experience does also bear testimony to. There is this clear evidence that men's own wisdom is no security to them from death; that if it were otherwise we should see some difference between the wise and politick men of the world, and others, with regard to the liableness to early and unexpected death; but how is it in fact? Eccles. ii: 16. *How dieth the wise man? as the fool.*

9. All wicked men's *pains* and *contrivance* they use to escape Hell, while they continue to reject Christ, and so remain wicked men, don't secure 'em from Hell one moment. Almost every natural man that hears of Hell, flatters himself that he shall escape it; he depends upon himself for his own security; he flatters himself in what he has done, in what he is now doing, or what he intends to do; every one lays out matters in his own mind how he shall avoid damnation, and flatters himself that he contrives well for himself, and that his schemes won't fail. They hear indeed that there are but few saved, and that the bigger part of men that have died heretofore are gone to Hell; but each one imagines that he lays out matters better for his own escape than others have done: he don't intend to come to that place of torment; he says within himself, that he intends to take care that shall be effectual, and to order matters so for himself as not to fail.

But the foolish children of men do miserably delude themselves in their own schemes, and in their confidence in their own strength and wisdom; they trust to nothing but a shadow. The bigger part of those that heretofore have lived under the same means of grace, and are now dead, are undoubt-edly gone to Hell: and it was not because they were not as wise as those that are now alive: it was not because they did not lay out matters as well for themselves to secure their own escape. If it were so, that we could come to speak with them, and could inquire of them, one by one, whether they expected when alive, and when they used to hear about Hell, ever to be the subjects of that misery, we doubtless should hear one and another reply, "No, I never intended to come here; I had laid out matters otherwise in my mind; I thought I should contrive well for myself; I thought my scheme good; I intended to take effectual care; but it came upon me unexpected; I did not look for it at that time, and in that manner; it came as a thief; death outwitted me; God's wrath was too quick for me; O my cursed foolishness! I was flattering myself, and pleasing myself with vain dreams of what I would do hereafter, and when I was saying peace and safety, then sudden destruction came upon me."

10. God has laid himself under no *obligation* by any promise to keep any natural man out of Hell one moment. God certainly has made no promises either of eternal life, or of any deliverance or preservation from eternal death, but what are contained in the Covenant of Grace, the promises that are given in Christ, in whom all the promises are yea and amen. But surely they have no interest in the promises of the Covenant of Grace that are not the children of the Covenant, and that don't believe in any of the promises of the Covenant, and have no interest in the *Mediator* of the Covenant.

So that whatever some have imagined and pretended about promises made to natural men's earnest seeking and knocking, 'tis plain and manifest that whatever pains a natural man takes in religion, whatever prayers he makes, till he believes in Christ, God is under no manner of obligation to keep him a *moment* from eternal destruction.

So that thus it is, that natural men are held in the hand of God over the pit of Hell; they have deserved the fiery pit, and are already sentenced to it; and God is dreadfully provoked, his anger is as great towards them as to those that are actually suffering the executions of the fierceness of his wrath in Hell, and they have done nothing in the least to appease or abate that anger, neither is God in the least bound by any promise to hold 'em up one moment; the Devil is waiting for them, Hell is gaping for them, the flames gather and flash about them, and would fain lay hold on them, and swallow them up; the fire pent up in their own hearts is struggling to break out; and they have no interest in any mediator, there are no means within reach that can be any security to them. In short, they have no refuge, nothing to take hold of, all that preserves them every moment is the mere arbitrary will, and uncovenanted unobliged forbearance of an incensed God.

## APPLICATION

The use may be of *awakening* to unconverted persons in this congregation. This that you have heard is the case of every one of you that are out of Christ. That world of misery, that lake of burning brimstone is extended abroad under you. *There* is the dreadful pit of glowing flames of the wrath of God; there is Hell's wide gaping mouth open; and you have nothing to stand upon, nor any thing to take hold of: there is nothing between you and Hell but the air; 'tis only the power and mere pleasure of God that holds you up.

You probably are not sensible of this; you find you are kept out of Hell, but don't see the hand of God in it, but look at other things, as the good state of your bodily constitution, your care of your own life, and the means you use for your own preservation. But indeed these things are nothing; if God should withdraw his hand, they would avail no more to keep you from falling, than the thin air to hold up a person that is suspended in it.

Your wickedness makes you as it were heavy as lead, and to tend downwards with great weight and pressure towards Hell; and if God should let you go, you would immediately sink and swiftly descend and plunge into the bottomless gulf, and your healthy constitution, and your own care and prudence, and best contrivance, and all your righteousness, would have no more influence to uphold you and keep you out of Hell, than a spider's web would have to stop a falling rock. Were it not that so is the sovereign pleasure of God, the earth would not bear you one moment; for you are a burden to it; the creation groans with you; the creature is made subject to the bondage of your corruption, not willingly; the sun don't willingly shine upon you to give you light to serve sin and Satan; the earth don't willingly yield her increase to satisfy your lusts; nor is it willingly a stage for your wickedness to be acted upon; the air don't willingly serve you for breath to maintain the flame of life in your vitals, while you spend your life in the service of God's enemies. God's creatures are good, and were made for men to serve God with, and don't willingly subserve to any other purpose, and groan when they are abused to purposes so directly contrary to their nature and end. And the world would spue you out, were it not for the sovereign hand of him who hath subjected it in hope. There are the black clouds of God's wrath now hanging directly over your heads, full of the dreadful storm, and big with thunder; and were it not for the restraining hand of God it would immediately burst forth upon you. The sovereign pleasure of God for the present stays his rough wind; otherwise it would come with fury, and your destruction would come like a whirlwind, and you would be like the chaff of the summer threshing floor.

The wrath of God is like great waters that are dammed for the present; they increase more and more, and rise higher and higher, till an outlet is given, and the longer the stream is stopped, the more rapid and mighty is its course, when once it is let loose. 'Tis true, that judgment against your evil works has not been executed hitherto; the floods of God's vengeance have been withheld; but your guilt in the meantime is constantly increasing, and you are every day treasuring up more wrath; the waters are continually rising and waxing more and more mighty; and there is nothing but the mere pleasure of God that holds the waters back that are unwilling to be stopped, and press hard to go forward; if God should only withdraw his hand from the flood-gate, it would immediately fly open, and the fiery floods of the fierceness and wrath of God would rush forth with inconceivable fury, and would come upon you with omnipotent power; and if your strength were ten thousand times greater than it is, yea ten thousand times greater than the strength of the stoutest, sturdiest devil in Hell, it would be nothing to withstand or endure it.

The bow of God's wrath is bent, and the arrow made ready on the string, and justice bends the arrow at your heart, and strains the bow, and it is nothing but the mere pleasure of God, and that of an angry God, without any promise or obligation at all, that keeps the arrow one moment from being made drunk with your blood.

Thus are all you that never passed under a great change of heart, by the mighty power of the spirit of God upon your souls; all that were never born again, and made new creatures, and raised from being dead in sin, to a state of new, and before altogether unexperienced light and life, (however you may have reformed your life in many things, and may have had religious affections, and may keep up a form of religion in your families and closets, and in the house of God, and may be strict in it,) you are thus in the hands of an angry God; 'tis nothing but his mere pleasure that keeps you from being this moment swallowed up in everlasting destruction.

However unconvinced you may now be of the truth of what you hear, by and by you will be fully convinced of it. Those that are gone from being in the like circumstances with you, see that it was so with them; for destruction came suddenly upon most of them, when they expected nothing of it, and while they were saying, *peace and safety:* Now they see, that those things that they depended on for peace and safety, were nothing but thin air and empty shadows.

The God that holds you over the pit of Hell, much as one holds a spider, or some loathsome insect, over the fire, abhors you, and is dreadfully provoked; his wrath towards you burns like fire; he looks upon you as worthy of nothing else, but to be cast into the fire; he is of purer eyes than to bear to have you in his sight; you are ten thousand times so abominable in his eyes as the most hateful venomous serpent is in ours. You have offended him infinitely more than ever a stubborn rebel did his prince: and yet 'tis nothing but his hand that holds you from falling into the fire every moment: 'tis to be ascribed to nothing else, that you did not go to Hell the last night; that you was suffered to awake again in this world, after you closed your eyes to sleep: and there is no other reason to be given why you have not dropped into Hell since you arose in the morning, but that God's hand has held you up: there is no other reason to be given why you have not gone to

Hell since you have sat here in the house of God, provoking his pure eyes by your sinful wicked manner of attending his solemn worship: yea, there is nothing else that is to be given as a reason why you don't this very moment drop down into Hell.

O sinner! Consider the fearful danger you are in: 'tis a great furnace of wrath, a wide and bottomless pit, full of the fire of wrath, that you are held over in the hand of that God, whose wrath is provoked and incensed as much against you as against many of the damned in Hell: you hang by a slender thread, with the flames of divine wrath flashing about it, and ready every moment to singe it, and burn it asunder; and you have no interest in any mediator, and nothing to lay hold of to save yourself, nothing to keep off the flames of wrath, nothing of your own, nothing that you can do, to induce God to spare you one moment.

# THE DEMIURGE'S LAUGH

## Robert Frost

It was far in the sameness of the wood;
    I was running with joy on the Demon's trail,
Though I knew what I hunted was no true god.
    It was just as the light was beginning to fail
That I suddenly heard—all I needed to hear:
It has lasted me many and many a year.

The sound was behind me instead of before,
    A sleepy sound, but mocking half,
As of one who utterly couldn't care.
    The Demon arose from his wallow to laugh,
Brushing the dirt from his eye as he went;
And well I knew what the Demon meant.

I shall not forget how his laugh rang out.
    I felt as a fool to have been so caught,
And checked my steps to make pretense
    It was something among the leaves I sought
(Though doubtful whether he stayed to see).
Thereafter I sat me against a tree.

# A POISON TREE

## William Blake

I was angry with my friend:
I told my wrath, my wrath did end.
I was angry with my foe:
I told it not, my wrath did grow.

And I watr'd it in fears,
Night & morning with my tears;
And I sunned it with smiles,
And with soft deceitful wiles.

And it grew both day and night,
Till it bore an apple bright;
And my foe beheld it shine,
And he knew that it was mine,

And into my garden stole
When the night had veil'd the pole:
In the morning glad I see
My foe outstretch'd beneath the tree.

# A LITTLE BOY LOST

## William Blake

"Nought loves another as itself,
"Nor venerates another so,
"Nor is it possible to Thought
"A greater than itself to know:

"And Father, how can I love you
"Or any of my brothers more?
"I love you like the little bird
"That picks up crumbs around the door."

The Priest sat by and heard the child,
In trembling zeal he siez'd his hair:
He led him by his little coat,
And all admir'd the Priestly care.

And standing on the altar high,
"Lo! what a fiend is here!" said he,
"One who sets reason up for judge
"Of our most holy Mystery."

The weeping child could not be heard,
The weeping parents wept in vain;
They strip'd him to his little shirt,
And bound him in an iron chain;

And burn'd him in a holy place,
Where many had been burn'd before;
The weeping parents wept in vain.
Are such things done on Albions shore.

*Satan Comes to the Gates of Hell* from Milton's *Paradise Lost* by William Blake.
(By permission of The Huntington Library, San Marino, California)

# THE SUITCASE

## Ezekial Mphahlele

One of these days he was going to take a desperate chance, Timi thought. He would not miss it if it presented itself. Many men had got rich by sheer naked chance. Couldn't it just be that he was destined to meet such a chance?

He sat on a pavement on a hot afternoon. It was New Year's Eve. And in such oppressive heat Timi had been sitting for over an hour. An insect got into his nostril and made him sneeze several times. Through the tears that filled his eyes the traffic seemed to dance about before him.

The grim reality of his situation returned to him with all its cold and aching pain after the short interlude with the insect. Today he had been led on something like a goose chase. He had been to three places where chance of getting work was promising. He had failed. At one firm he had been told, "We've already got a boy, Jim." At the second firm a tiny typist told him, "You're too big, John. The boss wants a small boy—about eighteen you know." Then she had gone on with her typing, clouding her white face with cigarette smoke. At the third place of call a short pudgy white man put down his price in a squeaking voice: "Two pounds ten a week." Three pounds ten a week, Timi had said. "Take it or leave it, my boy," the proprietor had said as his final word, and snorted to close the matter. Timi chuckled softly to himself at the thought of the pudgy man with fat white cheeks and small blinking eyes.

He was watching the movements of a wasp tormenting a worm. The wasp circled over the worm and then came down on the clumsy and apparently defenceless worm. It seemed to stand on its head as it stung the worm. The worm wriggled violently, seeming to want to fly away from the earth.

Then suddenly the worm stretched out, as though paralysed. The winged insect had got its prey. Timi felt pity for the poor worm. An unequal fight, an unfair fight, he thought. Must it always be thus, he asked—the well-armed and agile creatures sting the defenceless to death? The wasp was now dragging the worm; to its home, evidently.

He remembered he had nothing to take home. But the thought comforted him that his wife was so understanding. A patient and understanding wife. Yes, she would say, as she had often said, "Tomorrow's sun must rise, Timi. It rises for everyone. It may have its fortunes;" or "I will make a little fire, Timi. Our sages say even where there is no pot to boil there should be fire."

Now she was ill. She was about to have a baby; a third baby. And with nothing to take home for the last two months, his savings running out, he felt something must be done. Not anything that would get him into jail. No, not that. It wouldn't do for him to go to jail with his wife and children almost starving like that. No, he told himself emphatically.

A white man staggered past him, evidently drunk. He stopped a short way past Timi and turned to look at him. He walked back to Timi and held out a bottle of brandy before him, scarcely keeping firm on his legs.

"Here, John, drink this stuff. Happy New Year!" Timi shook his head.

"C'mon, be—be a s-sport, hic! No p-police to catch you, s-s-see?"

Timi shook his head again and waved him away.

"Huh, here's a bugger don't want to have a happy New Year, eh. Go t-to hell then."

The white man swung round brandishing his bottle as he tripped away.

If only that were money, Timi thought bitterly.

He remembered it was time he went home, and boarded a bus to Sophiatown. In the bus he found an atmosphere of revelry. The New Year spirit, he thought; an air of reckless abandon. Happy New Year! one shouted at intervals.

Timi was looking at a man playing a guitar just opposite him across the aisle. Here a girl was dancing to the rhythm of the music. The guitarist strummed away, clearly carried away in the flight of his own music. He coaxed, caressed and stroked his instrument. His long fingers played effortlessly on the strings. He glowered at the girl in front of him with hanging lower lip as she twisted her body seductively this way and that, like a young supple plant that the wind plays about with. Her breasts pushed out under a light sleeveless blouse. At the same time the guitarist bent his ear to the instrument as if to hear better its magic notes, or to whisper to it the secret of his joy.

Two young women came to sit next to Timi. One of them was pale, and seemed sick. The other deposited a suitcase in front between her leg and

Timi's. His attention was taken from the music by the presence of these two women. They seemed to have much unspoken between them.

At the next stop they rose to alight. Timi's one eye was fixed on the suitcase as he watched them go towards the door. When the bus moved a man who was sitting behind Timi exclaimed, "Those young women have left their case."

"No, it is mine," said Timi hastily.

"No. I saw them come in with it."

This is a chance . . . .

"I tell you it's mine."

"You can't tell me that."

Now there mustn't be any argument, or else . . . .

"Did you not see me come in with a case?"

I mustn't lose my temper, or else . . . .

"Tell the truth, my man, it bites no one."

"What more do you want me to say now?"

The people are looking at me now. By the gods, what can I do?

"It's his lucky day," shouted someone from the back, "let him be!"

"And if it is not his, how is this a lucky day?" asked someone else.

"Ha, ha, ha!" A woman laughed. "You take my thing, I take yours, he takes somebody else's. So we all have a lucky day, eh? Ha, ha, ha." She rocked with voluble laughter, seeming to surrender herself to it.

"Oh, leave him alone," an old voice came from another quarter, "only one man saw the girls come in with a suitcase, and only one man says it is his. One against one. Let him keep what he has, the case. Let the other man keep what he has, the belief that it belongs to the girls." There was a roar of laughter. The argument melted in the air of a happy New Year, of revelry and song.

Timi felt a great relief. He had won.

The bus came to a stop and he alighted. He did not even hear someone behind him in the bus cry, "That suitcase will yet tell whom it belongs to, God is my witness!" Why can't people mind their own affairs? He thought of all those people looking at him.

Once out of the bus he was seized by a fit of curiosity, anxiousness and expectancy. He must get home quickly and see what is in the case.

It was a chance, a desperate chance, and he had taken it. That mattered to him most as he paced up the street.

Timi did not see he was about to walk into a crowd of people. They were being searched by the police, two white constables. He was jolted into attention by the shining of a badge. Quickly he slipped into an open backyard belonging to a Chinese. Providence was with him, he thought, as he ran to stand behind the great iron door, his heart almost choking him.

He must have waited there for fifteen minutes, during which he could see all that was happening out there in the street. The hum and buzz so common to Good Street rose to a crescendo; so savage, so coldblooded, so menacing. Suddenly he got a strange and frightening feeling that he had excited all this noise, that he was the centre around which these angry noises whirled and circled, that he had raised a hue and cry.

For one desperate second he felt tempted to leave the case where he squatted. It would be so simple for him, he thought. Yes, just leave the case there and have his hands, no, more than that, his soul, freed of the burden. After all, it was not his.

Not his. This thought reminded him that he had done all this because it was not his. The incident in the bus was occasioned by the stark naked fact that the case was not his. He felt he must get home soon because it was not his. He was squatting here like an outlaw, because the case was not his. Why not leave it here then, after all these efforts to possess it and keep it? There must surely be valuable articles in it. Timi mused. It was so heavy. There must be. It couldn't be otherwise. Else why had Providence been so kind to him so far? Surely the spirits of his ancestors had pity on him; with a sick wife and hungry children. Then the wild, primitive determination rose in him; the blind determination to go through with a task once begun, whether a disaster can be avoided in time or not, whether it is to preserve worthless or valuable articles. No, he was not going to part with the case.

The pick-up van came and collected the detained men and women. The police car started up the street. Timi came out and walked on the pavement, not daring to look behind, lest he lose his nerve and blunder. He knew he was not made for all this sort of thing. Pitso was coming up the pavement in the opposite direction. Lord, why should it be Pitso at this time? Pitso, the gas-bag, the notorious talker whose appearance always broke up a party. They met.

"Greetings! You seem to be in a hurry, Timi?" Pitso called out in his usual noisy and jovial fashion. "Are you arriving or going?"

"Arriving." Timi did not want to encourage him.

"Ha, since when have you been calling yourself A.J.B.?"

"Who says I'm A.J.B.?"

"There my friend." Pitso pointed at the large initials on the case, and looked at his friend with laughing eyes.

"Oh, it's my cousin's." Timi wished he could wipe a broad stupid grin off the large mouth of this nonentity. He remembered later how impotent and helpless he felt now. For Pitso and his grin were inseparables, like Pitso and his mouth. Just now he wished he wouldn't look so uneasy. "I'm sorry, Pitso, my wife isn't well, and I must hurry." He passed on. Pitso looked at his friend, his broad mouth still smiling blankly.

The Chevrolet came to stop just alongside the pavement. Then it moved on, coasting idly and carelessly.

"Hey!" Timi looked to his left. Something seemed to snap inside him and release a lump shooting up to his throat. "Stop, *jong!*" The driver waved to him.

There they were, two white constables and an African in plain clothes in the back seat. Immediately he realised it would be foolish to run. Besides, the case should be his. He stopped. The driver went up to him and wrenched the suitcase from Timi's hand. At the same time he caught him by the shoulder and led him to the car, opening the back door for Timi. The car shot away to the police-station.

His knees felt weak when he recognised the black man next to him. It was the same man who was the first to argue that the case was not Timi's in the bus. By the spirits, did the man have such a strong sense of justice as to call God to be witness? Even on New Year's Eve? Or was he a detective? No, he could have arrested him on the bus. The man hardly looked at Timi. He just looked in front of him in a self-righteous posture, as it struck Timi.

Timi got annoyed; frantically annoyed. It was a challenge. He would face it. Things might turn round somewhere. He felt he needed all the luck fate could afford to give him.

At the police-station the two constables took the case into a small room. After a few minutes they came out, with what Timi thought was a strange communication of feelings between them as they looked at each other.

"*Kom, kom, jong!*" One of them said, although quite gently. They put the case in front of him.

"Whose case is this?"

"Mine."

"Do you have your things in here?"

"My wife's things."

"What are they?"

"I think she has some of her dresses in it."

"Why do you say you *think?*"

"Well, you see, she just packed them up in a hurry, and asked me to take them to her aunt; but I didn't see her pack them."

"Hm. You can recognise your wife's clothing?"

"Some of it." Why make it so easy for him? And why was there such cold amusement in the white man's eyes?

The constable opened the suitcase, and started to unpack the articles singly.

"Is this your wife's?" It was a torn garment.

"Yes."

"And this? And this?" Timi answered yes to both. Why did they pack such torn clothing? The constable lifted each one up before Timi. Timi's thoughts were racing and milling round in his head. What trick was fate about to play him? He sensed there was something wrong. Had he been a dupe?

The constable, after taking all the rags out, pointed to an object inside. *"And is this also your wife's?"* glaring at Timi with aggressive eyes.

Timi stretched his neck to see.

It was a ghastly sight. A dead baby that could not have been born more than twelve hours before. A naked, white, curly-haired image of death. Timi gasped and felt sick and faint. They had to support him to the counter to make a statement. He told the truth. He knew he had gambled with chance; the chance that was to cost him eighteen months' hard labour.

# THE AUTOPSY

## Georg Heym

*Translated by Michael Hamburger*

The dead man lay naked and alone on a white table in the great theater, in the oppressive whiteness, the cruel sobriety of the operating theater that seemed to be vibrating still with the screams of unending torment.

The noon sun covered him and caused the livid spots on his forehead to awaken; it conjured up a bright green out of his naked belly and made it swell like a great sack filled with water.

His body was like the brilliant calyx of a giant flower, a mysterious plant from the Indian jungles which someone had shyly laid down at the altar of death.

Splendid shades of red and blue grew along his loins, and the great wound below his navel, which emitted a terrible odor, split open slowly in the heat like a great red furrow.

The doctors entered. A few kindly men in white coats, with duelling scars and gold pince-nez.

They went up to the dead man and looked at him with interest and professional comments.

They took their dissecting instruments out of white cupboards, white boxes full of hammers, bonesaws with strong teeth, files, horrible batteries of tweezers, little cases full of enormous needles that seemed to cry out incessantly for flesh like the curved beaks of vultures.

They commenced their gruesome work. They were like terrible torturers. The blood flowed over their hands which they plunged ever more deeply into the cold corpse, pulling out its contents, like white cooks drawing a goose.

The intestines coiled around their arms, greenish-yellow snakes, and the

Reprinted by permission of Michael Hamburger.

excrement dripped on their coats, a warm, putrid fluid. They punctured the bladder. Cold urine glittered inside it like a yellow wine. They poured it into large bowls; it had a sharp and caustic stench like ammonia. But the dead man slept. Patiently he suffered them to tug him this way and that, to pull at his hair. He slept.

And while the blows of the hammer resounded on his head, a dream, the remnant of love in him, awoke like a torch shining into his night.

In front of the large window a great wide sky opened, full of small white clouds that floated in the light, in the afternoon quiet, like small white gods. And the swallows traveled high up in the blue, trembling in the warm July sun.

The dead man's black blood trickled over the blue putrescence of his forehead. It condensed in the heat to a terrible cloud, and the decay of death crept over him with its brightly colored talons. His skin began to flow apart, his belly grew white as an eel's under the greedy fingers of the doctors, who were bathing their arms up to the elbows in his moist flesh.

Decay pulled the dead man's mouth apart. He seemed to smile. He dreamed of a blissful star, of a fragrant summer evening. His dissolving lips quivered as though under a light kiss.

How I love you. I loved you so much. Shall I tell you how much I loved you? When you walked through the poppy fields, yourself a fragrant poppy flame, you had drawn the whole evening into yourself. And your dress that blew about your ankles was like a wave of fire in the glow of the setting sun. But you inclined your head in the light, and your hair still burned and flamed with all my kisses.

So you walked away, looking back at me all the time. And the lamp in your hand swayed like a glowing rose in the dusk long after you had gone.

I shall see you again tomorrow. Here, under the chapel window; here, where the candlelight pours through and changes your hair into a golden forest; here, where the narcissi cling to your ankles, tender as tender kisses.

I shall see you again every night at the hour of dusk. We shall never leave each other. How I love you! Shall I tell you how much I love you?

And the dead man trembled softly with bliss on his white mortuary table, while the iron chisel in the doctor's hand broke open the bones of his temple.

*"Even God likes a good joke."*

# VIII

# HUMOR

# THE LATEST DECALOGUE

## Arthur Hugh Clough

Thou shalt have one God only; who
Would be at the expense of two?
No graven images may be
Worshipped, except the currency:
Swear not at all; for for thy curse
Thine enemy is none the worse:
At church on Sunday to attend
Will serve to keep the world thy friend:
Honour thy parents; that is, all
From whom advancement may befall:
Thou shalt not kill; but needst not strive
Officiously to keep alive:
Do not adultery commit;
Advantage rarely comes of it:
Thou shalt not steal; an empty feat,
When it's so lucrative to cheat:
Bear not false witness; let the lie
Have time on its own wings to fly:
Thou shalt not covet; but tradition
Approves all forms of competition.

The sum of all is, thou shalt love,
If any body, God above:
At any rate shall never labour
*More* than thyself to love thy neighbour.

# WARTY BLIGGENS,
# THE TOAD

## Don Marquis

i met a toad
the other day by the name
of warty bliggens
he was sitting under
a toadstool
feeling contented
he explained that when the cosmos
was created
that toadstool was especially
planned for his personal
shelter from sun and rain
thought out and prepared
for him

do not tell me
said warty bliggens
that there is not a purpose
in the universe
the thought is blasphemy

a little more
conversation revealed
that warty bliggens
considers himself to be
the center of the said
universe

the earth exists
to grow toadstools for him
to sit under
the sun to give him light
by day and the moon
and wheeling constellations
to make beautiful
the night for the sake of
warty bliggens

to what act of yours
do you impute
this interest on the part
of the creator
of the universe
i asked him
why is it that you
are so greatly favored

ask rather
said warty bliggens
what the universe
has done to deserve me
if i were a
human being i would
not laugh
too complacently
at poor warty bliggens
for similar
absurdities
have only too often
lodged in the crinkles
of the human cerebrum

                              archy

# THROUGH
# THE LOOKING GLASS

## Lewis Carroll

There was a book lying near Alice on the table, and while she sat watching the White King (for she was still a little anxious about him, and had the ink all ready to throw over him, in case he fainted again), she turned over the leaves, to find some part that she could read, "for it's all in some language I don't know," she said to herself.

It was like this:

### YKCOWABBBAL
'Twas brillig, and the slithy toves
Did gyre and gimble in the wabe;
All mimsy were the borogoves,
And the mome raths outgrabe.

"Beware the Jabberwock, my son!
The jaws that bite, the claws that catch!
Beware the Jubjub bird, and shun
The frumious Bandersnatch!"

She puzzled over this for some time, but at last a bright thought struck her. "Why, it's a looking-glass-book, of course! And if I hold it up to a glass, the words will all go the right way again."

This was the poem that Alice read:

### JABBERWOCKY
'Twas brillig, and the slithy toves
    Did gyre and gimble in the wabe;
All mimsy were the borogoves,
    And the mome raths outgrabe.

"Beware the Jabberwock, my son!
    The jaws that bite, the claws that catch!
Beware the Jubjub bird, and shun
    The frumious Bandersnatch!"

He took his vorpal sword in hand:
  Long time the manxome foe he sought—
So rested he by the Tumtum tree,
  And stood awhile in thought.

And as in uffish thought he stood,
  The Jabberwock, with eyes of flame,
Came whiffling through the tulgey wood,
  And burbled as it came!

One, two! One, two! And through and through
  The vorpal blade went snicker-snack!
He left it dead, and with its head
  He went galumphing back.

"And hast thou slain the Jabberwock?
  Come to my arms, my beamish boy!
O frabjous day! Callooh! Callay!"
  He chortled in his joy.

'Twas brillig, and the slithy toves
  Did gyre and gimble in the wabe;
All mimsy were the borogoves,
  And the mome raths outgrabe.

"It seems very pretty," she said when she had finished it, "but it's *rather* hard to understand!" (You see she didn't like to confess, even to herself, that she couldn't make it out at all.) "Somehow it seems to fill my head with ideas—only I don't exactly know what they are! However, *somebody* killed *something:* that's clear, at any rate——". . . .

Humpty Dumpty took the book, and looked at it carefully. "That seems to be done right——" he began.

"You're holding it upside down!" Alice interrupted.

"To be sure I was!" Humpty Dumpty said gayly, as she turned it round for him. "I thought it looked a little queer. As I was saying, that *seems* to be done right—though I haven't time to look it over thoroughly just now—and that shows that there are three hundred and sixty-four days when you might get un-birthday presents——"

"Certainly," said Alice.

"And only *one* for birthday presents, you know. There's glory for you!"

"I don't know what you mean by 'glory,'" Alice said.

Humpty Dumpty smiled contemptuously. "Of course you don't—till I tell you. I meant 'there's a nice knock-down argument for you!'"

"But 'glory' doesn't mean 'a nice knock-down argument,'" Alice objected.

"When *I* use a word," Humpty Dumpty said in rather a scornful tone, "it means just what I choose it to mean—neither more nor less."

"The question is," said Alice, "whether you *can* make words mean so many different things."

"The question is," said Humpty Dumpty, "which is to be master—that's all."

Alice was too much puzzled to say anything, so after a minute Humpty Dumpty began again. "They've a temper, some of them—particularly verbs, they're the proudest—adjectives you can do anything with, but not verbs—however, *I* can manage the whole lot of them! Impenetrability! That's what I say!"

"Would you tell me, please," said Alice, "what that means?"

"Now you talk like a reasonable child," said Humpty Dumpty, looking very much pleased. "I meant by 'impenetrability' that we've had enough of that subject, and it would be just as well if you'd mention what you mean to do next, as I suppose you don't mean to stop here all the rest of your life."

"That's a great deal to make one word mean," Alice said, in a thoughtful tone.

"When I make a word do a lot of work like that," said Humpty Dumpty, "I always pay it extra."

"Oh!" said Alice. She was too much puzzled to make any other remark.

"Ah, you should see 'em come round me of a Saturday night," Humpty Dumpty went on, wagging his head gravely from side to side: "for to get their wages, you know."

(Alice didn't venture to ask what he paid them with; and so you see I can't tell *you*.)

"You seem very clever at explaining words, sir," said Alice. "Would you kindly tell me the meaning of the poem called 'Jabberwocky?' "

"Let's hear it," said Humpty Dumpty. "I can explain all the poems that ever were invented—and a good many that haven't been invented just yet."

This sounded very hopeful, so Alice repeated the first verse.

" 'Twas brillig, and the slithy toves
    Did gyre and gimble in the wabe:
  All mimsy were the borogoves,
    And the mome raths outgrabe."

"That's enough to begin with," Humpty Dumpty interrupted: "there are plenty of hard words there, *'Brillig'* means four o'clock in the afternoon—the time when you begin *broiling* things for dinner."

"That'll do very well," said Alice: "and *'slithy?'* "

"Well, *'slithy'* means lithe and slimy. 'Lithe' is the same as 'active.' You see it's like a portmanteau—there are two meanings backed up into one word."

"I see it now," Alice remarked thoughtfully: "and what are *'toves?'* "

"Well, *'toves'* are something like badgers—they're something like lizards —and they're something like corkscrews."

"They must be very curious-looking creatures."

"They are that," said Humpty Dumpty, "also they make their nests under sun-dials—also they live on cheese."

"And what's to *'gyre'* and to *'gimble'?*"

"To *'gyre'* is to go round and round like a gyroscope. To *'gimble'* is to make holes like a gimblet."

"And *'the wabe'* is the grass-plot round a sun-dial, I suppose?" said Alice, surprised at her own ingenuity.

"Of course it is. It's called *'wabe,'* you know, because it goes a long way before it, and a long way behind it——"

"And a long way beyond it on each side," Alice added.

"Exactly so. Well then. *'mimsy'* is flimsy 'and miserable' (there's another portmanteau for you). And a *'borogove'* is a thin shabby-looking bird with its feathers sticking out all round—something like a live mop."

"And then *'mome raths?'* " said Alice. "I'm afraid I'm giving you a great deal of trouble."

"Well, a *'rath'* is a sort of green pig: but *'mome'* I'm not certain about. I think it's short for 'from home'—meaning that they'd lost their way, you know."

"And what does *'outgrabe'* mean?"

"Well, *'outgribing'* is something between bellowing and whistling, with a kind of sneeze in the middle: however, you'll hear it done, maybe—down in the wood yonder—and when you've once heard it you'll be *quite* content. Who's been repeating all that hard stuff to you?"

"I read it in a book," said Alice.

# MILO

## Joseph Heller

April had been the best month of all for Milo. Lilacs bloomed in April and fruit ripened on the vine. Heartbeats quickened and old appetites were renewed. In April a livelier iris gleamed upon the burnished dove. April was spring, and in the spring Milo Minderbinder's fancy had lightly turned to thoughts of tangerines.

"Tangerines?"

"Yes, sir."

"My men would love tangerines," admitted the colonel in Sardinia who commanded four squadrons of B-26s.

"There'll be all the tangerines they can eat that you're able to pay for with money from your mess fund," Milo assured him.

"Casaba melons?"

"Are going for a song in Damascus."

"I have a weakness for casaba melons. I've always had a weakness for casaba melons."

"Just lend me one plane from each squadron, just one plane, and you'll have all the casabas you can eat that you've money to pay for."

"We buy from the syndicate?"

"And everybody has a share."

"It's amazing, positively amazing. How can you do it?"

"Mass purchasing power makes the big difference. For example, breaded veal cutlets."

"I'm not so crazy about breaded veal cutlets," grumbled the skeptical B-25 commander in the north of Corsica.

From *Catch-22*. Copyright © 1955, by Joseph Heller. Reprinted by permission of Simon & Schuster, Inc.

"Breaded veal cutlets are very nutritious," Milo admonished him piously. "They contain egg yolk and bread crumbs. And so are lamb chops."

"Ah, lamb chops," echoed the B-25 commander. "Good lamb chops?"

"The best," said Milo, "that the black market has to offer."

"Baby lamb chops?"

"In the cutest little pink paper panties you ever saw. Are going for a song in Portugal."

"I can't send a plane to Portugal. I haven't the authority."

"I can, once you lend the plane to me. With a pilot to fly it. And don't forget—you'll get General Dreedle."

"Will General Dreedle eat in my mess hall again?"

"Like a pig, once you start feeding him my best white fresh eggs fried in my pure creamery butter. There'll be tangerines too, and casaba melons, honeydews, filet of Dover sole, baked Alaska, and cockles and mussels."

"And everybody has a share?"

"That," said Milo, "is the most beautiful part of it."

"I don't like it," growled the uncooperative fighter-plane commander, who didn't like Milo either.

"There's an uncooperative fighter-plane commander up north who's got it in for me," Milo complained to General Dreedle. "It takes just one person to ruin the whole thing, and then you wouldn't have your fresh eggs fried in my pure creamery butter any more."

General Dreedle had the uncooperative fighter-plane commander transfered to the Solomon Islands to dig graves and replaced him with a senile colonel with bursitis and a craving for litchi nuts who introduced Milo to the B-17 general on the mainland with a yearning for Polish sausage.

"Polish sausage is going for peanuts in Cracow," Milo informed him.

"Polish sausage," sighed the general nostalgically. "You know, I'd give just about anything for a good hunk of Polish sausage. Just about anything."

"You don't have to give *anything*. Just give me one plane for each mess hall and a pilot who will do what he's told. And a small down payment on your initial order as a token of good faith."

"But Cracow is hundreds of miles behind the enemy lines. How will you get to the sausage?"

"There's an international Polish sausage exchange in Geneva. I'll just fly the peanuts into Switzerland and exchange them for Polish sausage at the open market rate. They'll fly the peanuts back to Cracow and I'll fly the Polish sausage back to you. You buy only as much Polish sausage as you want through the syndicate. There'll be tangerines too, with only a little artificial coloring added. And eggs from Malta and Scotch from Sicily. You'll be paying the money to yourself when you buy from the syndicate, since you'll own a share, so you'll really be getting everything you buy for nothing. Doesn't that make sense?"

"Sheer genius. How in the world did you ever think of it?"

"My name is Milo Minderbinder. I am twenty-seven years old."

Milo Minderbinder's planes flew in from everywhere, the pursuit planes, bombers and cargo ships streaming into Colonel Carthcart's field with pilots at the controls who would do what they were told. The planes were decorated with flamboyant squadron emblems illustrating such laudable ideals as Courage, Might, Justice, Truth, Liberty, Love, Honor and Patriotism that were painted out at once by Milo's mechanics with a double coat of flat white and replaced in garish purple with the stenciled name M & M ENTERPRISES, FINE FRUITS AND PRODUCE. The "M & M" in "M & M ENTERPRISES" stood for Milo & Minderbinder, and the & was inserted, Milo revealed candidly, to nullify any impression that the syndicate was a one-man operation. Planes arrived for Milo from airfields in Italy, North Africa and England, and from Air Transport Command stations in Liberia, Ascension Island, Cairo and Karachi. Pursuit planes were traded for additional cargo ships or retained for emergency invoice duty and small-parcel service; trucks and tanks were procured from the ground forces and used for short-distance road hauling. Everybody had a share, and men got fat and moved about tamely with toothpicks in their greasy lips. Milo supervised the whole expanding operation by himself. Deep otter-brown lines of preoccupation etched themselves permanently into his careworn face and gave him a harried look of sobriety and mistrust. Everybody but Yossarian thought Milo was a jerk, first for volunteering for the job of mess officer and next for taking it so seriously. Yossarian also thought that Milo was a jerk; but he also knew that Milo was a genius.

One day Milo flew away to England to pick up a load of Turkish halvah and came flying back from Madagascar leading four German bombers filled with yams, collards, mustard greens and black-eyed Georgia peas. Milo was dumfounded when he stepped down to the ground and found a contingent of armed M.P.s waiting to imprison the German pilots and confiscate their planes. *Confiscate!* The mere word was anathema to him, and he stormed back and forth in excoriating condemnation, shaking a piercing finger of rebuke in the guilt-ridden faces of Colonel Cathcart, Colonel Korn and the poor battle-scarred captain with the submachine gun who commanded the M.P.s.

"Is this Russia?" Milo assailed them incredulously at the top of his voice. *"Confiscate?"* he shrieked, as though he could not believe his own ears. "Since when is it the policy of the American government to confiscate the private property of its citizens? Shame on you! Shame on all of you for even thinking such a horrible thought."

"But Milo," Major Danby interrupted timidly, "we're at war with Germany, and those are German planes."

"They are no such thing!" Milo retorted furiously. "Those planes belong to the syndicate, and everybody has a share. *Confiscate?* How can you possibly confiscate your own private property? *Confiscate,* indeed! I've never heard anything so depraved in my whole life."

And sure enough, Milo was right, for when they looked, his mechanics had painted out the German swastikas on the wings, tails and fuselages with double coats of flat white and stenciled in the words M & M ENTERPRISES, FINE FRUITS AND PRODUCE. Right before their eyes he had transformed his syndicate into an international cartel.

Milo's argosies of plenty now filled the air. Planes poured in from Norway, Denmark, France, Germany, Austria, Italy, Yugoslavia, Romania, Bulgaria, Sweden, Finland, Poland—from everywhere in Europe, in fact, but Russia, with whom Milo refused to do business. When everybody who was going to had signed up with M & M Enterprises, Fine Fruits and Produce, Milo created a wholly owned subsidiary, M & M Enterprises, Fancy Pastry, and obtained more airplanes and more money from the mess funds for scones and crumpets from the British Isles, prune and cheese Danish from Copenhagen, éclairs, cream puffs, Napoleons and *petits fours* from Paris, Reims and Grenoble, *Kugelhopf,* pumpernickel and *Pfefferkuchen* from Berlin, *Linzer* and *Dobos Torten* from Vienna, *Strudel* from Hungary and *baklava* from Ankara. Each morning Milo sent planes aloft all over Europe and North Africa hauling long red tow signs advertising the day's specials in large square letters: "EYE ROUND, 79¢ . . . WHITING, 21¢." He boosted cash income for the syndicate by leasing tow signs to Pet Milk, Gaines Dog Food, and Noxzema. In a spirit of civic enterprise, he regularly allotted a certain amount of free aerial advertising space to General Peckem for the propagation of such messages in the public interest as NEATNESS COUNTS, HASTE MAKES WASTE, and THE FAMILY THAT PRAYS TOGETHER STAYS TOGETHER. Milo purchased spot radio announcements on Axis Sally's and Lord Haw Haw's daily propaganda broadcasts from Berlin to keep things moving. Business boomed on every battlefront.

Milo's planes were a familiar sight. They had freedom of passage everywhere, and one day Milo contracted with the American military authorities to bomb the German-held highway bridge at Arvieto and with the German military authorities to defend the highway bridge at Orvieto with anti-aircraft fire against his own attack. His fee for attacking the bridge for America was the total cost of the operation plus six per cent, and his fee from Germany for defending the bridge was the same cost-plus-six agreement augmented by a merit bonus of a thousand dollars for every American plane he shot down. The consummation of these deals represented an important victory for private enterprise, he pointed out, since the armies of both countries were socialized institutions. Once the contracts were signed, there seemed to be no point in using the resources of the syndicate to bomb and defend the bridge, inasmuch as both governments had ample men and material right there to do so and were perfectly happy to contribute them, and in the end Milo realized a fantastic profit from both halves of his project for doing nothing more than signing his name twice.

The arrangements were fair to both sides. Since Milo did have freedom of passage everywhere, his planes were able to steal over in a sneak attack without alerting the German antiaircraft gunners; and since Milo knew about the attack, he was able to alert the German antiaircraft gunners in sufficient time for them to begin firing accurately the moment the planes came into range. It was an ideal arrangement for everyone but the dead man in Yossarian's tent, who was killed over the target the day he arrived.

"I didn't kill him!" Milo kept replying passionately to Yossarian's angry protest. "I wasn't even there that day, I tell you. Do you think I was down there on the ground firing an antiaircraft gun when the planes came over?"

"But you organized the whole thing, didn't you?" Yossarian shouted back at him in the velvet darkness cloaking the path leading past the still vehicles of the motor pool to the open-air movie theater.

"And I didn't organize anything," Milo answered indignantly, drawing great agitated sniffs of air in through his hissing, pale twitching nose. "The Germans have the bridge, and we were going to bomb it, whether I stepped into the picture or not. I just saw a wonderful opportunity to make some profit out of the mission, and I took it. What's so terrible about that?"

"What's so terrible about it? Milo, a man in my tent was killed on that mission before he could even unpack his bags."

"But I didn't kill him."

"You got a thousand dollars extra for it."

"But I didn't kill him. I wasn't even there, I tell you. I was in Barcelona buying olive oil and skinless and boneless sardines, and I've got the purchase orders to prove it. And I didn't get the thousand dollars. That thousand dollars went to the syndicate, and everybody got a share, even you." Milo was appealing to Yossarian from the bottom of his soul. "Look, I didn't start this war, Yossarian, no matter what that lousy Wintergreen is saying. I'm just trying to put it on a businesslike basis. Is anything wrong with that? You know, a thousand dollars ain't such a bad price for a medium bomber and a crew. If I can persuade the Germans to pay me a thousand dollars for every plane they shoot down, why shouldn't I take it?"

"Because you're dealing with the enemy, that's why. Can't you understand that we're fighting a war? People are dying. Look around you, for Christ's sake!"

Milo shook his head with weary forbearance. "And the Germans are not our enemies," he declared. "Oh, I know what you're going to say. Sure, we're at war with them. But the Germans are also members in good standing of the syndicate, and it's my job to protect their rights as shareholders. Maybe they did start the war, and maybe they are killing millions of people, but they pay their bills a lot more promptly than some allies of ours I could name. Don't you understand that I have to respect the sanctity of my contract with Germany? Can't you see it from my point of view?"

"No," Yossarian rebuffed him harshly.

Milo was stung and made no effort to disguise his wounded feelings. It was a muggy, moonlit night filled with gnats, moths, and mosquitoes. Milo lifted his arm suddenly and pointed toward the open-air theater, where the milky, dust-filled beam bursting horizontally from the projector slashed a conelike swath in the blackness and draped in a fluorescent membrane of light the audience tilted on the seats there in hypnotic sags, their faces focused upward toward the aluminized movie screen. Milo's eyes were liquid with integrity, and his artless and uncorrupted face was lustrous with a shining mixture of sweat and insect repellent.

"Look at them," he exclaimed in a voice choked with emotion. "They're my friends, my countrymen, my comrades in arms. A fellow never had a better bunch of buddies. Do you think I'd do a single thing to harm them if I didn't have to? Haven't I got enough on my mind? Can't you see how upset I am already about all that cotton piling up on those piers in Egypt?" Milo's voice splintered into fragments, and he clutched at Yossarian's shirt front as though drowning. His eyes were throbbing visibly like brown caterpillars. "Yossarian, what am I going to do with so much cotton? It's all your fault for letting me buy it."

The cotton was piling up on the piers in Egypt, and nobody wanted any. Milo had never dreamed that the Nile Valley could be so fertile or that there would be no market at all for the crop he had bought. The mess halls in his syndicate would not help; they rose up in uncompromising rebellion against his proposal to tax them on a per capita basis in order to enable each man to own his own share of the Egyptian cotton crop. Even his reliable friends the Germans failed him in this crisis: they preferred ersatz. Milo's mess halls would not even help him store the cotton, and his warehousing costs skyrocketed and contributed to the devastating drain upon his cash reserves. The profits from the Orvieto mission were sucked away. He began writing home for the money he had sent back in better days; soon that was almost gone. And new bales of cotton kept arriving on the wharves at Alexandria every day. Each time he succeeded in dumping some on the world market for a loss it was snapped up by canny Egyptian brokers in the Levant, who sold it back to him at the original contract price, so that he was really worse off than before.

M & M Enterprises verged on collapse. Milo cursed himself hourly for his monumental greed and stupidity in purchasing the entire Egyptian cotton crop, but a contract was a contract and had to be honored, and one night, after a sumptuous evening meal, all Milo's fighters and bombers took off, joined in formation directly overhead and began dropping bombs on the group. He had landed another contract with the Germans, this time to bomb his own outfit. Milo's planes separated in a well-co-ordinated attack and bombed the fuel stocks and the ordnance dump, the repair hangars and the B-25 bombers resting on the lollipop-shaped hardstands at the field. His crews spared the landing strip and the mess halls so that they could land safely when their work was done and enjoy a hot snack before retiring. They bombed with their landing lights on, since no one was shooting back. They bombed all four squadrons, the officers' club and the Group Head-quarters building. Men bolted from their tents in sheer terror and did not know in which direction to turn. Wounded soon lay screaming everywhere. A cluster of fragmentation bombs exploded in the yard of the officers' club and punched jagged holes in the side of the wooden building and in the bellies and backs of a row of lieutenants and captains standing at the bar. They doubled over in agony and dropped. The rest of the officers fled toward the two exits in panic and jammed up the doorways like a dense, howling dam of human flesh as they shrank from going farther.

Colonel Cathcart clawed and elbowed his way through the unruly, bewildered mass until he stood outside by himself. He stared up at the sky in stark astonishment and horror. Milo's planes, ballooning serenely in over the blossoming treetops with their bomb bay doors open and wing flaps down and with their monstrous, bug-eyed, blinding, fiercely flickering eerie landing lights on, were the most apocalyptic sight he had ever beheld. Colonel Cathcart let go a stricken gasp of dismay and hurled himself head-long into his jeep, almost sobbing. He found the gas pedal and the ignition and sped toward the airfield as fast as the rocking car would carry him, his huge flabby hands clenched and bloodless on the wheel or blaring his horn tormentedly. Once he almost killed himself when he swerved with a banshee screech of tires to avoid plowing into a bunch of men running crazily toward the hills in their underwear with their stunned faces down and their thin arms pressed high around their temples as puny shields. Yellow, orange and red fires were burning on both sides of the road. Tents and trees were in flames, and Milo's planes kept coming around interminably with their blinking white landing lights on and their bomb bay doors open. Colonel Cathcart almost turned the jeep over when he slammed the brakes on at the control tower. He leaped from the car while it was still skidding dangerously and hurtled up the flight of steps inside, where three men were busy at the instruments and the controls. He bowled two of them aside in his lunge for the nickel-plated microphone, his eyes glittering wildly and his beefy face contorted with stress. He squeezed the microphone in a bestial grip and began shouting hysterically at the top of his voice,

"Milo, you son of a bitch! Are you crazy? What the hell are you doing? Come down! Come down!"

"Stop hollering so much, will you?" answered Milo, who was standing there right beside him in the control tower with a microphone of his own. "I'm right here." Milo looked at him with reproof and turned back to his work. "Very good, men, very good," he chanted into his microphone. "But I see one supply shed still standing. That will never do, Purvis—I've spoken to you about that kind of shoddy work before. Now, you go right back there this minute and try it again. And this time come in slowly . . . slowly. Haste makes waste, Purvis. Haste makes waste. If I've told you that once, I must have told you that a hundred times. Haste makes waste."

The loud-speaker overhead began squawking. "Milo, this is Alvin Brown. I've finished dropping my bombs. What should I do now?"

"Strafe," said Milo.

"*Strafe?*" Alvin Brown was shocked.

"We have no choice," Milo informed him resignedly. "It's in the contract."

"Oh, okay, then," Alvin Brown acquiesced. "In that case I'll strafe."

This time Milo had gone too far. Bombing his own men and planes was more than even the most phlegmatic observer could stomach, and it looked like the end for him. High-ranking government officials poured in to investigate. Newspapers inveighed against Milo with glaring headlines, and Congressmen denounced the atrocity in stentorian wrath and clamored for punishment. Mothers with children in the service organized into militant groups and demanded revenge. Not one voice was raised in his defense. Decent people everywhere were affronted, and Milo was all washed up until he opened his books to the public and disclosed the tremendous profit he had made. He could reimburse the government for all the people and property he had destroyed and still have enough money left over to continue buying Egyptian cotton. Everybody, of course, owned a share. And the sweetest part of the whole deal was that there really was no need to reimburse the government at all.

"In a democracy, the government is the people," Milo explained. "We're people, aren't we? So we might just as well keep the money and eliminate the middleman. Frankly, I'd like to see the government get out of war altogether and leave the whole field to private industry. If we pay the government everything we owe it, we'll only be encouraging government control and discouraging other individuals from bombing their own men and planes. We'll be taking away their incentive."

Milo was correct, of course, as everyone soon agreed but a few embittered misfits like Doc Daneeka, who sulked cantankerously and muttered offensive insinuations about the morality of the whole venture until Milo mollified him with a donation, in the name of the syndicate, of a lightweight aluminum collapsible garden chair that Doc Daneeka could fold up conveniently and carry outside his tent each time Chief White Halfoat came inside his tent and carry back inside his tent each time Chief White Halfoat came out. Doc Daneeka had lost his head during Milo's bombardment; instead of running for cover, he had remained out in the open and performed his duty, slithering along the ground through shrapnel, strafing and incendiary bombs like a furtive, wily lizard from casualty to casualty, administering tourniquets, morphine, splints and sulfanilamide with a dark and doleful visage, never saying one word more than he had to and reading in each man's bluing wound a dreadful portent of his own decay. He worked himself relentlessly into exhaustion before the long night was over and came down with a sniffle the next day that sent him hurrying querulously into the medical tent to have his temperature taken by Gus and Wes and to obtain a mustard plaster and vaporizer.

Doc Daneeka tended each moaning man that night with the same glum and profound and introverted grief he showed at the airfield the day of the Avignon mission when Yossarian climbed down the few steps of his plane naked, in a state of utter shock, with Snowden smeared abundantly all over his bare heels and toes, knees, arms and fingers, and pointed inside wordlessly toward where the young radiogunner lay freezing to death on the floor beside the still younger tail-gunner who kept falling back into a dead faint each time he opened his eyes and saw Snowden dying.

Doc Daneeka draped a blanket around Yossarian's shoulders almost tenderly after Snowden had been removed from the plane and carried into an ambulance on a stretcher. He led Yossarian toward his jeep. McWatt helped, and the three drove in silence to the squadron medical tent, where McWatt and Doc Daneeka guided Yossarian inside to a chair and washed Snowden off him with cold wet balls of absorbent cotton. Doc Daneeka gave him a pill and a shot that put him to sleep for twelve hours. When Yossarian woke up and went to see him, Doc Daneeka gave him another pill and a shot that put him to sleep for another twelve hours. When Yossarian woke up again and went to see him, Doc Daneeka made ready to give him another pill and a shot.

"How long are you going to keep giving me those pills and shots?" Yossarian asked him.

"Until you feel better."

"I feel all right now."

Doc Daneeka's fragile suntanned forehead furrowed with surprise. 'Then why don't you put some clothes on? Why are you walking around naked?"

"I don't want to wear a uniform any more."

Doc Daneeka accepted the explanation and put away his hypodermic syringe. "Are you sure you feel all right?"

"I feel fine. I'm just a little logy from all those pills and shots you've been giving me."

Yossarian went about his business with no clothes on all the rest of that day and was still naked late the next morning when Milo, after hunting everywhere else, finally found him sitting up a tree a small distance in back of the quaint little military cemetery at which Snowden was being buried. Milo was dressed in his customary business attire—olive-drab trousers, a fresh olive-drab shirt and tie, with one silver first lieutenant's bar gleaming on the collar, and a regulation dress cap with a stiff leather bill.

"I've been looking all over for you," Milo called up to Yossarian from the ground reproachfully.

"You should have looked for me in this tree," Yossarian answered. "I've been up here all morning."

"Come on down and taste this and tell me if it's good. It's very important."

Yossarin shook his head. He sat nude on the lowest limb of the tree and balanced himself with both hands grasping the bough directly above. He rufused to budge, and Milo had no choice but to stretch both arms about the trunk in a distasteful hug and start climbing. He struggled upward clumsily with loud grunts and wheezes, and his clothes were squashed and crooked by the time he pulled himself up high enough to hook a leg over the limb and pause for breath. His dress cap was askew and in danger of falling. Milo caught it just when it began slipping. Globules of perspiration glistened like transparent pearls around his mustache and swelled like opaque blisters under his eyes. Yossarin watched him impassively. Cautiously Milo worked himself around in a half circle so that he could face Yossarian. He unwrapped tissue paper from something soft, round and brown and handed it out to Yossarian.

"Please taste this and let me know what you think. I'd like to serve it to the men."

"What is it?" asked Yossarin, and took a big bite.

"Chocolate-covered cotton."

Yossarian gagged convulsively and sprayed his big mouthful of chocolate-covered cotton right out into Milo's face. "Here, take it back!" he spouted angrily. "Jesus Christ! Have you gone crazy? You didn't even take the goddam seeds out."

"Give it a chance, will you?" Milo begged. "It can't be that bad. Is it really that bad?"

"It's even worse."

"But I've got to make the mess halls feed it to the men."

"They'll never be able to swallow it."

"They've got to swallow it," Milo ordained with dictatorial grandeur, and almost broke his neck when he let go with one arm to wave a righteous finger in the air.

"Come on out here," Yossarian invited him. "You'll be much safer, and you can see everything."

Gripping the bough above with both hands, Milo began inching his way out on the limb sideways with utmost care and apprehension. His face was rigid with tension, and he sighed with relief when he found himself seated securely beside Yossarian. He stroked the tree affectionately. "This is a pretty good tree," he observed admiringly with proprietary gratitude.

"It's the tree of life," Yossarian answered, waggling his toes, "and of knowledge of good and evil, too."

Milo squinted closely at the bark and branches. "No it isn't," he replied. "It's a chestnut tree. I ought to know. I sell chestnuts."

"Have it your way."

They sat in the tree without talking for several seconds, their legs dangling and their hands almost straight up on the bough above, the one completely nude but for a pair of crepe-soled sandals, the other completely dressed in a coarse olive-drab woolen uniform with his tie knotted tight. Milo studied Yossarian diffidently through the corner of his eye, hesitating tactfully.

"I want to ask you something," he said at last. "You don't have any clothes on. I don't want to butt in or anything, but I just want to know. Why aren't you wearing your uniform?"

"I don't want to."

Milo nodded rapidly like a sparrow pecking. "I see, I see," he stated quickly with a look of vivid confusion. "I understand perfectly. I heard Appleby and Captain Black say you had gone crazy, and I just wanted to find out." He hesitated politely again, weighing his next question. "Aren't you ever going to put your uniform on again?"

"I don't think so."

Milo nodded with spurious vim to indicate he still understood and then sat silent, ruminating gravely with troubled misgiving. A scarlet-crested bird shot by below, brushing sure dark wings against a quivering bush. Yossarian and Milo were covered in their bower by tissue-thin tiers of sloping green and largely surrounded by other gray chestnut trees and a silver spruce. The sun was high overhead in a vast sapphire-blue sky beaded with low, isolated, puffy clouds of dry and immaculate white. There was no breeze, and the leaves about them hung motionless. The shade was feathery. Everything was at peace but Milo, who straightened suddenly with a muffled cry and began pointing excitedly.

"Look at that!" he exclaimed in alarm. "Look at that! That's a funeral going on down there. That looks like the cemetery. Isn't it?"

Yossarian answered him slowly in a level voice. "They're burying that kid who got killed in my plane over Avignon the other day. Snowden."

"What happened to him?" Milo asked in a voice deadened with awe.

"He got killed."

"That's terrible," Milo grieved, and his large brown eyes filled with tears. "That poor kid. It really is terrible." He bit his trembling lip hard, and his voice rose with emotion when he continued. "And it will get even worse if the mess halls don't agree to buy my cotton. Yossarian, what's the matter with them? Don't they realize it's their syndicate? Don't they know they've all got a share?"

"Did the dead man in my tent have a share?" Yossarian demanded caustically.

"Of course he did," Milo assured him lavishly. "Everybody in the squadron has a share."

"He was killed before he even got into the squadron."

Milo made a deft grimace of tribulation and turned away. "I wish you'd stop picking on me about that dead man in your tent," he pleaded peevishly. "I told you I didn't have anything to do with killing him. Is it my fault that I saw this great opportunity to corner the market on Egyptian cotton and got us into all this trouble? Was I supposed to know there was going to be a glut? I didn't even know what a glut was in those days. An opportunity to corner a market doesn't come along very often, and I was pretty shrewd to grab the chance when I had it." Milo gulped back a moan as he saw six uniformed pallbearers lift the plain pine coffin from the ambulance and set it gently down on the ground beside the yawning gash of the freshly dug grave. "And now I can't get rid of a single penny's worth," he mourned.

Yossarian was unmoved by the fustian charade of the burial ceremony, and by Milo's crushing bereavement. The chaplain's voice floated up to him through the distance tenuously in an unintelligible, almost inaudible monotone, like a gaseous murmur. Yossarian could make out Major Major by his towering and lanky aloofness and thought he recognized Major Danby mopping his brow with a handkerchief. Major Danby had not stopped shaking since his run-in with General Dreedle. There were strands of enlisted men molded in a curve around the three officers, as inflexible as lumps of wood, and four idle gravediggers in streaked fatigues lounging indifferently on spades near the shocking, incongruous heap of loose copper-red earth. As Yossarian stared, the chaplain elevated his gaze toward Yossarian beatifically, pressed his fingers down over his eyeballs in a manner of affliction, peered upward again toward Yossarian searchingly, and bowed his head, concluding what Yossarian took to be a climatic part of the funeral rite. The four men in fatigues lifted the coffin on slings and lowered it into the grave. Milo shuddered violently.

"I can't watch it," he cried, turning away in anguish. "I just can't sit here and watch while those mess halls let my syndicate die." He gnashed his teeth and shook his head with bitter woe and resentment. "If they had any loyalty, they would buy my cotton till it hurts so that they can keep right on buying my cotton till it hurts them some more. They would build fires and burn up their underwear and summer uniforms just to create a bigger demand. But they won't do a thing. Yossarian, try eating the rest of this chocolate-covered cotton for me. Maybe it will taste delicious now."

Yossarian pushed his hand away. "Give up, Milo. People can't eat cotton."

Milo's face narrowed cunningly. "It isn't really cotton," he coaxed. "I was joking. It's really cotton candy, delicious cotton candy. Try it and see."

"Now you're lying."

"I never lie!" Milo rejoindered with proud dignity.

"You're lying now."

"I only lie when it's necessary," Milo explained defensively, averting his eyes for a moment and blinking his lashes winningly. "This stuff is better than cotton candy, really it is. It's made out of real cotton. Yossarian, you've got to help me make the men eat it. Egyptian cotton is the finest cotton in the world."

"But it's indigestible," Yossarian emphasized. "It will make them sick, don't you understand? Why don't you try living on it yourself if you don't believe me?"

"I did try," admitted Milo gloomily. "And it made me sick."

The graveyard was yellow as hay and green as cooked cabbage. In a little while the chaplain stepped back, and the beige crescent of human forms began to break up sluggishly, like flotsam. The men drifted without haste or sound to the vehicles parked along the side of the bumpy dirt road. With their heads down disconsolately, the chaplain, Major Major and Major Danby moved toward their jeeps in an ostracized group, each holding himself friendlessly several feet away from the other two.

"It's all over," observed Yossarian.

"It's the end," Milo agreed despondently. "There's no hope left. And all because I left them free to make their own decisions. That should teach me a lesson about discipline the next time I try something like this."

"Why don't you sell your cotton to the government?" Yossarian suggested casually, as he watched the four men in streaked fatigues shoveling heaping bladefuls of the copper-red earth back down inside the grave.

Milo vetoed the idea brusquely. "It's a matter of principle," he explained firmly. "The government has no business in business, and I would be the last person in the world to ever try to involve the government in a business of mine. But the business of government *is* business," he remembered alertly and continued with elation. "Calvin Coolidge said that, and Calvin Coolidge was a President, so it must be true. And the government does have the responsibility of buying all the Egyptian cotton I've got that no one else wants so that I can make a profit, doesn't it?" Milo's face clouded almost as abruptly, and his spirits descended into a state of sad anxiety. "But how will I get the government to do it?"

"Bribe it," Yossarian said.

"Bribe it!" Milo was outraged and almost lost his balance and broke his neck again. "Shame on you!" he scolded severely, breathing virtuous fire down and upward into his rusty mustache through his billowing nostrils and prim lips. "Bribery is against the law, and you know it. But it's not against the law to make a profit, is it? So it can't be against the law for me to bribe someone in order to make a fair profit, can it? No, of course not!" He fell to brooding again, with a meek, almost pitiable distress. "But how will I know who to bribe?"

"Oh, don't you worry about that," Yossarian comforted him with a toneless snicker as the engines of the jeeps and ambulance fractured the drowsy silence and the vehicles in the rear began driving away backward. "You make the bribe big enough and they'll find you. Just make sure you do everything right out in the open. Let everyone know exactly what you want and how much you're willing to pay for it. The first time you act guilty or ashamed, you might get into trouble."

"I wish you'd come with me," Milo remarked. "I won't feel safe among people who take bribes. They're no better than a bunch of crooks."

"You'll be all right," Yossarian assured him with confidence. "If you run into trouble, just tell everybody that the security of the country requires a strong domestic Egyptian-cotton speculating industry."

"It does," Milo informed him solemnly. "A strong Egyptian-cotton speculating industry means a much stronger America."

"Of course it does. And if that doesn't work, point out the great number of American families that depend on it for income."

"A great many American families do depend on it for income."

"You see?" said Yossarian. "You're much better at it than I am. You almost make it sound true."

"It is true," Milo exclaimed with a strong trace of the old hauteur.

"That's what I mean. You do it with just the right amount of conviction."

"You're sure you won't come with me?"

Yossarian shook his head.

Milo was impatient to get started. He stuffed the remainder of the chocolate-covered cotton ball into his shirt pocket and edged his way back gingerly along the branch to the smooth gray trunk. He threw his arms about the trunk in a generous and awkward embrace and began shinnying down, the sides of his leather-soled shoes slipping constantly so that it seemed many times he would fall and injure himself. Halfway down, he changed his mind and climbed back up. Bits of tree bark stuck to his mustache, and his straining face was flushed with exertion.

"I wish you'd put your uniform on instead of going around naked that way," he confided pensively before he climbed back down again and hurried away. "You might start a trend, and then I'll never get rid of all this goldarned cotton."

# THE GINGER MAN

## J. P. Donleavy

**4**

There was a tugging at his leg. Slowly opening eyes to see the irate face of Marion looming over him on this Monday morn of chaos.

"Good God, what's happened to the house? Why weren't you at the station to meet me? Look at you. Gin. This is horrid. I had to take a taxi out here, do you hear me? A taxi, fifteen shillings."

"Now, now, for Christ's sake have some patience and let me explain everything."

"I say, explain? Explain what? There's nothing to explain, it's all quite evident."

Marion holding aloft the gin.

"All right, I'm not blind, I see it."

"O dear, this is frightful. Why you honestly are a cad. If Mommy and Daddy could only see what I've got to come back to. What are you doing on the table?"

"Shut up."

"I won't shut up and don't look at me like that. What are these feathers doing all over the place? Dishes broken on the floor. What were you doing?"

"Goat dance."

"How frightfully sordid it all is. Disgusting. Feathers in everything. You damn, damn drinker. Where did you get the money? Didn't meet me at the train. Why? Answer me."

"Shut up. Be quiet for the love of Jesus. The alarm didn't work."

"You're a liar. You were drinking, drinking, drinking. Look at the grease, the mess, the filth. And what's this?"

"A sea bird."

"Who paid for all this? You had smelly O'Keefe out here. I know you did, I can smell him."

"Just leave me alone."

"Did you pay the milk?"

"Yes, now sweet Jesus shut up, my head."

"So you paid it, did you? Here it is. Here it is. Exactly where I left it and the money gone. Lies. You blighter. You nasty blighter."

"Call me a bugger, I can't stand the gentility on top of the yelling."

"O stop it, stop it. I don't intend to go on living like this, do you hear me? Your brazen lies, one after the other and I was trying to get Father to do something for us and I come back to this."

"Your father. Your father is a sack of excrement, genteel excrement, as tight as they come. What has he been doing, playing battleship in the tub?"

Marion lunged, her slap landing across his jaw. The child began to scream in the nursery. Sebastian up off the table. He drove his first into Marion's face. She fell backward against the cupboard. Dishes crashing to the floor. In tattered underwear he stood at the nursery door. He kicked his foot through and tore off the lock to open it. Took the child's pillow from under its head and pressed it hard on the screaming mouth.

"I'll kill it, God damn it, I'll kill it, if it doesn't shut up."

Marion behind him, digging her nails into his back.

"You madman, leave the child alone, I'll get the police. I'll divorce you, you blackguard, coward, coward, coward."

Marion clasping the child to her breast. Sobbing, she lay her long English body and child across the bed. The room echoing the hesitations of her wailing voice. Sebastian walked white faced from the room, slamming the broken door, cutting off the sound of suffering from a guilty heart.

Dangerfield took a late morning bus to Dublin. Sat up the top side in front, clicking the teeth. Out there the mud flats and that windy golf course. North Bull Island shimmering in the sun. Cost money to leave Marion. Vulgar blood in her somewhere, may be from the mother. Mother's father kept a shop. Bad blood leaks out. I know it leaks out. And I ought to get out. One way on the boat. She doesn't have the nerve for divorce. I know her too well for that. Never gave me a lousy chance to explain the account. Let her rot out there. I don't care. Got to face the facts of this life. The facts, the facts. Could square things with her. She's good with the cheese dishes. Few days without food will weaken her. Maybe I'll come back with a tin of peaches and cream. She's always airing the house. Opening up the windows at every little fart. Tells me she never farts. At least mine come out with a bang.

Fairview Park looks like a wet moldy blanket. Feel a little better. O'Keefe broke a toilet bowl in that house. Fell into it when he was trying to sneak a look behind a woman's medicine chest. Long suffering O'Keefe, bent over tomes in the National Library studying Irish and dreaming of seduction.

Amiens Street Station, Dangerfield stepping down from the bus, crossing and using the ostrich step up the Talbot Street. My God, I think I see prostitutes with squinting eyes and toothless mouths. Don't relish a trip up an alley with one without wearing impenetrable armour and there is no armour at all in Dublin. I asked one how much it was and she said I had an evil mind. Invited her for a drink and she said the American sailors were rough and beat her up in the backs of taxicabs and told her to take a bath. She said she liked chewing gum. And when she had a few drinks she got frightfully crude. I was shocked. Asked me how big it was. I almost slapped her face. With it. Provocation I calls it. And told her to confess. Dublin has more than a hundred churches. I bought a map and counted them. Must be a nice thing to have faith. But I think a pot of Gold Label run from the barrel in the house of the aspidistras. Settle the nerves. No time to be nervous now. With youth on my side. I'm still a young man in the late twenties, although the Lord knows I've been through some trying times. A lot of people tell you, caution you. Now young man, don't get married without money, without a good job, without a degree. E. E. E. They are right.

Into the pub with stuffed foxes behind the potted plants. And the snug stained brown. Reach over and press this buzzer for action.

A young man's raw face flicked around the door.

"Good morning, Mr. Dangerfield."

"A fine spring morning, a double and some Woodbines."

"Certainy, sir. Early today?"

"Little business to attend to."

"It's always business isn't it."

"O aye."

Some fine clichés there. Should be encouraged. Too many damn people trying to be different. Coining phrases when a good platitude would do and save anxiety. If Marion wants to make the barbarous accusation that I took the milk money, it's just as well I took it.

A tray comes in the discreet door.

"On your bill, Mr. Dangerfield?"

"If you will, please."

"Grand to be having some decent weather and I think you're looking very well."

"Thank you. Yes, feel fine."

I think moments like sitting here should be preserved. I'd like friends to visit me at my house and maybe have a cocktail cabinet, but nothing vulgar. And Marion could make nice little bits. Olives. And kids playing on the lawn. Wouldn't mind a room a bit on the lines of this. Fox on the mantelpiece and funereal fittings. Outside, the world, I think is driven. And I'm right out in front. To keep friends, photographs and letters. Me too. And women stealing alimony for young lovers. Wrinkled buttocks astride rose wood chairs, weeping signing each check. Become a lover of women over fifty. They're the ones that's looking for it. Good for O'Keefe. But he might balk. A knowledgeable man but a botcher. And now get that check. I want to see dollars. Thousands of them. Want them all over me to pave the streets of me choosey little soul.

"Bye, bye."

"Bye now, Mr. Dangerfield. Good luck."

Across the Butt Bridge. Covered with torn newspapers and hulking toothless old men watching out the last years. They're bored. I know you've been in apprenticeships and that there was a moment when you were briefly respected for an opinion. Be in the sight of God soon. He'll be shocked. But there's happiness up there, gentlemen. All white and gold. Acetylene lighted sky. And when you go, go third class. You damn bastards.

And walking along Merrion Square. Rich up this way. Wriggle the fingers a bit. American flag hanging out there. That's my flag. Means money, cars and cigars. And I won't hear a word said against it.

Spinning up the steps. Big black door. With aplomb, approaching the receptionist's desk. Unfallow Irishwomen of middle age and misery. Belaboring poor micks headed for that land across the seas. Giving them the first taste of being pushed around. And ingratiating to the middle western college boy who bounces by.

"Could you tell me if the checks have arrived?"

"You're Mr. Dangerfield, aren't you?"

"I am."

"Yes the checks have arrived. I think yours is here somewhere. However, isn't there some arrangement with your wife? I don't think I can give it to you without her consent."

Dangerfield warming to irritated erection.

"I say, if you don't mind I will take that check immediately."

"I'm sorry, Mr. Dangerfield but I have had instructions not to give it to you without the permission of your wife."

"I say, I will take that check immediately."

Dangerfield's mouth a guillotine. This woman a little upset. Insolent bitch.

"I'm very sorry but I will have to ask Mr. Morgue."

"You will ask no one."

"I'm terribly sorry, but I will have to ask Mr. Morgue."

"What?"

"You must remember that I am in charge of handling these checks."

Dangerfield's fist swished through the air, landing with a bang on the desk. Receptionist jumped. And her jaw came down with a touch of obedience.

"You'll ask no one and unless that check is given me this instant I'll have you charged with theft. Do you understand me? Am I clear? I will not have an Irish serf interfering in my affairs. This irregularity will be reported to the proper authorities. I will take that check and no more nonsense."

Receptionist with mouth open. Trickle of spittle twisted on her jaw. An instant's hesitation and fear forced a nervous hand to deliver the white envelope. Dangerfield burning her with red eyes. A door opening in the hall. Several bog men, watching from the staircase, slipped hurriedly back to seats, caps over folded hands. A final announcement from Dangerfield.

"Now, God damn it, when I come in here again I want that check handed to me instantly."

From the door, a middle western accent.

"Say buddy, what's going on here?"

"Twiddle twat."

"What?"

Dangerfield suddenly convulsed with laughter. Spinning on his heel, he pushed open this Georgian door and hopped down the steps. The rich green of the park across the street. And through the tops of the trees, red brick buildings on the other side. Look at these great slabs of granite to walk on. How very nice and solid. Celtic lout. I'm all for Christianity but insolence must be put down. With violence if necessary. People in their place, neater that way. Eke. Visit my broker later and buy a French Horn and play it up the Balscaddoon road. About four a.m. And I think I'll step into this fine house here with ye oldish windows.

This public house is dark and comforting with a feeling of scholarship. With the back gate of Trinity College just outside. Makes me feel I'm close to learning and to you students who don't take the odd malt. Maybe I put too much faith in atmosphere.

Put the money away safely. A bright world ahead. Of old streets and houses, screams of the newly born and grinning happy faces escorting the lately dead. American cars speeding down Nassau Street and tweedy bodies of ex-Indian Army officers stuttering into the well-mannered gloom of the Kildare Street Club for a morning whiskey. The whole world's here. Women from Foxrock with less thick ankles and trim buttocks shod closely and cleanly with the badge of prosperity, strutting because they owned the world and on their way to coffee and an exhibition of paintings. I can't get enough. More. See Marion like that. Going to make money. Me. A sun out. With Jesus for birth control. This great iron fence around Trinity serves a good purpose. World in resurrection. Yellow banners in the sky, all for me, Sebastian Bullion Dangerfield.

> And dear God
> Give me strength
> To put my shoulder
> To the wheel
> And push
> Like the rest. . . .

## 6

O summer and soft wind. Relieves the heart and makes living cheaper. Get that fire out in the grate. Get it out. That's better.

There's the butcher a few houses up the street. A tram line goes by the window. And across the road is the most fantastic laundry with forty girls and great steaming vats. O I think they are a bunch for using just the little touch of acid.

Mr. and Mrs. Sebastian Dangerfield and their daughter, Felicity Wilton, late of Howth, are now residing at 1 Mohammed Road, The Rock, Co. Dublin.

It was decided to get out of the haunted house of Howth. But there were hesitations till the morning after the storm when Marion opened the kitchen door to get the milk and she screamed and Sebastian came running and they looked down into a mud stained sea into which had fallen the back garden and turf shed. They moved.

The new house was not new. And you didn't want to walk too fast in the front door or you'd find yourself going out the back. Mr. Egbert Skully took Mr. Dangerfield aside and said he was glad he could rent to an American because he and his wife had worked for twenty years in Macy's Department Store and loved New York and was pleased he could find tenants like themselves. And I hope you, your wife and little one will be happy here. I know it's a little small but I think you'll like the cozy quality, ha, you look like a gentleman, Mr. Dangerfield as likes his cozy comforts, and do you play golf? O aye. But my clubs are indisposed. Having them looked over by a professional for flaws, particular about alignment, you know. A very good idea, Mr. Dangerfield and perhaps my wife can give yours some recipes. Great.

Walls newly papered with brown flowers even feel soggy to the touch. And a nice brown, fourth-hand Axminster rug on the sitting room floor and a scabrous, blue settee. The kitchen was fine but the tap and sink were out the door. Up steep narrow stairs, a closet with plate sized skylight, the conservatory. And a toilet bowl wedged between two walls, the lavatory. Tory was a great suffix in this house. And the sitting room window two feet off the sidewalk was perfect for the neighbors passing by, so don't want to get caught with the pants down. But the tram rumbling by keeps one on one's guard.

A visit to the fuel merchant for coal to keep piled under the stairs. Marion got crates and covered them with table cloths for color and respectability. And my special maps one or two of which are rare and old. The one I have of a cemetery I keep under thick glass. And got the card table for a desk under the window. The laundry girls will take me mind off the awful grind of studying. They come out twice a day, hair in curlers and breasts like needles in these American uplift bras. Think the Bishop had something to say about that and rightly too. Then watch them line up for the tram, a row of steamed white faces. And some of them giving a giggle in this direction at the madman behind the curtain.

Facing the summer ahead. Living in this little house was calm. No drinking and minding the baba when Marion was off to shop. Had a cup of beef tea in the morning. Also see a rather pleasant creature up there in the window. Catch her looking in here with rather large brown eyes, no smiles or giggles. A little disdain, her dark hair straight and thick. And I think I see intelligence, a little embarrassing that look. Retreat into the kitchen. Most exciting.

Made a little case and filled it with books of law, a short life of Blessed Oliver Plunket and others on birds. Bottom shelf for business magazines for the big days ahead. And then a section for my extensive collection, which, God forgive me, I stole from Catholic Churches. But I did it because I needed strength in paupery. My favorites are, "This Thing Called Love," "Drink Is A Curse," and "Happiness In Death."

The first morning tram almost shakes one to the floor and Felicity gives the twisted cry from the conservatory. Growl back to sleep. Pull the legs up in the foetal crouch. Marion wearing my underwear. Sometimes the sun would sneak in. Then Marion beating barefoot on the linoleum. Entreaties. O do get up. Don't leave me to do everything every morning. In my heart where no one else can hear me I was saying, now for God's sake, Marion, be a good Britisher and get down there in that little nest of a kitchen and buzz on the coffee like a good girl and would you, while you're at it, kind of brown up a few pieces of bread and I wouldn't mind if maybe there was just the suggestion of bacon on it, only a suggestion, and have it all ready on the table and then I'll come down and act the good husband with, ah darling good morning, how are you, you're looking lovely this morning darling and younger every morning. A great one that last. But I come down martyred and mussed, feeble and fussed, heart and soul covered in cement.

But later in the morning great things were to be seen. Sound of horses on the cobble stones. Then up to the bedroom to look down in the street. These sleek black animals glistening in soft rain. Heads high, driving slits of steam in the morning air. Sometimes I see through the little glass windows, a lily on a pine box. Take me with you too. And I can't help murmuring from memory poems I read in the *Evening Mail:*

> Sleep thy last sleep,
> Free from care and sorrow.
> Rest where none weep,
> And we too, shall follow.

And I see the grinning faces popping out the windows of the cab, radiant with the importance of the dead. Hats being tipped along the road and hands moving in a quick sign of the cross. Whiskey passed from hand to hand. Green, greedy mouth is dead. A fiddle across the fields. Mushrooms fatten in the warm September rain. Gone away.

Then time to go for the paper. And back with it to the lavatory. Between the green peeling walls. Always feel I'm going to get stuck. One morning there was sunshine and I was feeling great. Sitting in there grunting and groaning, looking over the news, and then reach up and pull the chain. Downstairs in the kitchen, Marion screamed.

"I say, Marion, what is it?"

"For God's sake, stop it, stop it, Sebastian, you fool. What have you done?"

Moving with swift irritability down the narrow stairs, stumbling into the kitchen at the bottom. Perhaps things have gotten too much for Marion and she's gone mad.

"You idiot, Sebastian, look at me, look at the baby's things."

Marion trembling in the middle of the kitchen floor covered with strands of wet toilet paper and fecal matter. From a gaping patch in the ceiling poured water, plaster and excrement.

"God's miserable teeth."

"Oh damnable, damnable. Do something, you fool."

"For the love of Jesus."

Sebastian stalking away.

"How dare you walk away, you damnable rotter. This is horrible and I can't bear any more."

Marion broke into sobs, slammed into silence with the front door.

Walking past the parking lot, down the little hill to the station. Stand by this wall here and watch the trains go by. Just take a crap and look what happens. This damn Skully probably put in rubber pipes. Three pounds a week for a rat hole, with brown swamp grass on the walls and cardboard furniture. And Marion has to be standing right under it. Couldn't she hear it coming? And the sun's gone in and it looks like rain. Better get back to the house or it'll weaken my position. Get her a little present, a fashion magazine filled with richery.

Marion sitting in the easy chair sewing. Pausing at the door, testing the silence.

"I'm sorry, Marion."

Marion head bent. Sebastian tendering his gift.

"I really am sorry. Look at me, I've got a present for you. It's hot tamale with ink dressing, see."

"O."

"Nice?"

"Yes."

"Like the gold teeth of God?"

"Don't spoil it now."

"My little Marion. I'm such a bastard. I tell you the whole thing up there is just a bunch of roots."

"I'll have something to read in bed."

"I'm an incredible pig, Marion."

"Aren't these suits nice."

"Don't you hear me, Marion? I'm a pig."

"Yes, but I wish we were rich and had money. I want to travel. If we could only travel."

"Let me kiss you, Marion, at least."

Marion arose, embracing him with blond arms, driving her long groin against his and her tongue deep into his mouth.

# THE HIPPOPOTAMUS

## T. S. Eliot

*Similiter et omnes revereantur Diaconos, ut mandatum Jesu Christi;*
*et Episcopum, ut Jesum Christum, existentem filium Patris; Presbyteros*
*autem, ut concilium Dei et conjunctionem Apostolorum. Sine his Ecclesia*
*non vocatur; de quibus suadeo vos sic habeo.*

S. IGNATII AD TRALLIANOS.

*And when this epistle is read among you, cause that it be read also in*
*the church of the Laodiceans.*

The broad-backed hippopotamus
Rests on his belly in the mud;
Although he seems so firm to us
He is merely flesh and blood.

Flesh and blood is weak and frail,
Susceptible to nervous shock;
While the True Church can never fail
For it is based upon a rock.

The hippo's feeble steps may err
In compassing material ends,
While the True Church need never stir
To gather in its dividends.

The 'potamus can never reach
The mango on the mango-tree;
But fruits of pomegranate and peach
Refresh the Church from over sea.

At mating time the hippo's voice
Betrays inflexions hoarse and odd,
But every week we hear rejoice
The Church, at being one with God.

The hippopotamus's day
Is passed in sleep; at night he hunts;
God works in a mysterious way—
The Church can sleep and feed at once.

I saw the 'potamus take wing
Ascending from the damp savannas,
And quiring angels round him sing
The praise of God, in loud hosannas.

Blood of the Lamb shall wash him clean
And him shall heavenly arms enfold,
Among the saints he shall be seen
Performing on a harp of gold.

He shall be washed as white as snow,
By all the martyr'd virgins kist,
While the True Church remains below
Wrapt in the old miasmal mist.

# LETTERS FROM THE EARTH

## Mark Twain

The Creator sat upon the throne, thinking. Behind him stretched the illimitable continent of heaven, steeped in a glory of light and color; before him rose the black night of Space, like a wall. His mighty bulk towered rugged and mountain-like into the zenith, and His divine head blazed there like a distant sun. At His feet stood three colossal figures, diminished to extinction, almost, by contrast—archangels—their heads level with His ankle-bone.

When the Creator had finished thinking, He said, "I have thought. Behold!"

He lifted His hand, and from it burst a fountain-spray of fire, a million stupendous suns, which clove the blackness and soared, away and away and away, diminishing in magnitude and intensity as they pierced the far frontiers of Space, until at last they were but as diamond nailheads sparkling under the domed vast roof of the universe.

At the end of an hour the Grand Council was dismissed.

They left the Presence impressed and thoughtful, and retired to a private place, where they might talk with freedom. None of the three seemed to want to begin, though all wanted somebody to do it. Each was burning to discuss the great event, but would prefer not to commit himself till he should know how the others regarded it. So there was some aimless and halting conversation about matters of no consequence, and this dragged tediously along, arriving nowhere, until at last the archangel Satan gathered his courage together—of which he had a very good supply—and broke ground. He said: "We know what we are here to talk about, my lords,

From pp. 3–20 in *Letters from The Earth* (hardbound ed.) by Mark Twain, edited by Bernard DeVoto. Copyright © 1962 by The Mark Twain Company. Reprinted by permission of Harper & Row, Publishers, Inc.

and we may as well put pretense aside, and begin. If this is the opinion of the Council——"

"It is, it is!" said Gabriel and Michael, gratefully interrupting.

"Very well, then, let us proceed. We have witnessed a wonderful thing; as to that, we are necessarily agreed. As to the value of it—if it has any—that is a matter which does not personally concern us. We can have as many opinions about it as we like, and that is our limit. We have no vote. I think Space was well enough, just as it was, and useful, too. Cold and dark—a restful place, now and then, after a season of the overdelicate climate and trying splendors of heaven. But these are details of no considerable moment; the new feature, the immense feature, is——what, gentlemen?"

"The invention and introduction of automatic, unsupervised, self-regulating law for the government of those myriads of whirling and racing suns and worlds!"

"That is it!" said Satan. "You perceive that it is a stupendous idea. Nothing approaching it has been evolved from the Master Intellect before. Law—*Automatic* Law—exact and unvarying Law—requiring no watching, no correcting, no readjusting while the eternities endure! He said those countless vast bodies would plunge through the wastes of Space ages and ages, at unimaginable speed, around stupendous orbits, yet never collide, and never lengthen nor shorten their orbital periods by so much as the hundredth part of a second in two thousand years! That is the new miracle, and the greatest of all—*Automatic Law!* And He gave it a name—the LAW OF NATURE—and said Natural Law is the LAW OF GOD—interchangeable names for one and the same thing."

"Yes," said Michael, "and He said He would establish Natural Law—the Law of God—throughout His dominions, and its authority should be supreme and inviolable."

"Also," said Gabriel, "He said He would by and by create animals, and place them, likewise, under the authority of that Law."

"Yes," said Satan, "I heard Him, but did not understand. What is animals, Gabriel?"

"Ah, how should I know? How should any of us know? It is a new word."

[*Interval of three centuries, celestial time—the equivalent of a hundred million years, earthly time. Enter a Messenger-Angel.*]

"My lords, He is making animals. Will it please you to come and see?"

They went, they saw, and were perplexed. Deeply perplexed—and the Creator noticed it, and said, "Ask. I will answer."

"Divine One," said Satan, making obeisance, "what are they for?"

"They are an experiment in Morals and Conduct. Observe them, and be instructed."

There were thousands of them. They were full of activities. Busy, all busy—mainly in persecuting each other. Satan remarked—after examining one of them through a powerful microscope: "This large beast is killing weaker animals, Divine One."

"The tiger—yes. The law of his nature is ferocity. The law of his nature is the Law of God. He cannot disobey it."

"Then in obeying it he commits no offense, Divine One?"

"No, he is blameless."

"This other creature, here, is timid, Divine One, and suffers death without resisting."

"The rabbit—yes. He is without courage. It is the law of his nature—the Law of God. He must obey it."

"Then he cannot honorably be required to go counter to his nature and resist, Divine One?"

"No. No creature can be honorably required to go counter to the law of his nature—the Law of God."

After a long time and many questions, Satan said, "The spider kills the fly, and eats it; the bird kills the spider and eats it; the wildcat kills the goose; the—well, they all kill each other. It is murder all along the line. Here are countless multitudes of creatures, and they all kill, kill, kill, they are all murderers. And they are not to blame, Divine One?"

"They are not to blame. It is the law of their nature. And always the law of nature is the Law of God. Now—observe—behold! A new creature—and the masterpiece—*Man!*"

Men, women, children, they came swarming in flocks, in droves, in millions.

"What shall you do with them, Divine One?"

"Put into each individual, in differing shades and degrees, all the various Moral Qualities, in mass, that have been distributed, a single distinguishng characteristic at a time, among the nonspeaking animal world—courage, cowardice, ferocity, gentleness, fairness, justice, cunning, treachery, magnanimity, cruelty, malice, malignity, lust, mercy, pity, purity, selfishness, sweetness, honor, love, hate, baseness, nobility, loyalty, falsity, veracity, untruthfulness—each human being shall have all of these in him, and they will constitute his nature. In some, there will be high and fine characteristics which will submerge the evil ones, and those will be called good men; in others the evil characteristics will have dominion, and those will be called bad men. Observe—behold—they vanish!"

"Whither are they gone. Divine One?"

"To the earth—they and all their fellow animals."

"What is the earth?"

"A small globe I made, a time, two times and a half ago. You saw it, but did not notice it in the explosion of worlds and suns that sprayed from my hand. Man is an experiment, the other animals are another experiment.

Time will show whether they were worth the trouble. The exhibition is over; you may take your leave, my lords."

Several days passed by.

This stands for a long stretch of (our) time, since in heaven a day is as a thousand years.

Satan had been making admiring remarks about certain of the Creator's sparkling industries—remarks which, being read between the lines, were sarcasms. He had made them confidentially to his safe friends the other archangels, but they had been overheard by some ordinary angels and reported at Headquarters.

He was ordered into banishment for a day—the celestial day. It was a punishment he was used to, on account of his too flexible tongue. Formerly he had been deported into Space, there being nowhither else to send him, and had flapped tediously around there in the eternal night and the Arctic chill; but now it occurred to him to push on and hunt up the earth and see how the Human-Race experiment was coming along.

By and by he wrote home—very privately—to St. Michael and St. Gabriel about it.

## SATAN'S LETTER

This is a strange place, an extraordinary place, and interesting. There is nothing resembling it at home. The people are all insane, the other animals are all insane, the earth is insane, Nature itself is insane. Man is a marvelous curiosity. When he is at his very very best he is a sort of low grade nickel-plated angel; at his worst he is unspeakable, unimaginable; and first and last and all the time he is a sarcasm. Yet he blandly and in all sincerity calls himself the "noblest work of God." This is the truth I am telling you. And this is not a new idea with him, he has talked it through all the ages, and believed it. Believed it, and found nobody among all his race to laugh at it.

Moreover—if I may put another strain upon you—he thinks he is the Creator's pet. He believes the Creator is proud of him; he even believes the Creator loves him; has a passion for him; sits up nights to admire him; yes, and watch over him and keep him out of trouble. He prays to Him, and thinks He listens. Isn't it a quaint idea? Fills his prayers with crude and bald and florid flatteries of Him, and thinks He sits and purrs over these extravagancies and enjoys them. He prays for help, and favor, and protection, every day; and does it with hopefulness and confidence, too, although no prayer of his has ever been answered. The daily affront, the daily defeat, do not discourage him, he goes on praying just the same. There is something almost fine about this perseverance. I must put one more strain upon you: he thinks he is going to heaven!

He has salaried teachers who tell him that. They also tell him there is a hell, of everlasting fire, and that he will go to it if he doesn't keep the Commandments. What are the Commandments? They are a curiosity. I will tell you about them by and by.

## LETTER II

"I have told you nothing about man that is not true." You must pardon me if I repeat that remark now and then in these letters; I want you to take seriously the things I am telling you, and I feel that if I were in your place and you in mine, I should need that reminder from time to time, to keep my credulity from flagging.

For there is nothing about man that is not strange to an immortal. He looks at nothing as we look at it, his sense of proportion is quite different from ours, and his sense of values is so widely divergent from ours, that with all our large intellectual powers it is not likely that even the most gifted among us would ever be quite able to understand it.

For instance, take this sample: he has imagined a heaven, and has left entirely out of it the supremest of all his delights, the one ecstasy that stands first and foremost in the heart of every individual of his race—and of ours—sexual intercourse!

It is as if a lost and perishing person in a roasting desert should be told by a rescuer he might choose and have all longed-for things but one, and he should elect to leave out water!

His heaven is like himself: strange, interesting, astonishing, grotesque. I give you my word, it has not a single feature in it that he *actually values*. It consists—utterly and entirely—of diversions which he cares next to nothing about, here in the earth, yet is quite sure he will like in heaven. Isn't it curious? Isn't it interesting? You must not think I am exaggerating, for it is not so. I will give you details.

Most men do not sing, most men cannot sing, most men will not stay where others are singing if it be continued more than two hours. Note that.

Only about two men in a hundred can play upon a musical instrument, and not four in a hundred have any wish to learn how. Set that down.

Many men pray, not many of them like to do it. A few pray long, the others make a short cut.

More men go to church than want to.

To forty-nine men in fifty the Sabbath Day is a dreary, dreary bore.

Of all the men in a church on a Sunday, two-thirds are tired when the service is half over, and the rest before it is finished.

The gladdest moment for all of them is when the preacher uplifts his hands for the benediction. You can hear the soft rustle of relief that sweeps the house, and you recognize that it is eloquent with gratitude.

All nations look down upon all other nations.

All nations dislike all other nations.

All white nations despise all colored nations, of whatever hue, and oppress them when they can.

White men will not associate with "niggers," nor marry them.

They will not allow them in their schools and churches.

All the world hates the Jew and will not endure him except when he is rich.

I ask you to note all those particulars.

Further. All sane people detest noise.

All people, sane or insane, like to have variety in their life. Monotony quickly wearies them.

Every man, according to the mental equipment that has fallen to his share, exercises his intellect constantly, ceaselessly, and this exercise makes up a vast and valued and essential part of his life. The lowest intellect, like the highest, possesses a skill of some kind and takes a keen pleasure in testing it, proving it, perfecting it. The urchin who is his comrade's superior in games is as diligent and as enthusiastic in his practice as are the sculptor, the painter, the pianist, the mathematician and the rest. Not one of them could be happy if his talent were put under an interdict.

Now then, you have the facts. You know what the human race enjoys, and what it doesn't enjoy. It has invented a heaven, out of its own head, all by itself: guess what it is like! In fifteen hundred eternities you couldn't do it. The ablest mind known to you or me in fifty million aeons couldn't do it. Very well, I will tell you about it.

1. First of all, I recall to your attention the extraordinary fact with which I began. To wit, that the human being, like the immortals, naturally places sexual intercourse far and away above all other joys—yet he has left it out of his heaven! The very thought of it excites him; opportunity sets him wild; in this state he will risk life, reputation, everything—even his queer heaven itself—to make good that opportunity and ride it to the overwhelming climax. From youth to middle age all men and all women prize copulation above all other pleasures combined, yet it is actually as I have said: it is not in their heaven; prayer takes its place.

They prize it thus highly; yet, like all their so-called "boons," it is a poor thing. At its very best and longest the act is brief beyond imagination—the imagination of an immortal, I mean. In the matter of repetition the man is limited—oh, quite beyond immortal conception. We who continue the act and its supremest ecstasies unbroken and without withdrawal for centuries, will never be able to understand or adequately pity the awful poverty of these people in that rich gift which, possessed as we possess it, makes all other possessions trivial and not worth the trouble of invoicing.

2. In man's heaven *everybody sings!* The man who did not sing on earth sings there; the man who could not sing on earth is able to do it there. This universal singing is not casual, not occasional, not relieved by intervals of quiet; it goes on, all day long, and every day, during a stretch of twelve hours. And *everybody stays;* whereas in the earth the place would be empty in two hours. The singing is of hymns alone. Nay, it is of *one* hymn alone. The words are always the same, in number they are only about a dozen, there is no rhyme, there is no poetry: "Hosannah, hosannah, hosannah, Lord God of Sabaoth, 'rah! 'rah! 'rah! siss!—boom! . . . a-a-ah!"

3. Meantime, every person is playing on a harp—those millions and millions!—whereas not more than twenty in the thousand of them could play an instrument in the earth, or ever wanted to.

Consider the deafening hurricane of sound—millions and millions of voices screaming at once and millions and millions of harps gritting their teeth at the same time! I ask you: is it hideous, is it odious, is it horrible?

Consider further: it is a praise service; a service of compliment, of flattery, of adulation! Do you ask who it is that is willing to endure this strange compliment, this insane compliment; and who not only endures it, but likes it, enjoys it, requires it, *commands* it? Hold your breath!

It is God! This race's God, I mean. He sits on his throne, attended by his four and twenty elders and some other dignitaries pertaining to his court, and looks out over his miles and miles of tempestuous worshipers, and smiles, and purrs, and nods his satisfaction northward, eastward, southward; as quaint and naïve a spectacle as has yet been imagined in this universe, I take it.

It is easy to see that the inventor of the heavens did not originate the idea, but copied it from the show-ceremonies of some sorry little sovereign State up in the back settlements of the Orient somewhere.

All sane white people hate noise; yet they have tranquilly accepted this kind of a heaven—without thinking, without reflection, without examination —and they actually want to go to it! Profoundly devout old gray-headed men put in a large part of their time dreaming of the happy day when they will lay down the cares of this life and enter into the joys of that place. Yet you can see how unreal it is to them, and how little it takes a grip upon them as being fact, for they make no practical preparation for the great change: you never see one of them with a harp, you never hear one of them sing.

As you have seen, that singular show is a service of praise: praise by hymn, praise by prostration. It takes the place of "church." Now then, in the earth these people cannot stand much church—an hour and a quarter is the limit, and they draw the line at once a week. That is to say, Sunday. One day in seven; and even then they do not look forward to it with longing. And so—consider what their heaven provides for them: "church" that lasts forever, and a Sabbath that has no end! They quickly weary of this brief hebdomadal Sabbath here, yet they long for that eternal one; they dream of it, they talk about it, they *think* they think they are going to enjoy it—with all their simple hearts they think they think they are going to be happy in it!

It is because they do not think at all; they only think they think. Whereas they can't think; not two human beings in ten thousand have anything to think with. And as to imagination—oh, well, look at their heaven! They accept it, they approve it, they admire it. That gives you their intellectual measure.

4. The inventor of their heaven empties into it all the nations of the earth, in one common jumble. All are on an equality absolute, no one of them ranking another; they have to be "brothers"; they have to mix together, pray together, harp together, hosannah together—whites, niggers, Jews, everybody—there's no distinction. Here in the earth all nations hate each other, and every one of them hates the Jew. Yet every pious person adores that heaven and wants to get into it. He really does. And when he is in a holy rapture he thinks he thinks that if he were only there he would take all the populace to his heart, and hug, and hug, and hug!

He is a marvel—man is! I would I knew who invented him.

5. Every man in the earth possesses some share of intellect, large or small; and be it large or be it small he takes pride in it. Also his heart swells at mention of the names of the majestic intellectual chiefs of his race, and he loves the tale of their splendid achievements. For he is of their blood, and in honoring themselves they have honored him. Lo, what the mind of man can do! he cries; and calls the roll of the illustrious of all the ages; and points to the imperishable literatures they have given to the world, and the mechanical wonders they have invented, and the glories wherewith they have clothed science and the arts; and to them he uncovers, as to kings, and gives to them the profoundest homage, and the sincerest, his exultant heart can furnish—thus exalting intellect above all things else in his world, and enthroning it there under the arching skies in a supremacy unapproachable. And then he contrives a heaven that hasn't a rag of intellectuality in it anywhere!

Is it odd, is it curious, is it puzzling? It is exactly as I have said, incredible as it may sound. This sincere adorer of intellect and prodigal rewarder of its mighty services here in the earth has invented a religion and a heaven which pay no compliments to intellect, offer it no distinctions, fling to it no largess: in fact, never even mention it.

By this time you will have noticed that the human being's heaven has been thought out and constructed upon an absolutely definite plan; and that this plan is, that it shall contain, in labored detail, each and every imaginable thing that is repulsive to a man, and not a single thing he likes!

Very well, the further we proceed the more will this curious fact be apparent.

Make a note of it: in man's heaven there are no exercises for the intellect, nothing for it to live upon. It would rot there in a year—rot and stink. Rot and stink—and at that stage become holy. A blessed thing: for only the holy can stand the joys of that bedlam.

## LETTER III

You have noticed that the human being is a curiosity. In times past he has had (and worn out and flung away) hundreds and hundreds of religions; today he has hundreds and hundreds of religions, and launches not fewer than three new ones every year. I could enlarge that number and still be within the facts.

One of his principal religions is called the Christian. A sketch of it will interest you. It is set forth in detail in a book containing two million words, called the Old and New Testaments. Also it has another name—The Word of God. For the Christian thinks every word of it was dictated by God—the one I have been speaking of.

It is full of interest. It has noble poetry in it; and some clever fables; and some blood-drenched history; and some good morals; and a wealth of obscenity; and upwards of a thousand lies.

This Bible is built mainly out of the fragments of older Bibles that had their day and crumbled to ruin. So it noticeably lacks in originality, necessarily. Its three or four most imposing and impressive events all happened in earlier Bibles; all its best precepts and rules of conduct came also from those Bibles; there are only two new things in it: hell, for one, and that singular heaven I have told you about.

What shall we do? If we believe, with these people, that their God invented these cruel things, we slander him; if we believe that these people invented them themselves, we slander them. It is an unpleasant dilemma in either case, for neither of these parties has done *us* any harm.

For the sake of tranquillity, let us take a side. Let us join forces with the people and put the whole ungracious burden upon *him*—heaven, hell, Bible and all. It does not seem right, it does not seem fair; and yet when you consider that heaven, and how crushingly charged it is with everything that is repulsive to a human being, how can we believe a human being invented it? And when I come to tell you about hell, the strain will be greater still, and you will be likely to say, No, a man would not provide that place, for either himself or anybody else; he simply couldn't.

That innocent Bible tells about the Creation. Of what—the universe? Yes, the universe. In six days!

God did it. He did not call it the universe—that name is modern. His whole attention was upon this world. He constructed it in five days—and then? It took him only one day to make twenty million suns and eighty million planets!

What were they for—according to his idea? To furnish light for this little toy-world. That was his whole purpose; he had no other. One of the twenty million suns (the smallest one) was to light it in the daytime, the rest were to help one of the universe's countless moons modify the darkness of its nights.

It is quite manifest that he believed his fresh-made skies were diamond-sown with those myriads of twinkling stars the moment his first-day's sun sank below the horizon; whereas, in fact, not a single star winked in that black vault until three years and a half after that memorable week's formidable industries had been completed.[1] Then one star appeared, all solitary and alone, and began to blink. Three years later another one appeared. The two blinked together for more than four years before a third joined them. At the end of the first hundred years there were not yet twenty-five stars twinkling in the wide wastes of those gloomy skies. At the end of a thousand years not enough stars were yet visible to make a show. At the end of a million years only half of the present array had sent their light over the telescopic frontiers, and it took another million for the rest to follow suit, as the vulgar phrase goes. There being at that time no telescope, their advent was not observed.

For three hundred years, now, the Christian astronomer has known that his Deity didn't make the stars in those tremendous six days; but the Christian astronomer does not enlarge upon that detail. Neither does the priest.

In his Book, God is eloquent in his praises of his mighty works, and calls them by the largest names he can find—thus indicating that he has a strong, and just admiration of magnitudes; yet he made those millions of prodigious suns to light this wee little orb, instead of appointing this orb's little sun to dance attendance upon them. He mentions Arcturus in his Book—you remember Arcturus; we went there once. It is one of this earth's night lamps!—that giant globe which is fifty thousand times as large as this earth's sun, and compares with it as a melon compares with a cathedral.

However, the Sunday school still teaches the child that Arcturus was created to help light this earth, and the child grows up and continues to believe it long after he has found out that the probabilities are against its being so.

[1] It takes the light of the nearest star (61 Cygni) three and a half years to come to the earth, traveling at the rate of 186,000 miles per second. Arcturus had been shining 200 years before it was visible from the earth. Remoter stars gradually became visible after thousands and thousands of years—THE EDITOR [M. T.]

According to the Book and its servants the universe is only six thousand years old. It is only within the last hundred years that studious, inquiring minds have found out that it is nearer a hundred million.

During the Six Days, God created man and the other animals.

He made a man and a woman and placed them in a pleasant garden, along with the other creatures. They all lived together there in harmony and contentment and blooming youth for some time; then trouble came. God had warned the man and the woman that they must not eat of the fruit of a certain tree. And he added a most strange remark: he said that if they ate of it they should surely die. Strange, for the reason that inasmuch as they had never seen a sample of death they could not possibly know what he meant. Neither would he nor any other god have been able to make those ignorant children understand what was meant, without furnishing a sample. The mere word could have no meaning for them, any more than it would have for an infant of days.

Presently a serpent sought them out privately, and came to them walking upright, which was the way of serpents in those days. The serpent said the forbidden fruit would store their vacant minds with knowledge. So they ate it, which was quite natural, for man is so made that he eagerly wants to know; whereas the priest, like God, whose imitator and representative he is, has made it his business from the beginning to keep him *from* knowing any useful thing.

Adam and Eve ate the forbidden fruit, and at once a great light streamed into their dim heads. They had acquired knowledge. What knowledge— useful knowledge? No—merely knowledge that there was such a thing as good, and such a thing as evil, and how to do evil. They couldn't do it before. Therefore all their acts up to this time had been without stain, without blame, without offense.

But now they could do evil—and suffer for it; now they had acquired what the Church calls an invaluable possession, the Moral Sense; that sense which differentiates man from the beast and sets him above the beast. In- stead of below the beast—where one would suppose his proper place would be, since he is always foul-minded and guilty and the beast always clean- minded and innocent. It is like valuing a watch that must go wrong, above a watch that can't.

The Church still prizes the Moral Sense as man's noblest asset today, although the Church knows God had a distinctly poor opinion of it and did what he could in his clumsy way to keep his happy Children of the Garden from acquiring it.

Very well, Adam and Eve now knew what evil was, and how to do it. They knew how to do various kinds of wrong things, and among them one principal one—the one God had his mind on principally. That one was the art and mystery of sexual intercourse. To them it was a magnificent discovery, and they stopped idling around and turned their entire attention to it, poor exultant young things!

In the midst of one of these celebrations they heard God walking among the bushes, which was an afternoon custom of his, and they were smitten with fright. Why? Because they were naked. They had not known it before. They had not minded it before; neither had God.

In that memorable moment immodesty was born; and some people have valued it ever since, though it would certainly puzzle them to explain why.

Adam and Eve entered the world naked and unashamed—naked and pure-minded; and no descendant of theirs has ever entered it otherwise. All have entered it naked, unashamed, and clean in mind. They have entered it modest. They had to acquire immodesty and the soiled mind; there was no other way to get it. A Christian mother's first duty is to soil her child's mind, and she does not neglect it. Her lad grows up to be a missionary, and goes to the innocent savage and to the civilized Japanese, and soils their minds. Whereupon they adopt immodesty, they conceal their bodies, they stop bathing naked together.

The convention miscalled modesty has no standard, and cannot have one, because it is opposed to nature and reason, and is therefore an artificiality and subject to anybody's whim, anybody's diseased caprice. And so, in India the refined lady covers her face and breasts and leaves her legs naked from the hips down, while the refined European lady covers her legs and exposes her face and her breasts. In lands inhabited by the innocent savage the refined European lady soon gets used to full-grown native stark-nakedness, and ceases to be offended by it. A highly cultivated French count and countess—unrelated to each other—who were marooned in their nightclothes, by shipwreck, upon an uninhabited island in the eighteenth century, were soon naked. Also ashamed—for a week. After that their nakedness did not trouble them, and they soon ceased to think about it.

You have never seen a person with clothes on. Oh, well, you haven't lost anything.

To proceed with the Biblical curiosities. Naturally you will think the threat to punish Adam and Eve for disobeying was of course not carried out, since they did not create themselves, nor their natures nor their impulses nor their weaknesses, and hence were not properly subject to anyone's commands, and not responsible to anybody for their acts. It will surprise you to know that the threat was carried out. Adam and Eve were punished, and that crime finds apologists unto this day. The sentence of death was executed.

As you perceive, the only person responsible for the couple's offense escaped; and not only escaped but became the executioner of the innocent.

In your country and mine we should have the privilege of making fun of this kind of morality, but it would be unkind to do it here. Many of these people have the reasoning faculty, but no one uses it in religious matters.

The best minds will tell you that when a man has begotten a child he is morally bound to tenderly care for it, protect it from hurt, shield it from disease, clothe it, feed it, bear with its waywardness, lay no hand upon it save in kindness and for its own good, and never in any case inflict upon it a wanton cruelty. God's treatment of his earthly children, every day and every night, is the exact opposite of all that, yet those best minds warmly justify these crimes, condone them, excuse then, and indignantly refuse to regard them as crimes at all, when *he* commits them. Your country and mine is an interesting one, but there is nothing there that is half so interesting as the human mind.

Very well, God banished Adam and Eve from the Garden, and eventually assassinated them. All for disobeying a command which he had no right to utter. But he did not stop there, as you will see. He has one code of morals for himself, and quite another for his children. He requires his children to deal justly—and gently—with offenders, and forgive them seventy-and-seven times; whereas he deals neither justly nor gently with anyone, and he did not forgive the ignorant and thoughtless first pair of juveniles even their first small offense and say, "You may go free this time, I will give you another chance."

On the contrary! He elected to punish *their* children, all through the ages to the end of time, for a trifling offense committed by others before they were born. He is punishing them yet. In mild ways? No, in atrocious ones.

You would not suppose that this kind of a Being gets many compliments. Undeceive yourself: the world calls him the All-Just, the All-Righteous, the All-Good, the All-Merciful, the All-Forgiving, the All-Truthful, the All-Loving, the Source of All Morality. These sarcasms are uttered daily, all over the world. But not as conscious sarcasms. No, they are meant seriously: they are uttered without a smile.

# NEVER CRY WOLF

## Farley Mowat

My infatuation with the study of animate nature grew rapidly into a full-fledged love affair. I found that even the human beings with whom the study brought me into contact could be fascinating too. My first mentor was a middle-aged Scotsman who gained his livelihood delivering ice, but who was in fact an ardent amateur mammalogist. At a tender age he had developed mange, or leprosy, or some other such infantile disease, and had lost all his hair, never to recover it—a tragedy which may have had a bearing on the fact that, when I knew him, he had already devoted fifteen years of his life to a study of the relationship between summer molt and incipient narcissism in pocket gophers. This man had become so intimate with gophers that he could charm them with sibilant whistles until they would emerge from their underground retreats and passively allow him to examine the hair on their backs.

Nor were the professional biologists with whom I later came into contact one whit less interesting. When I was eighteen I spent a summer doing field work in the company of another mammalogist, seventy years of age, who was replete with degrees and whose towering stature in the world of science had been earned largely by an exhaustive study of uterine scars in shrews. This man, a revered professor at a large American university, knew more about the uteri of shrews than any other man has ever known. Furthermore he could talk about his subject with real enthusiasm. Death will find me long before I tire of contemplating an evening spent in his company during which he enthralled a mixed audience consisting of a fur trader, a Cree Indian matron, and an Anglican missionary, with an hour-long monologue on sexual aberrations in female pygmy shrews. (The trader misconstrued the tenor of the discourse; but the missionary, inured by years of humorless dissertations, soon put him right.)

My early years as a naturalist were free and fascinating, but as I entered manhood and found that my avocation must now become my vocation, the walls began to close in. The happy days of the universal scholar who was able to take a keen interest in all phases of natural history were at an end, and I was forced to recognize the unpalatable necessity of specializing, if I was to succeed as a professional biologist. Nevertheless, as I began my academic training at the university, I found it difficult to choose the narrow path.

For a time I debated whether or not to follow the lead of a friend of mine who was specializing in scatology—the study of the excretory droppings of animals—and who later became a high-ranking scatologist with the United States Biological Survey. But although I found the subject mildly interesting, it failed to rouse my enthusiasm to the pitch where I could wish to make it my lifework. Besides, the field was overcrowded.

My personal predelictions lay towards studies of living animals in their own habitat. Being a literal fellow, I took the word *biology*—which means the study of life—at its face value. I was sorely puzzled by the paradox that many of my contemporaries tended to shy as far away from living things as they could get, and chose to restrict themselves instead to the aseptic atmosphere of laboratories where they used dead—often very dead—animal material as their subject matter. In fact, during my time at the university it was becoming unfashionable to have *anything* to do with animals, even dead ones. The new biologists were concentrating on statistical and analytical research, whereby the raw material of life became no more than fodder for the nourishment of calculating machines.

My inability to adjust to the new trends had an adverse effect upon my professional expectations. While my fellow students were already establishing themselves in various esoteric specialties, most of which they invented for themselves on the theory that if you are the *only* specialist in a given field you need fear no competition, I was still unable to deflect my interests from the general to the particular. As graduation approached I found that the majority of my contemporaries were assured of excellent research jobs while I seemed to have nothing particular to offer in the biological marketplace. It was, therefore, inevitable that I should end up working for the Government.

The die was cast one winter's day when I received a summons from the Dominion Wildlife Service informing me that I had been hired at the munificent salary of one hundred and twenty dollars a month, and that I "would" report to Ottawa at once.

I obeyed this peremptory order with hardly more than a twitch of subdued rebelliousness, for if I had learned anything during my years at the university it was that the scientific hierarchy requires a high standard of obedience, if not subservience, from its acolytes.

Two days later I arrived in the windswept, gray-souled capital of Canada and found my way into the dingy labyrinth which housed the Wildlife Service. Here I presented myself to the Chief Mammalogist, whom I had known as a school chum in more carefree days. But alas, he had now metamorphosed into a full-blown scientist, and was so shrouded in professional dignity that it was all I could do to refrain from making him a profound obeisance.

Through the next several days I was subjected to something called "orientation"—a process which, so far as I could see, was designed to reduce me to a malleable state of hopeless depression. At any rate, the legions of Dantesque bureaucrats whom I visited in their gloomy, Formalin-smelling dens, where they spent interminable hours compiling dreary data or originating meaningless memos, did nothing to rouse in me much devotion to my new employment. The only thing I actually *learned* during this period was that, by comparison with the bureaucratic hierarchy in Ottawa, the scientific hierarchy was a brotherhood of anarchy.

This was driven home one memorable day when, having at last been certified as fit for inspection, I was paraded into the office of the Deputy Minister, where I so far forgot myself as to address him as "Mister." My escort of the moment, all white-faced and trembling, immediately rushed me out of the Presence and took me by devious ways to the men's washroom. Having first knelt down and peered under the doors of all the cubicles to make absolutely certain we were alone and could not be overheard, he explained in an agonized whisper that I must never, on pain of banishment, address the Deputy as anything but "Chief," or, barring that, by his Boer War title of "Colonel."

Military titles were *de rigeur*. All memos were signed Captain-this or Lieutenant-that if they originated from the lower echelons; or Colonel-this and Brigadier-that if they came down from on high. Those members of the staff who had not had the opportunity to acquire even quasi-military status were reduced to the expedient of inventing suitable ranks—field ranks if they were senior men, and subaltern ranks for the juniors. Not everyone took this matter with due solemnity, and I met one new employee in the fishery sections who distinguished himself briefly by sending a memo up to the Chief signed "J. Smith, Acting Lance-Corporal." A week later this foolhardy youth was on his way to the northernmost tip of Ellesmere Island, there to spend his exile living in an igloo while studying the life history of the nine-spined stickleback.

Levity was not looked upon with favor anywhere in those austere offices, as I discovered for myself while attending a conference concerning my first assignment.

A tentative list of the material requirements for this assignment lay on the conference table, surrounded by many grave countenances. It was a formidable document, made out in quintuplicate—as was the official rule—and imposingly headed:

DESIDERATA FOR THE LUPINE PROJECT

Having already been unnerved by the gravity of the gathering, I lost my head completely when the assembly began to consider the twelfth item listed in this horrendous document:

*Paper, toilet, Government standard: 12 rolls.*

An austere suggestion by the representative of the Finance Department that, in the interest of economy, the quantity of this item might be reduced, providing the field party (which was me) exercised all due restraint, sent me into an hysterical spasm of giggling. I mastered myself almost instantly, but it was too late. The two most senior men, both "majors," rose to their feet, bowed coldly, and left the room without a word.

The Ottawa ordeal drew toward its end; but the climax was still to come. One early spring morning I was called to the office of the senior officer who was my direct chief, for a final interview before departing "into the field."

My chief sat behind a massive desk whose dusty surface was littered with yellowing groundhog skulls (he had been studying rates of tooth decay in groundhogs ever since he joined the Department in 1897). At his back hung the frowning, bearded portrait of an extinct mammalogist who glared balefully down upon me. The smell of Formalin swirled about like the fetid breath of an undertaker's back parlor.

After a long silence, during which he toyed portentously with some of his skulls, my chief began his briefing. There was a solemnity about the occasion which would have done justice to the briefing of a special agent about to be entrusted with the assassination of a Head of State.

"As you are aware, Lieutenant Mowat," my chief began, "the *Canis lupus* problem has become one of national importance. Within this past year alone this Department has received no less than thirty-seven memoranda from Members of the House of Commons, all expressing the deep concern of their constituents that we ought to do something about the wolf. Most of the complaints have come from such civic-minded and disinterested groups as various Fish and Game clubs, while members of the business community

—in particular the manufacturers of some well-known brands of ammunition—have lent their weight to the support of these legitimate grievances of the voting public of this Great Dominion, because their grievance is the complaint that the wolves are killing all the deer, and more and more of our fellow citizens are coming back from more and more hunts with less and less deer.

"As you may possibly have heard, my predecessor supplied the Minister with an explanation of this situation in which it was his contention that there were fewer deer because the hunters had increased to the point where they outnumbered the deer about five to one. The Minister, in all good faith, read this fallacious statement in the House of Commons, and he was promptly shouted down by Members howling 'Liar!' and 'Wolf-lover!'

"Three days later my predecessor retired to civilian life, and the Minister issued a press statement: 'The Department of Mines and Resources is determined to do everything in its power to curb the carnage being wreaked upon the deer population by hordes of wolves. A full-scale investigation of this vital problem, employing the full resources of the Department, is to be launched at once. The people of this country can rest assured that the Government of which I have the honor to be a member will leave no stone unturned to put an end to this intolerable situation.' "

At this juncture my chief seized a particularly robust groundhog skull and began rhythmically clacking its jaws together as if to emphasize his final words:

"You, Lieutenant Mowat, have been chosen for this great task! It only remains for you to go out into the field at once and tackle this work in a manner worthy of the great traditions of this Department. The wolf, Lieutenant Mowat, is *your* problem!"

Somehow I staggered to my feet, and with an involuntary motion brought my right hand up in a smart salute before fleeing from the room.

I fled from Ottawa too . . . that self-same night, aboard a Canadian Air Force transport plane. My immediate destination was Churchill, on the western shore of Hudson Bay; but beyond that, somewhere in the desolate wastes of the subarctic Barren Lands, lay my ultimate objective—the wolf himself.

# FIRST CONFESSION

## X. J. Kennedy

Blood thudded in my ears. I scuffed,
   Steps stubborn, to the telltale booth
Beyond whose curtained portal coughed
   The robed repositor of truth.

The slat shot back. The universe
   Bowed down his cratered dome to hear
Enumerated my each curse,
   The sip snitched from my old man's beer,

My sloth pride envy lechery,
   The dime held back from Peter's Pence
With which I'd bribed my girl to pee
   That I might spy her instruments.

Hovering scale-pans when I'd done
   Settled their balance slow as silt
While in the restless dark I burned
   Bright as a brimstone in my guilt

Until as one feeds birds he doled
   Seven Our Fathers and a Hail
Which I to double-scrub my soul
   Intoned twice at the altar rail

First Confession," copyright 1951 by X. J. Kennedy from *Nude Descending a Staircase* by X. J. Kennedy. Reprinted by permission of Doubleday & Company, Inc.

Where Sunday in seraphic light
   I knelt, as full of grace as most,
And stuck my tongue out at the priest:
   A fresh roost for the Holy Ghost.

*"Till human voices wake us, and we drown."*

*T. S. Eliot*

# IX
## ALIENATION

# RICHARD CORY

## E. A. Robinson

Whenever Richard Cory went down town,
We people on the pavement looked at him:
He was a gentleman from sole to crown,
Clean favored, and imperially slim.

And he was always quietly arrayed,
And he was always human when he talked;
But still he fluttered pulses when he said,
"Good-morning," and he glittered when he walked.

And he was rich—yes, richer than a king—
And admirably schooled in every grace:
In fine, we thought that he was everything
To make us wish that we were in his place.

So on we worked, and waited for the light,
And went without the meat, and cursed the bread;
And Richard Cory, one calm summer night,
Went home and put a bullet through his head.

"Richard Cory" is reprinted by permission of Charles Scribner's Sons from *The Children of the Night* by Edwin Arlington Robinson (1897).

# MR. FLOOD'S PARTY

## E. A. Robinson

Old Eben Flood, climbing alone one night
Over the hill between the town below
And the forsaken upland hermitage
That held as much as he should ever know
On earth again of home, paused warily.
The road was his with not a native near;
And Eben, having leisure, said aloud,
For no man else in Tilbury Town to hear:

"Well, Mr. Flood, we have the harvest moon
Again, and we may not have many more;
The bird is on the wing, the poet says,
And you and I have said it here before.
Drink to the bird." He raised up to the light
The jug that he had gone so far to fill,
And answered huskily: "Well, Mr. Flood,
Since you propose it, I believe I will."

Alone, as if enduring to the end
A valiant armor of scarred hopes outworn,
He stood there in the middle of the road
Like Roland's ghost winding a silent horn.
Below him, in the town among the trees,
Where friends of other days had honored him,

*Caged* by Raymond Keller

*The Media: Man* by Raymond Keller

*The Mouth* by Raymond Keller

*Man, Myth, and Madness* by Jill Dunner and Jill Bohlander

A phantom salutation of the dead
Rang thinly till old Eben's eyes were dim.

Then, as a mother lays her sleeping child
Down tenderly, fearing it may awake,
He set the jug down slowly at his feet
With trembling care, knowing that most things break;
And only when assured that on firm earth
It stood, as the uncertain lives of men
Assuredly did not, he paced away,
And with his hand extended paused again:

"Well, Mr. Flood, we have not met like this
In a long time; and many a change has come
To both of us, I fear, since last it was
We had a drop together. Welcome home!"
Convivially returning with himself,
Again he raised the jug up to the light;
And with an acquiescent quaver said:
"Well, Mr. Flood, if you insist, I might.

"Only a very little, Mr. Flood—
For auld lang syne. No more, sir; that will do."
So, for the time, apparently it did,
And Eben evidently thought so too;
For soon amid the silver loneliness
Of night he lifted up his voice and sang,
Secure, with only two moons listening,
Until the whole harmonious landscape rang—

"For auld lang syne." The weary throat gave out;
The last word wavered, and the song was done.
He raised again the jug regretfully
And shook his head, and was again alone.
There was not much that was ahead of him,
And there was nothing in the town below—
Where strangers would have shut the many doors
That many friends had opened long ago.

# THE SOUND OF SILENCE

## Paul Simon

Hello, darkness, my old friend,
I've come to talk with you again.
Because a vision softly creeping,
Left its seeds while I was sleeping,
And the vision that was planted in my brain
Still remains
Within the sound of silence.

In restless dreams I walked alone,
Narrow streets of cobblestone,
'Neath the halo of a street lamp,
I turned my collar to the cold and damp
When my eyes were stabbed by the flash of a neon light
That split the night.
And touched the sound of silence.

And in the naked light I saw
Ten thousand people, maybe more,
People talking without speaking,
People hearing without listening,
People writing songs that voices never share . . .
And no one dare
Disturb the sound of silence.

"Fools," said I, "you do not know,
Silence like a cancer grows."
"Hear my words that I might teach you,
Take my arms that I might reach you."
But my words like silent rain-drops fell,
And echoed in the wells of silence.

And the people bowed and prayed
to the neon god they made.
And the sign flashed out its warning
In the words that it was forming.
And the signs said, "The words of the prophets are written
on the subway walls
And tenement halls,
And whisper'd in the sounds of silence."

# MUCH MADNESS
# IS DIVINEST SENSE

## Emily Dickinson

Much Madness is divinest Sense—
To a discerning Eye—
Much Sense—the starkest Madness—
'Tis the Majority
In this, as All, prevail—
Assent—and you are sane—
Demur—you're straightway dangerous—
And handled with a Chain—

# RINGING THE BELLS

## Anne Sexton

And this is the way they ring
the bells in Bedlam
and this is the bell-lady
who comes each Tuesday morning
to give us a music lesson
and because the attendants make you go
and because we mind by instinct,
like bees caught in the wrong hive,
we are the circle of the crazy ladies
who sit in the lounge of the mental house
and smile at the smiling woman
who passes us each a bell,
who points at my hand
that holds my bell, E flat,
and this is the gray dress next to me
who grumbles as if it were special
to be old, to be old,
and this is the small hunched squirrel girl
on the other side of me
who picks at the hairs over her lip,
who picks at the hairs over her lip all day,
and this is how the bells really sound,
as untroubled and clean
as a workable kitchen,

and this is always my bell responding
to my hand that responds to the lady
who points at me, E flat;
and although we are no better for it,
they tell you to go. And you do.

# WILLIAM FAULKNER'S SPEECH OF ACCEPTANCE UPON THE AWARD OF THE NOBEL PRIZE FOR LITERATURE

*Delivered in Stockholm on the tenth of December,*
*nineteen hundred fifty*

I feel that this award was not made to me as a man, but to my work—a life's work in the agony and sweat of the human spirit, not for glory and least of all for profit, but to create out of the materials of the human spirit something which did not exist before. So this award is only mine in trust. It will not be difficult to find a dedication for the money part of it commensurate with the purpose and significance of its origin. But I would like to do the same with the acclaim too, by using this moment as a pinnacle from which I might be listened to by the young men and women already dedicated to the same anguish and travail, among whom is already that one who will some day stand here where I am standing.

Our tragedy today is a general and universal physical fear so long sustained by now that we can even bear it. There are no longer problems of the spirit. There is only the question: When will I be blown up? Because of this, the young man or woman writing today has forgotten the problems of the human heart in conflict with itself which alone can make good writing because only that is worth writing about, worth the agony and the sweat.

He must learn them again. He must teach himself that the basest of all things is to be afraid; and, teaching himself that, forget it forever, leaving no room in his workshop for anything but the old verities and truths of the heart, the old universal truths lacking which any story is ephemeral and doomed—love and honor and pity and pride and compassion and sacrifice. Until he does so, he labors under a curse. He writes not of love but of lust, of defeats in which nobody loses anything of value, of victories without

Reprinted by permission of Random House, Inc.

hope and, worst of all, without pity or compassion. His griefs grieve on no universal bones, leaving no scars. He writes not of the heart but of the glands.

Until he relearns these things, he will write as though he stood among and watched the end of man. I decline to accept the end of man. It is easy enough to say that man is immortal simply because he will endure: that when the last ding-dong of doom has clanged and faded from the last worthless rock hanging tideless in the last red and dying evening, that even then there will still be one more sound: that of his puny inexhaustible voice, still talking. I refuse to accept this. I believe that man will not merely endure: he will prevail. He is immortal, not because he alone among creatures has an inexhaustible voice, but because he has a soul, a spirit capable of compassion and sacrifice and endurance. The poet's, the writer's, duty is to write about these things. It is his privilege to help man endure by lifting his heart, by reminding him of the courage and honor and hope and pride and compassion and pity and sacrifice which have been the glory of his past. The poet's voice need not merely be the record of man, it can be one of the props, the pillars to help him endure and prevail.

# THE CAGED SKYLARK

## Gerard Manley Hopkins

As a dare-gale skylark scanted in a dull cage
  Man's mounting spirit in his bone-house, mean house, dwells—
  That bird beyond the remembering his free fells;
This in drudgery, day-labouring-out life's age.

Though aloft on turf or perch or poor low stage,
  Both sing sometímes the sweetest, sweetest spells,
  Yet both droop deadly sómetimes in their cells
Or wring their barriers in bursts of fear or rage.

Not that the sweet-fowl, song-fowl, needs no rest—
Why, hear him, hear him babble and drop down to his nest,
  But his own nest, wild nest, no prison.

Man's spirit will be flesh-bound when found at best,
But uncumberèd: meadow-down is not distressed
  For a rainbow footing it nor he for his bónes rísen.

# A NOISELESS
# PATIENT SPIDER

## Walt Whitman

A noiseless patient spider,
I mark'd where on a little promontory it stood isolated,
Mark'd how to explore the vacant vast surrounding,
It launch'd forth filament, filament, filament, out of itself,
Ever unreeling them, ever tirelessly speeding them.

And you O my soul where you stand,
Surrounded, detached, in measureless oceans of space,
Ceaselessly musing, venturing, throwing, seeking the spheres to
    connect them,
Till the bridge you will need be form'd, till the ductile anchor hold,
Till the gossamer thread you fling catch somewhere, O my soul.

# A FLAT ONE

## W. D. Snodgrass

Old Fritz, on this rotating bed
For seven wasted months you lay
Unfit to move, shrunken, gray,
No good to yourself or anyone
But to be babied—changed and bathed and fed.
    At long last, that's all done.

Before each meal, twice every night,
We set pads on your bedsores, shut
Your catheter tube off, then brought
The second canvas-and-black-iron
Bedframe and clamped you in between them, tight,
    Scared, so we could turn

You over. We washed you, covered you,
Cut up each bite of meat you ate;
We watched your lean jaws masticate
As ravenously your useless food
As thieves at hard labor in their chains chew
    Or insects in the wood.

Such pious sacrifice to give
You all you could demand of pain:
Receive this haddock's body, slain
For you, old tyrant; take this blood
Of a tomato, shed that you might live.
    You had that costly food.

You seem to be all finished, so
We'll plug your old recalcitrant anus
And tie up your discouraged penis
In a great, snow-white bow of gauze.
We wrap you, pin you, and cart you down below,
        Below, below, because

Your credit has finally run out.
On our steel table, trussed and carved,
You'll find this world's hardworking, starved
Teeth working in your precious skin.
The earth turns, in the end, by turn about
        And opens to take you in.

Seven months gone down the drain; thank God
That's through. Throw out the four-by-fours,
Swabsticks, the thick salve for bedsores,
Throw out the diaper pads and drug
Containers, pile the bedclothes in a wad,
        And rinse the cider jug

Half-filled with the last urine. Then
Empty out the cotton cans,
Autoclave the bowls and spit pans,
Unhook the pumps and all the red
Tubes—catheter, suction, oxygen;
        Next, wash the empty bed.

—All this Dark Age machinery
On which we had tormented you
To life. Last, we collect the few
Belongings: snapshots, some odd bills,
Your mail, and half a pack of Luckies we
        Won't light you after meals.

Old man, these seven months you've lain
Determined—not that you would live—
Just to not die. No one would give
You one chance you could ever wake
From that first night, much less go well again,
        Much less go home and make

Your living; how could you hope to find
A place for yourself in all creation?—
Pain was your only occupation.
And pain that should content and will

A man to give it up, nerved you to grind
   Your clenched teeth, breathing, till

  Your skin broke down, your calves went flat
  And your legs lost all sensation. Still,
  You took enough morphine to kill
  A strong man. Finally, nitrogen
Mustard: you could last two months after that;
   *It* would kill you then.

  Even then you wouldn't quit.
  Old soldier, yet you must have known
  Inside the animal had grown
  Sick of the world, made up its mind
To stop. Your mind ground on its separate
   Way, merciless and blind,

  Into these last weeks when the breath
  Would only come in fits and starts
  That puffed out your sections like the parts
  Of some enormous, damaged bug.
You waited, not for life, not for your death,
   Just for the deadening drug

  That made your life seem bearable.
  You still whispered you would not die.
  Yet in the nights I heard you cry
  Like a whipped child; in fierce old age
You whimpered, tears stood on your gun-metal
   Blue cheeks shaking with rage

  And terror. So much pain would fill
  Your room that when I left I'd pray
  That if I came back the next day
  I'd find you gone. You stayed for me—
Nailed to your own rapacious, stiff self-will.
   You've shook loose, finally.

  They'd say this was a worthwhile job
  Unless they tried it. It is mad
  To throw our good lives after bad;
  Waste time, drugs, and our minds, while strong
Men starve. How many young men did we rob
   To keep you hanging on?

I can't think we did *you* much good.
Well, when you died, none of us wept.
You killed for us, and so we kept
You, because we need to earn our pay.
No. We'd still have to help you try. We would
Have killed for you today.

# THE LOVE SONG OF J. ALFRED PRUFROCK

## T. S. Eliot

*S'io credesse che mia risposta fosse*
*A persona che mai tornasse al mondo,*
*Questa fiamma staria senza piu scosse.*
*Ma perciocche giammai di questo fondo*
*Non torno vivo alcun, s'i'odo il vero,*
*Senza tema d'infamia ti rispondo.*

Let us go then, you and I,
When the evening is spread out against the sky
Like a patient etherised upon a table;
Let us go, through certain half-deserted streets,
The muttering retreats
Of restless nights in one-night cheap hotels
And sawdust restaurants with oyster-shells:
Streets that follow like a tedious argument
Of insidious intent
To lead you to an overwhelming question. . .
Oh, do not ask, "What is it?"
Let us go and make our visit.

In the room the women come and go
Talking of Michelangelo.

The yellow fog that rubs its back upon the window-panes,
The yellow smoke that rubs its muzzle on the window-panes
Licked its tongue into the corners of the evening,
Lingered upon the pools that stand in drains,

Let fall upon its back the soot that falls from chimneys,
Slipped by the terrace, made a sudden leap,
And seeing that it was a soft October night,
Curled once about the house, and feel asleep.

And indeed there will be time
For the yellow smoke that slides along the street,
Rubbing its back upon the window-panes;
There will be time, there will be time
To prepare a face to meet the faces that you meet;
There will be time to murder and create,
And time for all the works and days of hands
That lift and drop a question on your plate;
Time for you and time for me,
And time yet for a hundred indecisions,
And for a hundred visions and revisions,
Before the taking of a toast and tea.

In the room the women come and go
Talking of Michelangelo.

And indeed there will be time
To wonder, "Do I dare?" and, "Do I dare?"
Time to turn back and descend the stair,
With a bald spot in the middle of my hair—
(They will say: "How his hair is growing thin!")
My morning coat, my collar mounting firmly to the chin,
My necktie rich and modest, but asserted by a simple pin—
(They will say: "But how his arms and legs are thin!")
Do I dare
Disturb the universe?
In a minute there is time
For decisions and revisions which a minute will reverse.

For I have known them all already, known them all:
Have known the evenings, mornings, afternoons,
I have measured out my life with coffee spoons;
I know the voices dying with a dying fall
Beneath the music from a farther room.
    So how should I presume?

And I have known the eyes already, known them all—
The eyes that fix you in a formulated phrase,
And when I am formulated, sprawling on a pin,
When I am pinned and wriggling on the wall,

Then how should I begin
To spit out all the butt-ends of my days and ways?
   And how should I presume?

And I have known the arms already, known them all—
Arms that are braceleted and white and bare
(But in the lamplight, downed with light brown hair!)
Is it perfume from a dress
That makes me so digress?
Arms that lie along a table, or wrap about a shawl.
   And should I then presume?
   And how should I begin?

     .    .    .    .    .

Shall I say, I have gone at dusk through narrow streets
And watched the smoke that rises from the pipes
Of lonely men in shirt-sleeves, leaning out of windows? . . .

I should have been a pair of ragged claws
Scuttling across the floors of silent seas.

     .    .    .    .    .

And the afternoon, the evening, sleeps so peacefully!
Smoothed by long fingers,
Asleep . . . tired . . . or it malingers,
Stretched on the floor, here beside you and me.
Should I, after tea and cakes and ices,
Have the strength to force the moment to its crisis?
But though I have wept and fasted, wept and prayed,
Though I have seen my head (grown slightly bald)
    brought in upon a platter,
I am no prophet—and here's no great matter;
I have seen the moment of my greatness flicker,
And I have seen the eternal Footman hold my coat,
    and snicker,
And in short, I was afraid.

And would it have been worth it, after all,
After the cups, the marmalade, the tea,
Among the porcelain, among some talk of you and me,
Would it have been worth while,
To have bitten off the matter with a smile,
To have squeezed the universe into a ball
To roll it toward some overwhelming question,
To say: "I am Lazarus, come from the dead,
Come back to tell you all, I shall tell you all"—

If one, settling a pillow by her head,
   Should say: "That is not what I meant at all;
   That is not it, at all."

And would it have been worth it, after all,
Would it have been worth while,
After the sunsets and the dooryards and the sprinkled streets,
After the novels, after the teacups, after the skirts that
      trail along the floor—
And this, and so much more?—
It is impossible to say just what I mean!
But as if a magic lantern threw the nerves in patterns on
     a screen:
Would it have been worth while
If one, settling a pillow or throwing off a shawl,
And turning toward the window, should say:
   "That is not it at all,
   That is not what I meant, at all."

.     .     .     .     .

No! I am not Prince Hamlet, nor was meant to be;
Am an attendant lord, one that will do
To swell a progress, start a scene or two,
Advise the prince; no doubt, an easy tool,
Deferential, glad to be of use,
Politic, cautious, and meticulous;
Full of high sentence, but a bit obtuse;
At times, indeed, almost ridiculous—
Almost, at times, the Fool.

I grow old . . . I grow old . . .
I shall wear the bottoms of my trousers rolled.

Shall I part my hair behind? Do I dare to eat a peach?
I shall wear white flannel trousers, and walk upon the beach.
I have heard the mermaids singing, each to each.

I do not think that they will sing to me.

I have seen them riding seaward on the waves
Combing the white hair of the waves blown back
When the wind blows the water white and black.

We have lingered in the chambers of the sea
By sea-girls wreathed with seaweed red and brown
Till human voices wake us, and we drown.

# STRANGER
# IN THE VILLAGE

## James Baldwin

From all available evidence no black man had ever set foot in this tiny Swiss village before I came. I was told before arriving that I would probably be a "sight" for the village; I took this to mean that people of my complexion were rarely seen in Switzerland, and also that city people are always something of a "sight" outside of the city. It did not occur to me—possibly because I am an American—that there could be people anywhere who had never seen a Negro.

It is a fact that cannot be explained on the basis of the inaccessibility of the village. The village is very high, but it is only four hours from Milan and three hours from Lausanne. It is true that it is virtually unknown. Few people making plans for a holiday would elect to come here. On the other hand, the villagers are able, presumably, to come and go as they please—which they do: to another town at the foot of the mountain, with a population of approximately five thousand, the nearest place to see a movie or go to the bank. In the village there is no movie house, no bank, no library, no theater; very few radios, one jeep, one station wagon; and, at the moment, one typewriter, mine, an invention which the woman next door to me here had never seen. There are about six hundred people living here, all Catholic—I conclude this from the fact that the Catholic church is open all year round, whereas the Protestant chapel, set off on a hill a little removed from the village, is open only in the summertime when the tourists arrive. There are four or five hotels, all closed now, and four or five *bistros,* of which, however, only two do any business during the winter. These two do not do a great deal, for life in the village seems to end around nine or ten o'clock.

There are a few stores, butcher, baker, *épicerie,* a hardware store, and a money-changer—who cannot change travelers' checks, but must send them down to the bank, an operation which takes two or three days. There is something called the *Ballet Haus,* closed in the winter and used for God knows what, certainly not ballet, during the summer. There seems to be only one schoolhouse in the village, and this for the quite young children; I suppose this to mean that their older brothers and sisters at some point descend from these mountains in order to complete their education—possibly, again, to the town just below. The landscape is absolutely forbidding, mountains towering on all four sides, ice and snow as far as the eye can reach. In this white wilderness, men and women and children move all day, carrying washing, wood, buckets of milk or water, sometimes skiing on Sunday afternoons. All week long boys and young men are to be seen shoveling snow off the rooftops, or dragging wood down from the forest in sleds.

The village's only real attraction, which explains the tourist season, is the hot spring water. A disquietingly high proportion of these tourists are cripples, or semi-cripples, who come year after year—from other parts of Switzerland, usually—to take the waters. This lends the village, at the height of the season, a rather terrifying air of sanctity, as though it were a lesser Lourdes. There is often something beautiful, there is always something awful, in the spectacle of a person who has lost one of his faculties, a faculty he never questioned until it was gone, and who struggles to recover it. Yet people remain people, on crutches or indeed on deathbeds; and wherever I passed, the first summer I was here, among the native villagers or among the lame, a wind passed with me—of astonishment, curiosity, amusement, and outrage. That first summer I stayed two weeks and never intended to return. But I did return in the winter, to work; the village offers, obviously, no distractions whatever and has the further advantage of being extremely cheap. Now it is winter again, a year later, and I am here again. Everyone in the village knows my name, though they scarcely ever use it, knows that I come from America—though, this, apparently, they will never really believe: black men come from Africa—and everyone knows that I am the friend of the son of a woman who was born here, and that I am staying in their chalet. But I remain as much a stranger today as I was the first day I arrived, and the children shout *Neger! Neger!* as I walk along the streets.

It must be admitted that in the beginning I was far too shocked to have any real reaction. In so far as I reacted at all, I reacted by trying to be pleasant—it being a great part of the American Negro's education (long before he goes to school) that he must make people "like" him. This smile-and-the-world-smiles-with-you routine worked about as well in this situation as it had in the situation for which it was designed, which is to say that it did not work at all. No one, after all, can be liked whose human weight and complexity cannot be, or has not been, admitted. My smile was simply another unheard-of phenomenon which allowed them to see my teeth—they did not, really, see my smile and I began to think that, should I take to snarling, no one would notice any difference. All of the physical characteristics of the Negro which had caused me, in America, a very different and almost forgotten pain were nothing less than miraculous—or infernal—in the eyes of the village people. Some thought my hair was the color of tar, that it had the texture of wire, or the texture of cotton. It was jocularly suggested that I might let it all grow long and make myself a winter coat. If I sat in the sun for more than five minutes some daring creature was certain to come along and gingerly put his fingers on my hair, as though he were afraid of an electric shock, or put his hand on my hand, astonished that the color did not rub off. In all of this, in which it must be conceded there was the charm of genuine wonder and in which there was certainly no element of intentional unkindness, there was yet no suggestion that I was human: I was simply a living wonder.

I knew that they did not mean to be unkind, and I know it now; it is necessary, nevertheless, for me to repeat this to myself each time that I walk out of the chalet. The children who shout *Neger!* have no way of knowing the echoes this sound raises in me. They are brimming with good humor and the more daring swell with pride when I stop to speak with them. Just the same, there are days when I cannot pause and smile, when I have no heart to play with them; when, indeed, I mutter sourly to myself, exactly as I muttered on the streets of a city these children have never seen, when I was no bigger than these children are now: *Your* mother *was a nigger.* Joyce is right about history being a nightmare—but it may be the nightmare from which no one *can* awaken. People are trapped in history and history is trapped in them.

There is a custom in the village—I am told it is repeated in many villages —of "buying" African natives for the purpose of converting them to Christianity. There stands in the church all year round a small box with a slot for money, decorated with a black figurine, and into this box the villagers drop their francs. During the *carnaval* which precedes Lent, two village children have their faces blackened—out of which bloodless darkness their blue eyes shine like ice—and fantastic horsehair wigs are placed on their blond heads; thus disguised, they solicit among the villagers for money for the missionaries in Africa. Between the box in the church and the blackened children, the village "bought" last year six or eight African natives. This was reported to me with pride by the wife of one of the *bistro* owners and I was careful to express astonishment and pleasure at the solicitude shown by the village for the souls of black folk. The *bistro* owner's wife beamed with a pleasure far more genuine than my own and seemed to feel that I might now breathe more easily concerning the souls of at least six of my kinsmen.

I tried not to think of these so lately baptized kinsmen, of the price paid for them, or the peculiar price they themselves would pay, and said nothing about my father, who having taken his own conversion too literally never, at bottom, forgave the white world (which he described as heathen) for having saddled him with a Christ in whom, to judge at least from their treatment of him, they themselves no longer believed. I thought of white men arriving for the first time in an African village, strangers there, as I am a stranger here, and tried to imagine the astounded populace touching their hair and marveling at the color of their skin. But there is a great difference between being the first white man to be seen by Africans and being the first black man to be seen by whites. The white man takes the astonishment as tribute, for he arrives to conquer and to convert the natives, whose inferiority in relation to himself is not even to be questioned; whereas I, without a thought of conquest, find myself among a people whose culture controls me, has even, in a sense, created me, people who have cost me more in anguish and rage than they will ever know, who yet do not even know of my existence. The astonishment with which I might have greeted them, should they have stumbled into my African village a few hundred years ago, might have rejoiced their hearts. But the astonishment with which they greet me today can only poison mine.

And this is so despite everything I may do to feel differently, despite my friendly conversations with the *bistro* owner's wife, despite their three-year-old son who has at last become my friend, despite the *saluts* and *bonsoirs* which I exchange with people as I walk, despite the fact that I know that no individual can be taken to task for what history is doing, or has done. I say that the culture of these people controls me—but they can scarcely be held responsible for European culture. America comes out of Europe, but these people have never seen America, nor have most of them seen more of Europe than the hamlet at the foot of their mountain. Yet they move with an authority which I shall never have; and they regard me, quite rightly, not only as a stranger in their village but as a suspect latecomer, bearing no credentials, to everything they have—however unconsciously—inherited.

For this village, even were it incomparably more remote and incredibly more primitive, is the West, the West onto which I have been so strangely grafted. These people cannot be, from the point of view of power, strangers anywhere in the world; they have made the modern world, in effect, even if they do not know it. The most illiterate among them is related, in a way that I am not, to Dante, Shakespeare, Michelangelo, Aeschylus, Da Vinci, Rembrandt, and Racine; the cathedral at Chartres says something to them which it cannot say to me, as indeed would New York's Empire State Building, should anyone here ever see it. Out of their hymns and dances come Beethoven and Bach. Go back a few centuries and they are in their full glory—but I am in Africa, watching the conquerors arrive.

The rage of the disesteemed is personally fruitless, but it is also absolutely inevitable; this rage, so generally discounted, so little understood even among the people whose daily bread it is, is one of the things that makes history. Rage can only with difficulty, and never entirely, be brought under the domination of the intelligence and is therefore not susceptible to any arguments whatever. This is a fact which ordinary representatives of the *Herrenvolk,* having never felt this rage and being unable to imagine it, quite fail to understand. Also, rage cannot be hidden, it can only be dissembled. This dissembling deludes the thoughtless, and strengthens rage and adds, to rage, contempt. There are, no doubt, as many ways of coping with the resulting complex of tensions as there are black men in the world, but no black man can hope ever to be entirely liberated from this internal warfare—rage, dissembling, and contempt having inevitably accompanied his first realization of the power of white men. What is crucial here is that, since white men represent in the black man's world so heavy a weight, white men have for black men a reality which is far from being reciprocal; and hence all black men have toward all white men an attitude which is designed, really, either to rob the white man of the jewel of his naïveté, or else to make it cost him dear.

The black man insists, by whatever means he finds at his disposal, that the white man cease to regard him as an exotic rarity and recognize him as a human being. This is a very charged and difficult moment, for there is a great deal of will power involved in the white man's naïveté. Most people are not naturally reflective any more than they are naturally malicious, and the white man prefers to keep the black man at a certain human remove because it is easier for him thus to preserve his simplicity and avoid being called to account for crimes committed by his forefathers, or his neighbors. He is inescapably aware, nevertheless, that he is in a better position in the world than black men are, nor can he quite put to death the suspicion that he is hated by black men therefore. He does not wish to be hated, neither does he wish to change places, and at this point in his uneasiness he can scarcely avoid having recourse to those legends which white men have created about black men, the most usual effect of which is that the white man finds himself enmeshed, so to speak, in his own language which describes hell, as well as the attributes which lead one to hell, as being as black as night.

Every legend, moreover, contains its residuum of truth, and the root function of language is to control the universe by describing it. It is of quite considerable significance that black men remain, in the imagination, and in overwhelming numbers in fact, beyond the disciplines of salvation; and this despite the fact that the West has been "buying" African natives for centuries. There is, I should hazard, an instantaneous necessity to be divorced from this so visibly unsaved stranger, in whose heart, moreover, one cannot guess what dreams of vengeance are being nourished; and, at the same time, there are few things on earth more atractive than the idea of the unspeakable liberty which is allowed the unredeemed. When, beneath the black mask, a human being begins to make himself felt one cannot escape a certain awful wonder as to what kind of human being it is. What one's imagination makes of other people is dictated, of course, by the laws of one's own personality and it is one of the ironies of black-white relations that, by means of what the white man imagines the black man to be, the black man is enabled to know who the white man is.

I have said, for example, that I am as much a stranger in this village today as I was the first summer I arrived, but this is not quite true. The villagers wonder less about the texture of my hair than they did then, and wonder rather more about me. And the fact that their wonder now exists on another level is reflected in their attitudes and in their eyes. There are the children who make those delightful, hilarious, sometimes astonishingly grave overtures of friendship in the unpredictable fashion of children; other children, having been taught that the devil is a black man, scream in genuine anguish as I approach. Some of the older women never pass without a friendly greeting, never pass, indeed, if it seems that they will be able to engage me in conversation; other women look down or look away or rather contemptuously smirk. Some of the men drink with me and suggest that I learn how to ski—partly, I gather, because they cannot imagine what I would look like on skis—and want to know if I am married, and ask questions about my *métier*. But some of the men have accused *le sale nègre* —behind my back—of stealing wood and there is already in the eyes of some of them that peculiar, intent, paranoiac malevolence which one sometimes surprises in the eyes of American white men when, out walking with their Sunday girl, they see a Negro male approach.

There is a dreadful abyss between the streets of this village and the streets of the city in which I was born, between the children who shout *Neger!* today and those who shouted *Nigger!* yesterday—the abyss is experience, the American experience. The syllable hurled behind me today expresses, above all, wonder: I am a stranger here. But I am not a stranger in America and the same syllable riding on the American air expresses the war my presence has occasioned in the American soul.

For this village brings home to me this fact: that there was a day, and not really a very distant day, when Americans were scarcely Americans at all but discontented Europeans, facing a great unconquered continent and strolling, say, into a marketplace and seeing black men for the first time. The shock this spectacle afforded is suggested, surely, by the promptness with which they decided that these black men were not really men but cattle. It is true that the necessity on the part of the settlers of the New World of reconciling their moral assumptions with the fact—and the necessity—of slavery enhanced immensely the charm of this idea, and it is also true that this idea expresses, with a truly American bluntness, the attitude which to varying extents all masters have had toward all slaves.

But between all former slaves and slave-owners and the drama which begins for Americans over three hundred years ago at Jamestown, there are at least two differences to be observed. The American Negro slave could not suppose, for one thing, as slaves in past epochs had supposed and often done, that he would ever be able to wrest the power from his master's hands. This was a supposition which the modern era, which was to bring about such vast changes in the aims and dimensions of power, put to death; it only begins, in unprecedented fashion, and with dreadful implications, to be resurrected today. But even had this supposition persisted with un-diminished force, the American Negro slave could not have used it to lend his condition dignity, for the reason that this supposition rests on another: that the slave in exile yet remains related to his past, has some means—if only in memory—of revering and sustaining the forms of his former life, is able, in short, to maintain his identity.

This was not the case with the American Negro slave. He is unique among the black men of the world in that his past was taken from him, almost literally, at one blow. One wonders what on earth the first slave found to say to the first dark child he bore. I am told that there are Haitians able to trace their ancestry back to African kings, but any American negro wishing to go back so far will find his journey through time abruptly arrested by the signature on the bill of sale which served as the entrance paper for his ancestor. At the time—to say nothing of the circumstances—of the enslavement of the captive black man who was to become the American Negro, there was not the remotest possibility that he would ever take power from his master's hands. There was no reason to suppose that his situation would ever change, nor was there, shortly, anything to indicate that his situation had ever been different. It was his necessity, in the words of E. Franklin Frazier, to find a "motive for living under American culture or die." The identity of the American Negro comes out of this extreme situation, and the evolution of this identity was a source of the most intoler-able anxiety in the minds and the lives of his masters.

For the history of the American Negro is unique also in this: that the question of his humanity, and of his rights therefore as a human being, became a burning one for several generations of Americans, so burning a question that it ultimately became one of those used to divide the nation. It is out of this argument that the venom of the epithet *Nigger!* is derived. It is an argument which Europe has never had, and hence Europe quite sincerely fails to understand how or why the argument arose in the first place, why its effects are so frequently disastrous and always so unpre-dictable, why it refuses until today to be entirely settled. Europe's black

possessions remained—and do remain—in Europe's colonies, at which remove they represented no threat whatever to European identity. If they
posed any problem at all for the European conscience, it was a problem
which remained comfortingly abstract: in effect, the black man, *as a man,*
did not exist for Europe. But in America, even as a slave, he was an
inescapable part of the general social fabric and no American could escape
having an attitude toward him. Americans attempt until today to make an
abstraction of the Negro, but the very nature of these abstractions reveals
the tremendous effects the presence of the Negro has had on the American
character.

When one considers the history of the Negro in America it is of the
greatest importance to recognize that the moral beliefs of a person, or a
people, are never really as tenuous as life—which is not moral—very often
causes them to appear; these create for them a frame of reference and a
necessary hope, the hope being that when life has done its worst they will
be enabled to rise above themselves and to triumph over life. Life would
scarcely be bearable if this hope did not exist. Again, even when the worst
has been said, to betray a belief is not by any means to have put oneself
beyond its power; the betrayal of a belief is not the same thing as ceasing
to believe. If this were not so there would be no moral standards in the
world at all. Yet one must also recognize that morality is based on ideas
and that all ideas are dangerous—dangerous because ideas can only lead
to action and where the action leads no man can say. And dangerous in
this respect: that confronted with the impossibility of remaining faithful to
one's beliefs, and the equal impossibility of becoming free of them, one can
be driven to the most inhuman excesses. The ideas on which American
beliefs are based are not, though Americans often seem to think so, ideas
which originated in America. They came out of Europe. And the establishment of democracy on the American continent was scarcely as radical a
break with the past as was the necessity, which Americans faced, of broadening this concept to include black men.

This was, literally, a hard necessity. It was impossible, for one thing, for
Americans to abandon their beliefs, not only because these beliefs alone
seemed able to justify the sacrifices they had endured and the blood that
they had spilled, but also because these beliefs afforded them their only
bulwark against a moral chaos as absolute as the physical chaos of the
continent it was their destiny to conquer. But in the situation in which
Americans found themselves, these beliefs threatened an idea which,
whether or not one likes to think so, is the very warp and woof of the
heritage of the West, the idea of white supremacy.

Americans have made themselves notorious by the shrillness and the
brutality with which they have insisted on this idea, but they did not invent
it; and it has escaped the world's notice that those very excesses of which

Americans have been guilty imply a certain, unprecedented uneasiness over the idea's life and power, if not, indeed, the idea's validity. The idea of white supremacy rests simply on the fact that white men are the creators of civilization (the present civilization, which is the only one that matters; all previous civilizations are simply "contributions" to our own) and are therefore civilization's guardians and defenders. Thus it was impossible for Americans to accept the black man as one of themselves, for to do so was to jeopardize their status as white men. But not so to accept him was to deny his human reality, his human weight and complexity, and the strain of denying the overwhelmingly undeniable forced Americans into rationalizations so fantastic that they approached the pathological.

At the root of the American Negro problem is the necessity of the American white man to find a way of living with the Negro in order to be able to live with himself. And the history of this problem can be reduced to the means used by Americans—lynch law and law, segregation and legal acceptance, terrorization and concession—either to come to terms with this necessity, or to find a way around it, or (most usually) to find a way of doing both these things at once. The resulting spectacle, at once foolish and dreadful, led someone to make the quite accurate observation that "the Negro-in-America is a form of insanity which overtakes white men."

In this long battle, a battle by no means finished, the unforeseeable effects of which will be felt by many future generations, the white man's motive was the protection of his identity; the black man was motivated by the need to establish an identity. And despite the terrorization which the Negro in America endured and endures sporadically until today, despite the cruel and totally inescapable ambivalence of his status in his country, the battle for his identity has long ago been won. He is not a visitor to the West, but a citizen there, an American; as American as the Americans who despise him, the Americans who fear him, the Americans who love him— the Americans who became less than themselves, or rose to be greater than themselves by virtue of the fact that the challenge he represented was inescapable. He is perhaps the only black man in the world whose relationship to white men is more terrible, more subtle, and more meaningful than the relationship of bitter possessed to uncertain possessor. His survival depended, and his development depends, on his ability to turn his peculiar status in the Western world to his own advantage and, it may be, to the very great advantage of that world. It remains for him to fashion out of his experience that which will give him sustenance, and a voice.

The cathedral at Chartres, I have said, says something to the people of this village which it cannot say to me; but it is important to understand that this cathedral says something to me which it cannot say to them. Perhaps they are struck by the power of the spires, the glory of the windows; but they have known God, after all, longer than I have known him, and in a different way, and I am terrified by the slippery bottomless well to be found in the crypt, down which heretics were hurled to death, and by the obscene, inescapable gargoyles jutting out of the stone and seeming to say that God and the devil can never be divorced. I doubt that the villagers think of the devil when they face a cathedral because they have never been identified with the devil. But I must accept the status which myth, if nothing else, gives me in the West before I can hope to change the myth.

Yet, if the American Negro has arrived at his identity by virtue of the absoluteness of his estrangement from his past, American white men still nourish the illusion that there is some means of recovering the European innocence, of returning to a state in which black men do not exist. This is one of the greatest errors Americans can make. The identity they fought so hard to protect has, by virtue of that battle, undergone a change: Americans are as unlike any other white people in the world as it is possible to be. I do not think, for example, that it is too much to suggest that the American vision of the world—which allows so little reality, generally speaking, for any of the darker forces in human life, which tends until today to paint moral issues in glaring black and white—owes a great deal to the battle waged by Americans to maintain between themselves and black men a human separation which could not be bridged. It is only now beginning to be borne in on us—very faintly, it must be admitted, very slowly, and very much against our will—that this vision of the world is dangerously inaccurate, and perfectly useless. For it protects our moral high-mindedness at the terrible expense of weakening our grasp of reality. People who shut their eyes to reality simply invite their own destruction, and anyone who insists on remaining in a state of innocence long after that innocence is dead turns himself into a monster.

The time has come to realize that the interracial drama acted out on the American continent has not only created a new black man, it has created a new white man, too. No road whatever will lead Americans back to the simplicity of this European village where white men still have the luxury of looking on me as a stranger. I am not, really, a stranger any longer for any American alive. One of the things that distinguishes Americans from other people is that no other people has ever been so deeply involved in the lives of black men, and vice versa. This fact faced, with all its implications, it can be seen that the history of the American Negro problem is not merely shameful, it is also something of an achievement. For even when the worst has been said, it must also be added that the perpetual challenge posed by this problem was always, somehow, perpetually met. It is precisely this black-white experience which may prove of indispensable value to us in the world we face today. This world is white no longer, and it will never be white again.

# DAYS WITH SOLEDAD
# IN NEW YORK

## Oscar Lewis

Rosa hurried along Eagle Avenue toward Soledad's house. It was almost nine o'clock and Soledad and her daughters had to be at the Public Health unit by nine-thirty. Rosa had agreed to go along as interpreter. Soledad lived in a four-story tenement in a Puerto Rican neighborhood in the Bronx. Her narrow, ground-floor railroad apartment consisted of a small living room in the front, a kitchen and bathroom in the rear, and two windowless bedrooms between. The living-room window, close to the street, was covered by a screen of heavy chicken wire. In the summertime when the window was kept open and the Venetian blind pulled up, passers-by could easily look into the apartment and Soledad could carry on conversations with her friends outside.

This April morning the blinds were closed. Rosa entered the tenement hallway, went directly to the kitchen door in the back, and knocked. Soledad's sister-in-law, Flora, a short, thin, pleasant-faced woman of about thirty, opened the door. "Good morning, Rosa," she said with a smile. "I'm coming along too, to see if they'll take the stitches out of Gabi's head." Gabriel, Felícita's seven-year-old son, had come from Puerto Rico a few days earlier to stay with his uncle Simplicio and Flora. The day he left Puerto Rico, Gabriel had fallen and cut his head, and the cut had required nine stitches.

Rosa sat down at the kitchen table. Although the kitchen was clean and cheerful-looking, she saw several cockroaches crawling on the walls and over the sink. On one side of the crowded room were a china cabinet, a large four-burner gas stove, and a table and three chairs. On the outer wall a combination sink and washtub was partially blocked by the refrigerator, making the washtub inaccessible. Soledad often washed clothes in the bathtub. The kitchen walls had just been painted a bright green. They were decorated with religious calendars, plastic flowers, a fancy match holder, a plaster plaque of brightly colored fruit, and a new set of aluminum pans. Fresh red-and-white curtains hung at the window. The linoleum, although worn, was scrubbed clean. On a shelf above the kitchen door stood an improvised altar for Saint Expedito, who brings luck to gamblers. On the altar, before a small straw cross, Soledad kept as an offering a glass of rum, cigarettes, coins, dice, playing cards, and bread and butter.

"Hello, Rosa, I'm almost ready," Soledad called from the far bedroom. "Just wait till I get shoes on these little bitches."

In a few minutes Soledad appeared with her three daughters and her nephew Gabriel. Soledad was an attractive, full-bodied mulatto woman, about five feet four inches in height. She had a broad face with high cheekbones, deep-set dark eyes and a short, slightly flat nose. Her hair, normally brown and kinky, had been straightened and tinted a coppery hue. Today she had it done up in two buns behind her ears.

"Well, let's go or we'll be late and then heaven knows when we'll get out," she said. "Those people fill out forms like the devil."

The three women walked together while the children, dressed in inexpensive though clean clothes and new shoes, skipped on ahead. Catín, Soledad's adopted daughter, was eight and a half years old. She was olive-skinned, with straight brown hair and large brown eyes. Her thin body and plain face had a pinched, sickly look and she walked with a limp because one leg was shorter than the other. Six-year-old Sarita, the prettiest of the sisters, was a slender, small-boned child, with blue eyes, white skin and abundant light-brown hair. Toya, who was only four years old but looked older and larger than Sarita, was an attractive, dark-skinned, robust child with a round face, bright black eyes and tightly curled black hair. Gabriel, also dark-skinned, with closely cropped black kinky hair and several front teeth missing, was dressed in a new gray wool suit, red plaid vest, white shirt and black shoes—the outfit he had worn on the plane.

"Oh, my God, I wonder what they'll tell me at the Health Bureau," Soledad said as they walked along. "If Catín is sick, I'm going to write my mother such a letter! She was the one in charge and she abandoned the child to go off with that *teenager*. She loves her husband more than her grandchild. But she'd better look out. If you harm a child you pay dearly for it. I wonder what came over my mother to take up with that *teenager*."

"He works, doesn't he?" Flora answered. "He gives her what she needs. That's what counts. Nothing else matters. Well, who am I to talk? When I first saw Simplicio he was a tiny boy, and now he's my husband."

"But, Flora, how can you compare your marriage to my mother's?"

Soledad protested. "The difference between you and Simplicio isn't so great."

"Well, everyone to his own taste," Flora replied. "Isn't that right?"

"Yes, everyone to his taste, but wait until that kid grows up," Soledad said cynically. "He's bound to meet some young girl and then a kick in the ass is all Nanda can expect. He'll get rid of her. As for me, I've always said I like old men. When I break up with a man, I don't want him to be able to call me 'old hag.' Let him look at himself and see who's younger."

They arrived at the Public Health unit and were told by the receptionist to take the elevator to the second floor.

"Oh, no, I won't go up in that!" Soledad protested. "Suppose it gets stuck between floors? I'm always dreaming that I'm in an elevator that keeps going up and down, up and down. Or else up and up without stopping."

"Oh, come on, Soledad!" Flora said, and they all crowded into the elevator.

They were given turn number 7 and sat down to wait. "*Ay,* I don't like to come to the doctor," Soledad said. "I wonder why I get so scared?"

To pass the time, Soledad began to tease Gabi. "What's the matter with you? You're trembling."

"I was born trembly," the boy answered.

"Ah, you're scared," Soledad said, taking his hands in hers. "That must mean you ran away from something in Puerto Rico. You've got a woman down there, haven't you? Whose wife did you steal, eh?"

"I didn't, Aunt Soledad, really I didn't do anything."

"Yes, you must have seduced some girl. We'll have to send you back to Puerto Rico."

"I won't go back," the boy said, looking worried. "I was hungry there, and everybody beat me, Cruz, Fela, and all of them. I won't go back."

"All right, you can stay here and be my pimp," Soledad said. "You love me, *papito,* don't you?" And she kissed him.

The boy wiped away the kiss. "I won't. I won't be your pimp."

"Oh, yes, you're going to be my man," Soledad insisted, pressing his little hand on her stomach.

"Don't be so fresh with him," Flora said. "He might begin to get fresh himself."

"Oh, when will we get out of here?" Soledad said impatiently. "I can't bear waiting." She fell silent for a few moments. Then she said, "You know, I made a vow to go on my knees from my house to Saint Peter's church if Catín comes out of this well. I wouldn't stop at the greatest sacrifice for my daughter. If He died nailed to the cross for His children, there's nothing wrong in my going to Saint Peter's on my knees. If I had money I'd have Catín treated by good doctors. I'd give my life for that child."

"Did I tell you what Nanda said when I wrote her that Catín was sick?" Flora asked.

"Yes. How could Nanda say that Catín got sick because I beat her! What wickedness! I never beat that child. If a person got sick from beatings, I'd be dead by now. Nanda gave me enough of those."

Finally Soledad's turn came. A tall Negro woman in a navy-blue uniform handed her paper jackets, saying, "Here, put these on the children." Then she began to fill out a form for Soledad, beginning with her name and address.

"And how many children have you?"

"Four."

"Names?"

Soledad gave the children's names, explaining that her son, Quique, was in Puerto Rico with his father.

"How come this little girl's last name is Alvarado?"

"Because she isn't my own daughter. I adopted her," Soledad answered.

"Well, I'd better put them all down as Ríos," the women said. "What's your husband's name?"

"My husband's dead."

"What did he die of?"

"In an accident." Soledad answered the woman's questions rather sullenly. "What busybodies these people are!" she said in an aside to Rosa. "You'd think I was being jailed for murder."

The attendant asked if Soledad was getting welfare aid. Soledad replied that she was not. "Don't you know you qualify for it?"

"Forget it," Soledad said shortly. "As long as I can work to support my children, I don't want *welfare*. Not the way they treat you."

"Have the children been in contact with anyone who had tuberculosis?" the woman asked.

"Well, yes, with a cousin of mine in Puerto Rico a long time ago. But it was the school doctor who told me to bring the children here." The attendant went out and a doctor came in to give the children the tuberculin test. He then sent them to an adjoining room for chest X-rays, telling them to come back for the results a week later, on Friday.

Before they left the Health Bureau, Soledad spoke to the attendant who had filled out their forms. "Could you take care of my nephew? All he needs is to have these stitches cut."

"No, not here," the woman answered. "You'll have to take him to a hospital for that."

"But we can pay," Soledad said.

"No, we can't do it here," the woman repeated impatiently, waving them out.

"What sons of the great whore they are, all of them! They should have a bomb dropped on them," Soledad exclaimed. "Look," she said when they were outside, "I'm going to cut Gabi's stitches myself. I just know they won't do it at the hospital either. They don't want to take care of him."

Sarita, skipping ahead, stopped in front of a chewing-gum vending machine. "*Mami,* give me a penny," she begged.

"A knife in your back is what you'll get," snapped her mother. "Let's go over to Third Avenue. I have to pawn my ring because I'm flat broke. That stupid husband of mine hasn't sent me a thing. I guess he expects me to live on air."

At the pawnshop Soledad stood admiring her ring while the proprietor waited on other customers.

When it was Soledad's turn, she held out her ring.

"How much do you want for it?" the pawnbroker asked.

"Seven."

"Four."

"All right. Give it to me and let's get it over with." She took the bills and the ticket and put them in her purse. "Let's go to the stationery store and buy some stamps," she said.

Inside the store some small religious pictures caught Soledad's eye. "Say, how much do these cost?"

"Thirty-five cents each."

"I'm going to buy one for Fernanda," she said. "You know, she's writing to me again. It's a miracle. The wings of her heart must have started fluttering." She chose a picture and wrote on the back of it, "Nanda, I am sending you this Saint Anthony so that he will get you lots of sweethearts. Save him as a keepsake from your daughter Soledad."

Leaving the store, she said to Rosa, "Saint Anthony gets sweethearts for you if you stand him on his head. But he's a bad saint. They say the men you get through him always beat you. I'm so unlucky with men, damn it! There hasn't been one good one except for Tavio, and he died. Good things never last."

They passed a Chinese woman and her two children. "Sainted Virgin, that woman looks like the devil's own mother!" Soledad said. "I wouldn't bear a baby to a Chinaman even if they tied me up. They say Chinese men are good husbands and all that, but they're so ugly!"

"I have to go home and cook Simplicio's dinner," Flora said abruptly. She took Gabriel by the hand and turned to leave.

"Yes, go along and take good care of your husband," Soledad called mockingly after her. Then she said to Rosa, "*Ay,* let's go to the park awhile so the children can get some sun. They're always shut up in the house."

When they reached the park Soledad broke into a run and raced the children to the swings. She picked each one up, set them on the swings and began pushing them. Then, smiling, she stopped Toya's swinging in order to hug the child. "This is *mami's* little girl. *Mami's* little Toya. Come, give me a real lover's kiss on the mouth like in the movies." Toya kissed her mother full on the mouth.

"Ummm, good!" Soledad said, licking her lips.

She went to Sarita, who was in the next swing. "Get down, get down!" Holding the child in her arms, she pulled down her panties and kissed her buttocks. Then she touched the little girl's vagina. "And who does this little kitchen belong to?"

"Don't be so fresh, *mami*," the little girl said, squirming free.

Soledad ran to Catín and hugged and kissed her. "*Ay,* this daughter is almost a young lady already."

"*Mami,* swing me on your lap," Catín said.

Soledad sat down on a swing and took Catín on her lap. As they swung, Soledad looked childishly happy; she laughed aloud like a little girl. After a time Catín slipped from her lap and ran with her sisters to the slides. Soledad began to swing high. When she tired of it she abruptly jumped from the swing and announced, "We're going now."

Outside the house they met Rosalía, an old, stout Negro woman who was a friend and neighbor. She was dressed in black as usual.

"Hello, my darling! How are you?" Soledad called, running up to hug and kiss the woman.

"Keep off, sugar, you aren't my husband," Rosalía said good-naturedly.

"You know you're my darling," Soledad answered as she hurried into the house. She unlocked the kitchen door and went straight to the bathroom. When Rosa and the girls came into the kitchen, they heard her urinating. "I can't hold my urine very long," she said when she came out. "They must have hurt my bladder when they operated on me."

Soledad went to her bedroom and threw herself face down on the big double bed. Because she seemed tired, Rosa tried to keep the girls in the kitchen, but after a few minutes they went to stand quietly beside the bed, looking at their mother with anxious faces. The room was very small and the bedroom set almost completely filled it. Between the bed and the matching dresser there was a space of only sixteen inches, and here the girls lined up. The foot of the bed was so close to the chest of drawers that the two bottom drawers could not be opened more than three inches. There was no closet; clothes were hung from hooks on the wall. Over the book-case headboard, a shelf held several suitcases and cartons. Underneath the shelf behind a short plastic curtain, a bar had been suspended to hold more clothing.

On top of the chest Soledad had arranged a number of religious objects to form an altar. In the center were statuettes of Jesus, the Sacred Heart, Saint Felícita, the Virgin of Carmen, and the dark-faced Saint Martin of

Porres. Around these figures were two candles in candleholders, a vase of artificial flowers, a small crucifix, a paperweight with the figure of Jesus, a gold ceramic incense burner, a bottle of French perfume and three gracefully draped rosaries. On the wall above the chest were eight religious pictures: the Virgin, Saint Martha, Saint Michael Archangel, the African Saint Barbara, the Heart of Jesus, the Child with the Torch, the Three Virtues—Faith, Hope and Charity—and a large Brazilian picture showing the Virgin as the Queen of the Sea who cast down stars that turned to roses.

Two prayer books lay open on the altar, one opened to "Prayers to the Guardian Angels," the other, a spiritist gospel, opened to "Instructions of the Spirits: In Gratitude for Children and Family Bonds." A glass of water to "catch evil spirits" stood next to the books. Each week Soledad poured the old water down the toilet and refilled the glass.

After watching her mother for several minutes, Catín said timidly, "What's the matter, *mami?*" Toya, who often demanded caresses, said, "*Mami,* please give me a kiss."

Soledad opened her eyes and said crossly, "Oh, go away and leave me alone! I'm all right." Seeing Rosa, she sat up and added, "I'll have to go to the old man. No matter how I stretch them, four dollars won't be enough for the whole week. Oh, I'm all screwed up!"

Suddenly she gathered the children into her arms. "But look at the treasures I have. Aren't my little girls pretty? There's just one thing missing, and that's my son, my only male child. I gave him my tits until he was five years old. Oh, Rosa, you don't know how much a mother loves her children! Look, want to see how beautiful Quique was when he was a baby?"

She got out a photograph album from a suitcase under the bed. Leafing through the album, she showed Rosa pictures of Quique at different ages. Then she came to some pictures of Octavio, her dead husband. In one photograph which had the words "My Heart Is Yours" inscribed on it, he was shown leaning against a counter. In another he and Soledad were together, she in a maternity dress and he proudly touching her stomach. On other pages Octavio's death was recorded. One showed his coffin covered with flowers; there were other photos of the grave. Soledad began to cry, silently at first. She shut the album, flung herself on the bed and sobbed, not caring who heard her. The children, who had wandered off to play, came running in.

"*Mami,* what's the matter? Why are you crying?"

Soledad drew Toya into her arms. "Come here, my little Toya. Where's your *papá?*"

"They killed him. They shot him dead."

"Yes, they did, they shot him dead." Soledad let the child go and turned to Rosa. "I loved that man and I still do," she said. "He was so affectionate, so nice to me. What a thing to happen! He's buried in the cemetery at La Esmeralda. We used to go there to talk and we'd play hide and seek and cowboys and Indians. He'd pretend to shoot me and I'd drop on the ground and then he'd pick me up."

Soledad fell silent for a moment, then stood up and freshened her makeup before the mirror. "Come out with me to call El Polaco," she said to Rosa. "I'll see if he asks me to go over. I just have to get hold of some money." The two women went to a telephone in a nearby store. Soledad dialed a number and then said engagingly. "Hello, lover, how are you? . . . Well, I was wondering about you, too. . . . You don't say! But that's no problem because I'll make it go down in no time at all. I'll be right over, *O.K.?* See you, darling."

Soledad hung up, and she and Rosa hurried back to the apartment. "Do me a favor, Rosa, and stay with the children? I'll just wash up and leave and come right back with some money." The children asked where she was going and she told them she had to buy something in El Barrio. She reminded Catín to tidy up the house and she warned all the girls that they must behave well. When she was gone, the children went back to playing with her old pocketbooks and shoes.

Rosa began to make the beds, and the three girls helped her. Catín tidied the jumble of cosmetics on Soledad's dresser—the small-sized jars and tubes of creams and pomades, the make-up lotion, hair spray, wave set, deodorant, nail polish, powder and perfumes, almost all of the Avon brand. There were also two large eau de cologne bottles and a small bottle of Lanvin perfume. A cracker tin held hair curlers and bobby pins, and a cardboard box was filled with several lipsticks, pins, jewelry, buttons, combs and odds and ends. There were several paperback books, love stories in Spanish and two in English that a neighbor had given to Soledad.

When the bedrooms were neat, Rosa and the girls washed the breakfast dishes and made lunch. Rosa fried some pork chops and bananas, setting aside enough for Soledad. After lunch Rosa lay down on the bed to rest and the girls crowded around her, hugging her and demanding to be kissed.

Rosa was teaching them the English alphabet when Soledad returned at two o'clock. She had been gone an hour and a half.

She came into the bedroom, gave the children some cookies she had bought and sent them to the kitchen, saying, "Don't come in here until I say so." She lit the two candles and knelt with bowed head in front of the altar for several minutes. She did this whenever she was unfaithful to her husband. As there were no prayers in either of her prayer books for a situation like this, she just remained silent until she felt better. When she left the bedroom to go to the kitchen to eat her lunch, her face was serious but she seemed calm.

"*Mami,* where have you been?" Catín asked.

"Don't ask questions. What a little busybody you are!"

"But what were you doing, *mami?*" Sarita said.

"Nothing. It's none of your business. Run away and play."

When the children had gone to the living room to watch television, Soledad said to Rosa, "Look, I got my fifteen dollars. It only takes a little while, because he comes right away."

Someone knocked on the kitchen door and Soledad opened it to Rosalía. "Hello, my love. You can't live without me, eh? What's new?"

"Oh, go to hell," Rosalía answered.

"Don't say that. I want you to take good care of your you-know-what, because it belongs to me."

"And since when have you become a lesbian, you shameless hussy?" Rosalía said, laughing. "Aren't you ashamed of yourself? How's your husband?"

"With a stiff one, I suppose, since I'm not there to give him anything."

"Have some respect, dirty mouth!"

"*Ay,* Rosalía, that's the way we talk in La Esmeralda. You talk even worse, because you're from Loíza Aldea, where people aren't civilized yet."

"Now look," Rosalía said, "I came here forty years ago. I've never been back to Puerto Rico and I never will go back. Not even when I die. I want to be buried here where it's cold so the worms won't eat me."

"I want to die in my own country. Me buried here? Oh no!"

"Do you know how much it costs to ship a body to Puerto Rico? About fifteen hundred dollars."

"Don't be a damn fool," Soledad said. "Do you think I'd let myself die here? What an idea! The minute I feel even a little bit sick, I'll fly back to Puerto Rico."

"I don't even remember what Puerto Rico's like. To tell you the truth, I don't even like to eat green bananas."

"Why, you shameless creature! You don't deserve to live. To think that a countrywoman from Loíza Aldea shouldn't like green bananas! There's nothing better than a dish of fresh-cut green bananas boiled with codfish. Oh, well, let's skip it. Want some coffee? Some soup? A banana?"

"No, no."

"Well then, eat—if that's what you want. Toya, come over here. Don't you want to make *caca?* Rosalía feels like eating some—"

"All kidding aside, I don't like to eat in anybody else's house," Rosalía said. "Not since I visited some people and found a gob of phlegm in the kitchen sink. I haven't eaten outside my own house since then."

"*Ave María!* Don't be so finicky. Water cleans anything."

"Oh no, I can't stand dirty habits, like people brushing their teeth over the kitchen sink. Listen, that girl of yours, the dark one, is getting fresh. She won't pay any attention to me any more."

"Tell Benedicto," Soledad said indifferently. "He's the one that spoils her. If I spank Toya, Benedicto practically eats me alive. He'd let her throw the doors out of the windows if she wanted to. But if Sarita, the white one, does anything at all, he spanks her right away. Do you think it's because of Toya's color that he likes her better? She's dark like him."

"That's what it is. You see, a white person sooner or later is going to call a Negro '*nigger.*' You mark my words. A white person will always throw your color up to you. Well, I have to go now. I'm waiting for my son and he's due to show up any minute."

"Oh, drop it, Rosalía," Soledad said. "Do you think that boy is still a baby? He must be twenty-eight years old. He's off some place with a girl. Or do you put out for him yourself?"

"Damn, it, Soledad, have a little more respect for my son!" Rosalía said in real annoyance. "I love that boy like he was God, girl."

"All right, you love him like God, *chica,* but for God's sake, let loose of him," Soledad answered.

A few minutes after Rosalía had gone there was another knock on the door, and Soledad opened it this time to Elfredo, a white-skinned, baby-faced, dark-haired young man. He was a numbers runner and Soledad bought a number from him almost every day. Today she asked for three numbers, paying fifteen cents each.

After she had finished her business with Elfredo, Soledad suggested that they go into the living room. She sent the children back to the kitchen and sat down with Elfredo on a bulky black sofa in front of the window. Rosa took a large blue chair in the opposite corner. This chair stood in front of the living-room door, which Soledad kept permanently locked. An orange chair in another corner was occupied by a life-sized doll dressed in black and yellow tulle. A false fireplace covered almost the entire left-hand wall; on the mantel was a profusion of photographs, ceramic figurines of a lion and a panther, a little boat in a stemmed glass, a set of toy animals and, in the center, an African voodoo doll which Benedicto had brought from Brazil. The plaster doll had two faces, a black one on one side and a brown one on the other. Soledad turned the faces around each week. She had more faith in this doll, she said, than in her two black saints. A coffee table that stood in front of the fireplace held a crocheted doily, a set of glass ashtrays shaped like butterflies, and various inexpensive ceramic objects. End tables holding similar objects stood beside each of the big chairs. On one of the end tables there was also a record player; a stack of records was piled on the shelf beneath. A television set occupied a corner between the coffee table and the sofa. The walls also were decorated with objects, a cheap tapestry of "The Last Supper," artificial flowers, ceramic plaques, small pictures, some tiny straw hats, and two necklaces of multi-colored plastic fruit with bracelets to match. On the window sill, partly hidden by the cretonne drapes, stood a green plant, some artificial flowers in a brightly painted vase, and a ceramic figure of a naked woman sitting on a beer barrel. A washable gray rug covered the small space in the center of the floor.

The television set was still turned on and they all watched a scene in which a young girl was contemplating suicide because her father had been killed for selling stolen goods and she was left alone and penniless.

"Dope! Idiot!" Soledad said, switching off the set impatiently. "How can she think of killing herself? She shouldn't be such a coward. You have to face whatever life brings. Hell, some people shit on themselves over every little thing that happens to them. I say put a good face to bad times. No trouble lasts a hundred years."

Elfredo looked at Soledad admiringly and said, "You know, Soledad, I wouldn't mind getting married to you."

"How can you say such a thing to me? And with all those sweethearts. Really, how can you? I have four children."

"That's nothing. If you love the hen, you love her chicks."

"You know very well that I have a husband."

"Yes, and I know something else, too. I know you aren't happy with him." He moved closer to Soledad on the sofa. "Come on, give me a kiss."

Soledad leaned back to avoid him but he kissed her on her closed lips anyway.

"I have to go now," he said. "It's getting late and I have to turn in these numbers. But I'll be back tomorrow and I'll be much hotter then."

"It's time for me to leave too," Rosa said. "Will you walk me to the bus, Elfredo?"

They went through the two darkened bedrooms. There was a strong stench of urine from the children's bed. "Those girls are real pissers," Soledad said. "I'll have to change their sheet tomorrow."

In the kitchen, the children were coloring pictures on the floor. Soledad said good-bye to Rosa and Elfredo and double-locked the door behind them.

# NIGHTMARE

## Malcolm X

When my mother was pregnant with me, she told me later, a party of hooded Ku Klux Klan riders galloped up to our home in Omaha, Nebraska, one night. Surrounding the house, brandishing their shotguns and rifles, they shouted for my father to come out. My mother went to the front door and opened it. Standing where they could see her pregnant condition, she told them that she was alone with her three small children, and that my father was away, preaching, in Milwaukee. The Klansmen shouted threats and warnings at her that we had better get out of town because "the good Christian white people" were not going to stand for my father's "spreading trouble" among the "good" Negroes of Omaha with the "back to Africa" preachings of Marcus Garvey.

My father, the Reverend Earl Little, was a Baptist minister, a dedicated organizer for Marcus Aurelius Garvey's U.N.I.A. (Universal Negro Improvement Association). With the help of such disciples as my father, Garvey, from his headquarters in New York City's Harlem, was raising the banner of black-race purity and exhorting the Negro masses to return to their ancestral African homeland—a cause which had made Garvey the most controversial black man on earth.

Still shouting threats, the Klansmen finally spurred their horses and galloped around the house, shattering every window pane with their gun butts. Then they rode off into the night, their torches flaring, as suddenly as they had come.

My father was enraged when he returned. He decided to wait until I was born—which would be soon—and then the family would move. I am not sure why he made this decision, for he was not a frightened Negro, as most then were, and many still are today. My father was a big, six-foot-four, very black man. He had only one eye. How he had lost the other one I have never known. He was from Reynolds, Georgia, where he had left school after the third or maybe fourth grade. He believed, as did Marcus Garvey, that freedom, independence and self-respect could never be achieved by the Negro in America, and that therefore the Negro should leave America to the white man and return to his African land of origin. Among the reasons my father had decided to risk and dedicate his life to help disseminate this philosophy among his people was that he had seen four of his six brothers die by violence, three of them killed by white men, including one by lynching. What my father could not know then was that of the remaining three, including himself, only one, my Uncle Jim, would die in bed, of natural causes. Northern white police were later to shoot my Uncle Oscar. And my father was finally himself to die by the white man's hands.

It has always been my belief that I, too, will die by violence. I have done all that I can to be prepared.

I was my father's seventh child. He had three children by a previous marriage—Ella, Earl, and Mary, who lived in Boston. He had met and married my mother in Philadelphia, where their first child, my oldest full brother, Wilfred, was born. They moved from Philadelphia to Omaha, where Hilda and then Philbert were born.

I was next in line. My mother was twenty-eight when I was born on May 19, 1925, in an Omaha hospital. Then we moved to Milwaukee, where Reginald was born. From infancy, he had some kind of hernia condition which was to handicap him physically for the rest of his life.

Louise Little, my mother, who was born in Grenada, in the British West Indies, looked like a white woman. Her father *was* white. She had straight black hair, and her accent did not sound like a Negro's. Of this white father of hers, I know nothing except her shame about it. I remember hearing her say she was glad that she had never seen him. It was, of course, because of him that I got my reddish-brown "mariny" color of skin, and my hair of the same color. I was the lightest child in our family. (Out in the world later on, in Boston and New York, I was among the millions of Negroes who were insane enough to feel that it was some kind of status symbol to be light-complexioned—that one was actually fortunate to be born thus. But, still later, I learned to hate every drop of that white rapist's blood that is in me.)

Our family stayed only briefly in Milwaukee, for my father wanted to find a place where he could raise our own food and perhaps build a business. The teaching of Marcus Garvey stressed becoming independent of the white man. We went next, for some reason, to Lansing, Michigan. My father bought a house and soon, as had been his pattern, he was doing freelance Christian preaching in local Negro Baptist churches, and during the week he was roaming about spreading word of Marcus Garvey.

He had begun to lay away savings for the store he had always wanted to own when, as always, some stupid local Uncle Tom Negroes began to funnel stories about his revolutionary beliefs to the local white people. This time, the get-out-of-town threats came from a local hate society called The Black Legion. They wore black robes instead of white. Soon, nearly everywhere my father went, Black Legionnaires were reviling him as an "uppity nigger" for wanting to own a store, for living outside the Lansing Negro district, for spreading unrest and dissension among "the good niggers."

As in Omaha, my mother was pregnant again, this time with my youngest sister. Shortly after Yvonne was born came the nightmare night in 1929, my earliest vivid memory. I remember being suddenly snatched awake into a frightening confusion of pistol shots and shouting and smoke and flames. My father had shouted and shot at the two white men who had set the fire and were running away. Our home was burning down around us. We were lunging and bumping and tumbling all over each other trying to escape. My mother, with the baby in her arms, just made it into the yard before the house crashed in, showering sparks. I remember we were outside in the night in our underwear, crying and yelling our heads off. The white police and firemen came and stood around watching as the house burned down to the ground.

My father prevailed on some friends to clothe and house us temporarily; then he moved us into another house on the outskirts of East Lansing. In those days Negroes weren't allowed after dark in East Lansing proper. There's where Michigan State University is located; I related all of this to an audience of students when I spoke there in January, 1963 (and had the first reunion in a long while with my younger brother, Robert, who was there doing postgraduate studies in psychology). I told them how East Lansing harassed us so much that we had to move again, this time two miles out of town, into the country. This was where my father built for us with his own hands a four-room house. This is where I really begin to remember things—this home where I started to grow up.

After the fire, I remember that my father was called in and questioned about a permit for the pistol with which he had shot at the white men who set the fire. I remember that the police were always dropping by our house, shoving things around, "just checking" or "looking for a gun." The pistol they were looking for—which they never found, and for which they wouldn't issue a permit—was sewed up inside a pillow. My father's .22 rifle and his shotgun, though, were right out in the open; everyone had them for hunting birds and rabbits and other game.

After that, my memories are of the friction between my father and mother. They seemed to be nearly always at odds. Sometimes my father would beat her. It might have had something to do with the fact that my mother had a pretty good education. Where she got it I don't know. But an educated woman, I suppose, can't resist the temptation to correct an uneducated man. Every now and then, when she put those smooth words on him, he would grab her.

My father was also belligerent toward all of the children, except me. The older ones he would beat almost savagely if they broke any of his rules—and he had so many rules it was hard to know them all. Nearly all my whippings came from my mother. I've thought a lot about why. I actually believe that as anti-white as my father was, he was subconsciously so afflicted with the white man's brainwashing of Negroes that he inclined to favor the light ones, and I was his lightest child. Most Negro parents in those days would almost instinctively treat any lighter children better than they did the darker ones. It came directly from the slavery tradition that the "mulatto," because he was visibly nearer to white, was therefore "better."

My two other images of my father are both outside the home. One was his role as a Baptist preacher. He never pastored in any regular church of his own; he was always a "visiting preacher." I remember especially his favorite sermon: "That little *black* train is a-comin' . . . an' you better get all your business right!" I guess this also fit his association with the back-to-Africa movement, with Marcus Garvey's "Black Train Homeward." My brother Philbert, the one just older than me, loved church, but it confused and amazed me. I would sit goggle-eyed at my father jumping and shouting as he preached, with the congregation jumping and shouting behind him, their souls and bodies devoted to singing and praying. Even at that young age, I just couldn't believe in the Christian concept of Jesus as someone divine. And no religious person, until I was a man in my twenties —and then in prison—could tell me anything. I had very little respect for most people who represented religion.

It was in his role as a preacher that my father had most contact with the Negroes of Lansing. Believe me when I tell you that those Negroes were in bad shape then. They are still in bad shape—though in a different way. By that I mean that I don't know a town with a higher percentage of complacent and misguided so-called "middle-class" Negroes—the typical status-symbol-oriented, integration-seeking type of Negroes. Just recently, I was standing in a lobby at the United Nations talking with an African ambassador and his wife, when a Negro came up to me and said, "You know me?" I was a little embarrassed because I thought he was someone I should remember. It turned out that he was one of those bragging, self-satisfied, "middle-class" Lansing Negroes. I wasn't ingratiated. He was the type who would never have been associated with Africa, until the fad of having African friends became a status-symbol for "middle-class" Negroes.

Back when I was growing up, the "successful" Lansing Negroes were such as waiters and bootblacks. To be a janitor at some downtown store was to be highly respected. The real "elite," the "big shots," the "voices of the race," were the waiters at the Lansing Country Club and the shoeshine boys at the state capitol. The only Negroes who really had any money were the ones in the numbers racket, or who ran the gambling houses, or who in some other way lived parasitically off the poorest ones, who were the masses. No Negroes were hired then by Lansing's big Oldsmobile plant, or the Reo plant. (Do you remember the Reo? It was manufactured in Lansing, and R. E. Olds, the man after whom it was named, also lived in Lansing. When the war came along, they hired some Negro janitors.) The bulk of the Negroes were either on Welfare, or W.P.A., or they starved.

The day was to come when our family was so poor that we would eat the hole out of a doughnut; but at that time we were much better off than most town Negroes. The reason was we raised much of our own food out there in the country where we were. We were much better off than the town Negroes who would shout, as my father preached, for the pie-in-the-sky and their heaven in the hereafter while the white man had his here on earth.

I knew that the collections my father got for his preaching were mainly what fed and clothed us, and he also did other odd jobs, but still the image of him that made me proudest was his crusading and militant campaigning with the words of Marcus Garvey. As young as I was then, I knew from what I overheard that my father was saying something that made him a "tough" man. I remember an old lady, grinning and saying to my father, "You're scaring these white folks to death!"

One of the reasons I've always felt that my father favored me was that to the best of my remembrance, it was only me that he sometimes took with him to the Garvey U.N.I.A. meetings which he held quietly in different people's homes. There were never more than a few people at any one time —twenty at most. But that was a lot, packed into someone's living room. I noticed how differently they all acted, although sometimes they were the same people who jumped and shouted in church. But in these meetings both they and my father were more intense, more intelligent and down to earth. It made me feel the same way.

I can remember hearing of "Adam driven out of the garden into the caves of Europe," "Africa for the Africans," "Ethiopians, Awake!" And my father would talk about how it would not be much longer before Africa would be completely run by Negroes—"by black men," was the phrase he always used. "No one knows when the hour of Africa's redemption cometh. It is in the wind. It is coming. One day, like a storm, it will be here."

I remember seeing the big, shiny photographs of Marcus Garvey that were passed from hand to hand. My father had a big envelope of them that he always took to these meetings. The pictures showed what seemed to me millions of Negroes thronged in parade behind Garvey riding in a fine car, a big black man dressed in a dazzling uniform with gold braid on it, and he was wearing a thrilling hat with tall plumes. I remember hearing that he had black followers not only in the United States but all around the world, and I remember how the meetings always closed with my father saying, several times, and the people chanting after him, "Up, you mighty race, you can accomplish what you will!"

I have never understood why, after hearing as much as I did of these kinds of things, I somehow never thought, then, of the black people in Africa. My image of Africa, at that time, was of naked savages, cannibals, monkeys and tigers and steaming jungles.

My father would drive in his old black touring car, sometimes taking me, to meeting places all around the Lansing area. I remember one daytime meeting (most were at night) in the town of Owosso, forty miles from Lansing, which the Negroes called "White City." (Owosso's greatest claim to fame is that it is the home town of Thomas E. Dewey.) As in East Lansing, no Negroes were allowed on the streets there after dark—hence the daytime meeting. In point of fact, in those days lots of Michigan towns were like that. Every town had a few "home" Negroes who lived there. Sometimes it would be just one family, as in the nearby county seat, Mason, which had a single Negro family named Lyons. Mr. Lyons had been a famous football star at Mason High School, was highly thought of in Mason, and consequently he now worked around that town in menial jobs.

My mother at this time seemed to be always working—cooking, washing, ironing, cleaning, and fussing over us eight children. And she was usually either arguing with or not speaking to my father. One cause of friction was that she had strong ideas about what she wouldn't eat—and didn't want *us* to eat—including pork and rabbit, both of which my father loved dearly. He was a real Georgia Negro, and he believed in eating plenty of what we in Harlem today call "soul food."

I've said that my mother was the one who whipped me—at least she did whenever she wasn't ashamed to let the neighbors think she was killing me. For if she even acted as though she was about to raise her hand to me, I would open my mouth and let the world know about it. If anybody was passing by out on the road, she would either change her mind or just give me a few licks.

Thinking about it now, I feel definitely that just as my father favored me for being lighter than the other children, my mother gave me more hell for the same reason. She was very light herself but she favored the ones who were darker. Wilfred, I know, was particularly her angel. I remember that she would tell me to get out of the house and "Let the sun shine on you so you can get some color." She went out of her way never to let me become afflicted with a sense of color-superiority. I am sure that she treated me this way partly because of how she came to be light herself.

I learned early that crying out in protest could accomplish things. My older brothers and sister had started to school when, sometimes, they would come in and ask for a buttered biscuit or something and my mother, impatiently, would tell them no. But I would cry out and make a fuss until I got what I wanted. I remember well how my mother asked me why I couldn't be a nice boy like Wilfred; but I would think to myself that Wilfred, for being so nice and quiet, often stayed hungry. So early in life, I had learned that if you want something, you had better make some noise.

Not only did we have our big garden, but we raised chickens. My father would buy some baby chicks and my mother would raise them. We all loved chicken. That was one dish there was no argument with my father about. One thing in particular that I remember made me feel grateful toward my mother was that one day I went and asked her for my own garden, and she did let me have my own little plot. I loved it and took care of it well. I loved especially to grow peas. I was proud when we had them on our table. I would pull out the grass in my garden by hand when the first little blades came up. I would patrol the rows on my hands and knees for any worms and bugs, and I would kill and bury them. And sometimes when I had everything straight and clean for my things to grow, I would lie down on my back between two rows, and I would gaze up in the blue sky at the clouds moving and think all kinds of things.

At five, I, too, began to go to school, leaving home in the morning along with Wilfred, Hilda, and Philbert. It was the Pleasant Grove School that went from kindergarten through the eighth grade. It was two miles outside the city limits, and I guess there was no problem about our attending because we were the only Negroes in the area. In those days white people in the North usually would "adopt" just a few Negroes; they didn't see them as any threat. The white kids didn't make any great thing about us, either. They called us "nigger" and "darkie" and "Rastus" so much that we thought those were our natural names. But they didn't think of it as an insult; it was just the way they thought about us.

One afternoon in 1931 when Wilfred, Hilda, Philbert, and I came home, my mother and father were having one of their arguments. There had lately been a lot of tension around the house because of Black Legion threats. Anyway, my father had taken one of the rabbits which we were raising, and ordered my mother to cook it. We raised rabbits, but sold them to whites. My father had taken a rabbit from the rabbit pen. He had pulled off the rabbit's head. He was so strong, he needed no knife to behead chickens or rabbits. With one twist of his big black hands he simply twisted off the head and threw the bleeding-necked thing back at my mother's feet.

My mother was crying. She started to skin the rabbit, preparatory to cooking it. But my father was so angry he slammed on out of the front door and started walking up the road toward town.

It was then that my mother had this vision. She had always been a strange woman in this sense, and had always had a strong intuition of things about to happen. And most of her children are the same way, I think. When something is about to happen, I can feel something, sense something. I never have known something to happen that has caught me completely off guard—except once. And that was when, years later, I discovered facts I couldn't believe about a man who, up until that discovery, I would gladly have given my life for.

My father was well up the road when my mother ran screaming out onto the porch. *"Early! Early!"* She screamed his name. She clutched up her apron in one hand, and ran down across the yard and into the road. My father turned around. He saw her. For some reason, considering how angry he had been when he left, he waved at her. But he kept on going.

She told me later, my mother did, that she had a vision of my father's end. All the rest of the afternoon, she was not herself, crying and nervous and upset. She finished cooking the rabbit and put the whole thing in the warmer part of the black stove. When my father was not back home by our bedtime, my mother hugged and clutched us, and we felt strange, not knowing what to do, because she had never acted like that.

I remember waking up to the sound of my mother's screaming again. When I scrambled out, I saw the police in the living room; they were trying to calm her down. She had snatched on her clothes to go with them. And all of us children who were staring knew without anyone having to say it that something terrible had happened to our father.

My mother was taken by the police to the hospital, and to a room where a sheet was over my father in a bed, and she wouldn't look, she was afraid to look. Probably it was wise that she didn't. My father's skull, on one side, was crushed in, I was told later. Negroes in Lansing have always whispered that he was attacked, and then laid across some tracks for a streetcar to run over him. His body was cut almost in half.

He lived two and a half hours in that condition. Negroes then were stronger than they are now, especially Georgia Negroes. Negroes born in Georgia had to be strong simply to survive.

It was morning when we children at home got the word that he was dead. I was six. I can remember a vague commotion, the house filled up with people crying, saying bitterly that the white Black Legion had finally gotten him. My mother was hysterical. In the bedroom, women were holding smelling salts under her nose. She was still hysterical at the funeral.

I don't have a very clear memory of the funeral, either. Oddly, the main thing I remember is that it wasn't in a church, and that surprised me, since my father was a preacher, and I had been where he preached people's funerals in churches. But his was in a funeral home.

And I remember that during the service a big black fly came down and landed on my father's face, and Wilfred sprang up from his chair and he shooed the fly away, and he came groping back to his chair—there were folding chairs for us to sit on—and the tears were streaming down his face. When we went by the casket, I remember that I thought that it looked as if my father's strong black face had been dusted with flour, and I wished they hadn't put on such a lot of it.

Back in the big four-room house, there were many visitors for another week or so. They were good friends of the family, such as the Lyons from Mason, twelve miles away, and the Walkers, McGuires, Liscoes, the Greens, Randolphs, and the Turners, and others from Lansing, and a lot of people from other towns, whom I had seen at the Garvey meetings.

We children adjusted more easily than our mother did. We couldn't see, as clearly as she did, the trials that lay ahead. As the visitors tapered off, she became very concerned about collecting the two insurance policies that my father had always been proud he carried. He had always said that families should be protected in case of death. One policy apparently paid off without any problem—the smaller one. I don't know the amount of it. I would imagine it was not more than a thousand dollars, and maybe half of that.

But after that money came, and my mother had paid out a lot of it for the funeral and expenses, she began going into town and returning very upset. The company that had issued the bigger policy was balking at paying off. They were claiming that my father had committed suicide. Visitors came again, and there was bitter talk about white people: how could my father bash himself in the head, then get down across the streetcar tracks to be run over?

So there we were. My mother was thirty-four years old now, with no husband, no provider or protector to take care of her eight children. But some kind of a family routine got going again. And for as long as the first insurance money lasted, we did all right.

Wilfred, who was a pretty stable fellow, began to act older than his age. I think he had the sense to see, when the rest of us didn't, what was in the wind for us. He quietly quit school and went to town in search of work. He took any kind of job he could find and he would come home, dog-tired, in the evenings, and give whatever he had made to my mother.

Hilda, who always had been quiet, too, attended to the babies. Philbert and I didn't contribute anything. We just fought all the time—each other at home, and then at school we would team up and fight white kids. Sometimes the fights would be racial in nature, but they might be about anything.

Reginald came under my wing. Since he had grown out of the toddling stage, he and I had become very close. I suppose I enjoyed the fact that he was the little one, under me, who looked up to me.

My mother began to buy on credit. My father had always been very strongly against credit. "Credit is the first step into debt and back into slavery," he had always said. And then she went to work herself. She would go into Lansing and find different jobs—in housework, or sewing—for white people. They didn't realize, usually, that she was a Negro. A lot of white people around there didn't want Negroes in their houses.

She would do fine until in some way or other it got to people who she was, whose widow she was. And then she would be let go. I remember how she used to come home crying, but trying to hide it, because she had lost a job that she needed so much.

Once when one of us—I cannot remember which—had to go for something to where she was working, and the people saw us, and realized she was actually a Negro, she was fired on the spot, and she came home crying, this time not hiding it.

When the state Welfare people began coming to our house, we would come from school sometimes and find them talking with our mother, asking a thousand questions. They acted and looked at her, and at us, and around in our house, in a way that had about it the feeling—at least for me—that we were not people. In their eyesight we were just *things,* that was all.

My mother began to receive two checks—a Welfare check and, I believe, a widow's pension. The checks helped. But they weren't enough, as many of us as there were. When they came, about the first of the month, one always was already owed in full, if not more, to the man at the grocery store. And, after that, the other one didn't last long.

We began to go swiftly downhill. The physical downhill wasn't as quick as the psychological. My mother was, above everything else, a proud woman, and it took its toll on her that she was accepting charity. And her feelings were communicated to us.

She would speak sharply to the man at the grocery store for padding the bill, telling him that she wasn't ignorant, and he didn't like that. She would talk back sharply to the state Welfare people, telling them that she was a grown woman, able to raise her children, that it wasn't necessary for them to keep coming around so much, meddling in our lives. And they didn't like that.

But the monthly Welfare check was their pass. They acted as if they owned us, as if we were their private property. As much as my mother would have liked to, she couldn't keep them out. She would get particularly incensed when they began insisting upon drawing us older children aside, one at a time, out on the porch or somewhere, and asking us questions, or telling us things—against our mother and against each other.

We couldn't understand why, if the state was willing to give us packages of meat, sacks of potatoes and fruit, and cans of all kinds of things, our mother obviously hated to accept. We really couldn't understand. What I later understood was that my mother was making a desperate effort to preserve her pride—and ours.

Pride was just about all we had to preserve, for by 1934, we really began to suffer. This was about the worst depression year, and no one we knew had enough to eat or live on. Some old family friends visited us now and then. At first they brought food. Though it was charity, my mother took it.

Wilfred was working to help. My mother was working, when she could find any kind of job. In Lansing, there was a bakery where, for a nickel, a couple of us children would buy a tall flour sack of day-old bread and cookies, and then walk the two miles back out into the country to our house. Our mother knew, I guess, dozens of ways to cook things with bread and out of bread. Stewed tomatoes with bread, maybe that would be a meal. Something like French toast, if we had any eggs. Bread pudding, sometimes with raisins in it. If we got hold of some hamburger, it came to the table more bread than meat. The cookies that were always in the sack with the bread, we just gobbled down straight.

But there were times when there wasn't even a nickel and we would be so hungry we were dizzy. My mother would boil a big pot of dandelion greens, and we would eat that. I remember that some small-minded neighbor put it out, and children would tease us, that we ate "fried grass." Sometimes, if we were lucky, we would have oatmeal or cornmeal mush three times a day. Or mush in the morning and cornbread at night.

Philbert and I were grown up enough to quit fighting long enough to take the .22 caliber rifle that had been our father's, and shoot rabbits that some white neighbors up or down the road would buy. I know now that they just did it to help us, because they, like everyone, shot their own rabbits. Sometimes, I remember, Philbert and I would take little Reginald along with us. He wasn't very strong, but he was always so proud to be along. We would trap muskrats out in the little creek in back of our house. And we would lie quiet until unsuspecting bullfrogs appeared, and we would spear them, cut off their legs, and sell them for a nickel a pair to people who lived up and down the road. The whites seemed less restricted in their dietary tastes.

Then, about in late 1934, I would guess, something began to happen. Some kind of psychological deterioration hit our family circle and began to eat away our pride. Perhaps it was the constant tangible evidence that we were destitute. We had known other families who had gone on relief. We had known without anyone in our home ever expressing it that we had felt prouder not to be at the depot where the free food was passed out. And, now, we were among them. At school, the "on relief" finger suddenly was pointed at us, too, and sometimes it was said aloud.

It seemed that everything to eat in our house was stamped Not To Be Sold. All Welfare food bore this stamp to keep the recipients from selling it. It's a wonder we didn't come to think of Not To Be Sold as a brand name.

Sometimes, instead of going home from school, I walked the two miles up the road into Lansing. I began drifting from store to store, hanging around outside where things like apples were displayed in boxes and barrels and baskets, and I would watch my chance and steal me a treat. You know what a treat was to me? Anything!

Or I began to drop in about dinnertime at the home of some family that we knew. I knew that they knew exactly why I was there, but they never embarrassed me by letting on. They would invite me to stay for supper, and I would stuff myself.

Especially, I liked to drop in and visit at the Gohannas' home. They were nice, older people, and great churchgoers. I had watched them lead the jumping and shouting when my father preached. They had, living with them—they were raising him—a nephew whom everyone called "Big Boy," and he and I got along fine. Also living with the Gohannas was old Mrs. Adcock, who went with them to church. She was always trying to help anybody she could, visiting anyone she heard was sick, carrying them something. She was the one who, years later, would tell me something that I remembered a long time: "Malcolm, there's one thing I like about you. You're no good, but you don't try to hide it. You are not a hypocrite."

The more I began to stay away from home and visit people and steal from the stores, the more aggressive I became in my inclinations. I never wanted to wait for anything.

I was growing up fast, physically more so than mentally. As I began to be recognized more around the town, I started to become aware of the peculiar attitude of white people toward me. I sensed that it had to do with my father. It was an adult version of what several white children had said at school, in hints, or sometimes in the open, which really expressed what their parents had said—that the Black Legion or the Klan had killed my father, and the insurance company had pulled a fast one in refusing to pay my mother the policy money.

When I began to get caught stealing now and then, the state Welfare people began to focus on me when they came to our house. I can't remember how I first became aware that they were talking of taking me away. What I first remember along that line was my mother raising a storm about being able to bring up her own children. She would whip me for stealing, and I would try to alarm the neighborhood with my yelling. One thing I have always been proud of is that I never raised my hand against my mother.

In the summertime, at night, in addition to all the other things we did, some of us boys would slip out down the road, or across the pastures, and go "cooning" watermelons. White people always associated watermelons with Negroes, and they sometimes called Negroes "coons" among all the other names, and so stealing watermelons became "cooning" them. If white boys were doing it, it implied that they were only acting like Negroes. Whites have always hidden or justified all of the guilts they could by ridiculing or blaming Negroes.

One Halloween night, I remember that a bunch of us were out tipping over those old country outhouses, and one old farmer—I guess he had tipped over enough in his day—had set a trap for us. Always, you sneak up from behind the outhouse, then you gang together and push it, to tip it over. This farmer had taken his outhouse off the hole, and set it just in *front* of the hole. Well, we came sneaking up in single file, in the darkness, and the two white boys in the lead fell down into the outhouse hole neck deep. They smelled so bad it was all we could stand to get them out, and that finished us all for that Halloween. I had just missed falling in myself. The whites were so used to taking the lead, this time it had really gotten them in the hole.

Thus, in various ways, I learned various things. I picked strawberries, and though I can't recall what I got per crate for picking, I remember that after working hard all one day, I wound up with about a dollar, which was a whole lot of money in those times. I was so hungry, I didn't know what to do. I was walking away toward town with visions of buying something good to eat, and this older white boy I knew, Richard Dixon, came up and asked me if I wanted to match nickels. He had plenty of change for my dollar. In about a half hour, he had all the change back, including my dollar, and instead of going to town to buy something, I went home with nothing, and I was bitter. But that was nothing compared to what I felt when I found out later that he had cheated. There is a way that you can catch and hold the nickel and make it come up the way you want. This was my first lesson about gambling: if you see somebody winning all the time, he isn't gambling, he's cheating. Later on in life, if I were continuously losing in any gambling situation, I would watch very closely. It's like the Negro in America seeing the white man win all the time. He's a professional gambler; he has all the cards and the odds stacked on his side, and he has always dealt to our people from the bottom of the deck.

About this time, my mother began to be visited by some Seventh Day Adventists who had moved into a house not too far down the road from us. They would talk to her for hours at a time, and leave booklets and leaflets and magazines for her to read. She read them, and Wilfred, who had started back to school after we had begun to get the relief food supplies, also read a lot. His head was forever in some book.

Before long, my mother spent much time with the Adventists. It's my belief that what mostly influenced her was that they had even more diet restrictions than she always had taught and practiced with us. Like us, they were against eating rabbit and pork; they followed the Mosaic dietary laws. They ate nothing of the flesh without a split hoof, or that didn't chew a cud. We began to go with my mother to the Adventist meetings that were held further out in the country. For us children, I know that the major attraction was the good food they served. But we listened, too. There were a handful of Negroes, from small towns in the area, but I would say that it was ninety-nine percent white people. The Adventists felt that we were living at the end of time, that the world soon was coming to an end. But they were the friendliest white people I had ever seen. In some ways, though, we children noticed, and, when we were back at home, discussed, that they were different from us—such as the lack of enough seasoning in their food, and the different way that white people smelled.

Meanwhile, the state Welfare people kept after my mother. By now, she didn't make it any secret that she hated them, and didn't want them in her house. But they exerted their right to come, and I have many, many times reflected upon how, talking to us children, they began to plant the seeds of division in our minds. They would ask such things as who was smarter than the other. And they would ask me why I was "so different."

I think they felt that getting children into foster homes was a legitimate part of their function, and the result would be less troublesome, however they went about it.

And when my mother fought them, they went after her—first, through me. I was the first target. I stole; that implied that I wasn't being taken care of by my mother.

All of us where mischievous at some time or another, I more so than any of the rest. Philbert and I kept a battle going. And this was just one of a dozen things that kept building up the pressure on my mother.

I'm not sure just how or when the idea was first dropped by the Welfare workers that our mother was losing her mind.

But I can distinctly remember hearing "crazy" applied to her by them when they learned that the Negro farmer who was in the next house down the road from us had offered to give us some butchered pork—a whole pig, maybe even two of them—and she had refused. We all heard them call my mother "crazy" to her face for refusing good meat. It meant nothing to them even when she explained that we had never eaten pork, that it was against her religion as a Seventh Day Adventist.

They were as vicious as vultures. They had no feelings, understanding, compassion, or respect for my mother. They told us, "She's crazy for refusing food." Right then was when our home, our unity, began to disintegrate.

We were having a hard time, and I wasn't helping. But we could have made it, we could have stayed together. As bad as I was, as much trouble and worry as I caused my mother, I loved her.

The state people, we found out, had interviewed the Gohannas family, and the Gohannas' had said that they would take me into their home. My mother threw a fit, though, when she heard that—and the home wreckers took cover for a while.

It was about this time that the large, dark man from Lansing began visiting. I don't remember how or where he and my mother met. It may have been through some mutual friends. I don't remember what the man's profession was. In 1935, in Lansing, Negroes didn't have anything you could call a profession. But the man, big and black, looked something like my father. I can remember his name, but there's no need to mention it. He was a single man, and my mother was a widow only thirty-six years old. The man was independent; naturally she admired that. She was having a hard time disciplining us, and a big man's presence alone would help. And if she had a man to provide, it would send the state people away forever.

We all understood without ever saying much about it. Or at least we had no objection. We took it in stride, even with some amusement among us, that when the man came, our mother would be all dressed up in the best that she had—she still was a good-looking woman—and she would act differently, lighthearted and laughing, as we hadn't seen her act in years.

It went on for about a year, I guess. And then, about 1936, or 1937, the man from Lansing jilted my mother suddenly. He just stopped coming to see her. From what I later understood, he finally backed away from taking on the responsibility of those eight mouths to feed. He was afraid of so many of us. To this day, I can see the trap that Mother was in, saddled with all of us. And I can also understand why he would shun taking on such a tremendous responsibility.

But it was a terrible shock to her. It was the beginning of the end of reality for my mother. When she began to sit around and walk around talking to herself—almost as though she was unaware that we were there—it became increasingly terrifying.

The state people saw her weakening. That was when they began the definite steps to take me away from home. They began to tell me how nice it was going to be at the Gohannas' home, where the Gohannas' and Big Boy and Mrs. Adcock had all said how much they liked me, and would like to have me live with them.

I liked all of them, too. But I didn't want to leave Wilfred. I looked up to and admired my big brother. I didn't want to leave Hilda, who was like my second mother. Or Philbert: even in our fighting, there was a feeling of brotherly union. Or Reginald, especially, who was weak with his hernia condition, and who looked up to me as his big brother who looked out for him, as I looked up to Wilfred. And I had nothing, either, against the babies, Yvonne, Wesley, and Robert.

As my mother talked to herself more and more, she gradually became less responsive to us. And less responsible. The house became less tidy. We began to be more unkempt. And usually, now, Hilda cooked.

We children watched our anchor giving way. It was something terrible that you couldn't get your hands on, yet you couldn't get away from. It was a sensing that something bad was going to happen. We younger ones leaned more and more heavily on the relative strength of Wilfred and Hilda, who were the oldest.

When finally I was sent to the Gohannas' home, at least in a surface way I was glad. I remember that when I left home with the state man, my mother said one thing: "Don't let them feed him any pig."

It was better, in a lot of ways, at the Gohannas'. Big Boy and I shared his room together, and we hit it off nicely. He just wasn't the same as my blood brothers. The Gohannas' were very religious people. Big Boy and I attended church with them. They were sanctified Holy Rollers now. The preachers and congregations jumped even higher and shouted even louder than the Baptists I had known. They sang at the top of their lungs, and swayed back and forth and cried and moaned and beat on tambourines and chanted. It was spooky, with ghosts and spirituals and "ha'nts" seeming to be in the very atmosphere when finally we all came out of the church, going back home.

The Gohannas' and Mrs. Adcock loved to go fishing, and some Saturdays Big Boy and I would go along. I had changed schools now, to Lansings's West Junior High School. It was right in the heart of the Negro community, and a few white kids were there, but Big Boy didn't mix much with any of our schoolmates, and I didn't either. And when we went fishing, neither he nor I liked the idea of just sitting and waiting for the fish to jerk the cork under the water—or make the tight line quiver, when we fished that way. I figured there should be some smarter way to get the fish— though we never discovered what it might be.

Mr. Gohannas was close cronies with some other men who, some Saturdays, would take me and Big Boy with them hunting rabbits. I had my father's .22 caliber rifle; my mother had said it was all right for me to take it with me. The old men had a set rabbit-hunting strategy that they had always used. Usually when a dog jumps a rabbit, and the rabbit gets away, that rabbit will always somehow instinctively run in a circle and return sooner or later past the very spot where he originally was jumped. Well, the old men would just sit and wait in hiding somewhere for the rabbit to come back, then get their shots at him. I got to thinking about it, and finally I thought of a plan. I would separate from them and Big Boy and I would go to a point where I figured that the rabbit, returning, would have to pass me first.

It worked like magic. I began to get three and four rabbits before they got one. The astonishing thing was that none of the old men ever figured out why. They outdid themselves exclaiming what a sure shot I was. I was about twelve, then. All I had done was to improve on their strategy, and it was the beginning of a very important lesson in life—that anytime you find someone more successful than you are, especially when you're both engaged in the same business—you know they're doing something that you aren't.

I would return home to visit fairly often. Sometimes Big Boy and one, or another, or both, of the Gohannas' would go with me—sometimes not. I would be glad when some of them did go, because it made the ordeal easier.

Soon the state people were making plans to take over all of my mother's children. She talked to herself nearly all of the time now, and there was a crowd of new white people entering the picture—always asking questions. They would even visit me at the Gohannas'. They would ask me questions out on the porch, or sitting out in their cars.

Eventually my mother suffered a complete breakdown, and the court orders were finally signed. They took her to the State Mental Hospital at Kalamazoo.

It was seventy-some miles from Lansing, about an hour and a half on the bus. A Judge McClellan in Lansing had authority over me and all of my brothers and sisters. We were "state children," court wards; he had the full say-so over us. A white man in charge of a black man's children! Nothing but legal, modern slavery—however kindly intentioned.

My mother remained in the same hospital at Kalamazoo for about twenty-six years. Later, when I was still growing up in Michigan, I would go to visit her every so often. Nothing that I can imagine could have moved me as deeply as seeing her pitiful state. In 1963, we got my mother out of the hospital, and she now lives there in Lansing with Philbert and his family.

It was so much worse than if it had been a physical sickness, for which a cause might be known, medicine given, a cure effected. Every time I visited her, when finally they led her—a case, a number—back inside from where we had been sitting together, I felt worse.

My last visit, when I knew I would never come to see her again—there —was in 1952. I was twenty-seven. My brother Philbert had told me that on his last visit, she had recognized him somewhat. "In spots," he said.

But she didn't recognize me at all.

She stared at me. She didn't know who I was.

Her mind, when I tried to talk, to reach her, was somewhere else. I asked, "Mama, do you know what day it is?"

She said, staring, "All the people have gone."

I can't describe how I felt. The woman who had brought me into the world, and nursed me, and advised me, and chastised me, and loved me, didn't know me. It was as if I was trying to walk up the side of a hill of feathers. I looked at her. I listened to her "talk." But there was nothing I could do.

I truly believe that if ever a state social agency destroyed a family, it destroyed ours. We wanted and tried to stay together. Our home didn't have to be destroyed. But the Welfare, the courts, and their doctor, gave us the one-two-three punch. And ours was not the only case of this kind.

I knew I wouldn't be back to see my mother again because it could make me a very vicious and dangerous person—knowing how they had looked at us as numbers and as a case in their book, not as human beings. And knowing that my mother in there was a statistic that didn't have to be, that existed because of a society's failure, hypocrisy, greed, and lack of mercy and compassion. Hence I have no mercy or compassion in me for a society that will crush people, and then penalize them for not being able to stand up under the weight.

I have rarely talked to anyone about my mother, for I believe that I am capable of killing a person, without hesitation, who happened to make the wrong kind of remark about my mother. So I purposely don't make any opening for some fool to step into.

Back then when our family was destroyed, in 1937, Wilfred and Hilda were old enough so that the state let them stay on their own in the big four-room house that my father had built. Philbert was placed with another family in Lansing, a Mrs. Hackett, while Reginald and Wesley went to live with a family called Williams, who were friends of my mother's. And Yvonne and Robert went to live with a West Indian family named McGuire.

Separated though we were, all of us maintained fairly close touch around Lansing—in school and out—whenever we could get together. Despite the artificially created separation and distance between us, we still remained very close in our feelings toward each other.

# THE METAMORPHOSIS

## Franz Kafka

I

As Gregor Samsa awoke one morning from uneasy dreams he found himself transformed in his bed into a gigantic insect. He was lying on his hard, as it were armor-plated, back and when he lifted his head a little he could see his dome-like brown belly divided into stiff arched segments on top of which the bed quilt could hardly keep in position and was about to slide off completely. His numerous legs, which were pitifully thin compared to the rest of his bulk, waved helplessly before his eyes.

What has happened to me? he thought. It was no dream. His room, a regular human bedroom, only rather too small, lay quiet between the four familiar walls. Above the table on which a collection of cloth samples was unpacked and spread out—Samsa was a commercial traveler—hung the picture which he had recently cut out of an illustrated magazine and put into a pretty gilt frame. It showed a lady, with a fur cap on and a fur stole, sitting upright and holding out to the spectator a huge fur muff into which the whole of her forearm had vanished!

Gregor's eyes turned next to the window, and the overcast sky—one could hear rain drops beating on the window gutter—made him quite melancholy. What about sleeping a little longer and forgetting all this nonsense, he thought, but it could not be done, for he was accustomed to sleep on his right side and in his present condition he could not turn himself over. However violently he forced himself towards his right side he always rolled on to his back again. He tried it at least a hundred times, shutting his eyes to keep from seeing his struggling legs, and only desisted when he began to feel in his side a faint dull ache he had never experienced before.

Oh God, he thought, what an exhausting job I've picked on! Traveling about day in, day out. It's much more irritating work than doing the actual business in the office, and on top of that there's the trouble of constant traveling, of worrying about train connections, the bed and irregular meals, casual acquaintances that are always new and never become intimate friends. The devil take it all! He felt a slight itching up on his belly; slowly pushed himself on his back nearer to the top of the bed so that he could lift his head more easily; identified the itching place which was surrounded by many small white spots the nature of which he could not understand and made to touch it with a leg, but drew the leg back immediately, for the contact made a cold shiver run through him.

He slid down again into his former position. This getting up early, he thought, makes one quite stupid. A man needs his sleep. Other commercials live like harem women. For instance, when I come back to the hotel of a morning to write up the orders I've got, these others are only sitting down to breakfast. Let me just try that with my chief; I'd be sacked on the spot. Anyhow, that might be quite a good thing for me, who can tell? If I didn't have to hold my hand because of my parents I'd have given notice long ago, I'd have gone to the chief and told him exactly what I think of him. That would knock him endways from his desk! It's a queer way of doing, too, this sitting on high at a desk and talking down to employees, especially when they have to come quite near because the chief is hard of hearing. Well, there's still hope; once I've saved enough money to pay back my parents' debts to him—that should take another five or six years—I'll do it without fail. I'll cut myself completely loose then. For the moment, though, I'd better get up, since my train goes at five.

He looked at the alarm clock ticking on the chest. Heavenly Father! he thought. It was half-past six o'clock and the hands were quietly moving on, it was even past the half-hour, it was getting on toward a quarter to seven. Had the alarm clock not gone off? From the bed one could see that it had been properly set for four o'clock; of course it must have gone off. Yes, but was it possible to sleep quietly through that ear-splitting noise? Well, he had not slept quietly, yet apparently all the more soundly for that. But what was he to do now? The next train went at seven o'clock; to catch that he would need to hurry like mad and his samples weren't even packed up, and he himself wasn't feeling particularly fresh and active. And even if he did catch the train he wouldn't avoid a row with the chief, since the firm's porter would have been waiting for the five o'clock train and would have long since reported his failure to turn up. The porter was a creature of the chief's, spineless and stupid. Well, supposing he were to say he was sick? But that would be most unpleasant and would look suspicious, since during his five years' employment he had not been ill once. The chief himself would be sure to come with the sick-insurance doctor, would reproach his parents with their son's laziness and would cut all excuses short by referring to the insurance doctor, who of course regarded all mankind as perfectly healthy malingerers. And would he be so far wrong on this occasion? Gregor really felt quite well, apart from a drowsiness that was utterly superfluous after such a long sleep, and he was even unusually hungry.

As all this was running through his mind at top speed without his being able to decide to leave his bed—the alarm clock had just struck a quarter to seven—there came a cautious tap at the door behind the head of his bed. "Gregor," said a voice—it was his mother's—"it's a quarter to seven. Hadn't you a train to catch?" That gentle voice! Gregor had a shock as he heard his own voice answering hers, unmistakably his own voice, it was true, but with a persistent horrible twittering squeak behind it like an undertone, that left the words in their clear shape only for the first moment and then rose up reverberating round them to destroy their sense, so that one could not be sure one had heard them rightly. Gregor wanted to answer at length and explain everything, but in the circumstances he confined himself to saying: "Yes, yes, thank you, Mother, I'm getting up now." The wooden door between them must have kept the change in his voice from being noticeable outside, for his mother contented herself with this statement and shuffled away. Yet this brief exchange of words had made the other members of the family aware that Gregor was still in the house, as they had not expected, and at one of the side doors his father was already knocking, gently, yet with his fist. "Gregor, Gregor," he called, "what's the matter with you?" And after a little while he called again in a deeper voice. "Gregor! Gregor!" At the other side door his sister was saying in a low, plaintive tone: "Gregor? Aren't you well? Are you needing anything?" He answered them both at once: "I'm just ready," and did his best to make his voice sound as normal as possible by enunciating the words very clearly and leaving long pauses between them. So his father went back to his breakfast, but his sister whispered: "Gregor, open the door, do." However, he was not thinking of opening the door, and felt thankful for the prudent habit he had acquired in traveling of locking all doors during the night, even at home.

His immediate intention was to get up quietly without being disturbed, to put on his clothes and above all eat his breakfast, and only then to consider what else was to be done, since in bed, he was well aware, his meditations would come to no sensible conclusion. He remembered that often enough in bed he had felt small aches and pains, probably caused by awkward postures, which had proved purely imaginary once he got up, and he looked forward eagerly to seeing this morning's delusions gradually fall away. That the change in his voice was nothing but the precursor of a severe chill, a standing ailment of commercial travelers, he had not the least possible doubt.

To get rid of the quilt was quite easy; he had only to inflate himself a little and it fell off by itself. But the next move was difficult, especially because he was so uncommonly broad. He would have needed arms and hands to hoist himself up; instead he had only the numerous little legs which never stopped waving in all directions and which he could not control in the least. When he tried to bend one of them it was the first to stretch itself straight; and did he succeed at last in making it do what he wanted, all the other legs meanwhile waved the more wildly in a high degree of unpleasant agitation. "But what's the use of lying idle in bed," said Gregor to himself.

He thought that he might get out of bed with the lower part of his body first, but this lower part, which he had not yet seen and of which he could form no clear conception, proved too difficult to move; it shifted so slowly; and when finally, almost wild with annoyance, he gathered his forces together and thrust out recklessly, he had miscalculated the direction and the stinging pain he felt informed him that precisely this lower part of his body was at the moment probably the most sensitive.

So he tried to get the top part of himself out first, and cautiously moved his head towards the edge of the bed. That proved easy enough, and despite its breadth and mass the bulk of his body at last slowly followed the movement of his head. Still, when he finally got his head free over the edge of the bed he felt too scared to go on advancing, for after all if he let himself fall in this way it would take a miracle to keep his head from being injured. And at all costs he must not lose consciousness now, precisely now; he would rather stay in bed.

But when after a repetition of the same efforts he lay in his former position again, sighing, and watched his little legs struggling against each other more wildly than ever, if that were possible, and saw no way of bringing any order into this arbitrary confusion, he told himself again that it was impossible to stay in bed and that the most sensible course was to risk everything for the smallest hope of getting away from it. At the same time he did not forget meanwhile to remind himself that cool reflection, the coolest possible, was much better than desperate resolves. In such moments he focused his eyes as sharply as possible on the window, but, unfortunately, the prospect of the morning fog, which muffled even the other side of the narrow street, brought him little encouragement and comfort. "Seven o'clock already," he said to himself when the alarm clock chimed again, "seven o'clock already and still such a thick fog." And for a little while he lay quiet, breathing lightly, as if perhaps expecting such complete repose to restore all things to their real and normal condition.

But then he said to himself: "Before it strikes a quarter past seven I must be quite out of this bed, without fail. Anyhow, by that time someone will have come from the office to ask for me, since it opens before seven." And he set himself to rocking his whole body at once in a regular rhythm, with the idea of swinging it out of the bed. If he tripped himself out in that way he could keep his head from injury by lifting it at an acute angle when he fell. His back seemed to be hard and was not likely to suffer from a fall on the carpet. His biggest worry was the loud crash he would not be able to help making, which would probably cause anxiety, if not terror, behind all the doors. Still, he must take the risk.

When he was already half out of the bed—the new method was more a game than an effort, for he needed only to hitch himself across by rocking to and fro—it struck him how simple it would be if he could get help. Two strong people—he thought of his father and the servant girl—would be amply sufficient; they would only have to thrust their arms under his convex back, lever him out of the bed, bend down with their burden and then be patient enough to let him turn himself right over on to the floor, where it was to be hoped his legs would then find their proper function. Well, ignoring the fact that the doors were all locked, ought he really to call for help? In spite of his misery he could not suppress a smile at the very idea of it.

He had got so far that he could barely keep his equilibrium when he rocked himself strongly, and he would have to nerve himself very soon for the final decision since in five minutes' time it would be a quarter past seven—when the front door bell rang. "That's someone from the office," he said to himself, and grew almost rigid, while his little legs only jigged about all the faster. For a moment everything stayed quiet. "They're not going to open the door," said Gregor to himself, catching at some kind of irrational hope. But then of course the servant girl went as usual to the door with her heavy tread and opened it. Gregor needed only to hear the first good morning of the visitor to know immediately who it was—the chief clerk himself. What a fate, to be condemned to work for a firm where the smallest omission at once gave rise to the gravest suspicion! Were all employees in a body nothing but scoundrels, was there not among them one single loyal devoted man who, had he wasted only an hour or so of the firm's time in a morning, was so tormented by conscience as to be driven out of his mind and actually incapable of leaving his bed? Wouldn't it really have been sufficient to send an apprentice to inquire—if any inquiry were necessary at all—did the chief clerk himself have to come and thus indicate to the entire family, an innocent family, that this suspicious circumstance could be investigated by no one less versed in affairs than himself? And more through the agitation caused by these reflections than through any act of will Gregor swung himself out of bed with all his strength. There was a loud thump, but it was not really a crash. His fall was broken to some extent by the carpet, his back, too, was less stiff than he thought, and so there was merely a dull thud, not so very startling. Only he had not lifted his head carefully enough and had hit it; he turned it and rubbed it on the carpet in pain and irritation.

"That was something falling down in there," said the chief clerk in the next room to the left. Gregor tried to suppose to himself that something like what had happened to him today might some day happen to the chief clerk; one really could not deny that it was possible. But as if in brusque reply to this supposition the chief clerk took a couple of firm steps in the next-door room and his patent leather boots creaked. From the right-hand room his sister was whispering to inform him of the situation: "Gregor, the chief clerk's here." "I know," muttered Gregor to himself; but he didn't dare to make his voice loud enough for his sister to hear it

"Gregor," said his father now from the left-hand room, "the chief clerk has come and wants to know why you didn't catch the early train. We don't know what to say to him. Besides, he wants to talk to you in person. So open the door, please. He will be good enough to excuse the untidiness of your room." "Good morning, Mr. Samsa," the chief clerk was calling amiably meanwhile. "He's not well," said his mother to the visitor, while his father was still speaking through the door, "he's not well, sir, believe me. What else would make him miss a train! The boy thinks about nothing but his work. It makes me almost cross the way he never goes out in the evenings; he's been here the last eight days and has stayed at home every single evening. He just sits there quietly at the table reading a newspaper or looking through railway timetables. The only amusement he gets is doing fretwork. For instance, he spent two or three evenings cutting out a little picture frame; you would be surprised to see how pretty it is; it's hanging in his room; you'll see it in a minute when Gregor opens the door. I must say I'm glad you've come, sir; we should never have got him to unlock the door by ourselves; he's so obstinate; and I'm sure he's unwell, though he wouldn't have it to be so this morning." "I'm just coming," said Gregor slowly and carefully, not moving an inch for fear of losing one word of the conversation. "I can't think of any other explanation, madam," said the chief clerk, "I hope it's nothing serious. Although on the other hand I must say that we men of business—fortunately or unfortunately—very often simply have to ignore any slight indisposition, since business must be attended to." "Well, can the chief clerk come in now?" asked Gregor's father impatiently, again knocking on the door. "No," said Gregor. In the left-hand room a painful silence followed this refusal, in the right-hand room his sister began to sob.

Why didn't his sister join the others? She was probably newly out of bed and hadn't even begun to put on her clothes yet. Well, why was she crying? Because he wouldn't get up and let the chief clerk in, because he was in danger of losing his job, and because the chief would begin dunning his parents again for the old debts? Surely these were things one didn't need to worry about for the present. Gregor was still at home and not in the least thinking of deserting the family. At the moment, true, he was lying on the carpet and no one who knew the condition he was in could seriously expect him to admit the chief clerk. But for such a small discourtesy, which could plausibly be explained away somehow later on, Gregor could hardly be dismissed on the spot. And it seemed to Gregor that it would be much more sensible to leave him in peace for the present than to trouble him with tears and entreaties. Still, of course, their uncertainty bewildered them all and excused their behavior.

"Mr. Samsa," the chief clerk called now in a louder voice, "what's the matter with you? Here you are, barricading yourself in your room, giving only 'yes' and 'no' for answers, causing your parents a lot of unnecessary trouble and neglecting—I mention this only in passing—neglecting your business duties in an incredible fashion. I am speaking here in the name of your parents and of your chief, and I beg you quite seriously to give me an immediate and precise explanation. You amaze me, you amaze me. I thought you were a quiet, dependable person, and now all at once you seem bent on making a disgraceful exhibition of yourself. The chief did hint to me early this morning a possible explanation for your disappearance —with reference to the cash payments that were entrusted to you recently— but I almost pledged my solemn word of honor that this could not be so. But now that I see how incredibly obstinate you are, I no longer have the slightest desire to take your part at all. And your position in the firm is not so unassailable. I came with the intention of telling you all this in private, but since you are wasting my time so needlessly I don't see why your parents shouldn't hear it too. For some time past your work has been most unsatisfactory; this is not the season of the year for a business boom, of course, we admit that, but a season of the year for doing no business at all, that does not exist, Mr. Samsa, must not exist."

"But, sir," cried Gregor, beside himself and in his agitation forgetting everything else, "I'm just going to open the door this very minute. A slight illness, an attack of giddiness, has kept me from getting up. I'm still lying in bed. But I feel all right again. I'm getting out of bed now. Just give me a moment or two longer! I'm not quite so well as I thought. But I'm all right, really. How a thing like that can suddenly strike one down! Only last night I was quite well, my parents can tell you, or rather I did have a slight presentiment. I must have showed some sign of it. Why didn't I report it at the office! But one always thinks that an indisposition can be got over without staying in the house. Oh sir, do spare my parents! All that you're reproaching me with now has no foundation; no one has ever said a word to me about it. Perhaps you haven't looked at the last orders I sent in. Anyhow, I can still catch the eight o'clock train, I'm much the better for my few hours' rest. Don't let me detain you here, sir; I'll be attending to business very soon, and do be good enough to tell the chief so and to make my excuses to him!"

And while all this was tumbling out pell-mell and Gregor hardly knew what he was saying, he had reached the chest quite easily, perhaps because of the practice he had had in bed, and was now trying to lever himself upright by means of it. He meant actually to open the door, actually to show himself and speak to the chief clerk; he was eager to find out what the others, after all their insistence, would say at the sight of him. If they were horrified then the responsibility was no longer his and he could stay quiet. But if they took it calmly, then he had no reason either to be upset, and could really get to the station for the eight o'clock train if he hurried. At first he slipped down a few times from the polished surface of the chest, but at length with a last heave he stood upright; he paid no more attention to the pains in the lower part of his body, however they smarted. Then he let himself fall against the back of a near-by chair, and clung with his little legs to the edges of it. That brought him into control of himself again and he stopped speaking, for now he could listen to what the chief clerk was saying.

"Did you understand a word of it?" the chief clerk was asking; "surely he can't be trying to make fools of us?" "Oh dear," cried his mother in tears, "perhaps he's terribly ill and we're tormenting him. Grete! Grete!" she called out then. "Yes Mother?" called his sister from the other side. They were calling to each other across Gregor's room. "You must go this minute for the doctor. Gregor is ill. Go for the doctor, quick. Did you hear how he was speaking?" "That was no human voice," said the chief clerk in a voice noticeably low beside the shrillness of the mother's. "Anna! Anna!" his father was calling through the hall to the kitchen, clapping his hands, "get a locksmith at once!" And the two girls were already running through the hall with a swish of skirts—how could his sister have got dressed so quickly?—and were tearing the front door open. There was no sound of its closing again; they had evidently left it open, as one does in houses where some great misfortune has happened.

But Gregor was now much calmer. The words he uttered were no longer understandable, apparently, although they seemed clear enough to him, even clearer than before, perhaps because his ear had grown accustomed to the sound of them. Yet at any rate people now believed that something was wrong with him, and were ready to help him. The positive certainty with which these first measures had been taken comforted him. He felt himself drawn once more into the human circle and hoped for great and remarkable results from both the doctor and the locksmith, without really distinguishing precisely between them. To make his voice as clear as possible for the decisive conversation that was now imminent he coughed a little, as quietly as he could, of course, since this noise too might not sound like a human cough for all he was able to judge. In the next room meanwhile there was complete silence. Perhaps his parents were sitting at the table with the chief clerk, whispering, perhaps they were all leaning against the door and listening.

Slowly Gregor pushed the chair towards the door, then let go of it, caught hold of the door for support—the soles at the end of his little legs were somewhat sticky—and rested against it for a moment after his efforts. Then he set himself to turning the key in the lock with his mouth. It seemed, unhappily, that he hadn't really any teeth—what could he grip the key with?—but on the other hand his jaws were certainly very strong; with their help he did manage to set the key in motion, heedless of the fact that he was undoubtedly damaging them somewhere, since a brown fluid issued from his mouth, flowed over the key and dripped on the floor. "Just listen to that," said the chief clerk next door; "he's turning the key." That was a great encouragement to Gregor; but they should all have shouted encouragement to him, his father and mother too: "Go on, Gregor," they should have called out, "keep going, hold on to that key!" And in the belief that they were all following his efforts intently, he clenched his jaws recklessly on the key with all the force at his command. As the turning of the key progressed he circled round the lock, holding on now only with his mouth, pushing on the key, as required, or pulling it down again with all the weight of his body. The louder click of the finally yielding lock literally quickened Gregor. With a deep breath of relief he said to himself: "So I didn't need the locksmith," and laid his head on the handle to open the door wide.

Since he had to pull the door towards him, he was still invisible when it was really wide open. He had to edge himself slowly round the near half of the double door, and to do it very carefully if he was not to fall plump upon his back just on the threshold. He was still carrying out this difficult manoeuvre, with no time to observe anything else, when he heard the chief clerk utter a loud "Oh!"—it sounded like a gust of wind—and now he could see the man, standing as he was nearest to the door, clapping one hand before his open mouth and slowly backing away as if driven by some invisible steady pressure. His mother—in spite of the chief clerk's being there her hair was still undone and sticking up in all directions—first clasped her hands and looked at his father, then took two steps towards Gregor and fell on the floor among her outspread skirts, her face quite hidden on her breast. His father knotted his fist with a fierce expression on his face as he meant to knock Gregor back into his room, then looked uncertainly round the living room, covered his eyes with his hands and wept till his great chest heaved.

Gregor did not go now into the living room, but leaned against the inside of the firmly shut wing of the door, so that only half his body was visible and his head above it bending sideways to look at the others. The light had meanwhile strengthened; on the other side of the street one could see clearly a section of the endlessly long, dark gray building opposite—it was a hospital—abruptly punctuated by its row of regular windows; the rain was still falling, but only in large singly discernible and literally singly splashing drops. The breakfast dishes were set out on the table lavishly, for breakfast was the most important meal of the day to Gregor's father, who lingered it out for hours over various newspapers. Right opposite Gregor on the wall hung a photograph of himself on military service, as a lieutenant, hand on sword, a carefree smile on his face, inviting one to respect his uniform and military bearing. The door leading to the hall was open, and one could see that the front door stood open too, showing the landing beyond and the beginning of the stairs going down.

"Well," said Gregor, knowing perfectly that he was the only one who had retained any composure, "I'll put my clothes on at once, pack up my samples and start off. Will you only let me go? You see, sir, I'm not obstinate, and I'm willing to work; traveling is a hard life, but I couldn't live without it. Where are you going, sir? To the office? Yes? Will you give a true account of all this? One can be temporarily incapacitated, but that's just the moment for remembering former services and bearing in mind that later on, when the incapacity has been got over, one will certainly work with all the more industry and concentration. I'm loyally bound to serve the chief, you know that very well. Besides, I have to provide for my parents and my sister. I'm in great difficulties, but I'll get out of them again. Don't make things any worse for me than they are. Stand up for me in the firm. Travelers are not popular there, I know. People think they earn sacks of money and just have a good time. A prejudice there's no particular reason for revising. But you, sir, have a more comprehensive view of affairs than the rest of the staff, yes, let me tell you in confidence, a more comprehensive view than the chief himself, who, being the owner, lets his judgment easily be swayed against one of his employees. And you know very well that the traveler, who is never seen in the office almost the whole year round, can so easily fall a victim to gossip and ill luck and unfounded complaints, which he mostly knows nothing about, except when he comes back exhausted from his rounds, and only then suffers in person from their evil consequences, which he can no longer trace back to the original causes. Sir, sir, don't go away without a word to me to show that you think me in the right at least to some extent!"

But at Gregor's very first words the chief clerk had already backed away and only stared at him with parted lips over one twitching shoulder. And while Gregor was speaking he did not stand still one moment but stole away towards the door, without taking his eyes off Gregor, yet only an inch at a time, as if obeying some secret injunction to leave the room. He was already at the hall, and the suddenness with which he took his last step out of the living room would have made one believe he had burned the sole of his foot. Once in the hall he stretched his right arm before him towards the staircase, as if some supernatural power were waiting there to deliver him.

Gregor perceived that the chief clerk must on no account be allowed to go away in this frame of mind if his position in the firm were not to be endangered to the utmost. His parents did not understand this so well; they had convinced themselves in the course of years that Gregor was settled for life in this firm, and besides they were so preoccupied with their immediate troubles that all foresight had forsaken them. Yet Gregor had this foresight. The chief clerk must be detained, soothed, persuaded and finally won over; the whole future of Gregor and his family depended on it! If only his sister had been there! She was intelligent; she had begun to cry while Gregor was still lying quietly on his back. And no doubt the chief clerk, so partial to ladies, would have been guided by her; she would have shut the door of the flat and in the hall talked him out of his horror. But she was not there, and Gregor would have to handle the situation himself. And without remembering that he was still unaware what powers of movement he possessed, without even remembering that his words in all possibility, indeed in all likelihood, would again be unintelligible, he let go the wing of the door, pushed himself through the opening, started to walk towards the chief clerk, who was already ridiculously clinging with both hands to the railing on the landing; but immediately, as he was feeling for a support, he fell down with a little cry upon all his numerous legs. Hardly was he down when he experienced for the first time this morning a sense of physical comfort; his legs had firm ground under them; they were completely obedient, as he noted with joy; they even strove to carry him forward in whatever direction he chose; and he was inclined to believe that a final relief from all his sufferings was at hand. But in the same moment as he found himself on the floor, rocking with suppressed eagerness to move, not far from his mother, indeed just in front of her, she, who had seemed so completely crushed, sprang all at once to her feet, her arms and fingers outspread, cried "Help, for God's sake, help!" bent her head down as if to see Gregor better, yet on the contrary kept backing senselessly away; had quite forgotten that the laden table stood behind her; sat upon it hastily, as if in absence of mind, when she bumped into it; and seemed altogether unaware that the big coffee pot beside her was upset and pouring coffee in a flood over the carpet.

"Mother, Mother," said Gregor in a low voice, and looked up at her. The chief clerk, for the moment, had quite slipped from his mind; instead, he could not resist snapping his jaws together at the sight of the streaming coffee. That made his mother scream again, she fled from the table and fell into the arms of his father, who hastened to catch her. But Gregor had now no time to spare for his parents; the chief clerk was already on the stairs; with his chin on the banisters he was taking one last backward look. Gregor made a spring, to be as sure as possible of overtaking him; the chief clerk must have divined his intention, for he leaped down several steps and vanished; he was still yelling "Ugh!" and it echoed through the whole staircase.

Unfortunately, the flight of the chief clerk seemed completely to upset Gregor's father, who had remained relatively calm until now, for instead of running after the man himself, or at least not hindering Gregor in his pursuit, he seized in his right hand the walking stick which the chief clerk had left behind on a chair, together with a hat and greatcoat, snatched in his left hand a large newspaper from the table and began stamping his feet and flourishing the stick and the newspaper to drive Gregor back into his room. No entreaty of Gregor's availed, indeed no entreaty was even understood, however humbly he bent his head his father only stamped on the floor the more loudly. Behind his father his mother had torn open a window, despite the cold weather, and was leaning far out of it with her face in her hands. A strong draught set in from the street to the staircase, the window curtains blew in, the newspapers on the table fluttered, stray pages whisked over the floor. Pitilessly Gregor's father drove him back, hissing and crying "Shoo!" like a savage. But Gregor was quite unpracticed in walking backwards, it really was a slow business. If he only had a chance to turn round he could get back to his room at once, but he was afraid of exasperating his father by the slowness of such rotation and at any moment the stick in his father's hand might hit him a fatal blow on the back or on the head. In the end, however, nothing else was left for him to do since to his horror he observed that in moving backwards he could not even control the direction he took; and so, keeping an anxious eye on his father all the time over his shoulder, he began to turn round as quickly as he could, which was in reality very slowly. Perhaps his father noted his good intentions, for he did not interfere except every now and then to help him in the manoeuvre from a distance with the point of the stick. If only he would have stopped making that unbearable hissing noise! It made Gregor quite lose his head. He had turned almost completely round when the hissing noise so distracted him that he even turned a little the wrong way again. But when at last his head was fortunately right in front of the doorway, it appeared that his body was too broad simply to get through the opening. His father, of course, in his present mood was far from thinking of such a thing as opening the other half of the door, to let Gregor have enough space. He had merely the fixed idea of driving Gregor back into his room as quickly as possible. He would never have suffered Gregor to make the circumstantial preparations for standing up on end and perhaps slipping his way through the door. Maybe he was now making more noise than ever to urge Gregor forward, as if no obstacle impeded him; to Gregor, anyhow, the noise in his rear sounded no longer like the voice of one single father; this was really no joke, and Gregor thrust himself—come what might—into the doorway. One side of his body rose up, he was tilted at an angle in the doorway, his flank was quite bruised, horrid blotches stained the white door, soon he was stuck fast and, left to himself, could not have moved at all, his legs on one side fluttered trembling in the air, those on the other were crushed painfully to the floor—when from behind his father gave him a strong push which was literally a deliverance and he flew far into the room, bleeding freely. The door was slammed behind him with the stick, and then at last there was silence.

## II

Not until it was twilight did Gregor awake out of a deep sleep, more like a swoon than a sleep. He would certainly have waked up of his own accord not much later, for he felt himself sufficiently rested and well-slept, but it seemed to him as if a fleeting step and a cautious shutting of the door leading into the hall had aroused him. The electric lights in the street cast a pale sheen here and there on the ceiling and the upper surfaces of the furniture, but down below, where he lay, it was dark. Slowly, awkwardly trying out his feelers, which he now first learned to appreciate, he pushed his way to the door to see what had been happening there. His left side felt like one single long, unpleasantly tense scar, and he had actually to limp on his two rows of legs. One little leg, moreover, had been damaged—and trailed uselessly behind him.

He had reached the door before he discovered what had really drawn him to it: the smell of food. For there stood a basin filled with fresh milk in which floated little sops of white bread. He could almost have laughed with joy, since he was now still hungrier than in the morning, and he dipped his head almost over the eyes straight into the milk. But soon in disappointment he withdrew it again; not only did he find it difficult to feed because of his tender left side—and he could only feed with the palpitating collaboration of his whole body—he did not like the milk either, although milk had been his favorite drink and that was certainly why his sister had set it there for him, indeed it was almost with repulsion that he turned away from the basin and crawled back to the middle of the room.

He could see through the crack of the door that the gas was turned on in the living room, but while usually at this time his father made a habit of reading the afternoon newspaper in a loud voice to his mother and occasionally to his sister as well, not a sound was now to be heard. Well, perhaps his father had recently given up this habit of reading aloud, which his sister had mentioned so often in conversation and in her letters. But there was the same silence all around, although the flat was certainly not empty of occupants. "What a quiet life our family has been leading," said Gregor to himself, and as he sat there motionless staring into the darkness he felt great pride in the fact that he had been able to provide such a life for his parents and sister in such a fine flat. But what if all the quiet, the comfort, the contentment were now to end in horror? To keep himself from being lost in such thoughts Gregor took refuge in movement and crawled up and down the room.

Once during the long evening one of the side doors was opened a little and quickly shut again, later the other side door too; someone had apparently wanted to come in and then thought better of it. Gregor now stationed himself immediately before the living room door, determined to persuade any hesitating visitor to come in or at least to discover who it might be; but the door was not opened again and he waited in vain. In the early morning, when the doors were locked, they had all wanted to come in, now that he had opened one door and the other had apparently been opened during the day, no one came in and even the keys were on the other side of the doors.

It was late at night before the gas went out in the living room, and Gregor could easily tell that his parents and his sister had all stayed awake until then, for he could clearly hear the three of them stealing away on tiptoe. No one was likely to visit him, not until the morning, that was certain; so he had plenty of time to meditate at his leisure on how he was to arrange his life afresh. But the lofty, empty room in which he had to lie flat on the floor filled him with an apprehension he could not account for, since it had been his very own room for the past five years—and with a half-unconscious action, not without a slight feeling of shame, he scuttled under the sofa, where he felt comfortable at once, although his back was a little cramped and he could not lift his head up, and his only regret was that his body was too broad to get the whole of it under the sofa.

He stayed there all night, spending the time partly in a light slumber, from which his hunger kept waking him up with a start, and partly in worrying and sketching vague hopes, which all led to the same conclusion, that he must lie low for the present and, by exercising patience and the utmost consideration, help the family to bear the inconvenience he was bound to cause them in his present condition.

Very early in the morning, it was still almost night, Gregor had the chance to test the strength of his new resolutions, for his sister, nearly fully dressed, opened the door from the hall and peered in. She did not see him at once, yet when she caught sight of him under the sofa—well, he had to be somewhere, he couldn't have flown away, could he?—she was so startled that without being able to help it she slammed the door shut again. But as if regretting her behavior she opened the door again immediately and came in on tiptoe, as if she were visiting an invalid or even a stranger. Gregor had pushed his head forward to the very edge of the sofa and watched her. Would she notice that he had left the milk standing, and not for lack of hunger, and would she bring in some other kind of food more to his taste? If she did not do it of her own accord, he would rather starve than draw her attention to the fact, although he felt a wild impulse to dart out from under the sofa, throw himself at her feet and beg her for something to eat. But his sister at once noticed, with surprise, that the basin was still full, except for a little milk that had been spilt all around it, she lifted it immediately, not with her bare hands, true, but with a cloth and carried it away. Gregor was wildly curious to know what she would bring instead, and made various speculations about it. Yet what she actually did next, in the goodness of her heart, he could never have guessed at. To find out what he liked she brought him a whole selection of food, all set out on an old newspaper. There were old, half-decayed vegetables, bones from last night's supper covered with a white sauce that had thickened; some raisins and almonds; a piece of cheese that Gregor would have called uneatable two days ago; a dry roll of bread, a buttered roll, and a roll both buttered and salted. Besides all that, she set down again the same basin, into which she had poured some water, and which was apparently to be reserved for his exclusive use. And with fine tact, knowing that Gregor would not eat in her presence, she withdrew quickly and even turned the key, to let him understand that he could take his ease as much as he liked. Gregor's legs all whizzed towards the food. His wounds must have healed completely, moreover, for he felt no disability, which amazed him and made him reflect how more than a month ago he had cut one finger a little with a knife and had still suffered pain from the wound only the day before yesterday. Am I less sensitive now? he thought, and sucked greedily at the cheese, which above all the other edibles attracted him at once and strongly. One after another and with tears of satisfaction in his eyes he quickly devoured the cheese, the vegetables and the sauce; the fresh food, on the other hand, had no charms for him, he could not even stand the smell of it and actually dragged away to some little distance the things he could eat. He had long finished his meal and was only lying lazily on the same spot when his sister turned the key slowly as a sign for him to retreat. That roused him at once, although he was nearly asleep, and he hurried under the sofa again. But it took considerable self-control for him to stay under the sofa, even for the short time his sister was in the room, since the large meal had swollen his body somewhat and he was so cramped he could hardly breathe. Slight attacks of breathlessness afflicted him and his eyes were starting a little out of his head as he watched his unsuspecting sister sweeping together with a broom not only the remains of what he had eaten but even the things he had not touched, as if these were now of no use to anyone, and hastily shoveling it all into a bucket, which she covered with a wooden lid and carried away. Hardly had she turned her back when Gregor came from under the sofa and stretched and puffed himself out.

In this manner Gregor was fed, once in the early morning while his parents and the servant girl were still asleep, and a second time after they had all had their midday dinner, for then his parents took a short nap and the servant girl could be sent out on some errand or other by his sister. Not that they would have wanted him to starve, of course, but perhaps they could not have borne to know more about his feeding than from hearsay, perhaps too his sister wanted to spare them such little anxieties wherever possible, since they had quite enough to bear as it was.

Under what pretext the doctor and the locksmith had been got rid of on that first morning Gregor could not discover, for since what he said was not understood by the others it never struck any of them, not even his sister, that he could understand what they said, and so whenever his sister came into his room he had to content himself with hearing her utter only a sigh now and then and an occasional appeal to the saints. Later on, when she had got a little used to the situation—of course she could never get completely used to it—she sometimes threw out a remark which was kindly meant or could be so interpreted. "Well, he liked his dinner today," she would say when Gregor had made a good clearance of his food; and when he had not eaten, which gradually happened more and more often, she would say almost sadly: "Everything's been left standing again."

But although Gregor could get no news directly, he overheard a lot from the neighboring rooms, and as soon as voices were audible, he would run to the door of the room concerned and press his whole body against it. In the first few days especially there was no conversation that did not refer to him somehow, even if only indirectly. For two whole days there were family consultations at every mealtime about what should be done; but also between meals the same subject was discussed, for there were always two members of the family at home, since no one wanted to be alone in the flat and to leave it quite empty was unthinkable. And on the very first of these days the household cook—it was not quite clear what and how much she knew of the situation—went down on her knees to his mother and begged leave to go, and when she departed, a quarter of an hour later, gave thanks for her dismissal with tears in her eyes as if for the greatest benefit that could have been conferred on her, and without any prompting swore a solemn oath that she would never say a single word to anyone about what had happened.

Now Gregor's sister had to cook too, helping her mother; true, the cooking did not amount to much, for they ate scarcely anything. Gregor was always hearing one of the family vainly urging another to eat and getting no answer but: "Thanks, I've had all I want," or something similar. Perhaps they drank nothing either. Time and again his sister kept asking his father if he wouldn't like some beer and offered kindly to go and fetch it herself, and when he made no answer suggested that she could ask the concierge to fetch it, so that he need feel no sense of obligation, but then a round "No" came from his father and no more was said about it.

In the course of that very first day Gregor's father explained the family's financial position and prospects to both his mother and sister. Now and then he rose from the table to get some voucher or memorandum out of the small safe he had rescued from the collapse of his business five years earlier. One could hear him opening the complicated lock and rustling papers out and shutting it again. This statement made by his father was the first cheerful information Gregor had heard since his imprisonment. He had been of the opinion that nothing at all was left over from his father's business, at least his father had never said anything to the contrary, and of course he had not asked him directly. At that time Gregor's sole desire was to do his utmost to help the family to forget as soon as possible the catastrophe which had overwhelmed the business and thrown them all into a state of complete despair. And so he had set to work with unusual ardor and almost overnight had become a commercial traveler instead of a little clerk, with of course much greater chances of earning money, and his success was immediately translated into good round coin which he could lay on the table for his amazed and happy family. These had been fine times, and they had never recurred, at least not with the same sense of glory, although later on Gregor had earned so much money that he was able to meet the expenses of the whole household and did so. They had simply got used to it, both the family and Gregor; the money was gratefully accepted and gladly given, but there was no special uprush of warm feeling. With his sister alone had he remained intimate, and it was a secret plan of his that she, who loved music, unlike himself, and could play movingly on the violin, should be sent next year to study at the Conservatorium, despite the great expense that would entail, which must be made up in some other way. During his brief visits home the Conservatorium was often mentioned in the talks he had with his sister, but always merely as a beautiful dream which could never come true, and his parents discouraged even these innocent references to it; yet Gregor had made up his mind firmly about it and meant to announce the fact with due solemnity on Christmas Day.

Such were the thoughts, completely futile in his present condition, that went through his head as he stood clinging upright to the door and listening. Sometimes out of sheer weariness he had to give up listening and let his head fall negligently against the door, but he always had to pull himself together again at once, for even the slight sound his head made was audible next door and brought all conversation to a stop. "What can he be doing now?" his father would say after a while, obviously turning towards the door, and only then would the interrupted conversation gradually be set going again.

Gregor was now informed as amply as he could wish—for his father tended to repeat himself in his explanations, partly because it was a long time since he had handled such matters and partly because his mother could not always grasp things at once—that a certain amount of investments, a very small amount it was true, had survived the wreck of their fortunes and had even increased a little because the dividends had not been touched meanwhile. And besides that, the money Gregor brought home every month—he had kept only a few dollars for himself—had never been quite used up and now amounted to a small capital sum. Behind the door Gregor nodded his head eagerly, rejoiced at this evidence of unexpected thrift and foresight. True, he could really have paid off some more of his father's debts to the chief with this extra money, and so brought much nearer the day on which he could quit his job, but doubtless it was better the way his father had arranged it.

Yet this capital was by no means sufficient to let the family live on the interest of it; for one year, perhaps, or at the most two, they could live on the principal, that was all. It was simply a sum that ought not to be touched and should be kept for a rainy day; money for living expenses would have to be earned. Now his father was still hale enough but an old man, and he had done no work for the past five years and could not be expected to do much; during these five years, the first years of leisure in his laborious though unsuccessful life, he had grown rather fat and become sluggish. And Gregor's old mother, how was she to earn a living with her asthma, which troubled her even when she walked through the flat and kept her lying on a sofa every other day panting for breath beside an open window? And was his sister to earn her bread, she who was still a child of seventeen and whose life hitherto had been so pleasant, consisting as it did in dressing herself nicely, sleeping long, helping in the housekeeping, going out to a few modest entertainments and above all playing the violin? At first whenever the need for earning money was mentioned Gregor let go his hold on the door and threw himself down on the cool leather sofa beside it, he felt so hot with shame and grief.

Often he just lay there the long nights through without sleeping at all, scrabbling for hours on the leather. Or he nerved himself to the great effort of pushing an armchair to the window, then crawled up over the window sill and, braced against the chair, leaned against the window panes, obviously in some recollection of the sense of freedom that looking out of a window always used to give him. For in reality day by day things that were even a little way off were growing dimmer to his sight; the hospital across the street, which he used to execrate for being all too often before his eyes, was now quite beyond his range of vision, and if he had not known that he lived in Charlotte Street, a quiet street but still a city street, he might have believed that his window gave on a desert waste where gray sky and gray land blended indistinguishably into each other. His quick-witted sister only needed to observe twice that the armchair stood by the window; after that whenever she had tidied the room she always pushed the chair back to the same place at the window and even left the inner casements open.

If he could have spoken to her and thanked her for all she had to do for him, he could have borne her ministrations better; as it was, they oppressed him. She certainly tried to make as light as possible of whatever was disagreeable in her task, and as time went on she succeeded, of course, more and more, but time brought more enlightenment to Gregor too. The very way she came in distressed him. Hardly was she in the room when she rushed to the window, without even taking time to shut the door, careful as she was usually to shield the sight of Gregor's room from the others, and as if she were almost suffocating tore the casements open with hasty fingers, standing then in the open draught for a while even in the bitterest cold and drawing deep breaths. This noisy scurry of hers upset Gregor twice a day; he would crouch trembling under the sofa all the time, knowing quite well that she would certainly have spared him such a disturbance had she found it at all possible to stay in his presence without opening the window.

On one occasion, about a month after Gregor's metamorphosis, when there was surely no reason for her to be still startled at his appearance, she came a little earlier than usual and found him gazing out of the window, quite motionless, and thus well placed to look like a bogey. Gregor would not have been surprised had she not come in at all, for she could not immediately open the window while he was there, but not only did she retreat, she jumped back as if in alarm and banged the door shut; a stranger might well have thought that he had been lying in wait for her there meaning to bite her. Of course he hid himself under the sofa at once, but he had to wait until midday before she came again, and she seemed more ill at ease than usual. This made him realize how repulsive the sight of him still was to her, and that it was bound to go on being repulsive, and what an effort it must cost her not to run away even from the sight of the small portion of his body that stuck out from under the sofa. In order to spare her that, therefore, one day he carried a sheet on his back to the sofa—it cost him four hours' labor—and arranged it there in such a way as to hide him completely, so that even if she were to bend down she could not see him. Had she considered the sheet unnecessary, she would certainly have stripped it off the sofa again, for it was clear enough that this curtaining and confining of himself was not likely to conduce to Gregor's comfort, but she left it where it was, and Gregor even fancied that he caught a thankful glance from her eye when he lifted the sheet carefully a very little with his head to see how she was taking the new arrangement.

For the first fortnight his parents could not bring themselves to the point of entering his room, and he often heard them expressing their appreciation of his sister's activities, whereas formerly they had frequently scolded her for being as they thought a somewhat useless daughter. But now, both of them often waited outside the door, his father and his mother, while his sister tidied his room, and as soon as she came out she had to tell them exactly how things were in the room, what Gregor had eaten, how he had conducted himself this time and whether there was not perhaps some slight improvement in his condition. His mother, moreover, began relatively soon to want to visit him, but his father and sister dissuaded her at first with arguments which Gregor listened to very attentively and altogether approved. Later, however, she had to be held back by main force, and when she cried out: "Do let me in to Gregor, he is my unfortunate son! Can't you understand that I must go to him?" Gregor thought that it might be well to have her come in, not every day, of course, but perhaps once a week; she understood things, after all, much better than his sister, who was only a child despite the efforts she was making and had perhaps taken on so difficult a task merely out of childish thoughtlessness.

Gregor's desire to see his mother was soon fulfilled. During the daytime he did not want to show himself at the window, out of consideration for his parents, but he could not crawl very far around the few square yards of floor space he had, nor could he bear lying quietly at rest all during the night, while he was fast losing any interest he had ever taken in food, so that for mere recreation he had formed the habit of crawling crisscross over the walls and ceiling. He especially enjoyed hanging suspended from the ceiling; it was much better than lying on the floor; one could breathe more freely; one's body swung and rocked lightly; and in the almost blissful absorption induced by this suspension it could happen to his own surprise that he let go and fell plump on the floor. Yet he now had his body much better under control than formerly, and even such a big fall did him no harm. His sister at once remarked the new distraction Gregor had found for himself—he left traces behind him of the sticky stuff on his soles wherever he crawled—and she got the idea in her head of giving him as wide a field as possible to crawl in and of removing the pieces of furniture that hindered him, above all the chest of drawers and the writing desk. But that was more than she could manage all by herself; she did not dare ask her father to help her; and as for the servant girl, a young creature of sixteen who had had the courage to stay on after the cook's departure, she could not be asked to help, for she had begged as an especial favor that she might keep the kitchen door locked and open it only on a definite summons; so there was nothing left but to apply to her mother at an hour when her father was out. And the old lady did come, with exclamations of joyful eagerness, which, however, died away at the door of Gregor's room. Gregor's sister, of course, went in first, to see that everything was in order before letting his mother enter. In great haste Gregor pulled the sheet lower and rucked it more in folds so that it really looked as if it had been thrown accidentally over the sofa. And this time he did not peer out from under it; he renounced the pleasure of seeing his mother on this occasion and was only glad that she had come at all. "Come in, he's out of sight," said his sister, obviously leading her mother in by the hand. Gregor could now hear the two women struggling to shift the heavy old chest from its place, and his sister claiming the greater part of the labor for herself, without listening to the admonitions of her mother who feared she might overstrain herself. It took a long time. After at least a quarter of an hour's tugging his mother objected that the chest had better be left where it was, for in the first place it was too heavy and could never be got out before his father came home, and standing in the middle of the room like that it would only hamper Gregor's movements, while in the second place it was not at all certain that removing the furniture would be doing a service to Gregor. She was inclined to think to the contrary; the sight of the naked walls made her own heart heavy, and why shouldn't Gregor have the same feeling, considering that he had been used to his furniture for so long and might feel forlorn without it. "And doesn't it look," she concluded in a low voice—in fact she had been almost whispering all the time as if to avoid letting Gregor, whose exact whereabouts she did not know, hear even the tones of her voice, for she was convinced that he could not understand her words—"doesn't it look as if we were showing him, by taking away his furniture, that we have given up hope of his ever getting better and are just leaving him coldly to himself? I think it would be best to keep his room exactly as it has always been, so that when he comes back to us he will find everything unchanged and be able all the more esasily to forget what has happened in between."

On hearing these words from his mother Gregor realized that the lack of all direct human speech for the past two months together with the monotony of family life must have confused his mind, otherwise he could not account for the fact that he had quite earnestly looked forward to having his room emptied of furnishing. Did he really want his warm room, so comfortably fitted with old family furniture, to be turned into a naked den in which he would certainly be able to crawl unhampered in all directions but at the price of shedding simultaneously all recollection of his human background? He had indeed been so near the brink of forgetfulness that only the voice of his mother, which he had not heard for so long, had drawn him back from it. Nothing should be taken out of his room; everything must stay as it was; he could not dispense with the good influence of the furniture on his state of mind; and even if the furniture did hamper him in his senseless crawling round and round, that was no drawback but a great advantage.

Unfortunately his sister was of the contrary opinion; she had grown accustomed, and not without reason, to consider herself an expert in Gregor's affairs as against her parents, and so her mother's advice was now enough to make her determined on the removal not only of the chest and the writing desk, which had been her first intention, but of all the furniture except the indispensable sofa. This determination was not, of course, merely the outcome of childish recalcitrance and of the self-confidence she had recently developed so unexpectedly and at such cost; she had in fact perceived that Gregor needed a lot of space to crawl about in, while on the other hand he never used the furniture at all, so far as could be seen. Another factor might have been also the enthusiastic temperament of an adolescent girl, which seeks to indulge itself on every opportunity and which now tempted Grete to exaggerate the horror of her brother's circumstances in order that she might do all the more for him. In a room where Gregor lorded it all alone over empty walls no one save herself was likely ever to set foot.

And so she was not to be moved from her resolve by her mother, who seemed moreover to be ill at ease in Gregor's room and therefore unsure of herself, was soon reduced to silence and helped her daughter as best she could to push the chest outside. Now, Gregor could do without the chest, if need be, but the writing desk he must retain. As soon as the two women had got the chest out of his room, groaning as they pushed it, Gregor stuck his head out from under the sofa to see how he might intervene as kindly and cautiously as possible. But as bad luck would have it, his mother was the first to return, leaving Grete clasping the chest in the room next door where she was trying to shift it all by herself, without of course moving it from the spot. His mother however was not accustomed to the sight of him, it might sicken her and so in alarm Gregor backed quickly to the other end of the sofa, yet could not prevent the sheet from swaying a little in front. That was enough to put her on the alert. She paused, stood still for a moment and then went back to Grete.

Although Gregor kept reassuring himself that nothing out of the way was happening, but only a few bits of furniture were being changed round, he soon had to admit that all this trotting to and fro of the two women, their little ejaculations and the scraping of furniture along the floor affected him like a vast disturbance coming from all sides at once, and however much he tucked in his head and legs and cowered to the very floor he was bound to confess that he would not be able to stand it for long. They were clearing his room out; taking away everything he loved; the chest in which he kept his fret saw and other tools was already dragged off; they were now loosening the writing desk which had almost sunk into the floor, the desk at which he had done all his homework when he was at the commercial academy, at the grammar school before that, and, yes, even at the primary school—he had no more time to waste in weighing the good intentions of the two women, whose existence he had by now almost forgotten, for they were so exhausted that they were laboring in silence and nothing could be heard but the heavy scuffling of their feet.

And so he rushed out—the women were just leaning against the writing desk in the next room to give themselves a breather—and four times changed his direction, since he really did not know what to rescue first, then on the wall opposite, which was already otherwise cleared, he was struck by the picture of the lady muffled in so much fur and quickly crawled up to it and pressed himself to the glass, which was a good surface to hold on to and comforted his hot belly. This picture at least, which was entirely hidden beneath him, was going to be removed by nobody. He turned his head towards the door of the living room so as to observe the women when they came back.

They had not allowed themselves much of a rest and were already coming; Grete had twined her arm around her mother and was almost supporting her. "Well, what shall we take now?" said Grete, looking round. Her eyes met Gregor's from the wall. She kept her composure, presumably because of her mother, bent her head down to her mother, to keep her from looking up, and said, although in a fluttering, unpremeditated voice: "Come, hadn't we better go back to the living room for a moment?" Her intentions were clear enough to Gregor, she wanted to bestow her mother in safety and then chase him down from the wall. Well, just let her try it! He clung to his picture and would not give it up. He would rather fly in Grete's face.

But Grete's words had succeeded in disquieting her mother, who took a step to one side, caught sight of the huge brown mass on the flowered wallpaper, and before she was really conscious that what she saw was Gregor screamed in a loud, hoarse voice: "Oh, God, oh God!" fell with outspread arms over the sofa as if giving up and did not move. "Gregor!" cried his sister, shaking her fist and glaring at him. This was the first time she had directly addressed him since his metamorphosis. She ran into the next room for some aromatic essence with which to rouse her mother from her fainting fit. Gregor wanted to help too—there was still time to rescue the picture—but he was stuck fast to the glass and had to tear himself loose; he then ran after his sister into the next room as if he could advise her, as he used to do; but then had to stand helplessly behind her; she meanwhile

searched among various small bottles and when she turned round started
in alarm at the sight of him; one bottle fell on the floor and broke; a
splinter of glass cut Gregor's face and some kind of corrosive medicine
splashed him; without pausing a moment longer Grete gathered up all the
bottles she could carry and ran to her mother with them; she banged the
door shut with her foot. Gregor was now cut off from his mother, who was
perhaps nearly dying because of him; he dared not open the door for fear
of frightening away his sister, who had to stay with her mother; there was
nothing he could do but wait; and harassed by self-reproach and worry he
began now to crawl to and fro, over everything, walls, furniture and ceiling,
and finally in his despair, when the whole room seemed to be reeling round
him, fell down on to the middle of the big table.

A little while elapsed, Gregor was still lying there feebly and all around
was quiet, perhaps that was a good omen. Then the doorbell rang. The
servant girl was of course locked in her kitchen, and Grete would have to
open the door. It was his father. "What's been happening?" were his first
words; Grete's face must have told him everything. Grete answered in a
muffled voice, apparently hiding her head on his breast: "Mother has been
fainting, but she's better now. Gregor's broken loose." "Just what I
expected," said his father, "just what I've been telling you, but you women
would never listen." It was clear to Gregor that his father had taken the
worst interpretation of Grete's all too brief statement and was assuming
that Gregor had been guilty of some violent act. Therefore Gregor must
now try to propitiate his father, since he had neither time nor means for an
explanation. And so he fled to the door of his own room and crouched
against it, to let his father see as soon as he came in from the hall that his
son had the good intention of getting back into his room immediately and
that it was not necessary to drive him there, but that if only the door were
opened he would disappear at once.

Yet his father was not in the mood to perceive such fine distinctions.
"Ah!" he cried as soon as he appeared, in a tone which sounded at once
angry and exultant. Gregor drew his head back from the door and lifted
it to look at his father. Truly, this was not the father he had imagined to
himself; admittedly he had been too absorbed of late in his new recreation
of crawling over the ceiling to take the same interest as before in what was
happening elsewhere in the flat, and he ought really to be prepared for
some changes. And yet, and yet, could that be his father? The man who
used to lie wearily sunk in bed whenever Gregor set out on a business
journey; who welcomed him back of an evening lying in a long chair in a
dressing gown; who could not really rise to his feet but only lifted his arms
in greeting, and on the rare occasions when he did go out with his family,
on one of two Sundays a year and on high holidays, walked between Gregor
and his mother, who were slow walkers anyhow, even more slowly than

they did, muffled in his old greatcoat, shuffling laboriously forward with the help of his crook-handled stick which he set down most cautiously at every step and, whenever he wanted to say anything, nearly always came to a full stop and gathered his escort around him? Now he was standing there in fine shape; dressed in a smart blue uniform with gold buttons, such as bank messengers wear; his strong double chin bulged over the stiff high collar of his jacket; from under his bushy eyebrows his black eyes darted fresh and penetrating glances; his onetime tangled white hair had been combed flat on either side of a shining and carefully exact parting. He pitched his cap, which bore a gold monogram, probably the badge of some bank, in a wide sweep across the whole room on to a sofa and with the tail-ends of his jacket thrown back, his hands in his trouser pockets, advanced with a grim visage towards Gregor. Likely enough he did not himself know what he meant to do; at any rate he lifted his feet uncommonly high, and Gregor was dumbfounded at the enormous size of his shoe soles. But Gregor could not risk standing up to him, aware as he had been from the very first day of his new life that his father believed only the severest measures suitable for dealing with him. And so he ran before his father, stopping when he stopped and scuttling forward again when his father made any kind of move. In this way they circled the room several times without anything decisive happening, indeed the whole operation did not even look like a pursuit because it was carried out so slowly. And so Gregor did not leave the floor, for he feared that his father might take as a piece of peculiar wickedness any excursion of his over the walls or the ceiling. All the same, he could not stay this course much longer, for while his father took one step he had to carry out a whole series of movements. He was already beginning to feel breathless, just as in his former life his lungs had not been very dependable. As he was staggering along, trying to concentrate his energy on running, hardly keeping his eyes open; in his dazed state never even thinking of any other escape than simply going forward; and having almost forgotten that the walls were free to him, which in this room were well provided with finely carved pieces of furniture full of knobs and crevices—suddenly something lightly flung landed close behind him and rolled before him. It was an apple; a second apple followed immediately; Gregor came to a stop in alarm; there was no point in running on, for his father was determined to bombard him. He had filled his pockets with fruit from the dish on the sideboard and was now shying apple after apple, without taking particularly good aim for the moment. The small red apples rolled about the floor as if magnetized and cannoned into each other. An apple thrown without much force grazed Gregor's back and glanced off harmlessly. But another following immediately landed right on his back and sank in; Gregor wanted to drag himself forward, as if this stratling, incredible pain could be left behind him; but he felt as if nailed to the spot and flattened himself out in a complete derangement of all his senses. With his last conscious look he saw the door of his room being torn open and his mother rushing out ahead of his screaming sister, in her underbodice, for her daughter had loosened her clothing to let her breathe more freely and recover from her swoon, he saw his mother rushing towards his father, leaving one after another behind her on the floor her loosened petticoats, stumbling over her petticoats straight to his father and embracing him, in complete union with him—but here Gregor's sight began to fail—with her hands clasped round his father's neck as she begged for her son's life.

# III

The serious injury done to Gregor, which disabled him for more than a month  the apple went on sticking in his body as a visible reminder, since no one ventured to remove it—seemed to have made even his father recollect that Gregor was a member of the family, despite his present unfortunate and repulsive shape, and ought not to be treated as an enemy, that, on the contrary, family duty required the suppression of disgust and the exercise of patience, nothing but patience.

And although his injury had impaired, probably for ever, his powers of movement, and for the time being it took him long, long minutes to creep across his room like an old invalid—there was no question now of crawling up the wall—yet in his own opinion he was sufficiently compensated for this worsening of his condition by the fact that towards evening the living-room door, which he used to watch intently for an hour or two beforehand, was always thrown open, so that lying in the darkness of his room, invisible to the family, he could see them all at the lamp-lit table and listen to their talk, by general consent as it were, very different from his earlier eaves-dropping.

True, their intercourse lacked the lively character of former times, which he had always called to mind with a certain wistfulness in the small hotel bedrooms where he had been wont to throw himself down, tired out, on damp bedding. They were now mostly very silent. Soon after supper his father would fall asleep in his armchair; his mother and sister would ad-monish each other to be silent; his mother, bending low over the lamp, stitched at fine sewing for an underwear firm; his sister, who had taken a job as a salesgirl, was learning shorthand and French in the evenings on the chance of bettering herself. Sometimes his father woke up, and as if quite unaware that he had been sleeping said to his mother: "What a lot of sewing you're doing today!" and at once fell asleep again, while the two women exchanged a tired smile.

With a kind of mulishness his father persisted in keeping his uniform on even in the house; his dressing gown hung uselessly on its peg and he slept fully dressed where he sat, as if he were ready for service at any moment and even here only at the beck and call of his superior. As a result, his uniform, which was not brand-new to start with, began to look dirty, despite all the loving care of the mother and sister to keep it clean, and Gregor often spent whole evenings gazing at the many greasy spots on the garment, gleaming with gold buttons always in a high state of polish, in which the old man sat sleeping in extreme discomfort and yet quite peacefully.

As soon as the clock struck ten his mother tried to rouse his father with gentle words and to persuade him after that to get into bed, for sitting there he could not have a proper sleep and that was what he needed most, since he had to go on duty at six. But with the mulishness that had obsessed him since he became a bank messenger he always insisted on staying longer at the table, although he regularly fell asleep again and in the end only with the greatest trouble could be got out of his armchair and into his bed. However insistently Gregor's mother and sister kept urging him with gentle reminders, he would go on slowly shaking his head for a quarter of an hour, keeping his eyes shut, and refuse to get to his feet. The mother plucked at his sleeve, whispering endearments in his ear, the sister left her lessons to come to her mother's help, but Gregor's father was not to be caught. He would only sink down deeper in his chair. Not until the two women hoisted him up by the armpits did he open his eyes and look at them both, one after the other, usually with the remark: "This is a life. This is the peace and quiet of my old age." And leaning on the two of them he would heave himself up, with difficulty, as if he were a great burden to himself, suffer them to lead him as far as the door and then wave them off and go on alone, while the mother abandoned her needlework and the sister her pen in order to run after him and help him farther.

Who could find time, in this overworked and tired-out family, to bother about Gregor more than was absolutely needful? The household was reduced more and more; the servant girl was turned off; a gigantic bony charwoman with white hair flying round her head came in morning and evening to do the rough work; everything else was done by Gregor's mother, as well as great piles of sewing. Even various family ornaments, which his mother and sister used to wear with pride at parties and celebrations, had to be sold, as Gregor discovered of an evening from hearing them all discuss the prices obtained. But what they lamented most was the fact that they could not leave the flat which was much too big for their present circumstances, because they could not think of any way to shift Gregor. Yet Gregor saw well enough that consideration for him was not the main difficulty preventing the removal, for they could have easily shifted him in some suitable box with a few air holes in it; what really kept them from moving into another flat was rather their own complete hopelessness and the belief that they had been singled out for a misfortune such as had never happened to any of their relations or acquaintances. They fulfilled to the uttermost all that the world demands of poor people, the father fetched breakfast for the small clerks in the bank, the mother devoted her energy to making underwear for strangers, the sister trotted to and fro behind the counter at the behest of customers, but more than this they had not the strength to do. And the wound in Gregor's back began to nag at him afresh when his mother and sister, after getting his father into bed, came back again, left their work lying, drew close to each other and sat cheek by cheek; when his mother, pointing towards his room, said: "Shut that door now, Grete," and he was left again in darkness, while next door the women mingled their tears or perhaps sat dry-eyed staring at the table.

Gregor hardly slept at all by night or by day. He was often haunted by the idea that next time the door opened he would take the family's affairs in hand again just as he used to do; once more, after this long interval, there appeared in his thoughts the figures of the chief and the chief clerk, the commercial travelers and the apprentices, the porter who was so dull-witted, two or three friends in other firms, a chambermaid in one of the rural hotels, a sweet and fleeting memory, a cashier in a milliner's shop, whom he had wooed earnestly but too slowly—they all appeared, together with strangers or people he had quite forgotten, but instead of helping him and his family they were one and all unapproachable and he was glad when they vanished. At other times he would not be in the mood to bother about his family, he was only filled with rage at the way they were neglecting him, and although he had no clear idea of what he might care to eat he would make plans for getting into the larder to take the food that was after all his due, even if he were not hungry. His sister no longer took thought to bring him what might especially please him, but in the morning and at noon before she went to business hurriedly pushed into his room with her foot any food that was available, and in the evening cleared it out again with one sweep of the broom, heedless of whether it had been merely tasted, or—as most frequently happened—left untouched. The cleaning of his room, which she now did always in the evenings, could not have been more hastily done. Streaks of dirt stretched along the walls, here and there lay balls of dust and filth. At first Gregor used to station himself in some particularly filthy corner when his sister arrived, in order to reproach her with it, so to speak. But he could have sat there for weeks without getting her to make any improvement; she could see the dirt as well as he did, but she had simply made up her mind to leave it alone. And yet, with a touchiness that was new to her, which seemed anyhow to have infected the whole family, she jealously guarded her claim to be the sole caretaker of Gregor's room. His mother once subjected his room to a thorough cleaning, which was achieved only by means of several buckets of water—all this dampness of course upset Gregor too and he lay widespread, sulky and motionless on the sofa—but she was well punished for it. Hardly had his sister noticed the changed aspect of his room that evening than she rushed in high dudgeon into the living room and, despite the imploringly raised hands of her mother, burst into a storm of weeping, while her parents—her father had of course been startled out of his chair—looked on at first in helpless amazement; then they too began to go into action; the father reproached the mother on his right for not having left the cleaning of Gregor's room to his sister; shrieked at the sister on his left that never again was she to be allowed to clean Gregor's room; while the mother tried to pull the father into his bedroom, since he was beyond himself with agitation; the sister, shaken with sobs, then beat upon the table with her small fists; and Gregor hissed loudly with rage because not one of them thought of shutting the door to spare him such a spectacle and so much noise.

Still, even if the sister, exhausted by her daily work, had grown tired of looking after Gregor as she did formerly, there was no need for his mother's intervention or for Gregor's being neglected at all. The charwoman was there. This old widow, whose strong bony frame had enabled her to survive the worst a long life could offer, by no means recoiled from Gregor. Without being in the least curious she had once by chance opened the door of his room and at the sight of Gregor, who, taken by surprise, began to rush to and fro although no one was chasing him, merely stood there with her arms folded. From that time she never failed to open his door a little for a moment, morning and evening, to have a look at him. At first she even used to call him to her, with words which apparently she took to be friendly, such as: "Come along, then, you old dung beetle!" or "Look at the old dung beetle, then!" To such allocutions Gregor made no answer, but stayed motionless where he was, as if the door had never been opened. Instead of being allowed to disturb him so senselessly whenever the whim took her, she should rather have been ordered to clean out his room daily, that charwoman! Once, early in the morning—heavy rain was lashing on the windowpanes, perhaps a sign that spring was on the way—Gregor was so exasperated when she began addressing him again that he ran at her, as if to attack her, although slowly and feebly enough. But the charwoman instead of showing fright merely lifted high a chair that happened to be beside the door, and as she stood there with her mouth wide open it was clear that she meant to shut it only when she brought the chair down on Gregor's back. "So you're not coming any nearer?" she asked, as Gregor turned away again, and quietly put the chair back into the corner.

Gregor was now eating hardly anything. Only when he happened to pass the food laid out for him did he take a bit of something in his mouth as a pastime, kept it there for an hour at a time and usually spat it out again. At first he thought it was chagrin over the state of his room that prevented him from eating, yet he soon got used to the various changes in his room. It had become a habit in the family to push into his room things there was no room for elsewhere, and there were plenty of these now, since one of the rooms had been let to three lodgers. These serious gentlemen—all three of them with full beards, as Gregor once observed through a crack in the door—had a passion for order, not only in their own room but, since they were now members of the household, in all its arrangements, especially in the kitchen. Superfluous, not to say dirty, objects they could not bear. Besides, they had brought with them most of the furnishings they needed. For this reason many things could be dispensed with that it was no use trying to sell but that should not be thrown away either. All of them found their way into Gregor's room. The ash can likewise and the kitchen garbage can. Anything that was not needed for the moment was simply flung into Gregor's room by the charwoman, who did everything in a hurry; fortunately Gregor usually saw only the object, whatever it was, and the hand that held it. Perhaps she intended to take the things away again as time and opportunity offered, or to collect them until she could throw them all out in a heap, but in fact they just lay wherever she happened to throw them, except when Gregor pushed his way through the junk heap and shifted it somewhat, at first out of necessity, because he had not room enough to crawl, but later with increasing enjoyment, although after such excursions, being sad and weary to death, he would lie motionless for hours. And since the lodgers often ate their supper at home in the common living room, the living-room door stayed shut many an evening, yet Gregor reconciled himself quite easily to the shutting of the door, for often enough on evenings when it was opened he had disregarded it entirely and lain in the darkest corner of his room, quite unnoticed by the family. But on one occasion the charwoman left the door open a little and it stayed ajar even when the lodgers came in for supper and the lamp was lit. They set themselves at the top end of the table where formerly Gregor and his father and mother had eaten their meals, unfolded their napkins and took knife and fork in hand. At once his mother appeared in the other doorway with a dish of meat and close behind her his sister with a dish of potatoes piled high. The food steamed with a thick vapor. The lodgers bent over the food set before them as if to scrutinize it before eating, in fact the man in the middle, who seemed to pass for an authority with the other two, cut a piece of meat as it lay on the dish, obviously to discover if it were tender or should be sent back to the kitchen. He showed satisfaction, and Gregor's mother and sister, who had been watching anxiously, breathed freely and began to smile.

The family itself took its meals in the kitchen. None the less, Gregor's father came into the living room before going into the kitchen and with one prolonged bow, cap in hand, made a round of the table. The lodgers all stood up and murmured something in their beards. When they were alone again they ate their food in almost complete silence. It seemed remarkable to Gregor that among the various noises coming from the table he could always distinguish the sound of their masticating teeth, as if this were a sign to Gregor that one needed teeth in order to eat, and that with toothless jaws even of the finest make one could do nothing. "I'm hungry enough," said Gregor sadly to himself, "but not for that kind of food. How these lodgers are stuffing themselves, and here am I dying of starvation!"

On that very evening—during the whole of his time there Gregor could not remember ever having heard the violin—the sound of violin-playing came from the kitchen. The lodgers had already finished their supper, the one in the middle had brought out a newspaper and given the other two a page apiece, and now they were leaning back at ease reading and smoking. When the violin began to play they pricked up their ears, got to their feet, and went on tiptoe to the hall door where they stood huddled together. Their movements must have been heard in the kitchen, for Gregor's father called out: "Is the violin-playing disturbing you, gentlemen? It can be stopped at once." "On the contrary," said the middle lodger, "could not Fräulein Samsa come and play in this room, beside us, where it is much more convenient and comfortable?" "Oh, certainly," cried Gregor's father, as if he were the violin-player. The lodgers came back into the living room and waited. Presently Gregor's father arrived with the music stand, his mother carrying the music and his sister with the violin. His sister quietly made everything ready to start playing; his parents, who had never let rooms before and so had an exaggerated idea of the courtesy due to lodgers, did not venture to sit down on their own chairs; his father leaned against the door, the right hand thrust between two buttons of his livery coat, which was formally buttoned up; but his mother was offered a chair by one of the lodgers and, since she left the chair just where he had happened to put it, sat down in a corner to one side.

Gregor's sister began to play; the father and mother, from either side, intently watched the movements of her hands. Gregor, attracted by the playing, ventured to move forward a little until his head was actually inside the living room. He felt hardly any surprise at his growing lack of consideration for the others; there had been a time when he prided himself on being considerate. And yet just on this occasion he had more reason than ever to hide himself, since owing to the amount of dust which lay thick in his room and rose into the air at the slightest movement, he too was covered with dust; fluff and hair and remnants of food trailed with him, caught on his back and along his sides; his indifference to everything was much too great for him to turn on his back and scrape himself clean on the carpet, as once he had done several times a day. And in spite of his condition, no shame deterred him from advancing a little over the spotless floor of the living room.

To be sure, no one was aware of him. The family was entirely absorbed in the violin-playing; the lodgers, however, who first of all had stationed themselves, hands in pockets, much too close behind the music stand so that they could all have read the music, which must have bothered his sister, had soon retreated to the window, half-whispering with downbent heads, and stayed there while his father turned an anxious eye on them. Indeed, they were making it more than obvious that they had been disappointed in their expectation of hearing good or enjoyable violin-playing, that they had had more than enough of the performance and only out of courtesy suffered a continued disturbance of their peace. From the way they all kept blowing the smoke of their cigars high in the air through nose and mouth one could divine their irritation. And yet Gregor's sister was playing so beautifully. Her face leaned sideways, intently and sadly her eyes followed the notes of music. Gregor crawled a little farther forward and lowered his head to the ground so that it might be possible for his eyes to meet hers. Was he an animal, that music had such an effect upon him? He felt as if the way were opening before him to the unknown nourishment he craved. He was determined to push forward till he reached his sister, to pull at her skirt and so let her know that she was to come into his room with her violin, for no one here appreciated her playing as he would appreciate it. He would never let her out of his room, at least, not so long as he lived; his frightful appearance would become, for the first time, useful to him; he would watch all the doors of his room at once and spit at intruders; but his sister should need no constraint, she should stay with him of her own free will; she should sit beside him on the sofa, bend down her ear to him and hear him confide that he had had the firm intention of sending her to the Conservatorium, and that, but for his mishap, last Christmas—surely Christmas was long past?—he would have announced it to everybody without allowing a single objection. After this confession his sister would be so touched that she would burst into tears, and Gregor would then raise himself to her shoulder and kiss her on the neck, which, now that she went to business, she kept free of any ribbon or collar.

"Mr. Samsa!" cried the middle lodger, to Gregor's father, and pointed, without wasting any more words, at Gregor, now working himself slowly forwards. The violin fell silent, the middle lodger first smiled to his friends with a shake of the head and then looked at Gregor again. Instead of driving Gregor out, his father seemed to think it more needful to begin by soothing down the lodgers, although they were not at all agitated and apparently found Gregor more entertaining than the violin-playing. He hurried towards them and, spreading out his arms, tried to urge them back into their own room and at the same time to block their view of Gregor. They now began to be really a little angry, one could not tell whether because of the old man's behavior or because it had just dawned on them at all unwittingly they had such a neighbor as Gregor next door. They demanded explanations of his father, they waved their arms like him, tugged uneasily at their beards, and only with reluctance backed towards their room. Meanwhile Gregor's sister, who stood there as if lost when her playing was so abruptly broken off, came to life again, pulled herself together all at once after standing for a while holding violin and bow in nervelessly hanging hands and staring at her music, pushed her violin into the lap of her mother, who was still sitting in her chair fighting asthmatically for breath, and ran into the lodgers' room to which they were now being shepherded by her father rather more quickly than before. One could see the pillows and blankets on the beds flying under her accustomed fingers and being laid in order. Before the lodgers had actually reached their room she had finished making the beds and slipped out.

The old man seemed once more to be so possessed by his mulish self-assertiveness that he was forgetting all the respect he should show to his lodgers. He kept driving them on and driving them on until in the very door of the bedroom the middle lodger stamped his foot loudly on the floor and so brought him to a halt. "I beg to announce," said the lodger, lifting one hand and looking also at Gregor's mother and sister, "that because of the disgusting conditions prevailing in this household and family"—here he spat on the floor with emphatic brevity—"I give you notice on the spot. Naturally I won't pay you a penny for the days I have lived here, on the contrary I shall consider bringing an action for damages against you, based on claims —believe me—that will be easily susceptible of proof." He ceased and stared straight in front of him, as if he expected something. In fact his two friends at once rushed into the breach with these words: "And we too give notice on the spot." On that he seized the door-handle and shut the door with a slam.

Gregor's father, groping with his hands, staggered forward and fell into his chair; it looked as if he were stretching himself there for his ordinary evening nap, but the marked jerkings of his head, which was as if uncontrollable, showed that he was far from asleep. Gregor had simply stayed quietly all the time on the spot where the lodgers had espied him. Disappointment at the failure of his plan, perhaps also the weakness arising from extreme hunger, made it impossible for him to move. He feared, with a fair degree of certainty, that at any moment the general tension would discharge itself in a combined attack upon him, and he lay waiting. He did not react even to the noise made by the violin as it fell off his mother's lap from under her trembling fingers and gave out a resonant note.

"My dear parents," said his sister, slapping her hand on the table by way of introduction, "things can't go on like this. Perhaps you don't realize that, but I do. I won't utter my brother's name in the presence of this creature, and so all I say is: we must try to get rid of it. We've tried to look after it and to put up with it as far as is humanly possible, and I don't think anyone could reproach us in the slightest."

"She is more than right," said Gregor's father to himself. His mother, who was still choking for lack of breath, began to cough hollowly into her hand with a wild look in her eyes.

His sister rushed over to her and held her forehead. His father's thoughts seemed to have lost their vagueness at Grete's words, he sat more upright, fingering his service cap that lay among the plates still lying on the table from the lodgers' supper, and from time to time looked at the still form of Gregor.

"We must try to get rid of it," his sister now said explicitly to her father, since her mother was coughing too much to hear a word, "it will be the death of both of you, I can see that coming. When one has to work as hard as we do, all of us, one can't stand this continual torment at home on top of it. At least I can't stand it any longer." And she burst into such a passion of sobbing that her tears dropped on her mother's face, where she wiped them off mechanically.

"My dear," said the old man sympathetically, and with evident understanding, "but what can we do?"

Gregor's sister merely shrugged her shoulders to indicate the feeling of helplessness that had now overmastered her during her weeping fit, in contrast to her former confidence.

"If he could understand us," said her father, half questioningly; Grete, still sobbing, vehemently waved a hand to show how unthinkable that was.

"If he could understand us," repeated the old man, shutting his eyes to consider his daughter's conviction that understanding was impossible, "then perhaps we might come to some agreement with him. But as it is——"

"He must go," cried Gregor's sister, "that's the only solution, Father. You must just try to get rid of the idea that this is Gregor. The fact that we've believed it for so long is the root of all our trouble. But how can it be Gregor? If this were Gregor, he would have realized long ago that human beings can't live with such a creature, and he'd have gone away on his own accord. Then we wouldn't have any brother, but we'd be able to go on living and keep his memory in honor. As it is, this creature persecutes us, drives away our lodgers, obviously wants the whole apartment to himself and would have us all sleep in the gutter. Just look, Father," she shrieked all at once, "he's at it again!" And in an access of panic that was quite incomprehensible to Gregor she even quitted her mother, literally thrusting the chair from her as if she would rather sacrifice her mother than stay so near to Gregor, and rushed behind her father, who also rose up, being simply upset by her agitation, and half-spread his arms out as if to protect her.

Yet Gregor had not the slightest intention of frightening anyone, far less his sister. He had only begun to turn round in order to crawl back to his room, but it was certainly a startling operation to watch, since because of his disabled condition he could not execute the difficult turning movements except by lifting his head and then bracing it against the floor over and over again. He paused and looked round. His good intentions seemed to have been recognized; the alarm had only been momentary. Now they were all watching him in melancholy silence. His mother lay in her chair, her legs stiffly outstretched and pressed together, her eyes almost closing for sheer weariness; his father and his sister were sitting beside each other, his sister's arm around the old man's neck.

Perhaps I can go on turning round now, thought Gregor, and began his labors again. He could not stop himself from panting with the effort, and had to pause now and then to take breath. Nor did anyone harass him, he was left entirely to himself. When he had completed the turn-round he began at once to crawl straight back. He was amazed at the distance separating him from his room and could not understand how in his weak state he had managed to accomplish the same journey so recently, almost without remarking it. Intent on crawling as fast as possible, he barely noticed that not a single word, not an ejaculation from his family, interfered with his progress. Only when he was already in the doorway did he turn his head round, not completely, for his neck muscles were getting stiff, but enough to see that nothing had changed behind him except that his sister had risen to her feet. His last glance fell on his mother, who was not quite overcome by sleep.

Hardly was he well inside his room when the door was hastily pushed shut, bolted and locked. The sudden noise in his rear startled him so much that his little legs gave beneath him. It was his sister who had shown such haste. She had been standing ready waiting and had made a light spring forward, Gregor had not even heard her coming, and she cried "At last!" to her parents as she turned the key in the lock.

"And what now?" said Gregor to himself, looking round in the darkness. Soon he made the discovery that he was now unable to stir a limb. This did not surprise him, rather it seemed unnatural that he should ever actually have been able to move on these feeble little legs. Otherwise he felt relatively comfortable. True, his whole body was aching, but it seemed that the pain was gradually growing less and would finally pass away. The rotting apple in his back and the inflamed area around it, all covered with soft dust, already hardly troubled him. He thought of his family with tenderness and love. The decision that he must disappear was one that he held to even more strongly than his sister, if that were possible. In this state of vacant and peaceful meditation he remained until the tower clock struck three in the morning. The first broadening of light in the world outside the window entered his consciousness once more. Then his head sank to the floor of its own accord and from his nostrils came the last faint flicker of his breath.

When the charwoman arrived early in the morning—what between her strength and her impatience she slammed all the doors so loudly, never mind how often she had been begged not to do so, that no one in the whole apartment could enjoy any quiet sleep after her arrival—she noticed nothing unusual as she took her customary peep into Gregor's room. She thought he was lying motionless on purpose, pretending to be in the sulks; she credited him with every kind of intelligence. Since she happened to have the long-handled broom in her hand she tried to tickle him up with it from the doorway. When that too produced no reaction she felt provoked and poked at him a little harder, and only when she had pushed him along the floor without meeting any resistance was her attention aroused. It did not take her long to establish the truth of the matter, and her eyes widened, she let out a whistle, yet did not waste much time over it but tore open the door of the Samsas' bedroom and yelled into the darkness at the top of her voice: "Just look at this, it's dead; it's lying here dead and done for!"

Mr. and Mrs. Samsa started up in their double bed and before they realized the nature of the charwoman's announcement had some difficulty in overcoming the shock of it. But then they got out of bed quickly, one on either side, Mr. Samsa throwing a blanket over his shoulders, Mrs. Samsa in nothing but her nightgown; in this array they entered Gregor's room. Meanwhile the door of the living room opened, too, where Grete had been sleeping since the advent of the lodgers; she was completely dressed as if she had not been to bed, which seemed to be confirmed also by the paleness of her face. "Dead?" said Mrs. Samsa, looking questioningly at the charwoman, although she could have investigated for herself, and the fact was obvious enough without investigation. "I should say so," said the charwoman, proving her words by pushing Gregor's corpse a long way to one side with her broomstick. Mrs. Samsa made a movement as if to stop her, but checked it. "Well," said Mr. Samsa, "now thanks be to God." He crossed himself, and the three women followed his example. Grete, whose eyes never left the corpse, said: "Just see how thin he was. It's such a long time since he's eaten anything. The food came out again just as it went in." Indeed, Gregor's body was completely flat and dry, as could only now be seen when it was no longer supported by the legs and nothing prevented one from looking closely at it.

"Come in beside us, Grete, for a little while," said Mrs. Samsa with a tremulous smile, and Grete, not without looking back at the corpse, followed her parents into their bedroom. The charwoman shut the door and opened the window wide. Although it was so early in the morning a certain softness was perceptible in the fresh air. After all, it was already the end of March.

The three lodgers emerged from their room and were surprised to see no breakfast; they had been forgotten. "Where's our breakfast?" said the middle lodger peevishly to the charwoman. But she put her finger to her lips and hastily, without a word, indicated by gestures that they should go into Gregor's room. They did so and stood, their hands in the pockets of their somewhat shabby coats, around Gregor's corpse in the room where it was now fully light.

At that the door of the Samsas' bedroom opened and Mr. Samsa appeared in his uniform, his wife, on one arm, his daughter on the other. They all looked a little as if they had been crying; from time to time Grete hid her face on her father's arm.

"Leave my house at once!" said Mr. Samsa, and pointed to the door without disengaging himself from the women. "What do you mean by that?" said the middle lodger, taken somewhat aback, with a feeble smile. The two others put their hands behind them and kept rubbing them together, as if in gleeful expectation of a fine set-to in which they were bound to come off the winners. "I mean just what I say," answered Mr. Samsa, and advanced in a straight line with his two companions towards the lodger. He stood his ground at first quietly, looking at the floor as if his thoughts were taking a new pattern in his head. "Then let us go, by all means," he said, and looked up at Mr. Samsa as if in a sudden access of humility he were expecting some renewed sanction for this decision. Mr. Samsa merely nodded briefly once or twice with meaning eyes. Upon that the lodger really did go with long strides into the hall, his two friends had been listening and had quite stopped rubbing their hands for some moments and now went scuttling after him as if afraid that Mr. Samsa might get into the hall before them and cut them off from their leader. In the hall they all three took their hats from the rack, their sticks from the umbrella stand, bowed in silence and quitted the apartment. With a suspiciousness which proved quite unfounded Mr. Samsa and the two women followed them out to the landing; leaning over the banister they watched the three figures slowly but surely going down the long stairs, vanishing from sight at a certain turn of the staircase on every floor and coming into view again after a moment or so; the more they dwindled, the more the Samsa family's interest in them dwindled, and when a butcher's boy met them and passed them on the stairs coming up proudly with a tray on his head, Mr. Samsa and the two women soon left the landing and as if a burden had been lifted from them went back into their apartment.

They decided to spend this day in resting and going for a stroll; they had not only deserved such a respite from work, but absolutely needed it. And so they sat down at the table and wrote three notes of excuse, Mr. Samsa to his board of management, Mrs. Samsa to her employer and Grete to the head of her firm. While they were writing, the charwoman came in to say that she was going now, since her morning's work was finished. At first they only nodded without looking up, but as she kept hovering there they eyed her irritably. "Well?" said Mr. Samsa. The charwoman stood grinning in the doorway as if she had good news to impart to the family but meant not to say a word unless properly questioned. The small ostrich feather standing upright on her hat, which had annoyed Mr. Samsa ever since she was engaged, was waving gaily in all directions. "Well, what is it then?" asked Mr. Samsa, who obtained more respect from the charwoman than the others.

"Oh," said the charwoman, giggling so amiably that she could not at once continue, "just this, you don't need to bother about how to get rid of the thing next door. It's been seen to already." Mrs. Samsa and Grete bent over their letters again, as if preoccupied; Mr. Samsa, who perceived that she was eager to begin describing it all in detail, stopped her with a decisive hand. But since she was not allowed to tell her story, she remembered the great hurry she was in, being obviously deeply huffed: "Bye, everybody," she said, whirling off violently, and departed with a frightful slamming of doors.

"She'll be given notice tonight," said Mr. Samsa, but neither from his wife nor his daughter did he get any answer, for the charwoman seemed to have shattered again the composure they had barely achieved. They rose, went to the window and stayed there, clasping each other tight. Mr. Samsa turned in his chair to look at them and quietly observed them for a little. Then he called out: "Come along, now, do. Let bygones be bygones. And you might have some consideration for me." The two of them complied at once, hastened to him, caressed him and quickly finished their letters.

Then they all three left the apartment together, which was more than they had done for months, and went by tram into the open country outside the town. The tram, in which they were the only passengers, was filled with warm sunshine. Leaning comfortably back in their seats they canvassed their prospects for the future, and it appeared on closer inspection that these were not at all bad, for the jobs they had got, which so far they had never really discussed with each other, were all three admirable and likely to lead to better things later on. The greatest immediate improvement in their condition would of course arise from moving to another house; they wanted to take a smaller and cheaper but also better situated and more easily run apartment than the one they had, which Gregor had selected. While they were thus conversing, it struck both Mr. and Mrs. Samsa, almost at the same moment, as they became aware of their daughter's increasing vivacity, that in spite of all the sorrow of recent times, which had made her cheeks pale, she had bloomed into a pretty girl with a good figure. They grew quieter and half unconsciously exchanged glances of complete agreement, having come to the conclusion that it would soon be time to find a good husband for her. And it was like a confirmation of their new dreams and excellent intentions that at the end of their journey their daughter sprang to her feet first and stretched her young body.

# RELUCTANCE

## Robert Frost

Out through the fields and the woods
    And over the walls I have wended;
I have climbed the hills of view
    And looked at the world, and descended;
I have come by the highway home,
    And lo, it is ended.

The leaves are all dead on the ground,
    Save those that the oak is keeping
To ravel them one by one
    And let them go scraping and creeping
Out over the crusted snow,
    When others are sleeping.

And the dead leaves lie huddled and still,
    No longer blown hither and thither;
The last lone aster is gone;
    The flowers of the witch hazel wither;
The heart is still aching to seek,
    But the feet question "Whither?"

Ah, when to the heart of man
    Was it ever less than a treason
To go with the drift of things,
    To yield with a grace to reason,
And bow and accept the end
    Of a love or a season?